Essays in International Economics

Essays in
International Economics

by J. Marcus Fleming

Deputy Director, Research Department
International Monetary Fund

with a Foreword by
Professor Harry G. Johnson

HARVARD UNIVERSITY PRESS
Cambridge, Massachusetts
1971

First published in 1971

SBN 674-26435-5

Printed in Great Britain

To my wife

Foreword
by Professor Harry G. Johnson

Professor of Economics
The London School of Economics and Political Science and
The University of Chicago

The field of international economics, and particularly international monetary economics, has been an extremely active and stimulating area of specialization for the economist with a keen interest in relevant policy questions during most of the postwar period. At the beginning of the period, the prevailing theory centred on the Joan Robinson-A. J. Brown elasticity approach to devaluation. That analysis was clearly inappropriate to the inflationary full employment conditions of the postwar period; its inadequacy led on the one hand to futile and unhelpful rantings against 'orthodoxy', on the other hand to the production of S. J. Alexander's 'absorption approach' and eventually, via controversy over the 'devaluation' versus the 'absorption' approach, to acceptance of some version of the synthesis earlier blocked out by James Meade. In the realm of practical policy, the major problem was the welfare effects of currency inconvertibility and the associated reliance on trade restrictions discriminatory among trading partners, and the problem of optimizing the use of such discriminatory restrictions, first breached by Ragnar Frisch.

Subsequently, with the restoration of currency convertibility towards the end of the 1950's, the liberalization of international trade through GATT negotiations, and the growing integration of international capital markets manifest overtly in the rise of the Eurodollar market, attention shifted to the problems of how to operate the system of fixed exchange rates re-established as part of postwar international economic reconstruction and embodied physically in the International Monetary Fund. In the first postwar decade, the Fund appeared largely irrelevant to economists concerned with their own nations' problems; thereafter the IMF system and its problems became matters of mounting international concern. From the late 1950's on, the chief problem appeared to be and was taken as that of providing for an adequate growth of international liquidity—a problem eventually resolved, or so one hopes, by the invention of Special Drawing Rights. In the latter half of the 1960's, however, it became increasingly apparent that adequate liquidity was not enough. Attention turned to the problem of adjustment of payments imbalances, first in the form of schemes of more or less ingenuity designed to permit countries to maintain their existing exchange rates via selection of a proper fiscal-monetary policy mix, forward-exchange-market intervention, compliance with guidelines for acceptable policies, and dual exchange rates for current and capital transactions, then, as the system passed quickly through a series of crises (eventuating in the sterling devaluation of 1967, the establishment of the two-tier gold market in 1968, and the franc devaluation and mark revaluation of 1969), in the form of proposals for introducing greater flexibility of exchange rates.

The author of the essays collected in this book, J. Marcus Fleming, has witnessed these various developments from the inside, so to speak, rather than the outside—first as a British Civil Servant, and then as a member of the Research Department of the International Monetary Fund. But, unlike many able economists who turn from academic pursuits to the service of policy formulation and research, he has not lost contact with his academic colleagues. On the contrary, he has continued to exercise a substantial influence on the development of academic thinking on international monetary affairs, in two major ways. The first, and overt, has been through his essays on international monetary problems, collected in this book. The second, and generally unknown but nonetheless important, has been through his regular participation in the private meetings of various groups of academic economists, academic economists and international monetary officials, and academic economists and international bankers and business men that have been going on since 1963 for the purpose of discussing the current problems of the international monetary system. In these meetings, his command both of the facts and of the relevant theory, together with his courtesy of manner and clarity of exposition, have commanded respect on all sides, and had an influence on the subsequent development of thought incalculable but perceptible.

The three parts into which the collection is divided correspond in subject-matter but not necessarily chronologically to the phases of concern about international monetary arrangements described above. The first essay in Part One was a revolutionary departure from the framework of analysis of discrimination initiated by Frisch, and immediately became a classic reference. It was in a real sense the progenitor of what is now known as 'the theory of second best'. The other two essays in the part deal with problems of considerable interest in the theory of commercial policy: the optimum use of tariffs as means of redistributing income among countries in a desirable direction, and the magnitude of the welfare losses imposed by tariffs. Part Two moves on to the problem of international liquidity and international monetary reform. These essays are important working papers contributed to the evolution of international thinking that eventually produced the Special Drawing Rights arrangement. They are distinguished, by contrast with much of the work then being published on the problem, by their knowledge of and attention to institutional detail, and by their recognition that the problem of providing adequate international reserves poses some of the most basic questions in general-equilibrium monetary theory. Part Three turns to the more recently recognized problem of adjustment. Some of these essays, in the nature of the case, constitute rather dated explorations in depth of proposals that turned out to be of only transient importance in the rapid evolution during the latter 1960's of the politics and economics of thinking on international monetary arrangements. Nevertheless, they are worth close study, if only because one never knows what proposals for reform may be revived in due course, and typically when a proposal is revived it is revived in virtually complete ignorance of the hard thought that was devoted to it on the last occasion. (Two examples of important suggestions that have flitted into and out of serious discussion circles in the past fifteen years are official forward-exchange-market intervention, and the so-called 'crawling peg', not to speak of the floating rate proposal itself.) It should also be mentioned that Chapter 9, 'Domestic Financial Policies under Fixed and under Floating Exchange Rates', was a pioneering piece of analysis that helped to stimulate research on what came to be known as 'the theory of the fiscal-monetary policy mix'.

Many economists, both academic and official, have written prolifically over the past decade or so on the problems of the international monetary system. Marcus Fleming's writings have been distinguished from most of this literature by his unwillingness to be content with the level of popular gimmickry, by his concern with fundamental economic theory, and above all, by his ability to relate pure monetary theory to institutional arrangements. It is a privilege to be allowed to write a Foreword to this collection of his work.

H. G. J.

The London School of Economics and Political Science

December, 1970

Contents

Foreword   page 7
Introduction   13

Part One: Trade Restrictions and Economic Welfare

1. On Making the Best of Balance-of-Payments Restrictions
   on Imports   23
2. The Optimal Tariff from an International Standpoint   49
3. The Loss from Trade Restriction   76

Part Two: International Monetary Reform

4. International Liquidity: Ends and Means   95
5. The Fund and International Liquidity   121
6. Use and Acceptance of Reserve Claims   161
7. Towards Assessing the Need for International Reserves   171

Part Three: Balance-of-Payments Policy and the Adjustment Process

8. Exchange Depreciation, Financial Policy and the Domestic   197
   Price Level
9. Domestic Financial Policies under Fixed and under Floating
   Exchange Rates   237
10. Official Intervention on the Forward Exchange Market   249
11. Guidelines for Balance-of-Payments Adjustment under the
    Par-Value System   268
12. Dual Exchange Rates for Current and Capital Transactions:
    A Theoretical Examination   296
13. Wider Margins of Exchange Rate Variation   326

Index   357

Introduction

The essays in this volume were written at intervals over twenty years, and, with the exception of the last two, have appeared in various journals. They include the bulk of my published work on international economic questions, apart from what has appeared as an anonymous ingredient in official publications.

Save for a few years of teaching in Columbia University, my working life has been spent in the public service, either national or international, but I have sought to make such contribution to economic thinking as time and opportunity allowed. It should go without saying that the opinions expressed in my publications are my own, and carry no implications as to the views of my employers, past or present.

Temperamental bent and the stimulus of my daily work have combined to interest me in the theoretical aspects of economic policy. Rather continuous contact with current policy problems as seen by the civil servant has, I believe, served as a useful corrective to what might otherwise have been an excessively abstract approach to economics; it has certainly helped to focus my attention on real issues. There is, however, another side of the ledger, and I am conscious that my official preoccupations have diverted my steps into a path somewhat apart from the main highway of academic thought, though hopefully within hailing distance of it.

The three essays comprising Part One below contain applications of welfare economic theory to international trade problems. My interest in welfare economics had been aroused, while I was in the Economic Section of the Cabinet Offices in Whitehall, by the appearance of Professor Lerner's *Economics of Control* in 1944, and further stimulated by the need to find rational solutions for the problems of pricing policy in Britain's nationalized enterprises.[1] In

---

[1] This interest found expression in such articles as my symposium with James Meade: 'Price and Output Policy of State Enterprise', *Economic Journal*, Vol. LIV, Dec. 1944; 'Production and Price Policy in Public Enterprise', *Economica*, Feb. 1950; and 'Optimal Production with Fixed Profits', *Economica*, Aug. 1953.

1948 and 1949 problems arose in the international sphere to which a similar welfare-economic approach appeared applicable, namely those connected with the efforts being made in the Organization for European Economic Co-operation to break away from bilateral payments arrangements in the direction of greater convertibility, first of all in a piecemeal fashion through the Basle transferability arrangements and later through the setting up of the European Payments Union. It seemed to me that the basic criterion of a good payments system was that it should provide an incentive to countries to adopt desirable policies with respect to trade in general and imports in particular. But in a world in which exchange rates (apart from occasional cataclysms) were fixed and in which practically all countries, save one, were keeping their international accounts in balance by import restrictions, it was by no means clear what the characteristics of a good (or least bad) trade policy might be, though such a policy would clearly have to be in some degree discriminatory. Professor Frisch had made an attempt to define a way of arriving at an optimal pattern of trade, but it appeared likely that an analysis more germane to a market economy could be made on the basis of welfare economics in the Cambridge tradition. This is what I tried to do in the essay reproduced in Chapter 1.

The essay in Chapter 2 was written in 1955, shortly after I became a staff member of the International Monetary Fund. By that time, the devaluations of 1949 had made possible so close an approach to equilibrium in international payments that restriction and discrimination, in the trade of industrial countries at any rate, could no longer be justified on grounds of balance-of-payments difficulty. However, per caput income differences between countries might, I thought, provide a justification for a more permanent type of restriction and discrimination favouring less developed countries. Following Professor Meade's lead, I tackled this question by attaching different values to the marginal utilities of money in different countries and worked out, on this basis, import and export tariffs that were optimal from an international standpoint. A similar type of analysis could easily be applied to problems of trade discrimination and of international commodity policy.

The essay appearing in Chapter 3, which was written about the same time as the foregoing, was stimulated by the desire to provide a meaningful indicator of the 'severity' of a tariff in the form of a

14

measure of the real income loss resulting from it. This exercise led to the comforting conclusion that even rather high trade barriers were likely, in most circumstances, to lead to rather small losses.

The essays appearing in Parts Two and Three, with the exception of that reproduced in Chapter 8, were written in the 1960s. Within each Part they are presented in chronological order.

The essays in Part Two are by-products of some of the thinking on international liquidity that went on in the International Monetary Fund prior to, and during the process of, designing a new instrument for creating international reserves, the Special Drawing Account, which was set up in 1969 and activated at the beginning of 1970. The first essay, reproduced in Chapter 4, takes a general view of the problem and follows the teleological approach to the concept of world need for reserves that comes naturally to a welfare economist. It was written in part out of my dissatisfaction with both the mode of analysis adopted and the rather negative conclusions arrived at in a previous Fund report entitled *International Reserves and Liquidity*, which had appeared in 1958. The first half of the essay is concerned primarily with the criteria for determining the optimal amount of world reserves and the effect on this amount of changes in various exogenous economic factors, in the distribution of reserves, and in the supply of other types of international liquidity. This analysis, which focusses attention on the behaviour rather than on the desires of governments with respect to reserves, is carried further in the essay contained in Chapter 7. This latter essay, written in 1966, separates out the influence on national policies of reserve stocks and reserve growth, and examines the interrelationships of the two; it also briefly treats the problem of quantifying the need for reserves.

The second half of the essay reproduced in Chapter 4 considers various techniques for creating international liquidity, and various types of liquidity-creating institution. Considerable emphasis is laid on the importance of countries' having obligations to hold the reserve assets created by the institution and to use these *pari passu* with other reserves, and of the issuing institution's having a power of long-term investment.

The subject matter of this part of Chapter 4 is investigated less generally, but in much greater depth, in the essay contained in Chapter 5, written in late 1963. Here the object is to see how

reserves might be created by the Fund with a minimum of alteration in the Articles of Agreement (much less alteration—or at least
supplementation—than was later involved in the Amendments of
1969 which set up the Special Drawing Account). The principal
conclusions are that the Fund could create reserves either as a
claim on the Fund arising as the counterpart of Fund investment
or through the extension to members of unconditional drawing
rights on the Fund. The resources to make this possible would be
provided either by quota increases or by borrowing arrangements,
which in turn might take the form either of lines of credit extended
by members to the Fund or of obligations by members to hold
loan claims on the Fund in proportion to reserves. The notion of
voluntary deposits with the Fund, at that time frequently advocated,
is heavily frowned upon. There is some tendency to favour investment over extension of drawing rights as a method of creating
reserves, the former technique being (in the case of short-term
investments) the more variable in time and the more selective in its
country distribution. In this connection, allusion is made to the
possibility of a link between development assistance and liquidity
creation.

The system of special drawing rights, adopted some five years
after the writing of this essay, differs considerably in form from any
of the techniques there suggested, but reproduces some of their
essential features. Special drawing rights resemble the 'drawing
rights' discussed in Chapter 5 and differ from claims on the Fund
created by way of investment in being distributed among participating members 'across the board' in proportion to quotas rather
than on a selective basis. However, they confer a right to obtain
currencies not, like 'drawing rights', from the Fund but, by way of
direct transfer, from other participants. The ability of participating
countries to use special drawing rights is guaranteed, not by the
ability of the Fund to draw on currencies subscribed in quota
increases or provided under lines of credit extended by members,
but by the obligation of other participants to accept transfer of
special drawing rights up to prescribed amounts, when designated
so to do, under the guidance of the Fund. The schemes outlined in
Chapter 5, like the special drawing rights scheme ultimately adopted,
involve a transfer of liquid claims between countries, but in the
case of the former the transfer is achieved indirectly through the

16

encashment of liquid claims by the Fund itself—the country whose currency is provided by the Fund adding to its drawing rights or loan claims and thus in effect receiving transfer of the claim that has been encashed—rather than directly, as in the latter case. The substantive difference between the two techniques is, however, small: the main purpose of putting transfers through the Fund, in the schemes in Chapter 5, was to determine the recipient or transferee, while in the special drawing rights scheme the same result has been achieved for direct transfers by the process of the designation of transferees by the Fund. A more important substantive difference between the extension of drawing rights proposed in Chapter 5 and the special drawing rights scheme, respectively, is that the former would have given rise to two types of reserve claims —drawing rights, which would have to be reconstituted through 'repurchase' after use, and loan claims, which would not—whereas the latter gives rise to only one kind of claim, subject to a reconstitution obligation which is not only more limited but is also potentially alterable. The greater elegance of this arrangement, as well as other advantages of the special drawing rights scheme, is made possible by the fact that though the Special Drawing Account has been set up within the Fund its financial functions, assets and obligations have been kept distinct from those of the original Fund. These are attributed to what is now called the 'General Account'.

The problems involved in balancing rights to use and obligations to accept international reserve claims, and in guiding their transfer, are examined in the essay, written in 1966, which appears in Chapter 6. This paper treats both the techniques ultimately adopted in the special drawing rights scheme and also certain alternatives that were ultimately rejected.

As Part Two is concerned with international liquidity, so Part Three deals with the balance-of-payments adjustment process, and in particular with the problems of implementing and adapting to changing circumstances the system of exchange stability, liberalization, and convertibility set up at Bretton Woods. In Chapter 11 in particular, an attempt is made to state with some precision the preconditions for successful operation of the system—the rules, as it were, of the Bretton Woods game.

Most of the essays in this Part provide evidence of my belief in the desirability of maintaining and increasing the flexibility of exchange rates if the advantages of full employment and price stability (so far as these are mutually compatible) are to be combined with those that derive from the freedom of international transactions.

Thus the essay reproduced in Chapter 8 of this volume, written in 1957, was intended to show that exchange rate devaluation need not lead to as much price inflation as was often alleged, provided that suitable 'flanking' measures affecting domestic expenditure were adopted. It is based on sets of numerical assumptions regarding foreign trade elasticities and other relevant parameters which appeared plausible for countries of different types. The argument can, of course, be made even more strongly in the very frequent case in which devaluation is an alternative to the imposition of import restrictions or is accompanied by liberalization of imports. Again, the essay in Chapter 9, written in 1962, was inspired by a feeling that the Canadian experiment with a floating exchange rate had been vitiated by a failure to observe that such an arrangement called for a different mix of fiscal and monetary policies from those that were appropriate under a regime of fixed exchange rates. And in a number of later essays I reveal certain leanings towards the device of a substantial widening of the permissible margin of exchange rate variation round the par value. Thus the essay in Chapter 11, written in 1967, indicates briefly how this device could fit into a general system of rules governing the operation of the par-value system, and finally, the essay in Chapter 13, written in 1969, examines at some length the pros and cons of wider margins.

Towards the 'crawling peg', or system of gradually moving parities, my attitude has always been much more reserved, as can be seen from the brief references thereto in Chapter 11. One reason for this reserve has been apprehension regarding the probable effect on speculative capital flows. More generally, the problems created for the balance-of-payments adjustment process by the steadily increasing international mobility of capital is a point which has received attention in the essays in Part Three as well as in those in Part Two. Thus the essay in Chapter 11 attempts to enunciate and to some extent evaluate a whole range of possible measures for controlling and guiding international capital flows. Two particular devices—forward market intervention and dual exchange rates for capital and current transactions—are examined in the essays appearing, respectively, in Chapters 10 and 12. The first of these essays, of which Robert Mundell is a co-author, describes a way of looking at the forward market which he and I found—and find—enlightening. The second, for which Michael Kuczynski supplied a mathematical appendix, attempts to analyse without advocacy a fascinating if unorthodox device.

I am grateful to Professor Mundell and to Mr Kuczynski for agreeing to the publication of these essays in this volume, and to the International Monetary Fund for authorizing the publication of the essays in Chapters 12 and 13.

I wish also to thank Professor Harry Johnson for contributing a Foreword, my wife, Gloria Fleming, for editing the essays, and my secretary, Miss Patricia Ferguson, for preparing the text for the printer.

Part One

Trade Restrictions and Economic Welfare

Chapter 1

On Making the Best of Balance-of-Payments Restrictions on Imports*

Part I—The Theory

INTRODUCTION

The title of this chapter very exactly describes its theme. No view is expressed or implied regarding the desirability, or otherwise, from the international standpoint, of the use of import restriction as a short- or medium-term stabilizer of the balance of payments. The fact that the principal stabilizing device of the orthodox gold standard—variation in employment, production and incomes—is now generally regarded with disfavour, makes it necessary to lean more heavily on such alternative techniques as remain available, e.g. import restriction, flexible exchange rates, international short-term credit flows of a compensatory type and the use of substantial gold reserves. Economists will differ in the relative emphasis they lay upon the various alternatives. That issue is not examined here. Our theme is a more limited one; given that import restrictions continue to be rather widely employed as a means of meeting medium-term disequilibria in the balance of payments, how would they have to be applied in order to reduce to a minimum their admitted diseconomies?

ASSUMPTIONS OF THE ECONOMIC MODEL

Assume that import restriction is the only method whereby a country can correct an adverse balance of payments. In each country full employment is maintained, and the level of factor prices is kept stable relative to the levels in other countries—thus excluding deflation and exchange depreciation as methods of restoring balance-of-payments equilibrium. Export subsidization or restriction and any

* Reprinted, with slight editing, from *The Economic Journal*, Vol. LXI, No. 241, March 1951.

kind of manipulation of capital movements are also excluded. Currency reserves are negligible, so that any balance-of-payments disequilibrium has to be at once corrected. All currencies are convertible. Import restrictions, however, can be applied with varying degrees of severity according to commodity and country of origin. Perfect competition prevails within each country, so that the severity of any import restriction is reflected in the margin between the price in the importing and that in the exporting country. Commodities exchange internationally at the prices prevailing in the country of export; any margin accrues to the importing country. The export-supply curves and the import-demand curves of the several commodities traded between the several pairs of countries are all given independently of each other and of the actual course of trade. (This assumption is later removed.) Export-supply conditions are such as to ensure that any expansion in the demand for a country's exports increases the value as well as the quantity exported. Considerations of space prevent examination of the exceptional cases where these supply conditions do not obtain.

WELFARE CONVENTIONS
It is assumed that there are no external economies of production or consumption, that producers equate value of marginal factor input with product price for each factor and product, that consumers secure an equi-marginal return in private utility from all forms of expenditure, and that increments in the general utility or welfare are made up of the sum of the increments of the private utilities of individuals. This allows us henceforward to speak of 'utility' without distinguishing whether it is private or general. Finally, it is assumed that the marginal utility of money expenditure is the same for each individual in whatever country he may live; or at least that it is, on the average, the same for those who gain by any given change in the economic situation as for those who lose. This implies that the marginal utility of any commodity to any individual can be measured by the price of that commodity within the country inhabited by the individual in question.

CRITERIA OF 'OPTIMIZATION' AND 'IMPROVEMENT'
The problem is to define the characteristics of an optimal structure of restrictions on imports of each commodity into each country

24

from each other country subject to the conditions of the model. In order to do this one has to be able to judge whether the change in the economic situation consequential on any alteration in an assumed initial structure of import restrictions is or is not an improvement.

Under the assumed conditions the net gain to the world from any small change in the economic situation can be measured by: (a) any increments in the output of any firm *minus*, (b) any increments in the input of any firm *plus*, (c) any increments in goods, services or claims received by any individual *minus*, (d) any increments in goods, services or claims supplied by any individual, all such increments being valued at the prices prevailing in the countries inhabited by the firm or individual in question. Most of these items will cancel out. All transfers between individuals or firms in the same country, or between individuals or firms in countries having the same price for the commodity or claim in question (there being no trade barriers between the countries in that commodity or claim) will count equally as gains and losses. Since we are here concerned with economic changes initiated by shifts in trade barriers, production changes are merely consequential and, since perfect competition prevails, each firm's increments of output will equal in value its increments in input. *The net gain to the world from the whole operation can therefore be measured by the sum of the increments of international trade in such items as are subject to import restriction, each increment being valued by the margin between the inland price in the importing country and that in the exporting country.* This margin will vary with the degree of restriction currently applied to the imports in question and will equal the specific import duty corresponding to that degree of restriction.[1]

The structure of import restrictions may be deemed optimal when no change in international trade quantities, capable of being brought about by a change in that structure, will yield a net gain by the above criterion. It is possible to define the characteristics of an optimal structure by considering a limited number of types of

---

[1] This amounts to defining an improvement as any change which increases the value of world output *less* the value of world input at constant market prices. An alternative definition would have been 'any change the gainers from which could (though they do not) over-compensate the losers'. Where, as in the case examined here, the economic model is such that the payment or non-payment of compensation in itself affects real world output these criteria diverge.

changes in international trade quantities or, as we shall call them, 'trade adjustments'.

TYPES OF EQUILIBRATED TRADE ADJUSTMENT

Starting from an initial position in which each country is in balance-of-payments equilibrium with the others taken as a group, but only because some or all countries are applying restrictions on imports, consider the following types of adjustment, each of which is so applied as to leave each country's over-all balance of payments unchanged:

(a) a change in a certain country's import of a certain commodity and a change of opposite sign in its import of a second commodity, both from the same exporting country;

(b) a change in a certain country's import of a certain commodity from a second country and a change of the same sign in the second country's import of a second commodity from the first country;

(c) a change in a certain country's import of a certain commodity from a second country, a change of the same sign in the second country's import of a second commodity from the third country and a change of the same sign in the third country's import of a third commodity from the first country;

(d) a change in a certain country's import of a certain commodity from a second country, a change of the same sign in the second country's import of a second commodity from a third country and a change of opposite sign in the first country's import of a third commodity from the third country.

Type (a) *adjustments* (*unilateral*)

Suppose that B's restrictions on imports of *m* from A are relaxed, while those on imports of *n* from A are intensified in such a way as to preserve unchanged any initial inequality of payments between A and B. The rise in the cost (at A prices) of A's imports of *m* must balance the fall in cost of its imports of *n*. The gain, if any, from the adjustment is measured by the rise in imports of *m*, weighted by the margin between B prices and A prices of *m*, *less* the fall in imports of *n*, weighted by the price margin of *n*. There will be a net gain only if the ratio of *m*'s price margin to *n*'s price margin is

higher than the rate at which imports of n fall as those of m rise. But the price margins of m and n depend on the severity of B's restrictions on imports of m and n respectively and the rate at which imports of n fall as those of m rise depends on the elasticities of supply from A to B of n and m respectively.

At this point it is convenient to introduce the notion of 'responsiveness of supply' by which is meant the ratio of the proportionate increase in quantity sold to the proportionate increase in the seller's money receipts. 'Responsiveness of supply' as thus defined is, of course, a function of the elasticity of supply with respect to price. Now, reverting to our example, the adjustment described will yield a net gain if, but only if, the ratio of the *ad valorem* tariff-equivalent of the import restriction on m to that of the import restriction on n exceeds the ratio of the responsiveness of supply (from A to B) of n to that of m. (In what follows the expression 'the "tariff"' is used to signify 'the tariff-equivalent of the import restriction'.) The situation will be incapable of improvement by Type (a) adjustments when the ratio of the percentage 'tariffs' on any pair of commodities imported by any country from any other country equals the reciprocal of the ratio of the corresponding export supply responsiveness.[2]

Type (b) *adjustments* (*bilateral*)

Suppose that A's restrictions on imports of p from B, and B's restrictions on imports of q from A are both relaxed in such a way as to leave unaffected A's balance of payments with B.

The mutual relaxation of import restrictions will give rise to an increase both in the value and in the volume of the exports both of p and q. So long as the price of each of these commodities in the importing country exceeds its price in the exporting country, i.e. so long as import restrictions are in force in both cases, the adjustment must, according to our criterion of meliorization, be beneficial. The mutual relaxation of import restrictions can therefore be continued with advantage up to the point at which one or other of the commodities is being imported entirely without restriction. At this point, according to the conditions of our model, the adjustment must stop (though if import subsidization had been permitted, it could have proceeded farther with advantage).

[2] See Appendix, paragraph 1.

Type (c) adjustments (trilateral)

Suppose that A relaxes restrictions on imports of r from C, B relaxes restrictions on imports of s from A and C relaxes restrictions on imports of t from B in such a way as to leave unchanged the balance-of-payments surplus or deficit of each country vis-à-vis the other pair. There will ensue an expansion in the value and volume of exports of r, s and t which can continue with advantage up to the point at which one of the three commodities—say t—is being imported without restriction. At this point, according to the conditions of our model, the adjustment must stop.

Type (d) adjustments (trilateral)

Suppose that C intensifies restrictions on imports of x from A, and relaxes restrictions on imports of y from B, while B relaxes restrictions on imports of z from A, in such a way as to leave unchanged the balance-of-payments surplus or deficit of each country vis-à-vis the remaining pair taken together. This implies that the decline in value of C's imports of x must equal the increase in value of its imports of y, which in turn must equal the increase in value of B's imports of z. Starting from a point at which C's 'tariff' on x is negligible, this type of adjustment can be carried either to a point at which it is abruptly brought to a stop by the disappearance of all import restrictions in B on z or in C on y, or to a point at which, thanks to the decline in B's 'tariff' on z and C's 'tariff' on y, and the increase in C's 'tariff' on x, it ceases to show a net advantage. This optimal point will be attained when C's percentage 'tariff' on x times the responsiveness of supply of x from A to C, equals C's percentage 'tariff' on y times the responsiveness of supply of y from B to C, plus B's percentage 'tariff' on z times the responsiveness of supply of z from A to B.[3]

OPTIMAL STRUCTURE OF IMPORT RESTRICTIONS

By combining advantageous adjustments of Types (a) and (b), applying them to all commodities traded between all pairs of countries, and pushing them to the point of maximum advantage, we reach a situation in which in each pair of countries one country is importing all commodities from the other without restriction, while the second country is imposing on commodities imported

[3] See Appendix, paragraph 2.

from the first percentage 'tariffs' inversely proportional to the corresponding responsiveness of export supply.

By proceeding similarly, in addition, with advantageous adjustments of Types (c) and (d), and by pursuing the practice, whenever advantageous adjustments are brought to an end by the elimination of one country's restrictions on imports from another, of initiating a new set of adjustments involving the restriction of the second country's imports from the first, it is always possible to arrive at a situation of the following kind:

All countries are ranged in an order, which we may term an order of 'strength', such that:

(i) each country is importing freely from countries 'weaker' than itself and restricting imports of all commodities from countries 'stronger' than itself;

(ii) the percentage 'tariffs' imposed by any country on the various commodities imported from any 'stronger' country are inversely proportional to the corresponding export supply responsiveness;

(iii) as between any three countries, the 'weak' country will be imposing on any commodity imported from the 'strong' country a percentage 'tariff' which, when multiplied by the corresponding export supply responsiveness, will equal the sum of (a) the percentage 'tariff' which it imposes on any commodity imported from the 'intermediate' country, times *the corresponding export supply responsiveness,* plus *(b) the percentage 'tariff' which the 'intermediate' country imposes on any commodity imported from the 'strong' country,* times *the corresponding export-supply responsiveness.*

Where all export-supply responsivenesses are equal each country should impose on all commodities imported from each 'stronger' country a uniform percentage 'tariff' equal to the sum of the percentage 'tariffs' applied by itself and by each 'intermediate' country on imports from the country immediately superior in order of 'strength'.

It could probably be demonstrated mathematically, given the relevant demand and supply conditions, that only one order of countries will satisfy the criteria set forth in italics above, i.e. that any situation satisfying these criteria is not merely a 'local' optimum but the absolute optimum subject to the conditions of the model. For suppose that, starting from a position which satisfies these criteria, some country is 'promoted' to a higher place in the order over the heads of a number of other countries. The 'promoted' country will have to remove any restrictions on imports from the 'demoted' countries, while the latter will impose some restrictions on imports from the 'promoted' country. Moreover, all countries of lower order will intensify their restrictions on imports from the 'promoted' country relative to the restrictions on imports from the 'demoted' countries. It seems impossible that both the 'promoted' and the 'demoted' countries will, under these conditions, maintain their over-all balance-of-payments positions unchanged. The 'promotion' will therefore not be permissible.

No advantage will be gained by proceeding to consider adjustments between four or more countries. Quadrilateral and multilateral adjustments can be resolved into a combination of notional trilateral adjustments of the kind already described, and can yield no improvement over the position already defined.

INTER-TRADE REPERCUSSIONS

We must now consider to what extent the results so far attained will be affected by the removal of the simplifying assumption on page 24 that each of the relevant export-supply curves and import-demand curves is unaffected by the volume of imports or exports in other commodities or with other countries.

The most important for our purpose of the possible interrelationships between particular trades are the following:

(i) an increased export of a particular commodity from one country to another may raise the supply curves of other commodities exported by the first country to the second, particularly in the short run;

(ii) increased exports from one country to a second may raise the supply curves of exports from the first country to third countries, particularly of the same commodities, and particularly in the short run;

(iii) increased imports by one country from a second country will tend to reduce the demand curves in the first country for imports from third countries, particularly imports of the same commodities.

EFFECT OF INTER-TRADE REPERCUSSIONS ON THE OPTIMAL STRUCTURE OF IMPORT RESTRICTIONS

Repercussion (i) affects the optimal relative 'tariffs' imposed by any

30

one country on the various commodities imported from another. Any commodity which is highly substitutable in the export country for other commodities exported to the same importing country should be restricted more severely by the latter than its supply responsiveness would otherwise warrant. This will tend to make optimal relative percentage 'tariffs' on different commodities imported from the same country more nearly equal than on the assumption of independent supply curves.

Repercussions (ii) and (iii) affect the desirability of carrying mutual trade between each pair of countries to the point at which only one of the two is restricting imports from the other. Suppose there are only three countries, A, B and C, ranged in that order, between which prevails a system of import restrictions of the type described on page 29. A and B begin to restrict imports from each other without altering the initial inequality in their bilateral balance of payments. Can this be advantageous? Both A and B will tend, in accordance with (iii), to take additional imports from C in substitution for each other's products. Moreover, in accordance with (ii), the contraction in A's and B's mutual exports should tend to lower the supply prices of their exports to C. C will then be able to increase its imports from A and B without detriment to its balance of payments.

Up to a point the advantage of the expansion in C's imports from A and B might outweigh the disadvantage of the contraction of B's imports from A and also—though for small adjustments this is unimportant—the contraction of A's imports from B. In the longer run, however, the effects of (ii) will become negligible, and a contraction of A's and B's mutual trade, though justifiable in the short run, might well be unjustifiable in the long run.

Suppose, now, that starting from the position described on page 29, countries B and C begin to contract their mutual imports while leaving their bilateral balance of payments unaltered. This will *not* lead automatically to any reduction in imports from A, since B's and C's imports from A are determined by their balance-of-payments position *vis-à-vis* A. It will, however, in the short run at any rate, probably lead to a decline in the supply prices of both B's and C's exports to A. Everything now depends on the elasticity of demand in A for imports from B and C respectively. If, as will normally be the case, this elasticity is in both cases higher than unity, A will *increase* its expenditure on imports from B and C, which will therefore be able to afford to expand their imports from A.

This operation will be advantageous only if the additional imports into C and B from A outweigh the fall in B's and C's mutual imports. It is clearly much less likely to be advantageous than the mutual restriction of imports between A and B previously considered. Import diversion plays no part in it. The effect of export diversion is indirect and is unlikely to be as beneficial as was export diversion in the case previously considered unless A's elasticity of demand for imports from B and C is at least 2. In the long run, this elasticity of demand may well be substantially higher than 2, but by that time the fall in B's and C's export-supply prices, resulting from their mutual contraction of trade, may have become negligible. It, therefore, seems most unlikely that any mutual restriction of imports by B and C will prove to be advantageous. The same applies, in even greater measure, to a mutual restriction of imports between A and C.

Consider now the effect of inter-trade repercussions on the optimum for trilateral adjustments as previously established. Start once more with countries, A, B and C in that order of strength, with a structure of import restrictions as described on page 29. Suppose that C imports more from A and less from B, thus forcing B to import less from A. A *small* trade adjustment of this sort, which leaves undisturbed each country's balance of payments with the other two combined, would, in the absence of the repercussions discussed below, have a negligible effect on welfare. Now the fall in B's imports from A will lead to an expansion in B's imports from C (repercussion (iii)) so that the fall of C's imports from B need no longer be so great in value as the rise of her imports from A. Moreover, the fall in B's exports to C may lead, in the short run, to a fall in the supply price of B's exports to A (repercussion (ii)) and (if A's demand is of more than unit elasticity) to an increase in B's export receipts from A, so that the fall in B's imports from A need no longer be as great in value as the fall of C's imports from B. These mitigations in the fall of C's imports from B, and of B's imports from A, constitute, for small adjustments, a net advantage. An extension of such an adjustment, however, as it got farther from the position defined on page 29, would create disadvantages which would, after a point, outweigh the advantages just mentioned.

To sum up, the examination of inter-trade repercussions alters our conception of an optimal structure of import barriers from that arrived at on the assumption of the independence of demand and supply curves,

(a) by mitigating the degree of inter-commodity discrimination in the restrictions to be imposed by any country on imports from a second country,

(b) by indicating a possible but doubtful advantage in some degree of mutual import restriction as between relatively 'strong' countries, and

(c) by reducing the degree of preference to be given by 'weaker' countries to imports from 'intermediate' countries over imports from 'stronger' countries.

Part II—The Theory Applied

Let us now examine to what extent various existing, projected or possible trade-and-payments arrangements satisfy the requirements of an optimal structure as set forth in Part I above.

NON-DISCRIMINATORY IMPORT RESTRICTION
Consider, first, the system under which balance-of-payments import restrictions are applied in a non-discriminatory manner, so as to be equivalent to a uniform tariff *vis-à-vis* all supplying countries. If, as was assumed in Part I, all currencies were fully convertible, each country, in so far as it acted unilaterally without exchanging concessions with other countries, and without taking account of their supply elasticities or other indirect repercussions, would have an incentive to apply its import restrictions in this way.

In a world in which exchange rates or internal money cost levels were sufficiently flexible to dispense with the necessity for balance-of-payments restrictions on imports, the principle of non-discrimination would undoubtedly be the right one. But, under the conditions of our model, which have to a considerable extent prevailed in reality in the post-war period,[4] any system constructed on this principle would operate in a most unsatisfactory way. Starting from the supposition that, in the absence of import restrictions, one set of countries would be in balance-of-payments surplus and another set in deficit, imagine that the deficit countries seek to restore equilibrium in their external accounts by non-discriminatory restrictions

[4] Up to the time of writing in 1950, that is.

33

on imports from all other countries, including each other. Not merely will these restrictions reduce the export income of the original deficit countries and force them to intensify their restrictions, but they will also transform countries originally in approximate balance into deficit countries, and force them, in turn, to apply import restrictions. If non-discriminatory import restrictions were the only way of correcting disequilibria, this process would continue until every country but one was applying import restrictions of a greater or lesser degree of severity.

Clearly, such a situation is very far removed from that described on page 29 as optimal. Each country, other than the 'strongest' country, would be withholding from each other country goods less valuable to itself than those which it could have obtained in exchange. 'Strong' countries would be restricting imports from 'weak' countries, thus enforcing unnecessary hardships on the latter without benefit to themselves. 'Weak' countries would be giving no preference to imports from 'intermediate' countries over imports from 'strong' countries, thus imposing on 'intermediate' countries a sacrifice which outweighs the benefit which they themselves derive from buying in the cheapest market.

BILATERAL BALANCING OF PAYMENTS
Compared with this the regime of trade-and-payments bilateralism, with limited currency convertibility, as practised in Europe and South America since the war, has considerable advantages. Under such a regime payments between a pair of countries, or 'monetary areas', are canalized ultimately through the two central banks concerned and, after offsetting, eventuate in a net addition to or subtraction from the balance held by one of the control banks with the other. If one of the pair has a continuing balance-of-payments surplus with the other, it accumulates in the other's currency a balance which it can use only if it can transform its surplus with the other into a deficit.

Such an arrangement gives each country an incentive to expand imports from the other, and particularly the surplus country from the deficit country, and thus tends to favour a bilateral expansion of trade, of the type discussed on page 27 above, to the point at which one of the two countries has abandoned all balance-of-payments restrictions on imports from the other.

MITIGATIONS OF BILATERALISM

The weakness of trade-and-payments bilateralism, of course, is in its failure to take advantage of trilateral adjustments, i.e. its tendency to eliminate or unduly to reduce bilateral surpluses and deficits. There are, however, three channels through which a measure of trade-and-payments multilateralism is frequently achieved within the general framework of the bilateral system:

(1) The existence of substantial or indefinite credit margins under bilateral agreements permits a—sometimes considerable—departure from strict bilateral balancing of payments. A country may be running a deficit with a second country, and a surplus with a third, both financed out of bilateral credit. Where, however, there is a persistent imbalance in bilateral accounts, the surplus country will probably seek to impose limits on the credit which it provides.

(2) If a substantial proportion of a country's exports consists of 'essentials' or 'dollar-worthy' items, it may succeed in maintaining bilateral surpluses without giving credit, by inducing its bilateral trading partners to settle their deficits in gold or hard currency. The second country, however, will desire, in these circumstances, to impose on imports from the first country restrictions which, if the first country is, from the 'world' standpoint, relatively 'weak', may be far more severe than is appropriate according to our formula. In practice, however, the second country may be deterred from applying the criterion of 'dollar essentiality' to its purchases from the first country by fear that the latter may retaliate by ceasing to import freely from the former.

(3) Under an arrangement which has assumed particular importance in connection with the use of sterling a country may permit the transfer of balances in its currency from holders resident in a second country to holders resident in a third country. The first country is likely to offer this facility provided that the currency of the second country is at least as scarce to it as that of the third country; the second country is likely to make the transfer provided that the currency of the third country is at least as scarce to it as that of the first country; and the third country is likely to accept the transfer provided that the currency of the first country is at least as scarce to it as that of the second country. In this connection the 'scarcity' of a country's currency may be measured by the

severity of the restrictions which it is necessary, on balance-of-payments grounds, to impose on imports from that country.

This device of 'selective transferability' if fully exploited would enable all possible trilateral adjustments of Type (c), as defined on page 27, to take place. Whenever country B is restricting imports from country A, country C from country B and country A from country C, an expansion of exports from A to B, B to C and C to A will normally be advantageous to each of the countries concerned. The whole operation could be carried out in A-currency (with A allowing its transfer from C to B), in B-currency (with B allowing its transfer from A to C) or in C-currency (with C allowing its transfer from B to A).

Transferability of this kind would also enable trilateral adjustments of Type (d) to be carried to a certain point, though somewhat short of the optimum. Suppose, to start from the example in the previous paragraph, that the adjustment of Type (c) is brought to an end by the elimination of A's barriers against imports from C. Then C will probably find it worth while to start restricting imports from A if it is allowed to use its earnings of A-currency to purchase additional imports from B. B will be glad to accept A-currency, which will enable it to obtain additional imports from A. A will probably consent to the transfer of its currency from C to B, which will leave its aggregate exports and importing power unaffected; unless, indeed, it had hoped to extract from B gold or some currency scarcer than its own. If we can assume that A will not withhold its consent to the transfer for the sake of earning scarce currency from countries 'weaker' than itself, the Type (d) operation just described will continue to the point at which C is restricting imports from A as severely as from B.

As a result of selective transferability then, we might arrive at a situation in which countries were ranged in an unambiguous order of 'strength' and 'weakness' in which each country had practically eliminated restrictions against imports from all countries 'weaker' than itself, and in which each country, in restricting imports from countries 'stronger' than itself, was restricting imports from relatively 'strong' suppliers *at least* as severely as those from 'intermediate' suppliers. This not unsatisfactory result is, however, dependent on relatively 'strong' countries' refraining from either restricting imports from, or refusing transfers to, relatively 'weak' countries for the sake of earning gold or scarce currencies from them. In the post-war period countries did in fact refrain to a surprising extent from exercising their power to extract gold from bilateral debtors.

GROUP DISCRIMINATION BASED ON INTERNATIONAL PLANNING

Dissatisfaction with the contrasted evils of non-discriminatory restriction and of pure bilateralism has led to attempts to devise arrangements which would promote a modulated group discrimination of a desirable kind. The most intellectually audacious attempts of this sort are those by Professor Frisch in his articles 'On the Need for Forecasting a Multilateral Balance of Payments' in the *American Economic Review* of September 1947 and 'The Problem of Multicompensatory Trade' in the *Review of Economics and Statistics* of November 1948.

In the former article Frisch proposes:

(a) that information should be collected regarding the amounts of goods and services which countries would be able and willing to exchange with each other;

(b) that this information should be arranged in 'matrices', i.e. square tables in which the columns show the amounts (in value terms) which particular importing countries would import from the various exporting countries, and the rows show the amounts which particular exporting countries would export to the various importing countries;

(c) that some international authority (e.g. the ITO) should attempt, both by recommendatory and permissive action, to ensure that such cutting down in the various elements of this matrix of potential trade as is necessary to bring balance-of-payments surpluses and deficits within the limits permitted by international lending is carried out in such a way as to maximize the quantum of international trade.

This scheme is open to objection on grounds both of principle and practicability. It takes account only of the *quantum* of international trade and neglects its *quality*—as measured by the (proportionate) margin between the price of the goods in question in the importing country and their price in the exporting country.

37

The result is that no matter how essential may be the goods which a 'weak' country imports from a 'strong' country, the weak country must practically always be prepared to restrict them further if there is some intermediate country from which it can then expand its imports by an equal amount, thus enabling the latter in turn to expand imports from a 'strong' country.[5] It is extremely doubtful whether the results of such a maximization process would be preferable to the results of ordinary bilateralism qualified by 'selective transferability' of currencies.

The practical difficulties are those of:

(a) arriving at a matrix of potential trade, the elements of which are: (i) agreed between the importing and the exporting country and (ii) forecast with reasonable accuracy; and
(b) inducing the countries concerned to take the action deemed desirable by the international authority.

The problem of providing an incentive to countries to implement an 'optimal' structure of import restrictions arises, of course, whatever the principles on which the structure is designed. Where, as here, the pattern of trade is planned in quantitative terms, and if countries are unwilling to regulate their every import at the behest of an international authority, consideration might be given to a technique employed by the OEEC, viz. the extension of drawing rights on a bilateral basis. A 'drawing right' is a grant in the donor's more or less inconvertible currency and hence available for the purchase of only such imports as are normally purchasable with that currency. Since the right is liable to lapse or lose its value at the end of a stated period, the recipient has a strong incentive to develop a balance-of-payments deficit *vis-à-vis* the donor of an amount corresponding to the size of the grant. In the past this technique has been used in connection with the provision of United States aid to Europe. It could, however, be used as a method of implementing a planned pattern of bilateral surpluses and deficits without any country's being on balance a donor or a recipient, i.e. each country would receive as large a sum in drawing rights from some countries as it extended to others. Of course, even this technique merely shifts the problem of incentive back one stage, since

[5] This is what is implied in the priority which Frisch gives to 'first-order' over 'second-order' adjustments.

countries would have to be induced to accept the pattern of drawing rights assigned to them.

A further difficulty about any attempt to bring about an optimal structure of import restrictions by quantitative planning is that the characteristics of an optimal structure of import restrictions set forth on page 29 can be translated into quantitative terms only by making very artificial assumptions about elasticities of import demand and export supply. On the assumption that all export elasticities are infinite and all import elasticities equal and starting from an estimated trade pattern corresponding to universal free imports, each country would have to cut down its imports from each country stronger than itself by a proportion equal to the sum of the proportionate reductions imposed by any intermediate country on imports from the strong country and by the weak country on imports from the intermediate country.

FRISCH'S MULTI-COMPENSATORY TRADE SYSTEM
In the second article referred to above, Frisch makes new proposals which purport to take account of the 'quality' as well as of the quantity of trade. The essence of his scheme is as follows:

(a) all trade to be subject to import licence;
(b) all licence applications to be assigned a priority number (ranging from 9 to 0) by the exporting country and a priority number by the importing country and to be submitted for final approval to an International Bureau of Compensation;
(c) the Compensation Bureau to approve or disapprove applications in such a way as to satisfy certain criteria.

The first criterion is that the value of each country's imports should equal the value of its exports (with a predetermined deviation). The second criterion is not very clearly formulated. After considering a number of alternatives Frisch concludes:

'A plausible principle seems to be simply to put up as a goal the maximization of the global surplus, i.e. the maximization of the priority sum for imports *minus* the priority sum for exports, both taken as a total for all countries, the figures for each country being normalized, so as to let only the relative, and not the absolute, magnitudes of the priority numbers influence the result.'

The 'priority sum' for imports (or exports) is the sum of the products of the import (or export) priority numbers *times* the value of the imports (or exports) falling within the corresponding priority class. Frisch illustrates this principle by a mathematical formula, which however, seems scarcely to correspond with the verbal description. According to the formula what is to be maximized is the product of two terms, one of which is the aggregate value (at given prices) of the permitted trade, and the other is the sum of each country's 'surplus' (as defined in the quotation above) expressed as a proportion of its 'priority sum' for imports.[6]

The Frischian concepts cannot be compared with the formulae developed earlier in this article unless the principles governments are to follow in assigning priority numbers to imports and exports are specifically laid down and expressed in terms of market prices. Thus a given priority number (whether on imports or exports) might represent a given proportional excess of the value of the good in question in the internal market over its value in the international market. On this interpretation the appropriate criterion would be that of maximizing the 'global surplus', i.e. maximizing the excess of the priority sum for imports over the priority sum for exports— prices and priority numbers both being treated as constants. Bearing in mind that, on the assumptions of my system, export subsidization is not permitted and hence the priority number on exports must always be zero, this maximization criterion is identical with the optimization criterion employed elsewhere in this article.

Frisch's own verbal formulation appears to be vitiated by the 'normalization' procedure. This aims at preventing countries from gaining any advantage by manipulating the levels of their priority numbers, but could achieve this only by depriving the 'weaker' countries of the benefit of the preference to which they are entitled in export competition with the 'stronger' countries. Frisch's mathematical formula, on the other hand, reduces, when export priority numbers are taken as equal to zero, to the maximization of the quantum of aggregate trade which is open, as was shown above, to quite the opposite objection.

I take on trust Frisch's assurance that it is mathematically possible for the Compensation Bureau to tailor the import-licence applications originally submitted so as to satisfy both the balance-of-

[6] See Appendix, paragraph 3.

payments conditions and the maximization criterion—and I assume this remains true when my criterion is substituted for his. Even so, the scheme is fraught with what are I fear overwhelming practical difficulties.

THE CLEARING UNION APPROACH: INTERNATIONAL CONTROL OF NATIONAL IMPORT DUTIES

(a) *Variant One*

The methods so far discussed for bringing into effect an optimal structure of import restrictions have involved the regulation of trade on a quantitative basis. But the criteria for such an optimal structure are expressed in terms of rates of import duty having equivalent effect to the import restrictions in question, and it would be possible to get a much closer approximation to the ideal if import restrictions imposed for balance-of-payments reasons took the form of actual import duties. Schemes whereby such duties would be internationally controlled in the light of ideal criteria are most naturally conceived in the institutional framework of a clearing union, of the type, for example, of the recently founded European Payments Union.

In such a Union all surpluses and deficits arising out of bilateral payments arrangements are submitted periodically for offsetting, and the net deficits and surpluses thus accruing are settled by adjusting the accounts which each country keeps with the Union. Persistent net creditors accumulate credit balances, and persistent net debtors accumulate debit balances on the Union's books. Suppose that all countries are members of a Union of this type and that to each country is assigned a quota, proportional to the value of its external trade. Defining a country's 'normalized balance' as its balance, positive or negative, with the Union divided by its quota, it might be laid down that to each size of normalized balance should correspond a certain 'basic percentage' which will be negative, zero or positive according as the balance is negative, zero or positive, and which should vary with the size of the 'normalized balance', though not necessarily in proportion thereto. Countries would be deemed 'stronger' or 'weaker' according as their 'basic percentages' were more or less positive. Now each country would be required:

(a) to import without balance-of-payments restriction or import

41

duty from any country 'weaker' than, or equally 'strong' with, itself, and

(b) to impose on imports from any country 'stronger' than itself a percentage duty equal to the 'basic percentage' of the country from which it is importing *less* its own 'basic percentage'.

In order to avoid constant fluctuation in import duties it would be expedient that basic percentages should vary with normalized balances only at discrete intervals. Thus to each basic percentage would correspond a certain 'tranche' of credit which a country would have to run through before its 'basic percentage' would be altered. Under this scheme a structure of import duties would be established corresponding roughly to the optimal criterion on page 29, but making no allowance for differences in the responsiveness of supply of exports or for inter-trade repercussions. Short-term fluctuations in the balance of payments would be covered by the use of Union credit. Somewhat longer-term disequilibria, if not covered by international capital movements outside the Union, would be corrected by alterations in the structure of import duties.

Nothing has been said about any limits to the extent to which a country should be allowed to incur indebtedness to the Union. To set rigid limits would make it difficult to keep extreme net debtors within the system and would deprive the Union of its principal sanction for inducing 'weak' countries to apply the desired degree of discrimination in favour of intermediate countries. Unlimited credit facilities would deprive the 'weak' countries of any incentive to live within their means by the imposing of import duties appropriate to their position in the scale of 'strong' and 'weak' countries. The best solution might be to give the Union power to withhold further credit from countries which decline to adjust their import duties to the appropriate levels.

(b) *Variant Two*

To deny access to the resources of the Union is, however, something of a blunt instrument, and one which it would be difficult to apply to a country in a net creditor position in the Union. A more refined incentive to apply the correct degree of discrimination might be supplied by the following variant of the scheme outlined above.

For each country there would be a special rate called the 'rate of equivalence' between its own currency and the unit of account in terms of which members' balances with the clearing union are expressed. Each country's rate of equivalence (expressed as a proportion of its par of exchange in clearing units) would rise or fall with the state of its 'normalized balance' in a way rather similar to that previously described for the 'basic percentage'. When neither in debt nor in credit with the Union, a country's 'equivalence' would be equal to unity.

While payments and receipts between countries would continue to be netted bilaterally at par, the equivalences would be used for turning net bilateral surpluses and deficits into clearing units for the purpose of multilateral offsetting as follows. Surpluses and deficits incurred by a country *vis-à-vis* 'weaker' or equally 'strong' countries would be converted into clearing units at the first country's own rate of equivalence. Surpluses or deficits incurred *vis-à-vis* 'stronger' countries would be converted into clearing units at the rate of equivalence of the 'stronger' country. Each country would be required to impose a percentage duty on imports from each 'stronger' country equal to the proportionate excess of the 'stronger' country's equivalence over that of the importing country.[7] Countries would have some incentive to apply the degree of import discrimination required by this system in that it would correspond to the relative exchange rates actually effective for *marginal* transactions with the countries concerned.

THE CLEARING UNION APPROACH, COMBINED WITH QUANTITATIVE IMPORT RESTRICTIONS

Systems of the sort discussed in the last seven paragraphs are, of course, far from being practical politics at the present time. Import duties are frequently bound under international trade agreements and in any event governments are reluctant to use them in defence of the balance of payments because of (a) the difficulty of anticipating their precise effects on that balance, (b) inflexibility resulting from parliamentary control over taxation and (c) their effect in raising the internal prices of imported goods. Quantitative restriction of imports by means of quotas and individual licensing is more convenient from all these standpoints, though in respect of the last

[7] See Appendix, paragraph 4.

point, its superiority depends on its being buttressed by internal price control and rationing.

An attempt might be made to use the clearing union device—for example, the system of variable 'equivalence' described above—not to control import duties but merely to provide governments with an incentive to apply quantitative import restrictions with the right degree of severity and discrimination. The system, however, can provide the incentives for an appropriate discrimination only if countries are induced by their shortage of clearing units to apply import restrictions of an adequate over-all severity; and it would be very difficult for the Union management to determine whether a country's import restrictions were in fact falling so far short of the appropriate degree of severity as to warrant the denial of further access to the Union's resources.

THE QUESTION OF FUNDAMENTAL DISEQUILIBRIUM

Any scheme for making the best of import restrictions, involving, as it must, systematic discrimination in favour of 'weak' countries, is open to the objection that it reduces the incentive to such countries to remedy (e.g. by the adjustment of exchange rates) what may be a fundamental disequilibrium. Recognition that this is so may well deter 'stronger' countries from co-operating in building up the type of structure of import restrictions which would be optimal at current exchange rates. Yet it would be a pity if long-run adjustment could be secured only at the price of short-run frustration and waste.

The question therefore arises whether procedures for correcting fundamental disequilibrium could not be grafted on to the arrangements for ensuring that such import restrictions as are at any time necessary are applied with an optimal degree of discrimination. If some practicable system on clearing union lines could be devised for the latter purpose, it might also be made to serve the former. Countries which, in spite of the application of severe import restrictions, remain persistent net debtors are clearly marked out for devaluation, while persistent net creditors are equally clearly marked out for revaluation. Against the former at any rate, means of coercion lie to hand in the withdrawal both of credit facilities and of the preferential treatment hitherto accorded to their exports.

CONCLUSION

None of the arrangements examined in Part II of this essay have attempted to carry into effect *all* the features of an optimal system of import restrictions. They have in general ignored the desirability of adjusting the severity of import restrictions to the responsiveness of export supply of the commodities in question, and they have ignored the refinements rendered desirable by inter-trade repercussions. The system of bilateral agreements modified by selective currency transferability probably takes more account of these factors than the more formal multilateral arrangements subsequently examined.

The principal features of an optimal structure, however—the ordering of countries according to 'strength' with free imports from 'weaker' countries, and preference for 'intermediate' over 'strong' countries—are reproduced in all the schemes considered: (i) bilateralism *plus* selective transferability; (ii) international trade planning; (iii) Frisch's multi-compensatory system; and (iv) the various variants of the clearing union approach. My own preference is for schemes of type (i), as the most practicable, and of type (iv), as the nearest approximation to the ideal. I have no illusions as to the immediate practicability of the various clearing union schemes suggested, culminating as they do in a streamlined IMF *cum* ITO, but think it possible that some of the features roughly sketched in here may find a place in the international monetary and commercial system of the future—unless, indeed, that system is based on a much more continuous adjustment of exchange rates than has been assumed in the preparation of this essay.

Appendix

1. Let q_m and q_n denote the quantity of m and n respectively imported by B from A,

p_{mA} and p_{mB} denote the price of m in A and in B respectively,

p_{nA} and p_{nB} denote the price of n in A and in B respectively,

$E = \dfrac{dq}{dp} \cdot \dfrac{p}{q}$ denote 'elasticity of supply',

45

$$R = \frac{dq}{d(pq)} \cdot \frac{pq}{q} = \frac{1}{1+\dfrac{1}{E}} \text{ denote 'responsiveness of supply',}$$

$$T_m = \frac{p_{mB} - p_{mA}}{p_{mA}} \text{ denote the } \textit{ad valorem} \text{ tariff-equivalent of re-}$$

strictions in B on imports of m from A,

. G denote the gain in welfare from the trade adjustment in question.

Then
$$G = p_{mA}T_m\delta q_m + p_{nA}T_n\delta q_n.$$

But the balance of payments must not be altered.

Therefore
$$\delta(p_{mA}q_m) + \delta(p_{nA}q_n) = 0$$

and
$$G = p_{mA}\delta q_m \left(T_m - \frac{R_n}{R_m} T_n \right)$$

at the optimal point $G = 0$ and

$$\frac{T_m}{T_n} = \frac{R_n}{R_m}.$$

2. Adopting the same notation *mutatis mutandis* as in paragraph 1.

$$G = p_{xA}T_x\delta q_x + p_{yB}T_y\delta q_y + p_{zA}T_z\delta q_z.$$

The balance-of-payments conditions are:

$$-\delta(p_{xA}q_x) = \delta(p_{yB}q_y) = \delta(p_{zA}q_z).$$

Then
$$G = p_{xA}\delta q_x \left(T_x - \frac{R_y}{R_x}T_y - \frac{R_z}{R_x}T_z \right).$$

The optimal point will be attained when

$$R_xT_x = R_yT_y + R_zT_z.$$

3. Frisch (*Review of Economic Studies and Statistics*, November 1948) suggests maximizing the following expression

$$(A_1 + A_2 + \ldots + A_n) \sum_{i=1}^{n} \frac{(1B_i^1 + 2B_i^2 + \ldots) - (1A_i^1 + 2A_i^2 + \ldots)}{(1B_i^1 + 2B_i^2 + \ldots)}$$

where $i = 1, 2, \ldots n$ designate the individual countries, A_i being the total multi-compensatory export from i and B_i, the total multi-compensatory import into country i, the superscripts indicating the priority categories.

Using the same notation, and bearing in mind that my system admits no export subsidization and thus no export priorities, I suggest maximizing the following expression:

$$\sum_{i=1}^{n} 1B_i{}^1 + 2B_i{}^2 + \ldots nB_i{}^n.$$

4. C is restricting the import of x from A.

C is restricting the import of y from B.

B is restricting the import of z from A.

Let q_r denote the quantity of r ($= x, y, z$) imported from the appropriate country to the appropriate country,

p_{rQ} denote the price of r in Q ($=$ A, B, C),

E_Q denote the rate of equivalence of Q's currency, expressed as a proportion of its par of exchange,

T_r denote the *ad valorem* tariff-equivalent of the restriction or imports of r,

$R = \dfrac{\delta q_r}{\delta(P_r q_r)} \cdot \dfrac{P_r q_r}{q_r}$ denote the responsiveness of supply of r from

the appropriate country to the appropriate country.

The rule regarding import duties on page 43 of the text is:

$$T_x = \frac{E_A - E_C}{E_C}$$

$$T_y = \frac{E_B - E_C}{E_C}$$

$$T_z = \frac{E_A - E_B}{E_B}$$

From which it follows that:

$$T_x = T_y + T_z + T_y T_z.$$

This, though it differs from the formula for an optimal tariff structure arrived at in paragraph 2 above, can be deduced from the same criterion of optimization. The difference is due to the peculiar balance-of-payments conditions which characterize the system under consideration. The condition of optimization is:

$$p_{xA}T_x\delta q_x + p_{yB}T_y\delta q_y + p_{zA}T_z\delta q_z = 0.$$

And the balance-of-payments conditions are:

$$\delta(p_{xA}q_x) = -\delta(p_{zA}q_z),$$
$$\delta(p_{xA}q_x)E_A = -\delta(p_{yB}q_y)E_B.$$

From which it follows, if $R_x = R_y = R_z$, that

$$T_x = T_y + T_z + T_yT_z.$$

Chapter 2

The Optimal Tariff from an
International Standpoint*

In discussing questions of international commercial policy, economists generally assume as the ultimate objective the enhancement of the real income either of the world as a whole or of the particular country whose policies are under examination.[1]

Neither of these criteria is entirely suitable for the consideration, from an international standpoint, of certain types of measures affecting international trade, notably, protective measures undertaken by underdeveloped countries, i.e. countries of low per capita income. The criterion of purely national interest is obviously inadmissible from an international standpoint, while that of maximizing world real income is appropriate only when international real income transfers can be regarded as having no significant effect on welfare, that is, when the marginal utility (in the sense of the marginal welfare yield) of such income is equal in all countries.

Precisely what is meant by a real income transfer and by the marginal utility of such income depends on the definition of real income adopted. As we shall see later, where impediments to trade exist, a number of alternative definitions are available. In the vicinity of a free trade equilibrium position, however, the marginal utility

* Reprinted, with slight editing, from *The Review of Economics and Statistics*, Vol. XXXVIII, No. 1, February 1956.

[1] A major exception to this is furnished by Professor Meade's *Trade and Welfare*, where the possibility that marginal increments of income should be weighted by different marginal utilities in different countries is specifically taken into account. Professor Meade pioneered this approach in an unpublished paper on 'Discriminatory Reductions in Trade Barriers', read to the Economics Seminar in Princeton in 1952. The specific problem of the optimal tariff considered in the present chapter was in fact dealt with in *Trade and Welfare* (Mathematical Supplement XVI), a copy of which reached me only when the article of which this chapter is a reprint was in proof. Happily, to the extent that my treatment overlaps with that of Professor Meade, my conclusions agree with his. I believe I have carried the argument a step further by treating relative national marginal utilities of money as a specific function of relative price levels and hence of the tariff itself.

of income is likely, on any definition, to be substantially greater in countries of low, than in those of high per capita income.[2]

Differences in the marginal utility of income among different countries may also arise from rapid changes in their relative per capita incomes. At any given level of present income the marginal utility of income in a country is likely to be the higher, the higher the level of income to which it has, until recently, been accustomed.

One effect of allowing for differences of marginal utility of income among countries is to provide a justification for measures of protection which would otherwise be contrary to the general interest.

In the present essay I wish to reconsider the familiar problem of the optimal tariff, or, more precisely, the problem of optimal import and export duties, in a two-country case where the marginal utility of income is deemed to be the same for all individuals within each country but is liable to differ as between the countries.

TRADE EFFECT OF RAISING AN IMPORT DUTY

Consider a world consisting of two countries, A and B, within each of which full employment and perfect competition prevail. Trade between the two countries is kept in balance by movements in c, the ratio of A's factor price level to B's factor price level (both price levels being expressed, at current exchange rates, in terms of a single currency). B trades freely with A, and A exports freely to B, but A may impose a duty on imports from B. Provided that the relevant foreign trade elasticities[3] are such that, starting from a balanced trade position, any increase in A's relative factor price level, c, at a constant level of A's *ad valorem* import duty, T_m, tends to generate a deficit in A's trade balance—i.e. provided that c is stable—any small increase in T_m will be associated with a finite increase in c.

---

[2] This is likely to be true even on the assumption that the general level of commodity prices is roughly the same in the two classes of countries. In reality prices are likely, on average, to be higher in the richer (and more productive) countries, because their advantage in productivity is frequently less marked in home market industries (e.g. service) than in foreign trade industries. This will accentuate the discrepancies between the marginal utilities of income in the different countries.

[3] The elasticities referred to are exclusively price elasticities of import demand and export supply. Income elasticities are neglected throughout this essay as their introduction would unduly complicate the analysis, and, with full employment assumed, real income effects on trade are likely to be small.

50

This is demonstrated mathematically in the Appendix (part II, section A, subsection (c)), but it is fairly obvious on common-sense grounds. The rise in duty, taken by itself, would tend to create a surplus in A's trade balance. This surplus will tend, through the exchange rate or otherwise, to bring about a rise in A's relative factor price level. And since the increase in c tends to evoke a deficit in A's trade balance, there will in general be some increase in c which will suffice to preserve equilibrium between the two countries.

Now, as T_m rises from any given level, and as c correspondingly rises, A's exports will become more expensive to B, and B's market less attractive to A; so that x, the physical volume of A's exports to B, will decline.

As T_m and c rise, and x falls, m, the physical volume of A's imports, will also change. Whether m rises or falls, and the amount by which m rises or falls for a given fall in x, will depend entirely on foreign trade elasticities in B, irrespective of those in A. (While the elasticities in both countries help to determine the relationship between c and T_m, those in B alone suffice to determine at what rate m must change as x falls in order that trade be kept in balance.)

With x, m, and T_m defined as above, let p_{xb} and p_{mb} represent prices in B of A's exports to B, and A's imports from B respectively, expressed as a ratio of B's factor price level; and let η_b and ϵ_b represent, respectively, B's (negative) elasticity of import demand with respect to p_{mb} and B's elasticity of export supply with respect to p_{xb}. Then, assuming continuous relationships, the rate at which m declines as x declines (as T_m is raised), is given by the following formula:[4]

$$\frac{dm}{dx} = \frac{p_{xb}}{p_{mb}} \cdot \frac{\epsilon_b(\eta_b - 1)}{\eta_b(\epsilon_b + 1)}. \tag{1}$$

We have shown that, as A's *ad valorem* import duty increases, A's export volume will decline. It follows from equation (1) that the volume of A's imports will decline only if η_b, the elasticity of B's import demand, is greater than unity. If η_b is less than unity, A will actually be able to afford a higher volume of imports than before.[5] In any event the decline, if any, in the quantum of A's

[4] See Appendix II.A.b., equation (xi).

[5] Cf. Appendix II.A.b., equation (xviii), bearing in mind that, when $\eta_b < 1$, $k > 1$.

51

imports is bound to be somewhat less than the decline in the quantum of its exports (both quanta being measured at B prices).

WELFARE EFFECT OF RAISING AN IMPORT DUTY

Now assume that, both in country A and in country B, (1) the supply of factors of production is fixed, (2) there is no net foreign lending or borrowing, and (3) perfect resource allocation—including full employment and perfect competition—prevails. In these conditions the effect on general welfare of any small change in trade between A and B may be measured by adding together the resulting changes in the quantum of net national expenditure (at home market prices) in the two countries, multiplied, in each case, by the marginal utility of money expenditure, at the given prices, in the country in question. But, in each country, the change in the quantum of net national expenditure will equal the change in the quantum of net domestic output *minus* the change in the quantum balance of foreign trade. Moreover, with fixed-factor supply and perfect resource allocation within each country (as evidenced by an exact correspondence between the relative prices and the relative marginal rates of substitution of different products and factors on the domestic market), any small adaptive adjustment in either country will leave the quantum of net domestic output unchanged. Therefore, in each country, the change in the quantum of net national expenditure reduces to the (negative) change in the quantum balance of foreign trade, i.e. to the change in the quantum of imports *less* that in the quantum of exports.

It follows that the welfare change associated with a small increase in A's import duty will be measured by the sum of two terms representing respectively, for A and for B, the change in the quantum of imports *less* that in the quantum of exports, at the prices prevailing in the domestic market of the country in question, multiplied by the marginal utility of income (expenditure) at those prices, in that country. Thus

$$\frac{dW}{dT_m} = \phi_a \left(p_{ma} \frac{dm}{dT_m} - p_{xa} \frac{dx}{dT_m} \right) + \phi_b \left(p_{xb} \frac{dx}{dT_m} - p_{mb} \frac{dm}{dT_m} \right) \quad (2)$$

where W stands for welfare, ϕ_a and ϕ_b for the marginal utility of money in A and B respectively, and p_{xa} and p_{ma} for the home market prices, in A, of A's exports and imports, respectively. It is convenient that money be measured, in *both* countries, in terms of its equivalent, at current exchange rates, in factors of production in B; p and ϕ should be interpreted accordingly.[6]

Substituting for dx/dm from equation (1) we get:

$$\frac{dW}{dT_m} = p_{mb}\frac{dm}{dT_m}\left[T_m\phi_a - \frac{\eta_b+\epsilon_b}{\epsilon_b(\eta_b-1)}(\phi_a-\phi_b)\right] \tag{3}$$

where
$$T_m = \frac{p_{ma}}{p_{mb}} - 1.$$

The expression on the right-hand side of this equation contains two terms, the first of which, $p_{mb}(dm/dT_m)T_m\phi_a$, measures the rate of change in welfare corresponding to the rate of change in the quantum of world expenditure, at home market prices, as A's import duty rises. The rate of change in the quantum of world expenditure, in this sense, is defined as the sum of the rates of change in the quantum of net national expenditure, at home market prices, in A and in B respectively, i.e. as

$$\left(p_{ma}\frac{dm}{dT_m} - p_{xa}\frac{dx}{dT_m}\right) + \left(p_{xb}\frac{dx}{dT_m} - p_{mb}\frac{dm}{dT_m}\right).$$

This reduces to $\quad p_{mb}\dfrac{dm}{dT_m}\left(\dfrac{p_{ma}}{p_{mb}}-1\right) = p_{mb}\dfrac{dm}{dT_m}T_m.$

Let us call this the 'quantum effect'. At any given level of A's import duty, a further increase in the duty will entail a positive or negative quantum effect according as it brings about a rise or a fall in the physical volume of A's imports. Thus an increase in A's import duty will reduce the quantum of world expenditure as defined, only if the demand elasticity in B for imports from A is greater than unity. If η_b is less than unity and A's import volume *increases* with the rise in the import duty, the expenditure quantum will actually increase.

[6] Thus p_a represents price in A, and ϕ_a the marginal utility of money in A, in terms, not of A-currency, but of A-currency deflated by the price, in A-currency, of a unit of B's production factors.

The second term on the right-hand side of equation (3) is a product of two factors, one of which,

$$-p_{mb}\frac{dm}{dT_m}\cdot\frac{\eta_b+\epsilon_b}{\epsilon_b(\eta_b-1)}\bigg(=p_{mb}\frac{dm}{dT_m}-p_{xb}\frac{dx}{dT_m}\bigg),$$

measures the fall in B's expenditure quantum; while the other, $(\phi_a-\phi_b)$, measures the excess of the marginal utility of money expenditures in A over that of money expenditures in B. This term as a whole therefore represents the welfare gain corresponding to a quantum transfer from B to A, equal in amount to B's loss of expenditure quantum. When deflated by ϕ_a it may be called the 'transfer effect'. It is entirely dependent on the existence of a discrepancy between the marginal utility of money in A and B, and it disappears if these are equal. The transfer effect will be positive or negative according as the marginal utility of money is higher or lower in A than in B.[7]

If, in the free trade position, where T_m is zero, the marginal utility of money is lower in A than in B, the imposition by A of an infinitesimal duty on imports can *never* enhance welfare. The quantum effect will be negligible, the transfer effect negative. If, on the other hand, the marginal utility of income is higher in A than in B, the imposition of a small tax will *always* increase welfare because of the favourable transfer effect.

As A's import duty increases, the marginal utility of money in A will decline relative to that in B. This is because A's factor prices and incomes will rise relative to B's. To some extent this will be reflected in a rise in the prices of goods bought in A relative to those of goods bought in B, and to some extent in a combination of rising real income in A and falling real income in B. Both of these developments will tend to depress the marginal utility of money in A relative to B.

THE OPTIMAL IMPORT DUTY
Suppose now that η_b, the elasticity of B's import demand for A's exports, is greater than unity. In this case, as A's import duty rises,

---

[7] The formula for the transfer effect is
$$-p_{mb}\cdot\frac{dm}{dT_m}\cdot\frac{\eta_b+\epsilon_b}{\epsilon_b(\eta_b-1)}\cdot\bigg(1-\frac{\phi_b}{\phi_a}\bigg).$$
Since $dm/dT_m \gtreqless 0$ as $\eta_b \lesseqgtr 1$, this expression is positive or negative as $\phi_a \gtreqless \phi_b$.

A's imports will decline and the quantum effect will be increasingly negative. On the other hand, the transfer effect, if positive at the free trade position, will become decreasingly so until, finally, the two effects will cancel out, and the optimal level of A's import duty will have been reached.[8] Let τ_m stand for the optimal level of the *ad valorem* import duty T_m. Then the following relationship will prevail between the various foreign trade elasticities and the marginal utilities of money in the two countries.[9]

$$\tau_m = \frac{\eta_b + \epsilon_b}{\epsilon_b(\eta_b - 1)}\left(1 - \frac{\phi_b}{\phi_a}\right). \qquad (4)$$

If ϕ_b, the marginal utility of money in B, were arbitrarily set equal to zero, this formula would give

$$\tau_m = \frac{\eta_b + \epsilon_b}{\epsilon_b(\eta_b - 1)},$$

the familiar expression for an optimal import duty from the standpoint of the country imposing the duty. Since, in the case under examination, the marginal utility of money in B, at the optimal tariff level, though positive, is still somewhat lower than in A, the effect of taking B's welfare into account is to make the level of the internationally optimal tariff somewhat lower than that of the nationally optimal one.

But what happens if η_b, B's elasticity of import demand for A's exports, is lower than unity? Then, as A's import duty rises, the volume of its imports will actually increase. This will entail a positive quantum effect as well as a strong quantum transfer from B to A. So long as A's marginal utility of income is higher than B's, the operation will yield a gain of welfare on both counts. As the process continues a point will be reached at which marginal utilities of money will be equal in A and in B. From that point onwards, while a continued increase in A's import duty will continue to yield a positive quantum effect, the transfer effect will be negative.

[8] Save in a limiting case, discussed below, where a rise in T_m has no effect either on the quantum of imports into A or on the ratio of A's to B's factor prices.

[9] Now ϵ_a and η_a, representing respectively A's export supply elasticity and its import supply elasticity, are defined (by analogy with ϵ_b and η_b) as elasticities of quantity relative to price, where the import and export prices in question are themselves measured relative to A's factor price level.

Will a point arrive, as the duty is raised, at which the negative transfer effect on welfare cancels out the positive quantum effect? If such an optimal point exists it must fulfil the conditions of equation (4). But the 'meaning' of the equation now is that the expression $(1-\phi_b/\phi_a)$ must be sufficiently negative to ensure that when multiplied by the negative expression

$$\frac{(\eta_b+\epsilon_b)}{\epsilon_b(\eta_b-1)}$$

it equals T_m, the *ad valorem* import duty.

If B's welfare were arbitrarily disregarded, the rate at which welfare changes as the tariff rises, as given in the right-hand side of equation (3), would become

$$p_{mb} \cdot \frac{dm}{dT_m} \cdot \phi_a \left[T_m - \frac{(\eta_b+\epsilon_b)}{\epsilon_b(\eta_b-1)} \right];$$

and since

$$\frac{(\eta_b+\epsilon_b)}{\epsilon_b(\eta_b-1)}$$

is negative the expression as a whole would always be positive, i.e. no optimal point would be attainable. The higher the tariff the better things would be. When, however, account is taken of B's welfare an optimal point with a finite value for T_m will always be attainable, so long as the foreign trade elasticities are constant and have finite, non-zero values.

In order to demonstrate this, and in order to express τ_m as a function of the elasticities alone, we must define more precisely the dependence of ϕ_b/ϕ_a on T_m.

We have seen that as T_m rises, ϕ_b/ϕ_a grows with the ratio of A's to B's factor price level. Let it be regarded as equal to zc where z is the value of ϕ_b/ϕ_a at the free trade, zero duty, position, and c is the ratio of A's to B's factor price level expressed as a proportion of the value of that ratio at the free trade position.

Now, since, as A's import duty rises—η_b being less than unity—A's imports will increase in volume, c must grow more than in proportion to p_{ma}/p_{mb} (the ratio of the price of A's imports in A to their price in B): for only if p_{mb} rises relative to B's factor price level will an increased volume of exports be supplied by B, and only if p_{ma} falls relative to A's factor price level will an increased volume of imports be demanded in A.[10] At first, however, when T_m is small, even though c (and therefore ϕ_b/ϕ_a) rises proportionately faster than p_{ma}/p_{mb}, (ϕ_b/ϕ_a-1) will not rise proportionately as fast as T_m $(= p_{ma}/p_{mb}-1)$. Indeed, when $T_m = 0$, $\phi_b/\phi_a < 1$ and (ϕ_b/ϕ_a-1) is negative. However, when T_m becomes very large and both p_{ma}/p_{mb} and ϕ_b/ϕ_a rise substantially in excess of unity there must come a point at which (ϕ_b/ϕ_a-1) begins to rise proportionately faster than T_m.

At this point the right-hand side of equation (4), which starts off by being less than the left-hand side when T_m is low, will begin to rise proportionately faster than the left-hand side. Since the left-hand side can rise indefinitely, it follows that at some finite T_m the two sides of the equation will be equal. At this point the import duty will be optimal.

As we have seen, when $\eta_b > 1$, the effect of taking account of B's welfare (of conceiving welfare from an international point of view) is merely, in all normal cases, to reduce the size of the optimal import duty below the purely national optimum. When $\eta_b < 1$, however, the effect of taking account of B's welfare is to ensure that, for all save certain extreme cases discussed below, a finite optimal level of import duty actually exists.

Substituting for ϕ_b/ϕ_a in equation (4) we get $\tau_m = h(1-cz)$ where c signifies the ratio of A's price level to B's price level expressed as a proportion of the value of this ratio when $T_m = 0$, z signifies the value of ϕ_b/ϕ_a when $T_m = 0$, and

$$h \equiv \frac{\eta_b + \epsilon_b}{\epsilon_b(\eta_b - 1)}.$$

In the Appendix[11] it is shown that where all the foreign trade elasticities are assumed constant with respect to variations in T_m over the relevant range, the optimal import duty will conform to an equation of the following form:

$$\tau_m = h[1 - z(\tau_m+1)^k]$$

or $$hz(\tau_m+1)^k + \tau_m - h = 0 \qquad (5)$$

[10] Save in the limiting case, discussed below, where both ϵ_b and η_a are infinite.

[11] Appendix II.A.d. and II.A.c. That one and only one optimal value of T_m exists is shown in II.A.f.

57

where
$$k \equiv \frac{1}{\dfrac{\epsilon_a(\eta_b-1)(\epsilon_b+\eta_a)}{\eta_a(\eta_b+\epsilon_a)(1+\epsilon_b)}+1}.$$

Unless the import demand elasticities are so small that c exercises a negative effect on the balance of trade (i.e. unless the balance of trade is fundamentally unstable), k must be positive.

THE OPTIMAL EXPORT DUTY

Reasoning similar to that employed in the calculation of the optimal import tax can be applied to the calculation of the optimal export tax also. The latter exercise not only serves, to some extent, to verify the former, but casts some additional light upon the method employed.

Assuming perfect flexibility of relative prices and, in general, perfect competition within countries A and B, the situation resulting from the imposition in A of a uniform *ad valorem* export tax is identical, in all substantive respects, with that resulting from the imposition in A of a uniform *ad valorem* import tax of equal magnitude. For example, suppose a situation, with equilibrated payments between A and B, in which A is imposing a 10 per cent import duty. If A depreciates its exchange rate by 10 per cent and replaces its import duty by a 10 per cent export duty, then, with trade volumes in both directions unchanged, all prices in A and B will be exactly the same, in domestic currency, as in the original situation. The new situation like the old will be in equilibrium. Nothing substantive will be altered. All that will be changed is the nominal relationship between factor price levels in the two countries.

Since import duties and export duties have identical substantive effects one would expect the optimal export duty to be identical with the optimal import duty. This is in fact the case. As we shall see, equation (5) serves to determine the optimal export tax, as well as the optimal import tax. But the intermediate steps in arriving at this common formulation are different in the two cases. This is because, for any given level of export tax, c, the ratio of factor prices in the two countries, is different from what it is at the same level of import tax. Consequently, ϕ_b/ϕ_a, the relative marginal utility of money, is also different in the two cases.

Using a notation similar to that previously employed we can

express the welfare effect of any infinitesimal increment in A's export tax as follows:

$$\frac{dW}{dT_x} = p_{xa}\frac{dx}{dT_x}\phi_a\left[T_x-\left(\frac{h}{h+1}\right)\left(1-\frac{\phi_b}{\phi_a}\right)(T_x+1)\right]. \qquad (6)$$

The optimal export tax will be attained when the right-hand side of equation (6) takes the value of zero, i.e. when

$$T_x = h[1-\phi_b/\phi_a(1+T_x)]. \qquad (7)$$

Substituting, as before, zc for ϕ_b/ϕ_a, we find, as is shown in the Appendix,[12] that

$$\tau_x = h[1-z(\tau_x+1)^k] \qquad (8)$$

where

$$h \equiv \frac{\epsilon_b+\eta_b}{\epsilon_b(\eta_b-1)}$$

and

$$k \equiv \frac{1}{\dfrac{\epsilon_a(\eta_b-1)(\epsilon_b+\eta_a)}{\eta_a(\eta_b+\epsilon_a)(1+\epsilon_b)}+1}.$$

Equation (8) is clearly identical with equation (5), save that τ_x is substituted for τ_m.

Reverting to equation (6) we note that, as in equation (3), the right-hand side consists of a two-term expression, of which the first term represents the rate of change in welfare resulting from the rate of change in the quantum of world expenditure at home market prices, while the second represents that resulting from the quantum transfer from B to A. But whereas the effect on the quantum of world expenditure of raising an import tax may, as we have seen, be negative or positive, according as the elasticity of demand in B for imports from A is greater or less than unity, the effect on this quantum of raising an export tax must *always* be negative. This follows from the fact that the first term on the right-hand side of equation (8) has the same sign as dx/dT_x, and that the effect on the volume of A's exports of raising the export tax can only be negative.[13] The optimal export tax will be attained when the

[12] Appendix II.B.c.

[13] Raising T_x has the same substantive effect as raising T_m. But we have already seen that raising T_m, by raising c, must lower x. See also Appendix II.B.b.

favourable transfer effect is no longer sufficiently great to out-weigh the unfavourable quantum effect.

SIZE OF OPTIMAL TARIFF ON VARIOUS ASSUMPTIONS[14]

From equation (5) it may be seen that the higher is z—the ratio, at the free trade position, of the marginal utility of money in the outside world to the marginal utility of money in the country imposing the duty—the lower will be the optimal import duty.[15]

When $z = 0$, i.e. when the marginal utility of money in B is negligible, $\tau_m = h$, as we have already seen. As z rises τ_m falls until when $z = 1$—i.e. when the marginal utility of money is the same, in the free trade position, in A as in B—the optimal duty is zero.[16]

However, given z somewhere between 0 and 1, how will the level of the optimal tariff be affected by variations in the several foreign trade elasticities?

The fact that A's foreign trade elasticities enter into the determination of T_m in two ways—through their influence on h and their influence on k—makes it impossible, save in special cases, to make simple statements about their net effects on τ_m.

One critical situation is when B's elasticity of demand for imports from A is equal to unity. In this case changes in T_m will affect only the volume of A's exports, leaving the volume of A's imports unchanged. Since, however, A's exports have the same price in A as in B the optimal point will be attained only when the marginal utility of money is the same in the two countries. This will happen only when the ratio of A's factor price level to B's has risen from the free trade position by the same proportion as A's marginal utility of money in that position exceeds B's. But when $\eta_b = 1$ the proportionate increase in A's relative factor price level will equal the *ad valorem* tariff, T_m. That is, the optimal import duty will equal the proportionate excess, in the free trade position, of the

---

[14] Since, as we have seen, the optimal *ad valorem* import duty and the optimal *ad valorem* export duty are of equal size, all the results given in this section, though deduced from the formula for the former, are equally true of the latter.

[15] $\partial \tau_m / \partial z = -h(\tau_m + 1)^k / 1 + hzk(\tau_m + 1)^{k-1} < 0.$

[16] When $z = 1$, $h(\tau_m + 1)^k + \tau_m = h$. Therefore $\tau_m = 0$.

marginal utility of money in A over that in B. In symbols, when $\eta_b = 1$,

$$\tau_m = \frac{1-z}{z},$$

irrespective of the value of other foreign trade elasticities.

The foreign trade elasticities in A, η_a and ϵ_a, influence the height of the optimal tariff in a relatively straightforward way. This is because, having no effect on h, their influence is exercised exclusively through k (see equation 5). Now anything which tends to raise k without affecting h will tend to reduce τ_m.[17] An increase in A's export supply elasticity, ϵ_a, will tend to lower or to raise k, and therefore to raise or to lower τ_m, according as η_b is greater or less than unity. An increase in the elasticity of A's import demand, η_a, will have precisely the opposite effect. It will tend to raise or to lower τ_m according as η_b is less or greater than unity.

Now τ_m may lie anywhere between zero and infinity, but it tends towards the latter only when certain foreign trade elasticities are themselves extreme. There are three cases when $\tau_m = 0$, i.e. when the free trade position is optimal. One, already mentioned, is when the marginal utility of money at the free trade position is the same in both countries. The second is when B's foreign trade elasticities,

---

[17] Differentiating equation (5) with respect to k,

$$\frac{\partial \tau_m}{\partial k} = \frac{-zh(\tau_m+1)^k \log(\tau_m+1)}{zhk(\tau_m+1)^{k-1}+1}.$$

If $h > 0$ (i.e. if $\eta_b > 1$) the denominator is positive, the numerator negative. $\therefore \partial \tau_m / \partial k < 0$.

If $h < 0$, $\partial \tau_m / \partial k < 0$ if, but only if, $1 + zhk(\tau_m+1)^{k-1} < 0$.

Now when T_m is optimal (i.e. when $T_m = \tau_m$), $\dfrac{d^2 W}{dT_m^2} < 0$.

But $\dfrac{dW}{dT_m} = p_{mb} \dfrac{dm}{dT_m} \phi_a[T_m - h(1-zc)]$

$\therefore \dfrac{d^2 W}{dT_m^2} = p_{mb} \dfrac{dm}{dT_m} \phi_a \left(1 + hz \dfrac{dc}{dT_m}\right) = p_m \dfrac{dm}{dT_m} \phi a[1 + hzk(T_m+1)^{k-1}].$

But, when $\eta_b < 1$, $\dfrac{dm}{dT_m} > 0$.

$\therefore$ When $\dfrac{d^2 W}{dT_m^2} < 0$ and $\eta_b < 1$, $1 + hzk(T_m+1)^{k-1} < 0$.

$\therefore$ When $\eta_b < 1$, $1 + hzk(T_m+1)^{k-1} < 0$.

$\therefore$ Whether η_b is greater or less than 1, $\dfrac{d\tau_m}{dk} < 0$.

η_b and ϵ_b, are both infinite.[18] The third case is where η_a and η_b, the import demand elasticities in both countries, are so low that c, the factor price ratio, is tending to become unstable. At such a point the slightest tariff increase will tend to drive c up to infinity.[19]

Apart from certain trivial cases where changes in T_m have no effect whatever on trade and welfare,[20] there are two cases when the optimal tariff tends towards infinity. One is when $\epsilon_b = 0$ and ϵ_a and η_b are infinite.[21] In this case, as T_m rises, the volume of A's imports remains constant; only the volume of its exports declines. But, owing to the infinite elasticities of import demand and export supply in B and A respectively, the marginal utility of A's export goods in A relative to B remains constant at the level of $1/z$; T_m can therefore rise indefinitely with advantage. As T_m rises, however, its effect on the volume of A's exports is of dwindling importance.

The second case where the optimal tariff is infinite is where $\eta_b = 0$ and ϵ_b and η_a are infinite.[22] In this case, as T_m rises the volume of A's exports remains constant and only the volume of its imports increases. Here, again, thanks to the infinite elasticity of export supply and import demand for B's import goods, the ratio of the marginal utility of these goods in A to their marginal utility in B remains constant at $1/z$ no matter how high the tariff is raised. In this case, unlike the previous one, the effect of further tariff increases does not dwindle as the tariff is raised.

The foregoing discussion has been based on the assumption that foreign trade elasticities, while affecting the height of the optimal tariff, are themselves unaffected by the height of the tariff. Clearly, this is not realistic. It is difficult to say anything in general about the effect of changes in trade on the *slopes* of the export demand and import supply curves, but the *elasticities* will probably vary inversely with the volume of trade. Thus, when $\eta_b > 1$, as T_m rises x and m will decline and all foreign trade elasticities will probably increase. Again, when $\eta_b < 1$, as T_m rises x will decline but m will rise, and while η_b and ϵ_a will probably increase, η_a and ϵ_b will

---

[18] In this case $h = 0$, and $k = \eta_a/\epsilon_a + \eta_a$. There is no transfer effect and the quantum effect is negative.

[19] That is, $k = \infty$. Where $\epsilon_a = \epsilon_b = \infty$, this point will be attained when $\eta_a + \eta_b = 1$.

[20] That is, where $\epsilon_a = 0$, and where $\eta_a = 0$.

[21] Here $h = \infty$ and $k = 0$.

[22] Here $h = -1$, and $k = 1$.

probably decline. This last result is of great importance. As we have seen, when $\eta_b < 1$, ϵ_a exercises a negative and η_a a positive influence on the optimal tariff level, τ_m. Therefore, through its influence on these elasticities, a rise in the actual tariff T_m will tend to bring about a decline in the optimal tariff τ_m. In particular, in the case last considered the effect of tariff changes on the elasticities will almost certainly make it impossible for η_b to remain at zero, or for ϵ_b and η_a to remain at infinity, as T_m is raised and will thus ensure a finite value for τ_m.

When the foreign trade elasticities are less extreme than those discussed above they may, as a first approximation, be assumed to be constant. This will permit us to calculate the height of the optimal import (or export) duty on alternative assumptions, of a more or less 'realistic' kind, as to the numerical values of these elasticities and of z (the ratio, at the free trade position, of the marginal utility of money in B to that in A). A number of such alternatives is set forth in the following table:[23]

Case	η_a	ϵ_a	η_b	ϵ_b	z	$\tau_m = \tau_x$
1	1	2	4	10	$\begin{cases} \frac{1}{2} \\ \frac{1}{3} \end{cases}$	21% 29%
2	1	1	3	5	$\begin{cases} \frac{1}{2} \\ \frac{1}{3} \end{cases}$	32% 46%
3	$\frac{1}{2}$	$\frac{1}{2}$	2	5	$\begin{cases} \frac{1}{2} \\ \frac{1}{3} \end{cases}$	47% 71%
4	2	3	$1\frac{1}{2}$	5	$\begin{cases} \frac{1}{2} \\ \frac{1}{3} \end{cases}$	64% 103%
5	1	1	$\frac{1}{2}$	3	$\begin{cases} \frac{1}{2} \\ \frac{1}{3} \end{cases}$	102% 227%

In all cases, country A may be thought of as a poor country—or group of countries—exporting primary products, B as the rest of the world exporting to A mainly manufactures. In case 1, A is small and the foreign trade elasticities are those describing the response of quantity to price over a relatively long period. Cases 2 and 3

---

[23] The values of τ_m in this table are arrived at by successive approximation from the logarithmic form of equation (5), $k \log (\tau_m + 1) = \log \left(\dfrac{h - \tau_m}{h^2} \right)$. This logarithmic form is permissible since $(\tau_m + 1)^k = c$ is, by definition, positive.

are also those of a small country, with elasticities relating to the medium run and short run respectively. In cases 4 and 5, A is a large country—or perhaps a group of small countries with a common tariff—and the elasticities relate to the long and the short run respectively.

It does not appear to be far fetched to suppose that at a free trade position the marginal utility of money in a poor, underdeveloped country might be two or three times as high as in those parts of the 'rest of the world' likely to be adversely affected by any tariff which it may impose. If the elasticities are realistic, for the circumstances to which they are intended to apply, it would appear that the level of tariffs whose imposition by poor or recently impoverished countries can be justified on grounds of their redistributive effects is quite substantial.

This conclusion is, however, subject to a number of qualifications and safeguards:

(1) The optimal tariff, or equivalent restriction, is likely to be higher, for a given value of z, in the case of a large country's adopting it to meet a temporary emergency than in the case of a small country's adopting it as a permanent measure. However, a more realistic analysis would have to take account of the fact that B, the 'outside world', is subdivided into regions whose marginal utilities of money are widely divergent. In so far as the economy of country A is competitive with—rather than complementary to— the economies of other poor countries the optimal level of A's tariff would be higher than shown in our model.

(2) In so far as the imposition of tariffs by poor countries leads to retaliation by rich countries or in so far as it tends to discourage direct income transfers from rich to poor countries any benefit will be reduced and may be cancelled.

(3) While some level of tariff protection by poor countries is justifiable on abstract welfare-economic grounds, the subjective character of the criteria employed—in particular the value assigned to z—would make it difficult, if not impossible, to base any clear-cut international trade rules on the sort of considerations discussed in this paper. Nevertheless some weight might well be given, in a general way, to such distributional considerations in international

64

negotiations on trade barriers, schemes of commodity regulation, and so forth.

Appendix

Part I

NOTE ON THE CONCEPT OF REAL INCOME EFFECTS IN RELATION TO TARIFF CHANGES

In the foregoing treatment the effect on welfare of a change in import duty (or of a change in export duty) was analysed into a quantum effect and a transfer effect. The definition of a quantum effect is such that in a single geographical market in which perfect competition prevails it would be acceptable as a measure of the effect on real income, or, more precisely, on real expenditure. The fact that anything gives rise to a positive quantum change at contemporary prices is an indication that, if coupled with an appropriate inter-personal transfer of purchasing power, it would enable *everyone* to attain a more desired position. As is well known the compensation test may prove ambiguous if pre-change and post-change prices diverge substantially, but when the quantum change itself is infinitesimal the discrepancy between pre-change and post-change prices becomes negligible.

Where, as in our problem, the market is divided into two parts separated by trade barriers the quantum effect has serious drawbacks as an indication of the real income effect. It will be noticed that where the elasticity of import demand in B is less than unity, an increase in A's import duty will have a positive quantum effect. It would however seem paradoxical to say that an increase in A's import duty could increase world *real income*.

A somewhat stronger objection to the use of the quantum effect as a measure of the real income effect in such cases is that it may yield ambiguous and contradictory results not only—as criteria of real income change generally do—when the underlying disturbance is large but even when it is infinitesimally small. For example, as we have seen, when $\eta_b < 1$ a minute increase in A's import duty from the level of x per cent, in the absence of any other impediment to trade, would have precisely the same substantive effect as

an equal percentage increase in A's export duty from a level of
x per cent in the absence of any other impediment to trade. Yet the
former increase would yield a *positive*, the latter a *negative*, quantum
effect.

Every economic change affecting a group of persons can be
broken down, from a welfare standpoint, into a real income component and a distributional component: the latter being equal to
a notional transfer of income from those who gain to those who
lose by the change, carried to the point at which either all are
gainers or all are losers; and the former being the uniform gain or
loss remaining after this act of compensation. The differences
between alternative concepts of real income change are often most
clearly mirrored in the different sorts of income redistribution with
which they are respectively associated.

In an economy with perfect competition the distributional change
with which an infinitesimal quantum change is associated—that of
an infinitesimal interpersonal transfer of money at constant prices
—is realistic. That is to say, the source of the expenditure could be
shifted from person to person, and from region to region, by a
transfer of purchasing power without significantly altering prices.
The money transfer will evoke a corresponding quantum transfer.
But where two regions are separated by a tariff barrier such a
quantum transfer is no longer possible. If country A, which already
has an import duty, raises it slightly and tries to compensate country
B for the losses involved, it cannot do so by transferring a given
sum of money at approximately constant prices. Since the prices
of certain goods are, thanks to the tariff, significantly higher in A
than in B the goods released by a given reduction in expenditure
in A will not be sufficient to meet the extra demand for goods
resulting from an equivalent increase in expenditure in B.

It is probably closer to the accepted idea of real income to define
a real income change, if possible, with reference to a 'realistic'
compensation criterion (even though this should make it impossible
to measure real income change with reference to actual prices or
amounts actually traded). This we can do by conceiving real income
change not as the actual quantum change in A and in B but as what
the quantum change in A would be *if* the change in tariff were
accompanied by a real transfer from A to B sufficient to prevent
any net quantum change in B. The formula for this can be worked

out.[24] It is such that any increase in A's import duty (or export duty) must *reduce* world real income.

The use of a real income concept correlated with such a 'realistic' distributional component is, however, not always satisfactory; specifically, where the conditions of the model are such that the act of transferring income will itself bring the situation nearer to, or further from, a Paretian optimum. For this reason, in the paper reproduced in Chapter 1 above, dealing with a situation in which import restrictions were the only means of preserving equilibrium in international payments, so that any international transfer had to be effected by means of an intensification or relaxation of restrictions, I preferred, despite its imperfections, to use the quantum test of real income gain.[25]

However, no concept of real income will make the real income change an adequate measure of the welfare effect of any act of policy. And once we decide to take explicit account of differences in the marginal utility of income it is far simpler to argue, as I have done in the present essay, in terms of the quantum effect and the marginal utility of money, than in terms of some other concept of real income, the marginal utility of which is more difficult to define or to conceive.

Part II

A. THE OPTIMAL IMPORT DUTY

(a) Let m be the volume of A's imports from B,

x be the volume of A's exports to B,

p_m be the price in B of A's imports from B, divided by B's factor price level,

p_x be the price in B of A's exports to B, divided by B's factor price level,

[24] If dR/dT be the rate at which world real income, as defined in the text, changes as the import (or export) duty increases, then

$$\frac{dR}{dT} = -\frac{aT(T+1)\left[\frac{\eta_a(\epsilon_b+1)(k-1)}{\epsilon_b+\eta_a}-1\right]}{1+\frac{\epsilon_b\eta_a}{\epsilon_a\eta_b}\cdot\frac{\epsilon_a+\eta_b}{\epsilon_b+\eta_a}}.$$

[25] Had I used, instead of the quantum change, a concept of real income change based on a 'realistic' compensation test, I should have obtained in all cases a formula for optimal discrimination identical with that which I in fact obtained for the special case where export supply elasticities are infinite.

t_m be the ratio of the price in A (expressed in B-currency) to the price in B of A's imports from B,

$T_m = t_m - 1$ be the *ad valorem* import duty on A's imports from B,

c be the ratio of A's factor price level (expressed in B-currency) to B's factor price level,

W be a numerical indicator of general welfare,

ϕ_a be the marginal utility of money in A, i.e. the ratio of

(1) the partial derivative of W with respect to the amount of any commodity consumed in A to

(2) the home market price of that commodity in A, expressed in B-currency in B factor price units,

ϕ_b be the marginal utility of money in B,

τ_m be the optimal value of T_m,

z be the value of ϕ_b/ϕ_a when $T_m = 0$.

$m = m_s(p_m)$ be the export supply function in B,   (i)

$m = m_d(p_m t_m c^{-1})$ be the import demand function of A,   (ii)

$x = x_d(p_x)$ be the import demand function in B,   (iii)

$x = x_s(p_x c^{-1})$ be the export supply function in A,   (iv)

$e_b = m'_s \cdot p_m/m$ be the elasticity of supply of exports in B, (v)

$e_a = x'_s \cdot p_x c^{-1}/x$ be the elasticity of supply of exports in A, (vi)

$\eta_b = -x'_d \cdot p_x/x$ be the negative elasticity of demand for imports in B,   (vii)

$\eta_a = -m'_d \cdot p_m t_m c^{-1}/m$ be the negative elasticity demand for imports in A,   (viii)

$xp_x = mp_m,$ (ix)

$\phi_b/\phi_a = cz.$ (x)

Then, from equation (2) in the text (since $p_{xa} = p_{xb} = p_x$, $p_{mb} = p_m$, and $p_{ma} = t_m p_m$),

$$\frac{dW}{dT_m} = \phi_a\left(p_m t_m \frac{dm}{dT_m} - p_x \frac{dx}{dT_m}\right) + \phi_b\left(p_x \frac{dx}{dT_m} - p_m \frac{dm}{dT_m}\right)$$

$$= \phi_a p_m \frac{dm}{dT_m}\left[T_m - \left(\frac{p_x}{p_m} \cdot \frac{dx}{dm} - 1\right)\left(1 - \frac{\phi_b}{\phi_a}\right)\right].$$

Differentiating (i) and (iii) and substituting in (v), (vii) and (ix),

$$\frac{p_x}{p_m} \cdot \frac{dx}{dm} - 1 = h = \frac{\eta_b + \epsilon_b}{\epsilon_b(\eta_b - 1)}. \tag{xi}$$

From (x),

$$\left(1 - \frac{\phi_b}{\phi_a}\right) = (1 - cz)$$

$$\therefore \qquad \frac{dW}{dT_m} = \phi_a p_m \frac{dm}{dT_m}\left[T_m - h(1 - cz)\right]. \tag{xii}$$

(b) The next step is to determine dm/dT_m.

From (iii), (iv), (vi) and (vii),

$$\frac{dp_x}{dt_m} = \frac{p_x}{c} \cdot \frac{\epsilon_a}{\epsilon_a + \eta_b} \cdot \frac{dc}{dt_m}. \tag{xiii}$$

From (i), (ii), (v) and (vii),

$$\frac{dp_m}{dt_m} = -\frac{p_m}{t_m} \cdot \frac{\eta_a}{\epsilon_b + \eta_a} + \frac{p_m}{c} \cdot \frac{\eta_a}{\epsilon_b + \eta_a} \cdot \frac{dc}{dt_m}. \tag{xiv}$$

From (i), (iii), (v), (vii) and (ix),

$$m\frac{dp_m}{dt_m}(1 + \epsilon_b) = x\frac{dp_x}{dt_m}(1 - \eta_b). \tag{xv}$$

From (xiii), (xiv) and (xv),

$$\frac{dc}{dT_m} = \frac{dc}{dt_m} = \frac{ck}{t_m} \text{ where } k = \frac{1}{\dfrac{\epsilon_a(\eta_b - 1)(\epsilon_b + \eta_a)}{\eta_a(\epsilon_a + \eta_b)(1 + \epsilon_b)} + 1}. \tag{xvi}$$

From (xiv) and (xvi),

$$\frac{dp_m}{dt_m} = \frac{\eta_a(k - 1)}{\epsilon_b + \eta_a} \cdot \frac{p_m}{t_m}. \tag{xvii}$$

From (xvii), (i) and (v),

$$\frac{dm}{dT_m} = \frac{dm}{dt_m} = \frac{\epsilon_b \eta_a(k - 1)}{\epsilon_b + \eta_a} \cdot \frac{m}{t_m}. \tag{xviii}$$

Substituting from (xviii) in (xii),

$$\frac{dW}{dT_m} = \frac{\epsilon_b \eta_a(k - 1)}{\epsilon_b + \eta_a} \cdot \frac{\phi_a p_m m}{T_m + 1}[T_m - h(1 - cz)]. \tag{xix}$$

69

(c) Let us assume that foreign trade elasticities are such that in a model in which T_m is constant but the ratio of exports to imports (xp_x/mp_m) is variable, this ratio falls as c rises. To see what this implies replace equation (ix) above by the following:

$$s = \frac{xp_x}{mp_m}.$$

Then, from (i), (iii), (v) and (vii),

$$mp_m\frac{ds}{dc} = x(1-\eta_b)\frac{dp_x}{dc} - sm(1+\epsilon_b)\frac{dp_m}{dc}.$$

From (xiii) and (xiv) (remembering that $dt_m/dc = 0$),

$$\frac{ds}{dc} = \frac{s}{c}\left[\frac{\epsilon_a(1-\eta_b)}{\epsilon_a+\eta_b} - \frac{\eta_a(1+\epsilon_b)}{\epsilon_b+\eta_a}\right]$$

$$\therefore \qquad \frac{ds}{dc} < 0 \text{ when } \frac{\epsilon_a(\eta_b-1)(\epsilon_b+\eta_a)}{\eta_a(\epsilon_a+\eta_b)(1+\epsilon_b)} > -1.$$

But when
$$\frac{\epsilon_a(\eta_b-1)(\epsilon_b+\eta_a)}{\eta_a(\epsilon_a+\eta_b)(1+\epsilon_b)} > -1$$

$$k > 0,$$

and
$$k \gtrless 1 \text{ as } \eta_b \lessgtr 1.$$

$\therefore$ If, when T_m is constant and s variable, $ds/dc < 0$, it follows from (xvi) and (xviii) that, when $s = 1$ and T_m is variable,

$$\frac{dc}{dT_m} > 0 \text{ and } \frac{dm}{dT_m} \gtrless 0 \text{ as } \eta_b \lessgtr 1.$$

(d) In order to express c, m, p_m and ϕ_a in (xix) as functions of T_m, let us specify the export supply and import demand functions (i) to (iv) as constant-elasticity functions.

Let the units of A's factors of production, of A's imports from B, of A's exports to B, and of welfare, be chosen such that, when $T_m = 0$,

$$1 = c = p_m = p_x = t_m = \phi_b, \qquad \text{(xx)}$$

Then B's export supply function will be $m = ap_m\epsilon_b$, $\qquad$ (xxi)

A's import demand function will be $m = a(p_mt_mc^{-1})^{-\eta_a}$, $\qquad$ (xxii)

B's import demand function will be $x = ap_x^{-\eta_b}$, (xxiii)

and A's export supply function will be $x = a(p_x c^{-1})\epsilon^a$. (xxiv)

Then, from (xxiii) and (xxiv),

$$p_x = c^{\frac{\epsilon_a}{\eta_b + \epsilon_a}}.$$ (xxv)

From (xxi) and (xxii),

$$p_m = t_m^{\frac{-\eta_a}{\epsilon_b + \eta_a}} c^{\frac{\eta_a}{\epsilon_b + \eta_a}}.$$ (xxvi)

From (xxi), (xxiii) and (ix),

$$p_x^{1-\eta_b} = p_m^{1+\epsilon_b}.$$ (xxvii)

And from (xxv), (xxvi) and (xxvii),

$$c = t_m^k.$$ (xxviii)

Again, from (xxi), (xxvi) and (xxviii),

$$\frac{p_m m}{T_m + 1} = a t_m^{\left[\frac{\eta_a(\epsilon_b + 1)(k-1)}{\epsilon_b + \eta_a} - 1\right]}$$ (xxix)

Now $\phi_a = \phi_b / zc$.

But ϕ_b, the marginal utility in B of income in units of B factors of production, is approximately constant.

Therefore $\phi_a = (zc)^{-1}$. (xxx)

From (xix), (xxviii), (xxix) and (xxx),

$$\frac{dW}{dT_m} = \frac{\epsilon_b \eta_a(k-1)}{\epsilon_b + \eta_a} az^{-1} t_m^{\left[\frac{\eta_a(\epsilon_b + 1)(k-1)}{\epsilon_b + \eta_a} - 1 - k\right]} [T_m - h(1 - t_m^k z)].$$ (xxxi)

(e) Now T_m will be either at an extremum or at a point of inflection when $dW/dT_m = 0$, i.e. when $T_m = h(1 - t_m^k z)$.

At this point

$$\frac{d^2 W}{dT_m^2} = \frac{\epsilon_b \eta_a(k-1)}{\epsilon_b + \eta_a} az^{-1} t_m^{\left[\frac{\eta_a(\epsilon_b + 1)(k-1)}{\epsilon_b + \eta_a} - 1 - k\right]} [1 + hzk t_m^{k-1}].$$

But since $k \gtrless 1$ as $\eta_b \lessgtr 1$ and since $h \lessgtr 0$ as $\eta_b \lessgtr 1$

$\therefore k \gtrless 1$ as $h \lessgtr 0$.

When k < 1 and $h > 0$ (also $k > 0$),

clearly $\qquad\qquad\qquad d^2W/dT_m{}^2 < 0.$

When $k > 1$ and $h < 0$,

$$d^2W/dT_m{}^2 < 0,$$

provided that $\qquad\qquad hzkt_m{}^{k-1} < -1.$

But, when $dW/dT_m = 0$, $hzt_m{}^k = h + 1 - t_m.$

$\therefore \qquad\qquad\qquad hzkt_m{}^{k-1} < 1$

if $\qquad\qquad\qquad k(h+1) < -t(1-k).$

But $-t(1-k) > 0$

and, if $\qquad\qquad h = \dfrac{\eta_b + \epsilon_b}{\epsilon_b(\eta_b - 1)} < 0,$

then $\qquad\qquad\qquad \eta_b < 1,$

and $\qquad\qquad\qquad h < -1,$

so that $\qquad\qquad\qquad k(h+1) < 0.$

$\therefore$ when $\qquad\qquad T_m = h(1 - t^k z)$

$$\frac{d^2W}{dT_m{}^2} < 0,$$

and W is at a maximum.

(f) There is always one and only one value of T_m for which

$$X = T_m - h(1 - zt_m{}^k) = 0.$$

For when $T_m = 0$

$$X = -h(1-z) \gtrless 0 \text{ as } h \lessgtr 0$$

and as $\qquad\qquad\qquad T_m \to \infty$

$$X \to T_m[1 + hz(T_m)^{k-1}]$$

and $\qquad\qquad X \gtrless 0 \text{ as } h \gtrless 0 \text{ (and } k \lessgtr 1)$

$\therefore$ since X is a continuous function of T_m,

$$X = 0$$

at some level of T_m between 0 and ∞.

Moreover, there is only one value of T_m for which $x = 0$. For, if there were more than one such value of T_m, the sign of dx/dT_m would not be the same for all such values of T_m.

But $dx/dT_m = 1 + hzkt_m^{k-1}$, and, as shown at (d) above, when $h > 0$

$$1 + hzkt^{k-1} > 0$$

and when $h < 0$, and $x = T_m - h + hzt^k = 0$,

$$1 + hzkt^{k-1} < 0$$

irrespective of the value of T_m.

Thus, when $x = 0$, sign dx/dT_m is invariable with respect to T_m. Therefore there is one and only one value of T_m for which $x = 0$.

B. THE OPTIMAL EXPORT DUTY

(a) Let t_x be the ratio of the price in B to the price in A (expressed in the same currency) of A's exports to B.

$T_x = t_x - 1$ be the *ad valorem* export duty in A's exports to B.

Let other symbols by defined as in Section A above.

Let $T_m = 0$.

Let the following definitional equations take the place of equations (ii), (iv), (vi) and (viii).

$$m = m_d(p_m c^{-1}) \tag{ii-a}$$

$$x = x_s(p_x t_x^{-1} c^{-1}) \tag{iv-a}$$

$$\epsilon_a = x'_s \frac{(p_x t_x^{-1} c^{-1})}{x} \tag{vi-a}$$

$$\eta_a = -m'_d \frac{p_m c^{-1}}{m} \tag{viii-a}$$

Then

$$\frac{dW}{dT_x} = \phi_a\left(p_m \frac{dm}{dT_x} - p_x t^{-1} \frac{dx}{dT_x}\right) + \phi_b\left(p_x \frac{dx}{dT_x} - p_m \frac{dm}{dT}\right)$$

$$= \phi_a p_x t_x^{-1} \frac{dx}{dT_x}\left[T_x - t_x\left(1 - \frac{p_m}{p_x} \cdot \frac{dm}{dx}\right)\left(1 - \frac{\phi_b}{\phi_a}\right)\right].$$

From (x) and (xi)

$$\frac{dW}{dT_x} = \phi_a p_x t_x^{-1} \frac{dx}{dT_x}\left[Tx - tx\left(\frac{h}{h+1}\right)(1 - cz)\right]. \tag{xxxii}$$

73

(b) From (iii), (iv-a), (vi-a) and (vii),

$$\frac{dp_x}{dt_x} = \frac{\epsilon_a}{\epsilon_a + \eta_b} \cdot \frac{p_x}{c} \cdot \frac{dc}{dt_x} + \frac{\epsilon_a}{\epsilon_a + \eta_b} \cdot \frac{p_x}{t_x}. \tag{xxxiii}$$

From (i), (ii-a), (v) and (viii-a),

$$\frac{dp_m}{dt_x} = \frac{\eta_a}{\epsilon_b + \eta_a} \cdot \frac{p_m}{c} \cdot \frac{dc}{dt_x}. \tag{xxxiv}$$

From (i), (iii), (v), (vii) and (ix),

$$m \frac{dp_m}{dt_x} (1 + \epsilon_b) = x \frac{dp_x}{dt_x} (1 - \eta_b). \tag{xxxv}$$

From (xxxiii), (xxxiv) and (xxxv),

$$\frac{dc}{dT_x} = \frac{dc}{dt_x} = \frac{c}{t_x} (k - 1). \tag{xxxvi}$$

From (xxiii) and (xxxvi),

$$\frac{dp_x}{dt_x} = \frac{\epsilon_a k}{\epsilon_a + \eta_b} \cdot \frac{p_x}{t_x}. \tag{xxxvii}$$

From (xxxvii), (iii) and (vii),

$$\frac{dx}{dT_x} = \frac{dx}{dt_x} = -\frac{\eta_b \epsilon_a k}{\epsilon_a + \eta_b} \cdot \frac{x}{t_x}. \tag{xxxviii}$$

Assuming, as before that $k > 0$

$$\frac{dx}{dT_x} < 0.$$

(c) From (xxxviii) and (xxxii),

$$\frac{dW}{dT_x} = -\frac{\eta_b \epsilon_a k}{\epsilon_a + \eta_b} \cdot \frac{\phi_a p_x x}{t_x^2} \left[T_x - t_x \left(\frac{h}{h+1} \right) \left(1 - cz \right) \right]. \tag{xxxix}$$

$$\frac{dW}{dT_x} = 0$$

when
$$T_x = t_x \left(\frac{h}{h+1} \right) \left(1 - cz \right)$$
$$= h(1 - czt_x).$$

By reasoning similar to that in section A.e. it can be shown that, at this value of T_x, $d^2W/dT^2{}_x < 0$

$\therefore$
$$\tau_x = h(1 - czt_x). \tag{xl}$$

Let us, as before, assume export supply and import demand functions of constant elasticity.

Substitute for (xxii) and (xxiv) the following:

$$m = a(p_m c^{-1})^{-\eta_a}$$

$$x = a(p_x t^{-1} c^{-1})^{\varepsilon} a.$$

By reasoning similar to that in section A.d. it can be shown that

$$c = t_x^{k-1}. \tag{xli}$$

From (xl) and (xli),

$$\tau_x = h(1 - z t_x^k). \tag{xlii}$$

Chapter 3
The Loss from Trade Restriction*

THE PROBLEM
What is the order of magnitude of the real income loss inflicted on
the world as a whole by the imposition of a tariff in a particular
country after all adjustments, of prices or exchange rates, required
to maintain international payments in balance have been made?
The answer must, of course, depend on (a) the definition of real
income change, (b) the height of the tariff, and (c) the demand and
supply conditions prevailing in the country in question and in the
rest of the world, respectively. Is it possible, assuming full employment and—save for the tariff—perfectly competitive conditions
everywhere, and adopting a suitable definition of real income
change, to arrive at a formula expressing that loss as a function of
the amount of trade prevailing in the initial situation and the
foreign trade elasticities in the two areas? If so, the exercise may
have some value in suggesting the degree of importance to be
attached, in various circumstances, to the economic disadvantages
of trade barriers.

THE REAL INCOME CONCEPT
The first task is to find a suitable concept of real income. We are
going to measure real income differences between situations. But
there is no point in doing this unless such differences can be compared—at least in the sense that if the fall in the real income index
involved in moving from situation A to situation C exceeds the fall
in moving from A to B, there will be a fall in moving from B to C
also. This implies that real income superiority (equality, inferiority)
is a transitive relation—that real income is an ordinal magnitude.
In addition we want to be able to add real income changes affecting individual countries to arrive at a real income change for the

* Reprinted, with slight editing, from *Economia Internazionale*, Vol. IX, No. 4,
Nov., 1956.

world as a whole. This implies that real income must be a cardinal or numerical magnitude. Finally—and this is crucial—our numerical concept of real income must be capable of being measured by an index *based on such price and quantity data as are deducible from the assumptions of our model.* Now the only data deducible from our model are those relating to international transactions. But any tolerable real income index must take into account domestic as well as international transactions. The only solution is for the index to be such that, under the condition of our model, those elements in it that are based on home market transactions retain a constant aggregate value, and only those elements that are based on international transactions show a net change.

Fortunately, there exists a respectable real income concept that satisfies all these requirements.

For any country let us define the change in the 'national quantum' as the change in the quantum of consumption *plus* the change in the quantum of property acquired *less* the change in the quantum of work and 'waiting' supplied, by residents of the country. Then, by the equations of social accounting, the change in the national quantum will be equal to the change in the quantum of gross output, *less* the change in the quantum of gross input, *plus* the change in the quantum of imports, *less* the change in the quantum of exports, *plus* the change in the net acquisition from foreigners of claims, securities, etc. Now assuming that (a) full employment and perfectly competitive conditions prevail in each country's home market and (b) there are no external economies or diseconomies, then any small change in production in any country that results from a small change in a tariff or in foreign trade conditions generally (production and consumption functions remaining constant), will entail a zero net change in the quantum of output *less* the quantum of input, at contemporary home market prices. Therefore, if we neglect—as we do throughout the rest of this chapter—the possibility of international capital movements, and assume that international payments remain continuously in balance, any small change in a country's national quantum at contemporary home market prices that results from a small change in a tariff can be measured by the change in the quantum of imports *less* the change in the quantum of exports, both changes being valued at contemporary home market prices.

However, we are dealing in this essay not with infinitesimal but with sizeable changes such as would result from the institution of a very high import duty. If we are to handle changes of this magnitude while retaining the advantage that the purely 'domestic' elements in our real income index remain constant we have to construct our index of the 'national quantum' on the lines of Marshallian consumers' and producers' surplus analysis. That is to say we have to assume the possibility of a gradual transition, by a series of infinitesimal steps, between any two situations that are to be compared—in the case under examination, between a free trade situation and a situation in which one country has an import duty of given size. If for each country the change in the national quantum corresponding to each step of the transition is calculated at the (home market) prices prevailing at that step it will be equal to the net quantum change, at that step, in the country's imports-less-exports. And, for each country, the (weighted) sum of the national quantum changes for all the various steps in the transition will be equal to the (similarly weighted) sum, for all steps, of the net quantum changes in its imports-less-exports.

The question now is: does any satisfactory concept of real income exist that would permit the real income change resulting from the imposition of an import duty to be approximately measured by a weighted sum of infinitesimal national quantum changes such as has been described?

It follows from the work of Professor Hicks[1] that if the prices of the goods consumed by an individual are expressed as a proportion of his income (expenditure) the effect on his real income (expenditure) of any change in these prices can be approximately measured by gradually adjusting the prices from the pre-change to the post-change position, weighting the additional goods consumed at each step of the transition by the prices appropriate to that step, and adding the increments thus valued. If the income effects of the price changes were confined to commodities whose prices did not significantly change, the sum arrived at by this calculation would measure the change in money income at constant pre-change prices that the individual would regard as equivalent

[1] See, in particular, J. R. Hicks, 'Consumers' Surplus and Index Numbers', *Review of Economic Studies*, Vol. 9, Summer 1942; also J. R. Hicks, 'The Generalized Theory of Consumers' Surplus', *Review of Economic Studies*, Vol. 13(2), No. 34, 1945–46.

to the effect on his purchasing power of the assumed price change. In the more probable case that the income effects are not so confined the sum arrived at will slightly overestimate real income losses, and underestimate real income gains accruing to the individual from price changes.

This supplies us with the real income concept we require to deal with our tariff problem. Let the home market prices of each commodity in each country be deflated by an index of domestic factor prices (i.e. approximately by an index of national income or expenditure) whose value, at the free trade position, is unity and, as the import duty is gradually raised, let the infinitesimal changes in imports *less* exports be weighted by the associated home market prices deflated in this way. Then, for each country, the sum of the increments in imports-*less*-exports, thus weighted, will measure approximately the equivalent income change aggregated for all the individuals in the country, at constant free trade prices.

The formula we have chosen may be regarded as measuring the net amount of money that would be required, at constant free trade prices, to compensate people in the free trade situation for not moving to the post-tariff situation.[2] This gives a privileged status to the international distribution of income at the free trade position. Had the national factor price indices chosen to deflate commodity prices in each country been based not on the free trade level but on the post-tariff level of factor prices, the formula would have measured the net amount of money at post-tariff prices that people would have paid rather than return to the free trade situation. In measuring the real income effect on the world as a whole, such a formula would have given a greater weight than does the formula we have actually used to the real income effect on the tariff-imposing country.

Had we chosen the post-tariff level of prices as the basis for our real income concept we might have found in certain circumstances that the imposition of a tariff exercises a *positive* effect on world real income. Having chosen the free trade level of prices, however, we can be sure that the effect on the world as whole—though not necessarily on the tariff importing country—will be negative. We

---

[2] It can also be interpreted as measuring the effect of the establishment of the tariff on the general welfare assuming the marginal utility of money to be the same in both countries at the free trade situation. See Chapter 2 above.

shall therefore—by inverting the signs in our formula as described above—seek to measure the *loss* rather than the gain to world real income involved in the imposition of an import duty of given *ad valorem* magnitude in country A, assuming that the rest of the world (non-A) maintains free trade.

FORMULA FOR THE REAL INCOME LOSS

Let L_1 be the loss of real income in A,

L_2 be the loss of real income in non-A,

L be the loss of real income to the world as a whole resulting from the establishment of an import duty of given magnitude in A,

τ stand for the *ad valorem* magnitude of the import duty introduced in A,

T for the tariff level corresponding to any step in the transition from a position with tariff level zero to a position with tariff level τ,

t for $T+1$,

m and x for the physical quantity of A's imports and exports respectively,

tP_m and P_x for the domestic prices (inside the tariff wall) of A's imports and exports respectively,

c for the ratio of A's factor price level at tariff level T to the same at the free trade position.

All t, m, x, P_m, P_x and c are functions of T. Then

$$L_1 = \int_{T=0}^{\tau} c^{-1}\left(P_x \frac{dx}{dT} - tP_m \frac{dm}{dT} \right) dT \tag{1}$$

Since A's imports and exports are non-A's exports and imports respectively, and since at the free trade position prices are the same in A and in non-A,

$$L_2 = \int_{T=0}^{\tau} c_2^{-1}\left(P_m \frac{dm}{dT} - P_x \frac{dx}{dT} \right) dT \tag{2}$$

where c_2 stands for the ratio of non-A's factor price level at tariff-level T to the same at the free trade position.

Let all prices be expressed in terms of non-A factor units. Then $c_2 = 1$ and c stands for A's factor price level *relative to that of non-A* expressed as a proportion of the same ratio in the free trade position.

Equation (2) will then be rewritten

$$L_2 = \int_{T=0}^{\tau} \left(P_m \frac{dm}{dT} - P_x \frac{dx}{dT} \right) dT. \tag{3}$$

Let us assume that, both in A and non-A, the volume of imports and that of exports are determined by the home market prices, in terms of domestic factor units, of import goods and of export goods respectively. This implies that neither the domestic demand for import goods nor that for exportable goods is sensitive to changes in domestic real income and that the export and import demand curves are independent of each other.[3] Let us further assume that as the tariff (T) changes the value of A's exports and imports are kept in balance by changes in the relative factor price level (c).

Let p_m be the price in non-A of A's imports from non-A, divided by non-A's factor price level. Then, in the above conditions, it can be shown[4] that, for any value of T,

$$L_1 = \int_{T=0}^{\tau} X_1 dT$$

where $$X_1 = -rmp_m c^{-1}[1 - (h+1)t^{-1}] \tag{4}$$

and $$L_2 = \int_{T=0}^{\tau} X_2 dT$$

where $$X_2 = -rmp_m h t^{-1}. \tag{5}$$

[3] The assumed absence of income effects on the demand for foreign trade goods is rendered less implausible by the assumed maintenance of full employment in both countries. It is also in harmony with the condition required for the exactitude of our real income measure, namely that income effects on the demand for commodities whose prices change markedly should be negligible. See p. 79 above.

[4] See Appendix, section 1.

In equations (4) and (5)

$$h \text{ stands for } \frac{\eta_b + \epsilon_b}{\epsilon_b(\eta_b - 1)}$$

$$r \text{ stands for } \frac{\epsilon_b \eta_a(k-1)}{\epsilon_b + \eta_a}$$

$$k \text{ stands for } \frac{1}{\frac{\epsilon_a(\eta_b - 1)(\epsilon_a + \eta_b)}{\eta_a(\epsilon_a + \eta_b)(1 + \epsilon_b)} + 1}$$

where η_a and ϵ_a stand, respectively, for the total price elasticities of import-demand and export-supply in A, and η_b and ϵ_b for the corresponding elasticities in non-A.

From equations (4) and (5),

$$L = L_1 + L_2 = \int_{T=0}^{\tau} (X_1 + X_2) dT$$

where
$$X_1 + X_2 = -rmp_m[c^{-1} - (h+1)t^{-1}c^{-1} + ht^{-1}]. \tag{6}$$

In this equation, the value of imports ($p_m m$), the relative factor price level (c) and t are all functions of T. In order to express them as such, however, it is necessary to give a specific form to the export supply and import demand functions[5] in A and non-A respectively. The most manageable form is that of constant elasticity functions. Assuming constant foreign trade elasticities it can be shown[6] that

$$X_1 = -ra[t^{s-k} - (h+1)t^{s-k-1}] \tag{7}$$

and
$$X_2 = -raht^{s-1}$$

where h, k and r are defined as above,

$$s \text{ stands for } \frac{\eta_a(\epsilon_b + 1)(k-1),}{\epsilon_b + \eta_a}$$

---

[5] I.e., export supply and import demand, respectively, as functions of home market prices of export goods and import goods, respectively, both prices being expressed in domestic factor units.

[6] See Appendix, section 2.

and a stands for the value of A's imports (or exports) at the free trade position.

Now
$$L_1 = \int_{T=0}^{\tau} X_1 dT$$

and
$$L_2 = \int_{T=0}^{\tau} X_2 dT$$

Integrating X_1 and X_2 with respect to T we get

$$L_1 = -ra[(s-k+1)^{-1}(t_\tau^{s-k+1}-1)-(s-k)^{-1}(h+1)(t_\tau^{s-k}-1)] \quad (8)$$

and
$$L_2 = -ras^{-1}h(t_\tau^{s}-1) \quad (9)$$

where
$$t_\tau \equiv \tau+1$$

$$\therefore L = L_1 + L_2 =$$

$$-ra\left[\frac{1}{s-k+1}(t_\tau^{s-k+1}-1)-\frac{h+1}{s-k}(t_\tau^{s-k}-1)+\frac{h}{s}(t_\tau^{s}-1)\right]. \quad (10)$$

THE MAGNITUDE OF THE LOSS AND THAT OF THE FOREIGN TRADE ELASTICITIES

This formula is very complicated. It is clear, however, that non-A must incur a loss from the introduction of A's tariff, i.e. L_2 is always positive. Country A itself may either gain or lose depending on whether the tariff level is below or above the nationally optimal tariff. The world as a whole, however, must lose from the introduction of the tariff, i.e. L is always positive. That L_2 is positive can be seen from the facts that r and s have the same sign, that s and h have opposite signs, and that t_τ is greater than unity: thus $(t_\tau^{s}-1)$ has the same sign as $-ras^{-1}h$. That L is positive can also be shown algebraically. It can perhaps be seen intuitively, since (a) any change in the quantities of goods imported or exported that is equivalent to a transfer of goods from a country where their price (deflated by the factor price index) is higher to one where their deflated price is lower will, according to our formula, involve a loss, (b) at the free trade position deflated prices are the same in both countries and (c) deflated prices tend to fall in the country receiving or retaining more foreign trade goods and to rise in the country receiving or retaining less foreign trade goods. Thus *any*

83

ESSAYS IN INTERNATIONAL ECONOMICS

shift from the free trade position will involve a real income loss to the world.

The magnitude of this real income loss (L) does not vary in any simple way with the magnitude of the various foreign trade elasticities. It may, however, provide some sort of thread through the labyrinth to remember, in conformity with what is said immediately above, that the magnitude of the loss varies with (a) the magnitude of the divergence of the trade quanta from their free trade position and (b) the excess of the price of the goods in question in the country which exports more or imports less than in the free trade position over their price in the country that imports more or exports less than in the free trade position, both prices being deflated by national factor price indices, and the divergence between the deflated prices being averaged over a gradual transition from the free trade position to the full tariff position.

Now, for any given level of t, the influence exercised by the respective foreign trade elasticities on the magnitude of the loss resulting from the tariff may be divided into two parts: that which is independent of, and that which is mediated through their influence on A's relative price level (c). If c is assumed to rise with t but the relationship between t and c is assumed to be unaffected by the foreign trade elasticities, an increase in *any* of these elasticities η_a, η_b, ϵ_a, ϵ_b, will increase the divergence between the volume of imports or exports resulting from the application of the tariff and their volume at the free trade optimum. The *marginal* degree of loss on such trade diversion depends on the height of t and c and is assumed to be independent of the elasticities. But the inframarginal, and hence the average, degree of loss will be somewhat reduced. It is only, however, when the elasticities reach very high levels that the effect of higher elasticities on the average degree of loss begins to outweigh its effect on the volume traded. Until then the higher the elasticities the greater the loss.

But we must take account of the fact that the relationship between t and c itself depends on the size of the foreign trade elasticities. Now c will be greater or less than t (i.e. the percentage rise from the free trade position in the ratio of A's price-level to that of non-A will exceed or fall short of the *ad valorem* tariff) so long as η_b, the elasticity of non-A's demand for A's exports, is less or greater than 1. So long as $\eta_b > 1$ the precise bearing of the elasticities

84

THE LOSS FROM TRADE RESTRICTION

on the relation between c and t does not matter much; for, so long as $c < t$, any rise in c (t remaining unchanged) will have an ambiguous effect on the loss from the tariff. It will move A's export volume further from, but bring A's import volume nearer to, the optimal or free trade volume, creating a loss on the former, a gain on the latter account.

If, however, $\eta_b < 1$, and $c > t$ then any further increase in c, for a given level of t, will involve a loss by reason of its effect on trade in *both* directions—it will tend to reduce A's exports further and further below, and to raise A's imports further and further above, the optimal volume. The effect of the elasticities on the relation of c to t therefore becomes very important. Now, for any given level of tariff, c will be the greater the higher is ϵ_a, and the lower are η_a and η_b, while it will rise or fall with ϵ_b according as η_a is less or greater than 1.

It follows that, when $c > t$, the influence of η_a and η_b on the magnitude of the loss will be uncertain—in the sense of being dependent on complex conditions—a positive 'independent' influence being offset (and probably outweighed) by a negative influence through c. We can, however, say that up to high levels of elasticity, the higher is ϵ_a, A's export supply elasticity, the greater will be the loss from the tariff. Moreover, if η_a, A's import demand elasticity, falls short of unity, we can add that, up to high levels of elasticity, the higher is ϵ_b, non-A's export supply elasticity, the greater will be the real income loss from the tariff.

MAGNITUDE OF THE LOSS ON SPECIFIC ASSUMPTIONS
Let us now consider a number of special cases where particular values are assigned to the foreign trade elasticities.

When the elasticity of demand abroad for A's exports is unity (i.e. when $\eta_b = 1$) the loss from A's tariff can be expressed relatively simply:[7]

$$L = a\frac{\epsilon_a}{1+\epsilon_a}(t_\tau^{-1} + \log_\epsilon t_\tau - 1) \qquad (11)$$

[7] This loss is the net result of a gain in country A, and a loss in non-A as follows:

$$L_1 = -a\frac{\epsilon_a}{1+\epsilon_a}(1 - t_\tau^{-1})$$

and
$$L_2 = a\frac{\epsilon_a}{1+\epsilon_a}\log_\epsilon t_\tau$$

85

Since with $\eta_b = 1$ the volume of A's imports is unaffected by the height of the tariff the only other elasticity that affects the magnitude of the loss is A's own export supply elasticity (ϵ_a) which, as it increases, tends to increase the loss. When both η_b and ϵ_a are equal to unity the real income loss from a 100 per cent *ad valorem* tariff is equivalent to a loss of money income at free trade prices equal to 9·65 per cent of the value of A's imports in the free trade situation. (See Table 3.1.)

If all the foreign trade elasticities are raised to 2, the real income loss will rise slightly to 11·8 per cent of the free trade value of imports and as the elasticities are raised further in a uniform manner the real loss will increase slowly until, when the elasticities are in the neighbourhood of $10\frac{1}{2}$, the real loss reaches a (local) maximum in the neighbourhood of 20·7 per cent of the value of free-trade imports. Thereafter, however, as the elasticities are raised further the real loss tends to decline. This is because, while the decline in trade resulting from a given tariff is the greater the higher

TABLE 3.1. *The Case of Uniform Foreign Trade Elasticities and 100 Per Cent Tariff*

$$\eta_a = \eta_b = \epsilon_a = \epsilon_b \qquad t_\tau = 2$$

Elasticity (η_a, η_b, ϵ_a, ϵ_b)	Real Loss (L)	
1	0·0965	a
2	0·118	a
3	0·135	a
9	0·205	a
10	0·2064	a
10·5	0·2066	a
11	0·2061	a
15	0·195	a
20	0·172	a
50	(= 0·08	a)
100	(= 0·04	a)

the foreign trade elasticities, the average rate of loss per unit of trade foregone declines as these elasticities increase, and, after a certain point, the decline in the average loss outweighs the contraction of trade. When the elasticities are infinite the real income loss tends to zero, for though in these circumstances a tariff of any size at all will result in a complete disappearance of foreign trade the loss per unit will be negligible.

Apart from the case just mentioned the loss from the tariff is naturally negligible in conditions in which the tariff exercises a negligible effect on the volume of trade. This will happen when either the export supply elasticity (ϵ_a) or the import demand elasticity (η_a) in the tariff country, tends towards zero.

When the import demand elasticity in non-A (η_b) is unity, the loss from the tariff, as appears from equation (11), will increase with ϵ_a, and when ϵ_a is infinite will be twice as great as when ϵ_a is unity, i.e. for a tariff of 100 per cent it will amount to 19·3 per cent of A's free trade imports. (See Table 3.2.)

So long as η_b is greater than unity the real loss from a 100 per cent tariff is unlikely to be much greater than 20 per cent of a, and, as can be seen from Table 3.2 for a number of more or less 'realistic' sets of foreign trade elasticities, the loss will usually be much less than this.

TABLE 3.2

Case	η_a	ϵ_a	η_b	ϵ_b	t_τ[8]	L	
1	$\frac{1}{2}$	$\frac{1}{2}$	2	5	2	0·048	a
					3	0·110	a
2	1	1	3	5	2	0·080	a
					3	0·176	a
3	1	2	4	10	2	0·106	a
					3	0·234	a
4	Any amount	1	1	Any amount	2	0·0965	a
					3	0·216	a
5	1	1	∞	∞	2	0·0965	a
					3	0·216	a
6	2	3	$1\frac{1}{2}$	5	2	0·132	a
					3	0·282	a
7	1	1	$\frac{1}{2}$	3	2	0·215	a
					3	0·536	a
8	Any amount	∞	1	Any amount	2	0·193	a
					3	0·432	a
9	$\frac{1}{2}$	∞	$\frac{1}{2}$	∞	2	∞	
					3	∞	

It is when the import elasticity in non-A for A's exports is less than unity that the loss from the tariff is apt to rise to really high levels. So long as η_b is greater than unity, trade between A and

---

[8] $t_\tau = 2$ corresponds to a 100 per cent *ad valorem* tariff; $t_\tau = 3$ to a 200 per cent tariff.

ESSAYS IN INTERNATIONAL ECONOMICS

non-A can only become disturbed by a curtailment of both exports and imports and this very fact puts a limit on it. But when η_b is less than unity, trade can become disturbed not only by a curtailment of A's exports but also by an expansion of A's imports which may assume dimensions far greater than A's free trade level of imports.

Particularly if import demand elasticities are low both in A and in non-A and if non-A's export supply elasticity is high, the expansion of non-A's imports and the consequential loss of world real income may be very high indeed. As ϵ_a and ϵ_b tend to infinity and the sum of η_a and η_b falls to 1, the real loss tends to infinity.

This is because, in the assumed conditions, even a relatively small tariff in A will entail a big increase in A's price level or exchange rate relative to non-A's; so that A will obtain additional goods from non-A, whether in the form of exports withheld or of imports extorted, that are worth far more—when deflated by factor prices—in non-A than in A. As import demand elasticities in both areas decline towards the point at which exchange rate equilibrium becomes radically unstable, any tariff at all will send the relative price levels shooting off to infinity and the real income loss will likewise tend towards infinity. Be it noted, however, that the loss will fall exclusively on non-A and arises from the fact that the goods—both export-goods and import-goods—which A extracts from non-A by raising the tariff, are increasingly vital to non-A, and increasingly unimportant to A.

Appendix

1. Let m be the volume of A's imports from non-A,

   x be the volume of A's exports to non-A,

   p_m be the price in non-A of A's imports from non-A, divided by non-A's factor price level,

   p_x be the price in non-A of A's exports to non-A, divided by non-A's factor price level,

   t be the ratio of the price in A (expressed in non-A-currency) to the price in non-A of A's imports from non-A,

   $T = t-1$ be the *ad valorem* import duty on A's imports from non-A,

c be the ratio of A's factor price level (expressed in non-A-currency) to non-A's factor price level,

L be the real income loss resulting in the world as a whole from a transition from a situation where $T = 0$ to one where $T = \tau$,

L_1 be the real income loss resulting in A from this transition,

L_2 be the real income loss resulting in non-A from this transition.

Let $m = m_s(p_m)$ be the export supply function in non-A,   (i)

$m = m_d(p_m t c^{-1})$ be the import demand function of A,   (ii)

$x = x_d(p_x)$ be the import demand function in non-A,   (iii)

$x = x_s(p_x c^{-1})$ be the export supply function in A,   (iv)

$\epsilon_b = m'_s \cdot \dfrac{p_m}{m}$ be the elasticity of supply of exports in non-A,   (v)

$\epsilon_a = x'_s \cdot \dfrac{p_x c^{-1}}{x}$ be the elasticity of supply of exports in A,   (vi)

$\eta_b = -x'_d \cdot \dfrac{p_x}{x}$ be the negative elasticity of demand for imports in non-A,   (vii)

$\eta_a = -m'_d \cdot \dfrac{p_m t c^{-1}}{m}$ be the negative elasticity of demand for imports in A,   (viii)

$xp_x = mp_m$ (ix)

From page 81 of the text we know that

$$L_1 = \int_{T=0}^{\tau} X_1 dT \tag{x}$$

where $\quad X_1 \equiv c^{-1}\left(p_x \dfrac{dx}{dT} - tp_m \dfrac{dm}{dT} \right) = c^{-1}\left(p_x \dfrac{dx}{dt} - tp_m \dfrac{dm}{dt} \right).$ (xi)

$\therefore \qquad X_1 = c^{-1} p_m \dfrac{dm}{dt}\left(\dfrac{p_x}{p_m} \cdot \dfrac{dx}{dm} - t \right).$ (xii)

Differentiating (i), (iii) and (ix) and substituting from (v) and (vii)

$$\frac{p_x}{p_m} \cdot \frac{dx}{dm} = 1 + h \quad \text{where} \quad h \equiv \frac{\eta_b + \epsilon_b}{\epsilon_b(\eta_b - 1)}. \tag{xiii}$$

From (xii) and (xiii)

$$X_1 = c^{-1} p_m \frac{dm}{dt}(h + 1 - t). \tag{xiv}$$

From (iii), (iv), (vi) and (vii)

$$\frac{dp_x}{dt} = \frac{p_x}{c} \cdot \frac{\epsilon_a}{\epsilon_a + \eta_b} \cdot \frac{dc}{dt}. \tag{xv}$$

From (i), (ii), (v), (vii) and (viii)

$$\frac{dp_m}{dt} = -\frac{p_m}{t} \cdot \frac{\eta_a}{\epsilon_b + \eta_a} + \frac{p_m}{c} \cdot \frac{\eta_a}{\epsilon_b + \eta_a} \cdot \frac{dc}{dt}. \tag{xvi}$$

From (i), (iii), (v), (vii) and (ix)

$$m \frac{dp_m}{dt}(1 + \epsilon_b) = x \frac{dp_x}{dt}(1 - \eta_b). \tag{xvii}$$

From (xv), (xvi) and (xvii)

$$\frac{dc}{dt} = \frac{ck}{t} \quad \text{where} \quad k \equiv \frac{1}{\dfrac{\epsilon_a(\eta_b - 1)(\epsilon_a + \eta_b)}{\eta_a(\epsilon_a + \eta_b)(1 + \epsilon_b)} + 1}. \tag{xviii}$$

From (xvi) and (xviii)

$$\frac{dp_m}{dt} = \epsilon_b^{-1} r t^{-1} p_m \quad \text{where} \quad r = \frac{\epsilon_b \eta_a(k - 1)}{\epsilon_b + \eta_a}. \tag{xix}$$

From (xix), (i) and (v)

$$\frac{dm}{dt} = r t^{-1} m. \tag{xx}$$

From (xiv) and (xx)

$$X_1 = -r m p_m c^{-1}[1 - (h + 1)t^{-1}]. \tag{xxi}$$

Again from page 83 of the text

$$L_2 = \int_{T=0}^{\tau} X_2 dT \tag{xxii}$$

where
$$X_2 \equiv p_m \frac{dm}{dT} - p_x \frac{dx}{dT}. \qquad \text{(xxiii)}$$

By reasoning similar to that employed to determine X_1,

$$X_2 = -rmp_m ht^{-1} \qquad \text{(xxiv)}$$

and
$$X_1 + X_2 = -rmp_m[c^{-1} - (h+1)t^{-1}c^{-1} + ht^{-1}]. \qquad \text{(xxv)}$$

2. In order to express c, m, and p_m as functions of t let us specify the export supply and import demand functions (i) to (iv) as constant elasticity functions.

Let the units of A's factors of production, of A's imports from non-A of A's exports to non-A and of welfare, be so chosen that, when $T = 0$,

$$1 = c = p_m = p_x = t. \qquad \text{(xxvi)}$$

Then non-A's export supply function will be

$$m = ap_m^{\epsilon_b}, \qquad \text{(xxvii)}$$

A's import demand function will be

$$m = a(p_m tc^{-1})^{-\eta_a}, \qquad \text{(xxviii)}$$

non-A's import demand function will be

$$x = ap_x^{-\eta_b}, \qquad \text{(xxix)}$$

and A's export supply function will be

$$x = a(p_x t^{-1})^{\epsilon_a}. \qquad \text{(xxx)}$$

Then from (xxix) and (xxx)

$$p_x = c^{\frac{\epsilon_a}{\eta_b + \epsilon_a}}. \qquad \text{(xxxi)}$$

From (xxvii) and (xxviii)

$$p_m = t^{\frac{-\eta_a}{\epsilon_b + \eta_a}} c^{\frac{\eta_a}{\epsilon_b + \eta_a}}. \qquad \text{(xxxii)}$$

From (xxvii), (xxix) and (ix)

$$p_x^{1-\eta_b} = p_m^{1+\epsilon_b}. \qquad \text{(xxxiii)}$$

From (xxxi), (xxxii) and (xxxiii)

$$c = t^k. \qquad \text{(xxxiv)}$$

Again from (xxvii), (xxxii) and (xxxiv)

$$mp_m = at^s \quad \text{where} \quad s \equiv \frac{\eta_a(\epsilon_b + 1)(k-1)}{\epsilon_b + \eta_a}. \qquad \text{(xxxv)}$$

∴ From (xxi), (xxiv) and (xxv)

$$X_1 = -ar[t^{s-k} - (h+1)t^{s-k-1}]. \qquad \text{(xxxvi)}$$

Again from (xxiv) and (xxxv)

$$X_2 = -arht^{s-1} \qquad \text{(xxxvii)}$$

and from (xxv), (xxxvi) and (xxxvii)

$$X_1 + X_2 = -ar[t^{s-k} - (h+1)t^{s-k-1} + ht^{s-1}].$$

Part Two

International Monetary Reform

Chapter 4

International Liquidity: Ends and Means*

A country's external liquidity consists of such resources as are readily available to its monetary authorities for the purpose of financing deficits in its balance of payments and defending the stability of its rate of exchange. These resources may take the form of liquid assets, such as gold and foreign exchange, or of facilities for borrowing such assets from abroad.

The first part of this essay sets forth criteria for determining, in principle, the most desirable aggregate amount, composition, and, to a lesser extent, country distribution of external liquidity in the world. The second part deals with the instrumentalities that are, or might conceivably be, used to attain or approach these optima.

Much that has been written in the post-war period about the adequacy of world reserves or world liquidity would appear to rest on uncertain logical foundations. One frequent approach is to estimate a figure for required or optimal reserves, by starting from some past date when total reserves are supposed to have been roughly satisfactory and adjusting this total for the growth in the value of world trade between the base date and the present time. While the value of world trade is, admittedly, a relevant consideration, there are many other dynamic factors affecting the need for reserves. This is emphasized in many of the writings in which such historical comparisons appear.[1] It is not surprising, therefore, that calculations starting from different base dates, at each of which reserves may have been roughly satisfactory, yield enormously different results. Moreover,

* Reprinted, with slight editing, from International Monetary Fund *Staff Papers*, Vol. VIII, December 1961.

[1] For example, see United Nations, Department of Economic Affairs, *Measures for International Economic Stability* (New York, 1951) pp. 32–33; Roy F. Harrod, 'Imbalance of International Payments', *Staff Papers*, Vol. III, 1953–54, pp. 2–4; 'The Adequacy of Monetary Reserves', *Staff Papers*, Vol. III, 1953–54, pp. 198–213; International Monetary Fund, *International Reserves and Liquidity* (Washington, 1958) pp. 14–30; Robert Triffin, *Gold and the Dollar Crisis* (New Haven, 1960) pp. 38–41.

if it is possible to say that reserves were or were not adequate at the base date, one wonders if it is not possible to apply the same criteria to the present situation and judge the adequacy of present reserves less indirectly. Another approach is to estimate the world's need for reserves on the basis of the amounts that individual countries would need if they were to behave appropriately (by some standard) with respect to the various types of payments fluctuations they may have to face.[2] It should be fairly obvious, however, that any fruitful approach to this problem must be based not on how countries ought to behave but on how they actually behave. A third approach that is sometimes adopted is to estimate optimal world reserves by adding together the reserves that individual countries show, by their be-haviour, they would like to hold. Sometimes this seems to mean merely that whatever is, is right. Countries should have the reserves they effectively demand, and what they effectively demand is shown by what they actually have. In the more sophisticated variants of this theory, the adequacy or inadequacy of reserves, relative to the demand for them, is said to be shown by the policy reactions of governments.[3] This is getting nearer to the truth but is still somewhat wide of the mark. Policy reactions are relevant to the question of reserve adequacy, not so much because of their symptomatic signifi-cance (i.e. because they show that the country would like to have larger or smaller reserves) as because they have effects on the welfare both of the country in question and of other countries.

I. Criteria for Determining Amount, Composition, and Distribution of External Liquidity

Our own approach, therefore, is to go back to first principles and consider the probable effects of any change in liquidity on the eco-nomic welfare of the world. Liquidity is optimal if no change having a desirable effect on economic welfare can take place. Of course,

[2] Traces of this approach are found rather generally in the literature. However, it appears most prominently, perhaps, in 'The Adequacy of Monetary Reserves', *Staff Papers*, Vol. III, 1953–54, pp. 185–91.

[3] See *International Reserves and Liquidity* (cited above), pp. 42–43; Committee on the Working of the Monetary System, 'Memorandum of Evidence Submitted by Mr A. C. L. Day', *Principal Memoranda of Evidence*, Vol. 3 (London, 1960) pp. 71–76; T. de Vries, 'International Liquidity', *Economisch-Statistische Berichten*, September 24, 1958, pp. 728–33.

there are various types of international liquidity and near-liquidity, and the most desirable aggregate amount of liquidity will depend on the proportions in which these various types are combined, and on their distribution among countries. It will therefore be a function of the particular methods by which the amount of liquidity in the world is varied. However, to start with, we can ignore all that and assume only one type of international liquidity—a reserve asset of some sort —and one method by which the supply of this reserve asset can be varied, presumably by the act of some international organization or by some intergovernmental decision.

POLICY EFFECTS OF RESERVE CHANGES
As it happens, practically all the important economic effects of reserve changes come to pass by way of their effects on national policies; namely, monetary and budgetary policies, policies with respect to restrictions on international trade and capital movements, and policies with respect to exchange rates. The main exception to this is the direct effect that the amount of national reserves has on private international capital movements of a speculative type. But, even here, the direct effect is probably minor, owing to the widespread tendency of monetary authorities to offset the effects of such movements on the money supply and on interest rates. Since these movements tend to accentuate the inadequacy of already inadequate reserves by transferring them from countries that need them to countries that do not, their main importance probably is to reinforce the effect on government policies that changes in aggregate reserves would, in any event, tend to exercise.

Any increase in countries' reserves relative to the amounts that they consider it desirable to hold will encourage (1) more expansionary financial policies, particularly monetary policies, (2) less severe restrictions on imports and capital imports, and (3) less frequent resort to currency devaluation (or increased resort to revaluation). Since in any given country these reactions are likely to be stronger if that country is in an adverse than if it is in a favourable payments situation, an increase in actual, relative to desired, reserves will evoke an increased tendency to meet payments fluctuations by the use of reserves rather than by variations in financial policies, restrictive policies, or exchange rates.

Up to World War II, the adequacy of world reserves or of gold supplies was judged primarily with reference to effects on the stock of money and on the trend of prices. In the course of the inter-war period, however, with the spread of quotas and the breakdown of the gold standard, it became clear that the level of reserves acted not only on prices and employment but also on trade restrictions and exchange rates. In the early post-war period, when there was no longer any question of an automatic link between reserves and money supply, discussion tended to highlight the bearing of international liquidity on the freedom of international transactions. It is important, however, that all types of policy reaction should be held in mind simultaneously.

DIMINISHING MARGINAL UTILITY OF INCREASES IN RESERVES

An evaluation of increases in reserves involves both factual and ethical judgments, on which opinions may differ. Most people, however, would consider liberalization of imports to be, in general, desirable, and monetary expansion to be good or bad according as conditions are otherwise deflationary or inflationary. The effects on exchange rate policy would be good to the extent that exchange depreciations in the face of short-run or cyclical payments weakness are avoided, and bad in so far as adjustments to more fundamental disequilibria are postponed.[4] As reserves rise, in any given set of circumstances, the marginal effects of raising them further will probably dwindle, in the sense that a given increase from a high level will have a less powerful impact on policy and will react less quickly on the balance of payments than would a similar increase from a lower level. Moreover, their character will alter and their welfare significance will change. After abnormal restrictions on imports have been removed, further liberalization becomes less likely and less important. The higher the level of reserves, the less likely are the expansionary effects on monetary policy of further reserve increases to exercise a useful effect on the economy, and so on. Generally speaking, there is a diminishing, and ultimately a negative, marginal utility of reserve increases; it is this that ensures the existence at any time of an optimal level. In a generally deflationary situation, when

---

[4] There will, of course, be differences of view as to the relative emphasis to be put on price stability and full employment in judging the presence or absence of inflation, and as to the degree of exchange rate stability deemed desirable.

no amount of reserves can do much harm, the optimum will be a gentle eminence in a plateau; only in a generally inflationary situation will it be more like a peak.

TIME HORIZON OF EFFECTS OF RESERVE CHANGES

The policy effects of any general change in the level of international reserves, though partly temporary, may nevertheless extend quite far into the future; and some of them may be permanent. On certain assumptions, however, all the policy effects of a general change would be temporary. Starting from a position of constant prices, an increase in reserves would result in expansionary monetary policies, rising prices, a rising value of international transactions, and a rising demand for reserves, which would continue until the demand for reserves had caught up with the supply and the inflation came to a stop. In the end, according to this view, prices and reserves will have increased in the same proportion, and any increase in production or liberalization that may have occurred in the transition to the higher price level will be reversed. This, however, does not appear to be a realistic picture of how reserve changes act on the economy. Some of the effects of such changes—on restrictions, on exchange rates, on investment, on output, on ways of dealing with disequilibria—may well be virtually permanent.

In any event, the effects of any given reserve change clearly take a long time to manifest themselves in full. There is, first of all, the interval that probably elapses between the change in reserves and the change in official policies, then the time it takes for the policies themselves to take effect on activity and trade, and then the period during which prices are adjusting themselves. Finally, there is, possibly, a period during which costs adjust themselves to the new demand situation. One corollary of this is that to evaluate the effects of any once-for-all reserve change would require a forecast of its effects extending over several years. The making of such a forecast would be difficult enough under the most stable economic conditions. The difficulty is further increased by the fact that both the response of governments to given reserve changes and the desirability of given responses are constantly changing with changes in the general economic situation.

DYNAMIC FACTORS AFFECTING NEED FOR RESERVES

In the two preceding sections, we have spoken loosely of the demand

99

for reserves as if it were an absolute magnitude, and of the equality or inequality between the demand for and supply of reserves as being manifested by the trend in prices. However, it would be more in keeping with the analysis in this essay to regard the ratio between the demand for and the supply of reserves as tending to affect the policies adopted in a variety of spheres. If this is done, we can no longer hope to quantify the demand for reserves as such but only the *changes* in that demand. Thus, a country's demand for reserves may be said to increase if, without any change in the amount of its reserves, developments occur in its monetary, commercial, and exchange policies similar to those which would have been evoked by a decline in reserves. More precisely, if a country's demand for reserves rises (or falls) by the same amount that its supply rises (or falls), and if other factors affecting policies remain unchanged, the policies themselves will not alter. Other things being equal, a change in the demand for reserves will involve a similar change in the need for (i.e. the optimal level of) reserves. However, changes in economic conditions may alter the need for reserves quite apart from any effects they may have on the demand for reserves.

Space does not permit an extensive discussion of the various dynamic factors affecting the demand, or the need, for reserves. One obvious trend factor is the growth in the value of international transactions. Any increase in the level of these transactions, given their composition and degree of stability, will tend to evoke a proportionate increase both in the demand for and in the need for reserves.[5] Again, anything that increases the magnitude (relative to the value of international transactions) of international payments deficits of a short-run or cyclical character will tend to increase the demand, and the need, for reserves. On the other hand, the emergence of persistent disequilibria in international payments, though likely to evoke some of the policy reactions characterizing an increase in the demand for reserves, may not lead to any increase in optimal reserves since higher reserves, while tending to mitigate policies of deflation or restriction in deficit countries, would also tend to delay a desirable adjustment of over-valued currencies.

The emergence of deflationary tendencies in the world economy

---

[5] More precisely expressed, the increase in demand for reserves will tend to bear the same proportion to the pre-existing amount of reserves as that by which the value of transactions increases.

might well involve, at first, a substantial increase in the optimal level of reserves, both because of the international disequilibria with which it would probably be attended and because of the importance of assisting governments in their efforts to counteract the deflationary pressures. However, in the longer run, in so far as the deflationary tendencies, while themselves disappearing, leave behind them a permanent legacy of lower prices in the world, the need for reserves will be *pro tanto* reduced.

The initial effect of the emergence of inflationary conditions on the optimal level of reserves is more doubtful than the effect of deflationary tendencies: considerations of anticyclical policy would favour a reduction of reserves, while the attendant payments disequilibria would argue for an increase. In the longer run, the effect would be to increase the need for reserves.

Changes in policy attitudes directly affect the demand, and hence the need, for reserves. Thus the optimal level of reserves will be increased, at any rate initially,[6] by an intensification of the tendencies of governments to deflate or to restrict international transactions, and will be reduced in the opposite case. Changes in policy attitudes that intensify one of these tendencies while attenuating the other are ambiguous in their effects on optimal reserves.

IMPORTANCE OF RESERVE FLEXIBILITY

It follows from what we have been saying that, in considering the desirability of any once-for-all change in reserves, we have to anticipate not only a train of effects stretching into the future, but also the economic and political conditions under which these effects will operate. Clearly, such conditions are extremely difficult to predict with any approach to accuracy. In the circumstances, it would seem that the assessment of an optimal level of reserves must be an extremely hit-and-miss affair.

Our problem would be somewhat eased if we had at our disposal methods whereby the level of reserves, or of international liquidity, could be adjusted up or down at fairly frequent intervals. If this were the case, and if the economic effects of reserve changes followed with little or no delay the reserve changes themselves, we could take the leap of faith and assume that the liquidity needs of the farther

[6] If the change in official policies is not checked by a rise in reserves, the decline in prices may ultimately bring the optimal reserves down towards their original level.

future would be looked after by future adjustments in the supply of liquidity and that all that matters in determining the ideal level of present liquidity is the situation prevailing at present and expected to prevail in the immediate future. However, even complete flexibility in the means of adjusting international liquidity would not enable us to attain the thermostatic ideal of adjusting liquidity in the light of current requirements. Not only do the effects of reserve changes run on for a long time, but they probably do not reach their maximum intensity until after a considerable time lag. Financial authorities take time to react to changes in their external liquidity and, as has been emphasized particularly by Professor Friedman,[7] domestic financial policies themselves may take six months or more before they exercise their full effects on monetary demand. The reaction of reserve changes on trade restrictions and hence on trade may be somewhat speedier.

Friedman argues that, given the existence of this time lag between monetary changes and their effects, and given the impossibility—as he believes—of successfully predicting business conditions, it is better to renounce any attempt to regulate the stock of money for short-term stabilization purposes, and to be content with maintaining a steady moderate rate of growth of the money stock over time. A similar thesis might be advanced with respect to the supply of international liquidity—that the best course is to maintain a steady rate of growth corresponding to an assumed trend rate of growth in the need for such liquidity. However, Friedman's argument rests on a further premise—that in the long or medium run a stable relationship exists between the growth of money stock and that of money incomes. No such stable long-run relationship—e.g. between external reserves and the value of international transactions—exists in the international sphere. Quite apart from short cyclical fluctuations, considerable changes take place over longer periods both in the optimal and in the actual ratio of reserves to transactions. Thus even if a target rate of growth were fixed for international transactions, this would not suffice to determine the trend in the need for reserves.

[7] Milton Friedman, 'A Monetary and Fiscal Framework for Economic Stability', *American Economic Review*, Vol. XXXVIII, 1948, pp. 245–64; reprinted in Milton Friedman, *Essays in Positive Economics* (Chicago, 1953) pp. 133–56. See also *Employment, Growth, and Price Levels*, Hearings before the Joint Economic Committee of the Congress of the United States (86th Congress, First Session, May 25, 1959), Part 4.

On the other hand, it would seem unduly pessimistic to doubt the possibility of using intelligent anticipations regarding those elements in the economic situation that are relevant to the need for international liquidity in order to make adjustments in the supply of such liquidity that are, on the whole, worthwhile.

Nevertheless, awareness of the difficulty of predicting economic conditions over periods even as short as one to two years provides a useful warning against attempting to bring about wide variations in the supply of liquidity to meet the needs of temporary situations. Another consideration pointing in the same direction is that reserve changes in the vicinity of the optimum are probably much less effective in time of slump, when the optimum is high relative to the value of transactions, than in time of boom, when it is low. If, therefore, there is any difficulty in making actual reserves decline as steeply between slump and boom as would short-run optimal reserves, it is better to fall well short of the optimal level in time of slump than to exceed it appreciably in time of boom.

INTERNATIONAL DISTRIBUTION OF RESERVES

Our main concern in this essay is with the general level of reserves or external liquidity. However, the effects of raising or lowering the general level of reserves will differ according to the manner in which increases or decreases are distributed among the different countries. Some attention must therefore be paid to the effects of redistributing reserves as distinct from changing their aggregate magnitude. An increase in the reserves of any country will tend, sooner or later, to be passed on to other countries and thus be widely diffused. The attitudes of different countries towards the holding of reserves give rise, as long as they persist, to something like a normal reserve distribution towards which the actual reserve distribution, subject to the vicissitudes of international payments balances, will tend. Thus, most of the effects of any change in the distribution of reserves are likely to be temporary. However, they may well be important. A transfer of reserves from countries which would have used them to inflate unduly, or to maintain an over-valued exchange rate, to countries that will use them to avoid deflation, import restriction, or undue devaluation—or an increase in the reserves of the latter rather than of the former group of countries—will have beneficial effects. It is, however, seldom possible to withdraw liquidity selectively from those that are likely to make bad use of it, though it may be possible, if liquidity is in any case to be increased, to steer it in the first instance towards countries that will make good use of it.

A danger that frequently presents itself is that, if additional liquidity is provided to countries that need it and would make good initial use of it, there is a danger that it will, when diffused among countries in general, turn out to be excessive, e.g. too inflationary. This dilemma may occur even if no net increase takes place in the aggregate amount of liquidity, but merely a transfer from countries in whose possession it would otherwise have remained unused. Unless, therefore, the liquidity is transferred not from countries that would have kept it unused but from countries that would have used it in a relatively undesirable way, any improvement in the distribution of liquidity is likely to involve some decline in its optimal aggregate level.

CONDITIONAL AND UNCONDITIONAL LIQUIDITY

Thus far, we have been assuming that there is only one sort of international liquidity, which, while it can be created or destroyed at the will of some authority, is nevertheless, as long as it exists, unconditionally at the disposal of the country possessing it. Let us call this 'unconditional liquidity'. But there may be another broad category of liquidity consisting in a potential access to reserves, an access which, however, is subject to the observance of certain conditions as to the use to be made of it or as to the general policies to be pursued by the recipient. One usually thinks of such liquidity as consisting of borrowing facilities, but the use of assets also might be made subject to certain conditions, whereas access to borrowing facilities might be unconditional.

We now have two types of liquidity, the amounts of which have to be optimized. To make actual use of conditional liquidity involves transforming it into unconditional liquidity. In order to prevent a continual expansion of the latter at the expense of the former, means must be taken to ensure that the use of conditional liquidity is merely temporary. If this is done, and if access to conditional liquidity is controlled by a presumptively wise international authority, there can scarcely be too much conditional liquidity in the world. By hypothesis, it can be used only by countries that are pursuing suitable policies, and such countries should have all the liquidity they need.

There remain the rather tricky questions of how the fact that conditional liquidity is available will affect (1) the amount of unconditional liquidity that is needed and (2) the criteria on the basis of which that need is assessed. On the assumption, for the moment, that there is no change in the criteria as previously discussed, the existence of conditional liquidity—to some extent a substitute for unconditional liquidity—will of course reduce the need for the latter. However, the two types of liquidity are not perfect substitutes. The difficulties of utilizing conditional liquidity at short notice, its unsuitability as a war chest, the undesirability of accumulating too many repayment obligations, and the reluctance that some countries may feel at accepting the conditions under which it is made available —all these set a minimum to the demand and need for unconditional liquidity. Moreover, this reluctance to accept policy conditions suggests a new consideration to be taken into account in determining the optimal amount of reserves or unconditional liquidity. A reduction in the level of reserves that might lead some countries to impose undesirable restrictions on trade might lead others to dismantle their restrictions in order to obtain access to liquidity of the conditional variety. Therefore, the importance of minimizing restrictions and exchange rate instability argues less strongly than was previously suggested for keeping reserves higher than would be desirable in the interest of internal financial stability alone.

II. Methods for Controlling International Liquidity

Let us turn, now, to some of the concrete methods that are available —or might become available—for influencing and controlling the amount and distribution of international liquidity. And let us consider how far these various techniques can be used to bring the levels of unconditional and of conditional liquidity closer to the ideal. The possible methods fall into two main classes: those involving changes in the price of gold in terms of the principal currencies; and those involving the extension of credit, directly or indirectly, between monetary authorities. The second category of techniques is a vast one and splits into several subcategories. Thus, there may be arrangements affecting the proportion of external reserves that monetary authorities hold in the form of foreign exchange of various kinds, or arrangements between monetary authorities more specifically directed

105

towards the provision of mutual financial assistance. Again, and most important of all, there may be changes in the amount of resources entrusted to international credit institutions, in the credit policies of these institutions, and in the willingness of countries to make use of them.

GOLD REVALUATION

We may begin by considering gold revaluation as a method of altering the real value of international reserves. Article IV, Section 7, of the Articles of Agreement of the International Monetary Fund contains a provision whereby that institution can take the initiative in bringing about a uniform proportional change in the price of gold in terms of all member currencies. Now it is fairly obvious that this provision is unlikely, in practice, to be used to reduce the value of gold in terms of national currencies, thus reducing the real value of central bank reserves. The accounting difficulties that this would create for central banks, whose assets would be reduced relative to their liabilities, is a sufficient reason, as the world goes, why such an operation would never be undertaken. A uniform increase in the price of gold in terms of currencies and in the real value of gold reserves is theoretically possible, and might occur in some extreme situation or other. However, even an upvaluation of gold presents legal difficulties. To bring it about would require the consent of the United States and the United Kingdom[8] to the operation as a whole as well as the consent of each individual country to a change in its own par value. A general increase in the real value of gold reserves is much more likely to take place, as it did in the 1930s, as a result of a straggling sequence of devaluations on the part of individual currencies.

It is clear that, whether practicable or not as a once-for-all measure, gold revaluation would be a very cumbersome technique for adjusting the amount of international liquidity to an optimal level which, as we have seen, is itself likely to vary substantially in the short run with variations in the world payments situation and in the world demand situation. In addition, gold revaluation has certain side effects, some of which are helpful and some the reverse. A rise in the foreign-currency price of gold would lead not only to a once-for-all increase in the level of real reserves but also to an expansion of gold

[8] That is, the consent of 'every member which has ten per cent or more of the total of the quotas' (Article IV, Section 7).

production and thus to a rise in the rate of growth of reserves. This, while open to objection on grounds of tying up labour and capital in unnecessary mining operations, has a rather useful effect on the long-term trend of reserves. On the other hand, the anticipation of an increase in the price of gold would induce both private individuals and monetary authorities to switch from holding currencies to holding gold. Such speculative reactions, which were seen in a mild form during the 'gold scare' in the closing months of 1960, would have the perverse effect of drawing down the level of reserves at the very time when, by hypothesis, an increase in their real value is aimed at. The distribution by countries of reserve changes resulting from gold revaluation is clearly not very selective, being proportional to the existing distribution of gold stocks. The desirability of using gold revaluation as a means of acting on the level of reserves cannot, of course, be assessed without due consideration of alternative techniques. Even at this point, however, it would seem that, while it may be a useful or even indispensable instrument for very occasional use in bringing about changes in the long-term trend of reserves, it is not a suitable instrument for adjusting international liquidity to shorter-term changes in the need for it.

HOLDING OF FOREIGN EXCHANGE IN OFFICIAL RESERVES

The level and trend of international reserves and liquidity depend not only on gold stocks and production but also on the proportion of reserves that countries hold in the form of foreign exchange. Any increase in international liquidity resulting from an increase in the ratio of foreign exchange to gold will be partly—but only partly— offset by an increase in the need for liquidity that arises from the existence of short-term liabilities in the reserve-currency countries. The growth of reserves will then depend on such factors as national propensities to hold foreign exchange reserves, interest rates obtainable on official balances, the degree of confidence in the future gold value of reserve currencies, and the distribution of reserves as between two groups of countries: those which hold little or no foreign exchange (such as the reserve-currency countries themselves) and those which hold a high proportion of their reserves in this form. Those relationships are too complicated to go into here.[9] Suffice to say that

[9] For an interesting mathematical treatment of some aspects of this question, on simplified assumptions, see Peter B. Kenen, 'International Liquidity and the Balance of Payments of a Reserve-Currency Country', *The Quarterly Journal of Economics*, Vol. LXXIV, 1960, pp. 572–86.

there is no reason at all to think that, by itself, the practice of holding foreign exchange would give rise to anything approaching an optimal level of reserves or even a tolerably steady rate of growth of reserves. On the contrary, while I think Professor Triffin has exaggerated the inevitability of the collapse of the exchange standard,[10] it is obviously an extremely unstable system which is liable to lead to a great reduction in reserves whenever, as is likely from time to time, a principal reserve country runs into balance-of-payments difficulties and confidence in its currency declines.

It would be possible for the reserve-currency countries to remedy the worst instabilities of the system by offering to guarantee the value, in terms of gold or foreign currency, of all foreign central bank balances held in their respective currencies, provided the balances in question are held in an approved form. Even if the political difficulties of this course were overcome, however, it still would not provide a satisfactory method of regulating the volume of reserves. World liquidity would grow faster whenever the reserve-currency countries were in deficit and decline or grow less fast whenever they were in surplus.[11] In order to begin transforming the gold exchange system into some sort of reliable instrument for controlling the volume of world liquidity, it would be necessary to arrive at international agreements under which countries would assume obligations as to the proportions of their reserves to be held in the form of foreign exchange. The provisions regarding the composition of existing reserves might be different from those regarding the composition of reserve increases or decreases. Even so, it would be enormously difficult to reach any agreement of this kind in view of the very great differences of practice between countries in regard to the holding of foreign exchange. Some countries would want to stick to their present proportions, others to change them substantially. Moreover, to be effective for the purpose of controlling the level of world reserves, the agreement would have to contain not merely provisions as to initial

---

[10] In particular, I would dispute the proposition, suggested on page 67 of his *Gold and the Dollar Crisis*, that increases in the short-term monetary liabilities of key currency countries, matched by less than one-to-one increases in their own gross reserves, will necessarily tend to bring about a collapse of the system 'through the gradual weakening of foreigners' confidence in the key currencies'. It is surely not necessary, in order to maintain confidence, that key currency countries should have a 100 per cent reserve backing for their short-term liabilities.

[11] This is true on the assumption that the reserve-currency countries themselves hold a smaller proportion of their reserves in foreign exchange than do other countries.

proportions but also a mechanism for changing these proportions from time to time according to developing needs. It seems likely that such an agreement would be beyond the sphere of practical possibility. Moreover, the distributive effects of this method of controlling liquidity would be bad. Reserve increments would be concentrated, in the first instance, on the reserve-currency countries, which is not necessarily where they are most required. Other countries would be affected only when the diffusion process had run its course.

Just as one would not wish to preclude the possible need for a very occasional revaluation of gold for the purpose of accelerating the long-term trend of reserve growth, so the possibility of some sort of agreement regarding holdings of foreign exchange, should this appear expedient for the purpose of avoiding a possible collapse of the reserve structure, need not be entirely excluded. However, for adjusting international liquidity to needs in the short or medium run, or even for providing an adequate rate of growth of international liquidity over the longer run, we must turn to instrumentalities of a different order.

Whereas the holding of foreign exchange reserves by monetary authorities enhances international liquidity by increasing the aggregate amount of reserves, other forms of official lending reduce the need for liquidity by transferring reserves to the countries that require them most. This happens, for example, when central banks in a strong payments position extend credit to those in a weak payments position. Even when, as is usually the case, the exchange risk is assumed by the borrowing country, the asset acquired by the lending country cannot be a very liquid one if the terms of the loan are such as will meet the needs of the borrower; so that, as the liquidity of the borrower increases, that of the lender will decline. The improvement in the distribution of liquidity will result, however, in a temporary decline in the aggregate amount of liquidity required in the world. If permanent arrangements are set up for the provision of mutual aid by monetary authorities, not only will the distribution of liquidity be improved and the need for it reduced but the expectation of being able to receive such assistance, when required, will itself constitute an addition, of a sort, to the liquidity of potential borrowers. However, the setting up of permanent arrangements of this kind, presumably on a mutual basis, is already a halfway house to the setting up of an international credit institution and raises all the problems of such institutions, which we shall now proceed to consider.

109

ROLE OF INTERNATIONAL CREDIT INSTITUTIONS

As domestic banks can increase the supply of domestic liquidity, so international credit institutions can increase the supply of international liquidity. In the first place, such institutions provide a means—and possibly the only means—whereby credit can be made available, subject to the adoption by the borrowing countries of policies desirable from an international point of view. In other words, they constitute practically the sole source of that conditional liquidity which, we have said, should be available in virtually unlimited supply.

The effect of the existence of international financial institutions on the supply of external liquidity in the unconditional form, i.e. on the level of reserves, is more complex. In so far as these institutions absorb gold, and in so far as their operations lead countries to reduce their holdings of foreign exchange, such institutions tend to bring down reserves; but in so far as they incur liquid liabilities (including any liabilities to provide unconditional borrowing rights) that countries in effect include in their reserves, they tend to raise reserves. Since countries' holdings of foreign exchange *plus* that part of their claims on institutions which they regard as a substitute for foreign exchange are held in some positive relation to their gold holdings *plus* the part of their claims on institutions which they regard as a substitute for gold, the total amount of countries' reserves will depend on their holdings of gold *plus* the part of their claim on institutions which they regard as a substitute for gold. Therefore, the net effect of an institution's existence on the supply of unconditional liquidity in the world will be favourable as long as its holdings of gold (which are *ipso facto* withdrawn from national reserves) are less than the part of its liquid liabilities that is regarded by the holders as a substitute for gold reserves. The more the institution reduces its gold stock or increases its liquid liabilities, e.g. by expanding credit or contracting its nonliquid liabilities, the greater will be its expansionary effect on world reserves—though there will be some corresponding decline in the amount of discretionary lending facilities that remain outstanding.

It is obvious that the supply of liquidity can be varied more flexibly over time and distributed more selectively between countries by an international credit institution or institutions than by any other method. Within the limits of its resources, such an institution can behave like a central bank, increasing its willingness to lend, as well as its actual lending, during periods when an increase in liquidity

110

appears likely to be beneficial, and curtailing them at other times. By varying its willingness to lend it can affect the amount of conditional liquidity, and by varying its actual lending it can affect the amount of unconditional liquidity.

Again, to the extent that it has discretion in its lending operations, an international credit institution can steer liquidity—whether newly created or currently withdrawn from countries repaying their debts to the institution—towards those countries where it will do the most good and the least harm.

The amount of international liquidity that an institution can create depends to a considerable extent on the amount of resources that countries are willing to subscribe to it, lend to it, or deposit with it. Much also depends, however, on psychological attitudes. For example, the more countries are inclined to regard their claims on the organization as an integral part of their reserves, the more willing they are to borrow from the organization, and the more they regard their borrowing rights as a substitute for reserves, the more liquidity will be felt to exist, and the more will actually exist in the world. Finally, the legal structure and acquired functional characteristics of the institution in question will affect not only the amount and character of the liquidity it creates but also the variability of the liquidity through time and the extent to which it can be steered into appropriate channels.

DIFFERENTIATING CHARACTERISTICS OF INTERNATIONAL
CREDIT INSTITUTIONS

There are innumerable types of possible international credit institutions. Some of the apparent differences between them are matters of form rather than of substance. For example, there is far less difference than is commonly believed between the Keynesian Clearing Union plan, which took the form of a deposit bank, and the International Monetary Fund, which takes the form of an exchange fund, or 'bag of currencies', as it has been described. It is not a matter of fundamental importance whether a country's net claims against an institution are reckoned in the form of a 'bancor' balance, as in the Clearing Union, or in the form of an initial subscription *less* the institution's holdings of the country's currency, as in the International Monetary Fund.

The really substantive differences between international credit institutions relate to such matters as the following:

111

Manner in which institution is provided with resources
The institution may obtain its resources:

(1) through countries' voluntarily depositing gold or foreign exchange on long term or short term,

(2) through the calling up, in advance of actual use, of gold or foreign exchange subscribed by members in accordance with a general agreement, or

(3) through members' undertaking in advance (a) to provide gold, foreign exchange, or domestic currency, up to a given maximum amount, as and when required by the institution for it lending operations, or (b) to maintain a given proportion of their reserves in the form of claims on the institution, if necessary by depositing gold or foreign exchange.

The Bank for International Settlements, though it has a small subscribed capital, relies very largely on (1). Apart from an initial contribution by the United States, the European Payments Union operated on the basis of permanent lines of credit extended as necessary by special arrangement, whereby each member financed a portion of any cumulative payments surplus with other members of the Union (method 3a). The European Fund relies partly on (2) and partly on (3a).[12] Subscriptions to the International Monetary Fund, in so far as they consist of gold, fall into category (2); in so far as they consist of domestic currency, they have the same effect as undertakings of type (3a) since, as long as they remain unused in the possession of the Fund, the amounts subscribed are in effect re-lent to the subscribing members. Dr. Bernstein's suggestion for the use of stand-by arrangements to finance a special fund primarily concerned with offsetting capital movements[13] is an example of method (3a). Professor Triffin's scheme[14] for a renovated International Monetary Fund relies partly on (1) and partly on (3b), reinforced by a prohibition against holding more than a minimum amount of reserves in the form of balances with other countries.

[12] The part of its capital called up in advance of actual use consisted of part of the capital of the European Payments Union contributed by the U.S. Government: capital contributed by member governments is called up as required.

[13] Edward M. Bernstein, 'The Adequacy of United States Gold Reserves', *American Economic Review*, Vol. LI, 1961, pp. 439–54.

[14] Robert Triffin, *Gold and the Dollar Crisis* (New Haven, 1960) pp. 104–6.

By the use of method (3a)—uncalled subscriptions, stand-bys, domestic-currency subscriptions—an institution can obtain resources (i.e. acquire lending power) with less initial loss to national reserves of gold or foreign exchange than under methods (1), (2), or (3b), though the impact on external liquidity of raising resources by these methods will depend on the nature of the claims that countries thereby acquire on the institution itself. Method (3a) also gives the institution more power than do other methods to determine from which countries it will draw resources at any time, and hence which countries will incur a loss in gold and foreign exchange reserves corresponding to the gain in the borrowing countries. This, however, will affect the liquidity of the creditor countries only to the extent that claims on the institution are less than fully liquid.

Liquidity of liabilities

An important question, related to, but distinguishable from, that just discussed, is the degree of liquidity attaching to members' claims on the institution. Such claims may be convertible into gold or foreign exchange on demand, as is true of some Bank for International Settlements deposits. They may be automatically available to finance a proportion of any payments deficits with other members of the organization, as was the case in the European Payments Union. They may, in practice, be convertible almost without question into foreign currency when the need arises, and yet not be fully accepted as constituting reserves, as is true of creditor positions in the International Monetary Fund.[15] They may be time deposits. Or they may be highly illiquid, as in the case of the called-up capital of the European Fund.

The greater the liquidity of the claims that countries acquire on surrendering gold or foreign exchange to the institution under methods (1), (2), and (3b) outlined above, the less will be the initial net loss of liquidity in subscribing countries. More generally, any increase in the liquidity of such claims will increase the potential contribution of the institution to the supply of unconditional liquidity in the world, both directly and by making countries more willing to acquire such claims and thus provide the institution with

---

[15] To the extent that members have a creditor position in the Fund, they enjoy the 'overwhelming benefit of any doubt', in any request they make to draw a currency they need to make payments for current transactions, or to meet such capital outflows as the Fund may legitimately finance.

additional resources, when needed. This statement, however, needs qualification, insofar as the liquidity of its liabilities induces the institution, for its own protection, to maintain relatively high gold reserves, and to hedge round with burdensome conditions the credit facilities that it provides.

Certain devices are employed, or have been suggested, with the object of preserving the liquidity of claims on the institution while safeguarding the liquidity of the institution itself. Thus, though creditor positions in the International Monetary Fund are almost as useful for meeting payments deficits as if they were convertible on demand, various safeguards exist against any excessive or arbitrary drawing down of such positions. The repayment provisions of the Fund are such that even a member with a creditor position (not exceeding the gold portion of its subscription) can, in principle, draw on the Fund's resources to finance only half of its payments deficit, the other half having to be financed out of reserves, and must restore its creditor position, to the extent of its gold subscription, when its reserves recover.[16] Moreover, even creditor positions in excess of the gold subscription, if drawn upon by a member in a strong payments position, may be restored through drawings of its currency from the Fund by other members. The arrangement suggested by Triffin, described above as method (3b), is intended to achieve an even more complete reconciliation between the liquidity needs of the institution and those of its creditors. Such of the deposits in his New Model International Monetary Fund as are held not voluntarily but under the deposit requirement provision and are kept proportional to national reserves are unlikely to decline in aggregate amount, so that, though under all ordinary circumstances they would be usable by individual holders in conjunction with other reserves, they would present no threat to the liquidity of the institution, which need therefore maintain very little backing for them in the form of gold.[17]

[16] These provisions do not apply when a member's reserves are low, i.e. less than its quota.

[17] A difficulty with regard to this proposal has been raised by R. F. Harrod in 'A Plan for Increasing Liquidity: A Critique', *Economica*, Vol. XXVIII, 1961, p. 196. He argues that, since countries might feel unable to rely on being able to convert the new International Monetary Fund deposits in time of war, a requirement that they should hold a fraction of their reserves in such deposits would have the effect of increasing the hard core of reserves that they will insist on keeping untouched in

Netting of assets and liabilities

In certain institutions, such as the Bank for International Settlements or Triffin's New Model International Monetary Fund, a country can be simultaneously a creditor and a debtor, and its rights and obligations *vis-à-vis* the institution are determined by the amount of its gross claims and gross liabilities, respectively. In other institutions, such as the European Payments Union and the International Monetary Fund, a country's claims and liabilities are offset against each other, and its rights and obligations are determined by its net position. The main effect of the practice of netting claims against liabilities is to reduce the volume of claims and to increase the amount of unused borrowing facilities. Where, as in the European Payments Union, both creditor positions and borrowing rights are automatic, this has no very great significance. But where, as in the International Monetary Fund, the liquidity afforded by claims on the organization is much less conditional than that afforded by borrowing rights, the effect of the netting practice is to reduce the amount of virtually unconditional liquidity that arises from a given amount of lending.

Liquidity of members' borrowing rights

Corresponding to the differences that may exist in the liquidity of claims on international financial institutions, there are also possible differences in the liquidity—or the conditionality—of borrowing facilities. Thus, borrowing facilities may be subject to the discretion of the institution, as in the European Fund or the higher credit tranches of the International Monetary Fund, or they may be dependent on the payments deficits cleared through the organization, as in the European Payments Union, or they may be available on relatively easy conditions, as in the first credit tranche of the International Monetary Fund. One of the aspects of the International Monetary Fund system is that the Executive Board, if it so desired,

---

ordinary circumstances, and would thus bring about an initial reduction in their liquidity. It is difficult to know how much importance countries still attach nowadays to the possession of a war chest kept in the form of gold on national territory. Certainly, deposits with the International Monetary Fund should be no less safe than foreign exchange or gold held on earmark abroad. To the extent that the difficulty is a real one, it should not be impossible to circumvent or palliate it, e.g. by exempting a fixed amount of reserves in each country from fractional deposit requirements, or by suitable arrangements for geographical dispersion of the Fund's own gold holdings.

could extend the automaticity of its lending to larger and larger percentages of the quotas and thus, rather simply, transform conditional into unconditional liquidity.

Quantitative limitations on members' borrowing rights

The amounts that a member is allowed to borrow from the institution, in specific circumstances or subject to specific conditions, may depend, as in the case of the European Payments Union or the International Monetary Fund, on the amounts that it is obligated in other circumstances to lend to or through the institution, or they may be at the discretion of the institution, as in the Bank for International Settlements or Triffin's New Model Fund. The second system obviously confers on the institution greater flexibility in lending and a greater power to steer liquidity towards the countries that most require it. On the other hand, it is difficult to combine with any degree of automaticity in members' borrowing rights.

Conditions of repayment

Institutions also differ as regards the conditions governing repayment of their loans. Sometimes, the timing of repayment depends on the payments situation of the borrower, as in the case of mandatory repurchases from the International Monetary Fund, where the drawing country repays *pari passu* with a rise in its net reserves, or as in the case of the European Payments Union, where a predetermined fraction of any payments surpluses with other members served to finance an improvement in the member's position *vis-à-vis* the institution. More frequently, as in the case of the contractual repurchases from the International Monetary Fund, repayments become due on a more or less flexible time schedule. In this event, maturities may be on a short-term (as is usual with the Bank for International Settlements), a medium-term (as with the European Fund and the International Monetary Fund), or even a long-term basis. The shorter the period of repayment, the greater for the institution will be:

(1) its ability, for a given volume of lending, to redistribute liquidity between member countries,

(2) its liquidity,

(3) its ability to exercise pressure on borrowers to follow appropriate policies for the restoration of equilibrium, and possibly

116

(4) its ability to attract resources in the form of voluntary deposits.

On the other hand, if the maturities are too short, this may detract from the usefulness of the loan and give rise to difficulty in finding willing borrowers if an expansion of credit and liquidity should become desirable. From the standpoint of the borrower, provision for repayment over a longer term, or as and when the payments situation improves, would be more attractive.

Power of investment
Finally, institutions differ in the extent to which they are empowered, on their own initiative and at their own discretion, to acquire or withdraw investments in balances or securities. The International Monetary Fund is, in principle, passive with respect to demands for credit from member countries, and its powers of investment are narrowly circumscribed.[18] The powers of the Bank for International Settlements are quite extensive but must be exercised in agreement with the central banks of the countries concerned. Complete freedom of investment in national markets is probably an unrealizable ideal. A substantial power of investment, however, such as Triffin envisages for his New Model International Monetary Fund, might be very important if the demand for loans, on conditions or for maturities acceptable to the institution, should turn out to be too small to enable the institution to expand its liabilities, and hence the supply of unconditional liquidity, to the extent that would be desirable.

CHARACTERISTICS OF INTERNATIONAL FINANCIAL
INSTITUTIONS IN RELATION TO THEIR TASKS
One of the tasks of an international financial institution is to adjust its policies flexibly to short-term changes in the optimal level of international liquidity. To some extent this adjustment will be achieved if the institution is responsive to fluctuations in demand for the use of its resources. However, in the sphere of international, as of domestic, liquidity there is no close correspondence between the need for liquidity and the demand for credit. An institution will be in a better position to fulfil this part of its function the more flexible are its lending criteria, the less binding are the quantitative restrictions on its power to lend to particular countries, the greater is its

---

[18] Up to the present they have been used only to acquire earning assets.

power to vary the duration of its loans, and the greater is its power to conduct open market operations by buying and selling investments on its own initiative.

Another important function is that of adjusting to short-term changes in the optimal distribution of liquidity. The ability of the institution to influence the distribution of liquidity will be greater the freer it is to switch its assets—and, to a lesser extent, its liabilities —from country to country. It will, therefore, be better placed to fulfil this function the less it is hampered by quantitative limitations on lending to particular countries, the greater, and the more wide-spread geographically, is the volume of its short-term loans, the greater is its power of buying and selling investments, and the freer it is to draw resources from whichever countries are currently best able to supply them.

In the event of any widespread decline in the willingness of countries to hold foreign exchange in their reserves, it would be particularly important that the institution should be in a position to take up reserve currencies in large amounts and hold them for a fairly long period of years.

As we have said above (p. 104), the amount of conditional liquidity available to countries on suitable conditions should, in principle, be indefinitely large. If this result is to be achieved by means of an international financial institution, that institution must be able to induce countries to provide it with sufficient resources, and to give its members access to a sufficiently high proportion of these resources in conditional form without providing too much unconditional liquidity. The ability of the institution to raise resources will depend partly on its success in winning the confidence and support of member countries and partly on its possession of a technique of raising resources that is as painless as possible for the contributing countries, e.g. by stand-bys that will be called only when a country is in a strong position and which, when called, confer upon the country claims on the institution that are liquid or otherwise attractive in character. On the other hand, an institution whose liabilities are reserve-worthy may find it difficult, in certain circumstances, to create a sufficient amount of liquidity in conditional form without as a by-product generating too much unconditional liquidity. The provision of a sufficient amount of conditional liquidity with a given volume of resources will be easier if there are no quantitative limits on the amounts that can be lent to particular countries. On the other hand, countries may be more willing to provide the institution with reserves if they thereby acquire some additional rights to borrow, if necessary, from the institution; this is difficult to arrange without some quantitative allocation of borrowing facilities.

Finally, the characteristics of a monetary institution have a bearing on its ability to generate, over the long run, an adequate but not excessive volume of unconditional liquidity in the world without the necessity for any general adjustment, upwards or downwards, of the price of gold in terms of the principal currencies. Apart from the problem discussed above of how to avoid creating too much unconditional liquidity as a by-product of creating adequate conditional liquidity, there should be no great difficulty in holding down the amount of international liquidity to a desired level. If necessary, gold could be acquired by an institution in exchange for an illiquid liability, and simply sterilized. At the other extreme, there is probably no limit to the amount of unconditional liquidity that can be created on the basis of a given stock of monetary gold, provided:

(1) that countries can be induced to hold, or to undertake to hold, a sufficiently high proportion of their reserves in the form of claims on the institution,

(2) that it can be arranged, by some technique similar to those discussed above (p. 114), that countries only draw on their claims on the institution *pari passu* with their independently held reserves,

(3) that the institution is enabled, through the power of investment or long-term lending, to expand credit to the necessary extent, and

(4) that it need not cancel its claims on countries against their claims on it.

From what has been said, it is clear that, if an institution of the deposit bank type envisaged by Triffin were starting *de novo*, it would be somewhat better fitted than one of the type of the International Monetary Fund for expanding the amount of unconditional liquidity or reserves in the world on the basis of a given gold stock. Even an institution of the latter type, however, could do more than is commonly realized to increase international liquidity by making access to its resources more automatic, not only for creditors but to some extent for borrowers also, particularly if its powers of investment were extended and if it incurred liquid liabilities to members in a

ESSAYS IN INTERNATIONAL ECONOMICS

form that did not necessarily have to be cancelled against its claims on those members.

On the other hand, an institution of the deposit bank type might find it more difficult than one of the Fund type to extend an adequate amount of conditional liquidity in the form of borrowing facilities without expanding national reserves excessively. In the early post-war years, when the combination of inflationary pressures and widespread restrictions in the world created a need for conditional rather than unconditional liquidity, it was natural that an institution of the International Monetary Fund type should have been set up. Today, on the other hand, when the dwindling of inflationary pressures makes it safer to expand reserves, while weaknesses in the gold exchange standard make it more difficult to maintain their expansion, it is equally natural that the air should be thick with proposals for making over the Fund into something more closely resembling a deposit bank.

In conclusion, it may be well to warn the reader that the achievement of an optimal amount of liquidity, even if the technical means of attaining that objective were available, would probably not do much to remedy the economic ills of the world. The fact that there are multiple criteria for regulating liquidity is itself sufficient to indicate that no one criterion can be completely satisfied. Even apart from the multiplicity of criteria, the regulation of international liquidity is not a sufficiently powerful instrument to ensure, for example, the maintenance of a broadly satisfactory balance between inflation and deflation in the world. Other forms of international co-operation than that required to achieve optimal liquidity might well be more successful in preserving the balance in question. However, external liquidity has some, if only a limited, influence on the general economic situation and therefore merits, as much as many another question, such systematic consideration as the economist can give to it.

Chapter 5
The Fund and International Liquidity*

This essay is intended to indicate to what extent the International Monetary Fund, with its present policies and practices or with some modification of those policies and practices, is capable of dealing satisfactorily with certain problems of international liquidity described in the following sections. Throughout the discussion, the attempt is made to secure any given result with the minimum adaptation of present arrangements; but it has not been assumed that the Articles of Agreement of the Fund are incapable of amendment in cases where they would appear to impose an inescapable legal obstacle to useful developments. No assumption has been made as to whether action affecting the supply of international liquidity is now, or may soon become, desirable. The only question raised is whether and how such action, if it did become necessary, could be undertaken through the Fund, under either the existing or amended provisions of the Articles. The discussion of a particular course of action in this essay does not necessarily imply that it could be adopted without amendment of the Articles.

NATURE AND TYPES OF INTERNATIONAL LIQUIDITY

International liquidity consists essentially in the resources available to national monetary authorities to finance potential balance-of-payments deficits, i.e. in their command over compensatory official financing. It may consist in the possession of assets or in the ability to borrow internationally. Typical items entering into international liquidity are holdings of gold and convertible foreign exchange; but claims on international institutions or entitlements to borrow from international institutions, from foreign governments, or even from private sources abroad, may be included in the concept. Not only may international liquidity take various forms, but it may be of

* Reprinted, with slight editing, from International Monetary Fund *Staff Papers*, Vol. XI, No. 2, July 1964.

various qualities, so that it cannot be unambiguously measured even for a single country.

An important distinction must be drawn between assets or borrowing facilities that place financing unconditionally at the disposal of the possessing government (i.e. 'reserves') and those that confer only a possibility of obtaining financing, subject to conditions. There are three important types of conditions:

(a) those relating to circumstances with which the country using the liquidity is confronted,
(b) those relating to policies which that country should pursue, and
(c) those relating to the period for which the liquidity may be used, i.e. the period for which the financing is made available.

Type (a) is exemplified by the stipulation contained in the Articles of Agreement of the International Monetary Fund that countries may draw from the Fund only currencies which are 'presently needed for making in that currency payments which are consistent with the provisions of this Agreement'.[1] Type (b) is exemplified by the tranche policies of the Fund, under which requests for transactions in the higher credit tranches are likely to be favourably received only 'when the drawings or stand-by arrangements are intended to support a sound program aimed at establishing or maintaining the enduring stability of the member's currency at a realistic rate of exchange'.[2] Type (c) is exemplified by the repurchase provisions of the Fund Articles,[3] and by the policy requiring drawings to be repaid within three to five years at the outside.[4] Liquidity that is conditional in any of these senses may be somewhat less prized by the country possessing it than would be an equivalent amount of unconditional liquidity; but the imposition of such conditions may be for the general advantage of the international community, and may make countries having surpluses in their balances of payments readier to provide, or to facilitate the provision of, additional liquidity.

[1] Article V, Section 3(a)(i).

[2] International Monetary Fund, *Annual Report, 1962*, p. 31.

[3] Article V, Section 7.

[4] Executive Directors' Decision No. 102 (52/11), reproduced in *Selected Decisions of Executive Directors* (Washington, D.C., Second Issue, September 1963), pp. 21–24.

In what follows, 'conditional liquidity', when referred to without further qualification, means liquidity subject to conditions of type (b) —'policy conditionality'—and the main contrast will be between unconditional liquidity and liquidity that is conditional in this sense.

CRITERIA OF NEED FOR INTERNATIONAL LIQUIDITY

Any increase in the supply of liquidity—particularly unconditional liquidity or reserves—since it facilitates the financing of payments deficits, is likely to result in an increase in the magnitude or duration of such deficits.[5] There will be milder or slower resort to methods— such as exchange rate adjustment, the use of restrictions on imports or capital exports, and the application of deflationary internal financial policies—whereby these deficits would otherwise have been reduced or eliminated. In itself, any diminution in the use of restrictions, particularly restrictions on current transactions, may be considered desirable, and the same is true of any decline in the necessity for applying policies that result in unemployment and setbacks to economic growth. On the other hand, an expansion in liquidity can be considered undesirable to the extent that it gives rise to or perpetuates inflation, or leads to the obstinate retention of too favourable rates of exchange. Any given increase in international liquidity of the unconditional variety may have good results in some countries and bad results in others. This makes it more difficult not only to judge what 'the need' for international liquidity is, but also to obtain a consensus among the different countries of the world that any given expansion or contraction of liquidity is, in fact, desirable.

An increased supply of the type of liquidity of which the use is subject to policy conditions will have somewhat different results. While it will probably increase the amount and the financing of external deficits, even this is not certain. It will not so much reduce recourse to other measures of dealing with disequilibria as alter, presumably for the better, the nature of the measures taken. If this type of liquidity is wisely administered, there can in principle scarcely be too much of it available, although there is of course a limit to the amount that can appropriately be used. The fact that,

[5] This is merely a probable net effect of influences that pull in opposite directions. More liquidity in the hands of countries with payments surpluses promotes policies tending to reduce surpluses; more liquidity in the hands of deficit countries promotes policies tending to enhance deficits. It is surmised that the latter set of influences will prove the stronger.

123

in practice, liquidity subject to conditions tends to take the form of short- to medium-term drawing or borrowing facilities[6] makes this limit narrower than would otherwise be the case.

The various types of liquidity are to some extent substitutes for each other. The need for unconditional liquidity will therefore be the less, the greater is the amount of conditional liquidity that is available. The advantages of conditional liquidity from an international standpoint would appear to make it desirable in principle to ensure that the need for such liquidity is fully met before assessing and meeting the residual need for unconditional reserves. There are, however, limits to the extent to which conditional liquidity will be accepted by countries as a satisfactory substitute for unconditional liquidity.

Despite considerable divergence of views as to the present adequacy of international liquidity, it would probably be widely agreed:

(1) that over the longer run, in the absence of co-ordinated international action, the rate of growth of international liquidity, both conditional and unconditional, may become inadequate to meet the growing needs;

(2) that situations may arise in which it is desirable to vary substantially the amount and distribution of international liquidity; and

(3) that the potential instability of the system under which reserves are held in the form of foreign exchange on a purely voluntary basis may make it necessary to take steps at some time or another to avert the danger of a running down of official holdings of reserve currencies, or to provide an alternative holder for such currencies. The present study considers to what extent the Fund would be in a position, or might be enabled, to deal with these contingencies if they should arise.

TYPES OF LIQUIDITY ARISING FROM FUND POSITIONS
AND OPERATIONS

Members of the Fund, as such, possess liquidity of different kinds, in amounts that depend primarily on the size of their quotas, on their IMF positions, and on whether or not they have a stand-by arrangement with the Fund. All drawings are subject to a small transactions charge of $\frac{1}{2}$ of 1 per cent. On drawings beyond the gold tranche interest is paid varying with the amount of the drawings and

---

[6] See p. 125 below.

the length of time for which they have been outstanding. Under present policies, a member is entitled to receive the overwhelming benefit of any doubt for any drawing not exceeding its net IMF position, i.e. its gold tranche position *plus* any lending to the Fund.[7, 8] The liquidity that such a drawing confers is therefore almost as free from burdensome conditions as that resulting from the possession of gold or foreign exchange reserves. Such drawings, however, are still subject to the conditions that the member must be eligible to draw from the Fund and that the currency required must be needed for making payments consistent with the provisions of the Agreement. Though the 'overwhelming benefit of any doubt' applies also to this statutory proviso, there is an obligation on members to respect it. Broadly speaking, this implies that a member should not draw from the Fund except to meet a deficit or threat of a deficit—not, surely, a significant limitation on the usefulness of the drawing right in question. Drawings within that part of a member's gold tranche position which exceeds its gold subscription and represents the net use of its currency by the Fund, are not subject to any repurchase obligation. Drawings other than those just mentioned are subject both to the statutory repurchase obligations under Article V, Section 7(*b*), and to the obligations to repay within three years[9] or within a three-year to five-year period,[10] which are undertaken or imposed as a matter of Fund policy. Within the gold tranche, however, the force of these repurchase obligations is weakened by the ease with which new drawings can be made.

Drawings or stand-by arrangements beyond the gold tranche require a degree of justification that increases with the amount of drawings outstanding. The power to draw within the credit tranches

[7] A member's 'gold tranche position' is defined as its quota *minus* the Fund's holdings of its currency (if the result is positive); this includes the member's 'net creditor position', which is that part of its gold tranche position which exceeds 25 per cent of the member's quota. A member is said to be drawing in 'the credit tranches' to the extent that the drawing increases the Fund's holdings of its currency to a figure greater than its quota; each credit tranche is equivalent to one-fourth of the quota. Such a member's 'credit tranche position' is the difference between twice its quota and the Fund's holdings of its currency.

[8] This was true as of the time of writing (1964). Since the amendment of the Articles of Agreement of the Fund in 1969, Fund holdings under compensatory financing policies may be disregarded in calculating the gold tranche position. Drawings within the gold tranche are not merely accorded the overwhelming benefit of any doubt but are legally free from challenge. Gold tranche drawings are also no longer subject to the transactions charge.

[9] For drawings under stand-by arrangements.

[10] For other drawings.

therefore confers upon a member a type of liquidity that is subject in varying degrees to policy conditions. There is no fixed limit to the amount of conditional liquidity that a member may obtain in this way. However, without a special waiver, a member cannot draw within the credit tranches more than a sum equivalent to its quota, i.e. it cannot draw beyond the point at which the Fund is holding an amount of its currency equal to twice its quota.[11] Until recently, this has been taken as the practical limit to the amount of a member's drawing facilities, and hence to the amount of conditional liquidity available to it through the Fund. A new facility providing financing to compensate for export fluctuations, however, makes it likely that this limit will be exceeded from time to time in appropriate circumstances. The export compensatory financing facility itself provides a type of conditional liquidity, normally not exceeding 25 per cent of quota—one conditional, however, more upon the presence of certain circumstances (the occurrence of a shortfall in exports) than upon the adoption of appropriate policies by the drawing country. Since export compensatory drawings can be made even when the Fund's holdings on account of other drawings have reached twice the member's quota, and since the limit on other drawings is to be waived to the extent that drawings within the special compensatory tranche are still outstanding, the practical limit on total drawings beyond the gold tranche may now be equivalent to 125 per cent, rather than 100 per cent, of quota.[12]

Drawings under stand-by arrangements are usually subject to rather precise policy conditions, agreed at the time when the arrangement is granted.

Members not only have a claim that the Fund will in certain circumstances add to its holdings of their currencies, i.e. will permit them to draw, they also have an obligation, in other circumstances, to enable the Fund to reduce its holdings of their currencies. If they

[11] The amount a member may draw without a waiver is further limited to the equivalent of 25 per cent of its quota annually. Waivers of this limit are, however, regularly granted if the drawings are otherwise suitable.

[12] Since the revision of the Compensatory Financing Decision in 1963, drawings under the compensatory facility, which are now completely disregarded in determining the amounts that can be drawn under the regular credit tranche policies of the Fund, can rise to 50 per cent of quota. The same is true of a special facility introduced in 1969 for drawings to finance contributions to international buffer stock arrangements. Since drawings under the two special facilities combined may amount to 75 per cent of quota, the total amount of drawings beyond the gold tranche may now rise as high as 175 per cent of quota.

126

have drawn, they will have repurchase obligations. Even—and especially—if they have no drawings outstanding, they are liable to have their currencies drawn upon by other members. These obligations could constitute a liquidity hazard for the country in question. Where repurchase obligations arise under Article V, Section 7(*b*)— which provides, *inter alia*, for repayment more or less *pari passu* with the recovery in reserves—this hazard is nominal. Other repurchase commitments, setting a maximum period within which repayment is to be made, may make the hazard material. The liability of members to have their currencies drawn upon by other members—within the limits set by the Fund's holdings of their currencies—could be inconvenient to the members in question, were it not that:

(1) the Fund provides guidance to drawing members regarding the currencies to be drawn with a view to avoiding the drawing of currencies that are in a weak position, and

(2) as explained below, a member whose currency is drawn is compensated for any loss in other reserves by an enhancement of its Fund drawing facilities, usually in the form of highly liquid drawing facilities in the gold tranche.

There is, at first sight, a certain tension, or tendency to incompatibility, between the Fund's policy of making members' gold tranche positions liquid by enabling their possessors to draw them down freely, and its need to be able to add where necessary to the amount of such positions held by countries whose currencies are required for drawings. This tension, however, is largely resolved by three factors. First, even within the gold tranche, the drawing country must represent that it needs to draw in order to meet a payments problem. Second, the transactions charge, though small, tends to discourage drawings of a frivolous character. Finally, the Fund's policy regarding the currencies to be drawn is designed to secure an equitable and acceptable distribution of gold tranche positions.

It should be noted that all members' rights and obligations *vis-à-vis* the Fund—the size of quotas, of drawing facilities, of repurchase obligations, etc.—are fixed in terms of gold; their gold value is unaffected by exchange rate adjustments with the possible exception of a (theoretically conceivable but practically quite unlikely) uniform

127

change in par values.[13] The fact that gold tranche positions and amounts lent to the Fund possess a constant value in terms of gold, as well as being able to be freely drawn upon, renders them, objectively, a good substitute for gold reserves.

When a member country draws from the Fund, it obtains the currency of another member in exchange for its own currency. How does this operation affect the level and distribution of international liquidity, both conditional and unconditional? The answer to this question is complex and may be given in stages.

Take, first, the effect on liquidity derived from IMF positions. As we have seen, insofar as the member draws within the gold tranche, it forfeits a corresponding amount of quasi-unconditional liquidity in the Fund. Insofar as it draws beyond the gold tranche, however, it uses up conditional drawing facilities. The member whose currency is drawn, on the other hand, improves its position in the Fund. As a rule, such a country will already have a gold tranche position, and the improvement in its IMF position will constitute an increase in quasi-unconditional liquidity. Most Fund drawings nowadays are in the credit tranches rather than in the gold tranche, and the effects of such a drawing, *as far as IMF positions are concerned*, will normally be (a) to increase quasi-unconditional liquidity and (b) to reduce conditional liquidity.

In order to arrive at the effect on the amount and distribution of liquidity in *all* forms, however, we have to take account of the repercussions of drawings on countries' owned reserves of gold and foreign exchange. Here again we proceed by stages, and assume first that changes in reserve holdings are composed of gold and foreign exchange in the same proportions in each of the countries affected. Now, as a result of the drawing, the drawing country will be in a position either to increase its reserves or to finance an increased deficit. There will therefore be a rise in owned reserves either in the drawing country or in the countries from which it imports, and the currency drawn will be converted partly into gold and partly into reserve currencies. The country whose currency is drawn will experience a decline in reserves of equal magnitude, again partly in gold and partly in reserve currencies. There will (on the hypothesis adopted) be no change in aggregate holdings of reserve currencies and thus no change in aggregate owned reserves. The country whose

[13] See Article IV, Section 8.

currency has been drawn (the drawee country) will probably have approximately the same amount of unconditional liquidity as before, but its composition will be changed: it will experience an increase in its gold tranche position in the Fund and a reduction in owned reserves. The drawing country or its suppliers (taken together) will have more unconditional liquidity, in the form of gold and foreign exchange, and less drawing facilities (probably of a conditional character) in the Fund.

However, we must take account of the fact that the countries concerned do not necessarily have the same marginal propensity to hold foreign exchange in their reserves. If, for example, the drawing country (and most of its suppliers) has a high marginal propensity while the country whose currency is drawn has a low marginal propensity, the drawing will probably result in some increase in aggregate holdings of reserve currencies and hence in the total of gold and foreign exchange reserves.[14] The drawing in question is thus likely to result in a twofold increase in unconditional liquidity: (a) in the form of gold tranche positions and (b) in the form of foreign exchange reserves. This increase in unconditional liquidity will accrue to the drawing country and/or its supplying countries and to reserve-currency countries. If, on the other hand, a country with a low marginal propensity to hold foreign exchange in its reserves should draw on a country with a high marginal propensity, the opposite result would be likely to ensue, viz. a decline in the holding of foreign exchange reserves, constituting a partial offset to the increase in unconditional liquidity in the form of gold tranche positions. The owned reserves of drawing and/or supplying countries will rise. Those of reserve-currency countries will decline.

Either the drawing country, or the drawee country, or one of the suppliers of the latter, may itself be a reserve-currency country. Such countries tend typically—though not inevitably—to effect their reserve changes largely or exclusively in gold. Their marginal propensity to hold foreign exchange in reserves is very low. Thus, any drawing of a reserve currency from the Fund is likely to result in a rise in the holding of reserve currencies, including that of the drawee country. That country may well gain more unconditional

[14] Sometimes the drawing country, though not in general accustomed to hold a high proportion of foreign exchange in its reserves, tends to hold in this form a high proportion of reserves acquired from drawings. This makes more likely the outcome described in the following sentences.

liquidity *qua* reserve-currency country than it loses *qua* drawee; in this case, the rise in its quasi-automatic drawing rights will be only partially, if at all, offset by a decline in its other reserves.

Repayments of drawings (i.e. repurchases) have the opposite effects on countries' liquidity to those produced by drawings. Repurchases normally reduce gold tranche positions while restoring conditional drawing facilities, and may have analogous effects (in reverse) on the holding of foreign exchange reserves to those discussed for drawings.

Broadly speaking, we may say that a Fund drawing not only serves currently to finance a deficit by providing liquidity to a country that has immediate need of it, but also—if it is a drawing in the credit tranches—adds to the aggregate amount of liquidity available in unconditional form. It thus increases the ease of financing potential future deficits. Assuming that the Fund's drawing policies remain unchanged, the total of outstanding drawings is likely to increase at times when payments disequilibria are particularly large and frequent. At such times the need for reserves is greater, and it is not inappropriate that Fund transactions arising in response to this need should generate additional reserves.

WAYS OF INFLUENCING INTERNATIONAL LIQUIDITY
THROUGH CHANGES IN THE FUND'S READINESS TO
PROVIDE FINANCING

Let us now consider various methods by which the amounts of unconditional and of conditional liquidity, respectively, can be increased through the Fund.

Increases in quotas[15]

Increases in quotas in the Fund have a dual aspect. They increase the drawing facilities afforded by the Fund to its members—assuming no change in the Fund's policies governing drawings—and they simultaneously increase the resources available to the Fund to meet the drawing requirements of members. They thus affect the liquidity both of Fund members and of the Fund itself.

The immediate effect on the external liquidity of members is complex, but on balance expansionary. Twenty-five per cent of any

---

[15] What is said here regarding quota increases applies also, *grosso modo*, to new quotas, which may be regarded as quota increases from a zero level.

increase in quotas has normally to be paid in gold and the rest in domestic currency. The subscribing member's owned reserves are, of course, reduced by the payment of gold. In return, however, the member's potential drawing facilities increase by at least 125 per cent of the addition to its quota.[16] Where the member, just before the increase in its quota, has no drawings outstanding beyond its former gold tranche, one-fifth of the additional facilities—equivalent to 25 per cent of the addition to its quota—will consist of quasi-automatic drawing rights in the gold tranche, and the member will suffer virtually no decline in unconditional liquidity. Where, however, it has previously drawn beyond the gold tranche, less than one-fifth, if any, of the additional drawing facilities will be in the gold tranche and the member will suffer some decline in unconditional liquidity. Moreover, in either case, to the extent that the member finds the gold for its subscription, not out of its own holdings but by converting foreign exchange reserves, reserve-currency countries will suffer a secondary loss of gold reserves. On the other hand, conditional liquidity in the form of drawing facilities in the credit tranches will be increased by an amount lying between 100 and 125 per cent of the addition to member quotas—an increase which, for most members, is much more important than the deterioration in the composition, or decline in the amount, of their unconditional liquidity.

The foregoing discussion of the effects of quota increases on liquidity has proceeded on the assumptions that quasi-automatic drawing rights are available only to the extent of gold tranche positions, and that the acquisition of gold by the Fund in subscriptions is neither reduced under Article III, Section 4(a), nor offset by the use of gold owned by the Fund to acquire currencies or investments. The effects of removing these assumptions are discussed later in this paper.

So much for immediate effects. In the longer run it may be assumed that, with unchanged drawing policies, outstanding drawings in the credit tranches will come to represent as great, or almost as great, a proportion of the enhanced quotas as, in the absence of the quota

---

[16] The member, if a primary producing country, also acquires contingent drawing facilities under the compensatory financing and buffer stock financing decisions equal to 75 per cent of the addition to its quota.

increase, they would have represented of the old quotas.[17] When this adjustment has been accomplished, gold tranche positions will have increased in much the same proportion as quotas, and the increase in such positions will exceed the gold subscriptions associated with the increase in quotas. Nevertheless, as long as quasi-automatic drawing rights are confined to the gold tranche, it is very doubtful whether quota increases, even in the longer run, make any significant net contribution to the expansion of unconditional liquidity.

If, provisionally, one ignores any effect which the transfer of gold to the Fund may have on the amount of foreign exchange that members are willing to hold in their reserves, the Fund's net contribution to unconditional liquidity up to any point of time can be measured by the amount of members' gold tranche positions *less* the amount of gold still held by the Fund. At the end of 1963, the net contribution, thus measured, amounted to some $1600 million. Of this amount, $800 million was attributable to the fact that between 1956 and 1960 the Fund invested that amount of its gold in U.S. securities. The remaining $800 million, reflecting the Fund's ordinary transactions, particularly the amount of outstanding drawings in the credit tranches,[18] represented some $5\frac{1}{2}$ per cent of member quotas. This figure has varied between 3 per cent and 8 per cent of quotas during the past decade. Taking account of the indirect effect of the net transfer of gold by members to the Fund in reducing members' holdings of reserve currencies, and assuming that one-fourth of the gold so transferred[19] was obtained by the conversion of reserve currencies, the consequential reduction in foreign exchange reserves, and hence in total owned reserves, would appear to have amounted to some 4 per cent of total quotas. It will be seen that any net contribution of the Fund to unconditional liquidity as a result of ordinary transactions has thus far been insignificant.

As long as additions to Fund quotas roughly keep pace with the rising demand to use the Fund's drawing facilities and as long as present drawing policies and repurchase arrangements remain

---

[17] This will hold true if, but only if, the expansion of quotas does not outrun the demand for conditional drawing facilities.

[18] This figure is also influenced by the accumulated net earnings of the Fund which, by adding to the Fund's stock of currencies, tend to reduce the amount of gold tranche positions relative to the Fund's gold holdings.

[19] The gold transferred is made up of gold subscriptions *plus* repurchases in gold *minus* the Fund's use of gold to replenish its stock of currencies.

unchanged, there is no reason why there should be any great change in the average proportion that outstanding drawings in the credit tranches bear to quotas; under these conditions, quota expansion must be regarded almost exclusively as a means of increasing the supply of conditional, as distinct from unconditional, liquidity.

If quotas were increased more rapidly than the demand for drawing facilities, the proportion of outstanding drawings to quotas would tend to decline, and the contribution of the Fund to unconditional liquidity would tend to become negative—gold and foreign exchange reserves would decline faster than gold tranche positions would expand. On the other hand, the expansion in the supply of, relative to the demand for, conditional drawing facilities would reduce members' *need* for unconditional liquidity, and this is probably much more important than the above-mentioned effect on the supply of unconditional liquidity. To take a highly simplified example, suppose that with total quotas of 100, Fund gold holdings amount to 25, drawings outstanding in the credit tranches to 6, and gold tranche positions to 31, and that the transfer of 25 of gold to the Fund has caused a fall of 6 in members' foreign exchange reserves. The Fund's net contribution to conditional liquidity in the form of unused credit tranche positions would then be 94, and its contribution to unconditional liquidity would be 0. If, now, quotas were raised from 100 to 200, without any corresponding increase in the need for Fund drawing facilities, the Fund's gold holdings and the associated negative impact on members' foreign exchange reserves might both be doubled. Drawings outstanding in the credit tranches, however, would probably rise less than in proportion to quotas, say, by 3. Gold tranche positions would rise by only 28, against a loss of gold and foreign exchange reserves of 31, so that the Fund's contribution to unconditional liquidity would *decline* by 3. However, the rise of 97 in its contribution to conditional liquidity (drawing facilities in the credit tranches) would surely reduce the need for unconditional liquidity by far more than 3.

Regarded as a method of increasing the liquidity provided by the Fund, increases in quotas have the disadvantage that they tend to occur—if past experience is any guide—in large amounts at infrequent intervals. A general increase in quotas has thus far occurred only once in the Fund's history—in 1959—although, of course,

133

increases in individual quotas have occurred at other times.[20] It is true that these abrupt and infrequent expansions in conditional liquidity are only gradually utilized in drawings. Nevertheless, it is arguable that the abrupt increases in conditional—and reductions in unconditional—liquidity associated with increases in quotas should themselves be smoothed out over time.

One possible method would be for general increases in quotas to be considered annually; this, however, runs into the difficulty that countries are unwilling to seek authorization from their legislatures for such increases as often as once a year. A more promising variant would be for increases in quotas to be undertaken at less frequent intervals, say, once in five years, but to come into effect by annual instalments.

Changes in drawing policies

The Fund possesses considerable power to vary the conditions on which consent is given to drawings or to the granting and use of stand-by arrangements. In particular, it can alter the degree of scrutiny of applications for, or the severity of the conditions imposed on, drawings over any given range of IMF positions; or alter the amount of drawings (in relation to quotas) to which any given policy applies.

For example, if it were felt that the quasi-automatic drawing rights now applicable to the gold tranche were still not quite automatic enough to induce all members to regard them as fully equivalent to their other reserves, it might be possible to arrange, by permanent stand-by arrangements or otherwise, that members could draw within that tranche without their applications even having to be considered by the Executive Board. Members would still be under obligation to draw only to meet a payments deficit, and would consult with the Managing Director regarding the currencies to be drawn.[21]

Again, the proportion of a member's quota that may be drawn upon quasi-automatically could be altered. For example, drawings in, say, the first 5 per cent of quota beyond the gold tranche, instead

[20] Since this paper was written a second general increase in Fund quotas has taken place in 1965, and a third in 1970.

[21] This greater automatism of gold tranche drawings has since been achieved in 1969 by amendment of the Articles of Agreement, i.e. through the addition of a new subsection (*d*) to Section 3 of Article V.

of being granted on the condition (now applicable to the whole of the first credit tranche) that the member 'is making reasonable efforts to solve its problems' could be granted on the same conditions as apply to the gold tranche. If such a step were taken, there would be an immediate increase in the amount of quasi-unconditional liquidity made available to members through the Fund. Unless further steps were taken, however, this increase in unconditional liquidity would involve some decline in conditional liquidity, since the amount that could be drawn within the credit tranches, subject to policy conditions, would be *pro tanto* diminished. However, the substitution of unconditional for conditional liquidity would no doubt have an effect on countries' policies similar in kind, though not in degree, to that resulting from an outright increase in reserves.

Again, members might be permitted, through the exercise of the waiver power, to draw up to a higher maximum limit than is now customary,[22] subject however to suitable conditions. Here, obviously, the immediate effect would be to increase conditional liquidity. However, since the adoption of this policy would lead to increased drawings, it would also tend to enhance the quasi-unconditional gold tranche positions in the Fund of those countries whose currencies are drawn.

Clearly, the above-mentioned policies could be combined. For example, if gold tranche drawing rights were extended to the first 5 per cent of the member's quota beyond the gold tranche, the normal maximum of drawing facilities—apart from the compensatory financing facility—could be extended into the fifth credit tranche, e.g. to the point where the Fund would be holding 205 per cent of the member's quota. In this way, unconditional liquidity would be increased without any reduction in conditional liquidity.

The examples of changes in drawing policies given above have as their object an increase in the amount or automaticity of drawing facilities. It is easy to see how they could be applied in reverse so as to bring about the opposite result.

Each extension of quasi-automatic drawing rights gives rise to a once-for-all increase in unconditional liquidity, followed by re-current increases with each subsequent expansion of quotas. For

[22] I.e. beyond the point where Fund holdings of a member's currency, other than those acquired in connection with compensatory financing drawings and buffer stock financing drawings, equal 200 per cent of its quota.

example, the extension of quasi-automatic drawing rights to the first 5 per cent of quota beyond the gold tranche would yield an increase of \$600–750 million in quasi-unconditional liquidity,[23] and—if we assume a long-run constancy in the proportion of outstanding drawings to quotas—would mean that any subsequent general expansion in quotas would increase unconditional liquidity for this reason alone by some 4 or 5 per cent of the increase in quotas.

Now, suppose it were desired that the Fund should contribute to the expansion of conditional and unconditional liquidity, respectively, at specified annual rates. One way of achieving this result, in principle, would be to expand drawing facilities, both conditional and unconditional, through a liberalization of drawing policies, while keeping quotas constant. Such a course, however, would soon run the Fund into difficulties in finding the resources to implement the drawing facilities it offered. A more practical approach would be to increase quotas annually by an amount equal to the total increase in liquidity desired, while simultaneously extending quasi-automatic drawing facilities at the expense of conditional facilities. Since, as time went on, a given quota increase as such would generate a larger and larger increase in unconditional liquidity, the need for a progressive substitution of quasi-automatic for conditional drawing facilities would diminish and finally cease. Thus, suppose that the world 'needed' a Fund contribution to unconditional liquidity amounting to \$600 million per annum, and a contribution to conditional liquidity of an equal amount. In order to add \$1200 million to total liquidity, it would be necessary to expand quotas by some \$1280 million.[24] On the assumption that an increase in quotas under present conditions adds nothing to unconditional liquidity, the \$600 million of unconditional liquidity required would have to be obtained in the first year by extending quasi-automatic drawing facilities at the expense of conditional drawing facilities by an equivalent amount

[23] The lower figure is based on the assumption that the extension of quasi-automatic drawing rights would lead to no increase in drawings outstanding. The higher figure is based on the assumption that drawings in the credit tranches would be increased by the amount now outstanding in the first 5 per cent of quota beyond the gold tranche.

[24] It is assumed that the secondary reduction in foreign exchange reserves associated with the gold subscriptions amounts to 6 per cent of the addition to quotas (\$80 million), and that while the expansion in gold tranche positions resulting from additional drawings makes up this loss in unconditional liquidity, it limits the increase in conditional liquidity (credit tranche facilities) and hence total liquidity, to \$1200 million.

(i.e. less than 4 per cent of present quotas). In the second year, a further addition of $1280 million to quotas under the new drawing conditions would, of itself, add some $45 million to unconditional liquidity, thus reducing to $555 million the addition to unconditional liquidity for which a further substitution of quasi-automatic for conditional drawing facilities would be required. And so on. Once quasi-automatic drawing facilities had been extended approximately through two credit tranches, amounting to 50 per cent of quotas, all required further expansion in unconditional liquidity would be provided by quota increases.

Turning to the second of the objectives listed above (p. 124), the question arises whether drawing policies can be adjusted with sufficient speed and flexibility to make a significant contribution towards meeting cyclical or short-term variations in the need for international liquidity. Though changes no doubt occur fairly frequently in the detailed interpretation given to these policies, they have been formally altered on only a few occasions in the history of the Fund, and only once or twice in a restrictive sense. To some extent this is inevitable. An explicit change in drawing policies requires a laborious process of formulation, and after this process has been gone through, time is required before members can see what the change means in practice. Moreover, the adoption of more restrictive policies might be regarded by some members as a breach of the understanding on which they had previously requested increases in quotas. Nevertheless, some of the inflexibility could be remedied. For example, it is not necessary that the tranches with respect to which policies are formulated should always be multiples of 25 per cent of quota. Moreover, despite the difficulties mentioned above, a more systematic periodic reconsideration of drawing policies might be aimed at, with a view to their being tightened up at times when inflationary pressures prevail or when countries show an undue reluctance to adopt realistic rates of exchange, and relaxed at times when the tendency is toward deflation or when a spread of restrictions tends to curtail the volume of international trade and payments.

Changes in gold policies

The Fund acquires gold:

    (i) as part (normally 25 per cent) of initial quota subscriptions or of increases in quota subscriptions;

(ii) in a certain proportion of repurchases under Article V, Section 7(b), and Schedule B;

(iii) in some repurchases outside Article V, Section 7(b);

(iv) in charges under Article V, Section 8(f); and

(v) in sales of currency for gold under Article V, Section 6(a).

The Fund may use gold:

(a) to replenish its holdings of scarce currency under Article VII, Section 2(ii);

(b) to acquire income-earning investments under implied powers; or

(c) to repay loans contracted under Article VII, Section 2(i).

The Fund has little power to vary the rate at which it acquires gold, though: (1) in connection with an increase in a quota, the Fund may reduce the proportion of the increase to be paid in gold if the reserves of the member are less than its increased quota; and (2) it may be possible to induce members to include more or less gold in their repurchases outside Article V, Section 7(b). Apart, however, from the possibilities, discussed below, that the Fund might borrow gold or that it might secure repayment in gold of investments originally made in gold, the main scope for varying the Fund's gold holdings probably lies in the discretion it possesses with respect to the use of gold.

If the Fund uses its gold to purchase currencies that it needs for drawings, or if it induces members to repurchase in currencies—necessarily the currencies of net creditor countries—rather than in gold, the result in both cases is likely to be the same, namely, a decline in the Fund's holdings of gold (as compared to what they would otherwise have been) and an increase in its holdings of the currencies of net creditor countries. The effect on the liquidity of the members primarily concerned will be slight, the increase in their gold reserves being offset, or nearly so, by the decline in their gold tranche positions. However, the countries whose currencies have been bought will probably consider their ratio of gold to foreign exchange assets as having increased and therefore use a fraction of their gold acquisitions for the purpose of acquiring reserve currencies. In this case there will be a secondary expansion in the reserve positions of the reserve-currency countries.

Fund instruments of indebtedness confer on their holders unconditional liquidity similar to that conferred by a gold tranche position. If the Fund uses gold to repay indebtedness, the effects on international liquidity will therefore be similar to those of a use by the Fund of gold to acquire a creditor currency, i.e. mildly expansionary.

To reduce the gold proportion of subscriptions to the Fund would have a slightly greater expansionary effect than the use of gold to acquire creditor currencies. Some, at least, of the countries whose gold subscriptions are remitted are likely to have substantial amounts of drawings from the Fund outstanding. Such countries, had they paid subscriptions in gold, would have lost reserves and gained, not drawing facilities in the gold tranche, but merely conditional drawing facilities in the credit tranches. The remission of the gold subscription thus enhances their liquidity. Moreover, since they would probably have obtained the gold by selling foreign exchange, the remission avoids a drain on the reserves of the reserve-currency countries also. On the other hand, the substitution of holdings of currencies for holdings of gold tends to reduce the liquidity of the Fund.

All forms of substitution of holdings of currency for holdings of gold, especially the last mentioned, tend to reduce the liquidity of the Fund.

The expansion in international liquidity that can be achieved by reducing the Fund's gold stocks is therefore necessarily limited in amount and is of a once-for-all character. On the other hand, in the absence of acts (of replenishment or investment) specifically designed to return gold to countries' reserves, the Fund might gradually accumulate a stock of gold in excess of what it requires in the interests of its own liquidity. Such an accumulation would exercise on the growth of unconditional liquidity in the world a negative influence which, even if not strong, might well be undesirable.

The accumulation and decumulation of gold by the Fund could, in principle, be used as a means of bringing about variations in world liquidity but, for the reasons explained above, their effect is likely to be moderate and largely confined to reserve-currency countries. In any event, gold operations constitute a reasonably flexible instrument only in an expansionary direction. The Fund has no reliable means of acquiring gold in substantial quantities, save as a part of a general increase in quotas. One way of strengthening this instrument for use in a contractionary direction might be for the Fund to borrow gold. However, any contractionary effect of such borrowing on the external liquidity of member countries would, as has been shown, be a mild one. Another possible method for the Fund to acquire gold would be for it to obtain repayment in gold of short-term investments which it might possess.[25] The right to secure repayment in this form would be natural in the case of investments originally acquired through the payment of gold, and is indeed provided for in the case of the gold investments at present held by the Fund for income purposes. If the repayment were made in gold, the contractionary effect on world liquidity would be somewhat greater than if the repayment were made in currency.

Changes in repurchase provisions

The resources of the Fund are used to assist members in meeting temporary balance-of-payments deficits, including deficits arising out of seasonal, cyclical, or emergency situations. Under the Articles, members are obliged at the end of each year to repurchase on the basis of the development of their reserves. As a matter of Fund policy, members undertake to, or represent that they will, repay any drawings within three to five years of the date of drawing, and even earlier if the payments problem for which the drawings were made has been solved.

By an act of policy, the Fund could alter its terms of repayment for drawings in ways that would allow drawings, or certain classes of them, to remain outstanding for longer periods. For example, the outside limit for drawings could be made four to six years, or five to seven years, instead of the present three to five years. The longer the period specified as the limit for repurchases outside Article V, Section 7(*b*), the greater would be the proportion of drawings which would have to be repaid under the provisions of Article V, Section 7. It could indeed be argued that the logical terminus to the process of liberalizing repurchases would be the abandonment of all stipulations as to repayment other than those arising under Article V, Section 7.

Such measures, particularly if carried to the point of abolishing all repayment undertakings, are open to the objection that they weaken the Fund's ability to secure the adoption by drawing members of appropriate balance-of-payments policies. Under present policies, the Fund can say that it will renew drawings that fall due for repurchase only if suitable policies are adopted. Thus, the

[25] See the section, 'Investment by the Fund', p. 142, below.

effective conditionality of the use of the Fund's resources is linked to their revolving character. This objection would not, however, have great force with respect to drawings in the gold tranche, or in any other tranche to which quasi-automatic drawing rights may be extended, since in these tranches repayment provisions can easily be nullified by fresh drawings. The withdrawal of time limits on the use of the Fund's quasi-automatic drawing facilities would therefore merely formalize the actual state of affairs, and would have the advantage of strengthening the resemblance of these drawing facilities to other reserves held by members. There may therefore be a case for rendering inapplicable any repurchase obligations, other than those arising under Article V, Section 7(b), where the effect of such repurchases would be to reconstitute quasi-automatic drawing facilities.

Where conditional drawing facilities are concerned, there are still further objections to the elimination of repayment undertakings or to extending their terms unduly. To make repayment contingent entirely on a recovery in reserves might weaken the incentive for countries to achieve a payments surplus and a consequential rise in reserves. Moreover, as the duration of the drawing extends beyond five years, it becomes more and more questionable how far it can be regarded as bona fide balance-of-payments financing. The concept of balance-of-payments financing rests on the notion that countries should so act as to ensure that any deficits in the remaining (noncompensatory) items of the balance of payments are succeeded by equivalent surpluses in the foreseeable future. Where the balance of payments is concerned, it is difficult to forecast with any confidence a period more than five years ahead—though admittedly the possibilities of balance-of-payments planning vary greatly as between countries.

Any extension of the time allowed for the repayment of drawings along the lines discussed above would increase the degree of utilization of quotas (i.e. the average ratio of outstanding drawings to quota), and would thus increase the proportion of unconditional liquidity to conditional liquidity (as measured by the credit tranche positions remaining unused) provided by the Fund. It is unlikely, however, that any mere lengthening of repayment terms while retaining the repurchase provisions of Article V, Section 7(b), would make a significant contribution to the growth of unconditional liquidity or reserves. If this effect were desired, it would probably be

141

necessary for the Fund to transcend the sphere of balance-of-payments financing altogether and to provide, in addition to such financing, longer-term lending of noncompensatory kinds. It would probably be a wrong approach to the problem to seek to introduce a new type of long-term drawing facility that would be exempt from the repurchase provisions of Article V, Section 7(*b*), but would still be related to quotas and still be activated on the initiative of the drawing country. Since the primary purpose of the Fund's entry into the longer-term lending field would be less to accommodate the immediate borrowers than to enable the Fund to make a net contribution to the stock of reserves, it would be more appropriate to consider such longer-term lending under the head of investment by the Fund, which is the subject of the next section.

Investment by the Fund

By 'investments' are here meant essentially any securities (other than the Fund's own instruments of indebtedness) which the Fund might buy or sell but which would not count as holdings of a member's currency for the purpose of calculating drawing entitlements, repurchase obligations, etc., and would therefore leave unaffected such rights and obligations. Under implied powers, the Fund has used gold to the extent of $800 million to acquire investments, in the form of interest-bearing U.S. dollar securities redeemable on demand with a gold guarantee, for the purpose of maintaining the income of the organization and providing a certain reserve.

In what follows, we shall consider the consequences of extending the concept of investment by the Fund so that it may be undertaken for purposes relating not only to the Fund's income but also to international liquidity, and so that it may be financed not only out of the Fund's gold holdings but also out of its currency holdings (whether the currency of the country in which the investment is made or another) or by borrowing. For simplicity, it is assumed that the investments take the form of securities denominated in the currency of the country in which the investment is made (the 'country of investment'), but subject, like currency holdings under the Articles, to a gold-value guarantee; and that they are bought and sold from or through the government of the country of investment.

Since this is a type of operation not yet undertaken, it can be given any characteristics desired. However, in order that the power of

142

investment should be useful, we shall assume it to possess the following characteristics, the first of which follows from the definition given above. First, investments would not enter into the calculation of the Fund's holdings of currencies, or of the IMF position of the countries of investment, and would not as such affect their drawing rights (though the method of acquisition of the investments might do so). Second, the formal initiative as to the buying or selling of investments in any particular country would lie with the Fund, though the consent of the country of investment would be necessary both for purchases and for sales before maturity. Third, investments would be made on long term as well as on short term.

By virtue of the first characteristic listed above, investment would permit an increase in the amount of external liquidity, unconditional and conditional, available to Fund members at any given level of quotas. This effect would be most clearly seen if the Fund purchased an investment in a member country by using its ordinary holdings of that member's currency. The decline in these holdings would improve the IMF position of the country of investment, and thus increase its drawing facilities, without impairing the IMF position of any other member. The initial position of the country of investment would determine whether the drawing facilities acquired were quasi-unconditional gold tranche drawing rights or conditional facilities in the credit tranches.

If the Fund used its holdings of country B's currency to invest in country A, the effect would be the same as if it had used its holdings of A's currency for this purpose while at the same time A had made a drawing of B's currency. If, as might often be true for this kind of investment, A had initially a debtor IMF position and B a creditor position, the effect of the drawing element in the transaction would be to transform what would otherwise have been an expansion of conditional liquidity into an expansion of unconditional liquidity.

Again, if the investment in A were paid for out of the Fund's holdings of gold, the effect would be similar to a combination of an investment financed from the Fund's holdings of A's currency and a use of the Fund's gold to purchase A's currency. Generally speaking, the investment of gold would have a more expansionary effect on unconditional liquidity than any other kind of investment.

The second characteristic suggested for the power of investment, namely, that the Fund should have more initiative and freedom of action than with respect to drawings, is clearly a question of degree. While it would seem undesirable that member countries should be entitled to receive an amount of investment, or even a share in total investments, in any way related to quota, the solicitation of investment could not in practice be entirely excluded. Though for investments, as for drawings, the consent both of the Fund and of the country of investment (cf. the drawing country) would doubtless be necessary, nevertheless the fact that the initiative lay with the Fund should give the latter much more effective power in influencing the amount, timing, and distribution of investments than it has with respect to drawings.

The third characteristic proposed for investment, that it extend to assets of long as well as short maturity, is, of course, of fundamental importance for the Fund's ability to expand the total amount of credit—and hence the amount of unconditional liquidity created in the form of gold tranche drawing rights or instruments of the Fund's indebtedness, relative to the amount of short-term to medium-term conditional drawing facilities which it provides. Investment by the Fund is thus a third way of bridging the possible gap between what the Fund ought to contribute to the expansion of unconditional liquidity or reserves and what, if anything, it contributes as the counterpart to the use of its conditional drawing facilities. The other two possible ways of bridging this gap, as already explained, are an extension of quasi-automatic drawing rights beyond the gold tranche and a lengthening of the term of drawings.

Investment differs from an extension of quasi-automatic drawing rights beyond the gold tranche in five main respects:

(1) it can be distributed more selectively than an extension of automatic drawing rights, which would normally be applied to all members in proportion to their quotas;

(2) in so far as the investment is made with a currency other than that of the country of investment, it resembles an extension of automatic drawing rights *plus* an actual drawing;

(3) investment will create more drawing facilities free from repurchase obligations than will an equal extension of automatic drawing rights beyond the gold tranche;

(4) investment will constitute a bigger drain on the Fund's resources than will an equal extension of automatic drawing rights;[26]

(5) whereas an extension of automatic drawing rights beyond the gold tranche automatically increases the effectiveness of increases in quotas in expanding unconditional liquidity, investment does not. To achieve a similar result, investment would have to be increased *pari passu* with the increases in quotas.

Investment of the type outlined differs from the introduction of longer-term drawing rights mainly with respect to the first two characteristics of investment discussed above. Owing to these characteristics, Fund investment has the advantage over the provision of long-term drawing facilities that it could more easily be kept distinct from the Fund's everyday task of providing short-to-medium-term drawing facilities, and is therefore more likely to leave that valuable function unimpaired.

In one respect, investment might act more powerfully on a country's policies than either of the other two methods of expanding credit from the Fund, viz., if it is regarded by the country of investment as entering into its balance of payments as a positive item 'above the line'. An increase in liquidity that results from a payments surplus (or a decline in liquidity that results from a payments deficit) is likely to be more effective than one arising independently of the balance of payments.

Insofar as investment is employed for the purpose of enabling the Fund to contribute to a long-term expansion in the trend of unconditional liquidity, it would seem appropriate that it should take the form of a purchase of securities amortized over a long period of time—e.g. twenty years. While the Fund would, of course, not be precluded from holding long-term investments in the more highly developed countries, it would seem desirable that as high a proportion as possible should be held in those countries where the need for capital is, humanly speaking, greatest—namely, the less developed countries. Since the latter would be unlikely to use the proceeds of such investments to build up their own reserves, but would spend them on the products of the industrial countries, the effect on the

---

[26] Both (3) and (4) are attributable to the fact that, assuming that the investments are distributed between countries in the same proportions as would be an extension of quasi-automatic drawing rights, countries' IMF positions will be generally more positive in the former than in the latter case.

reserves of the industrial countries would probably be almost as great as if the investments had been made in these countries in the first place. Moreover, insofar as the object of expanding liquidity is to encourage the industrialized countries to adopt more expansionary financial policies, the underlying purpose would be better achieved by investing in the less developed than in the more highly developed countries, since in the former case increased liquidity would accrue to the industrialized countries in the form of export receipts, with a stimulating effect on incomes, and in the latter case it would accrue only in the form of greater ease in the money and securities markets. Investment by the Fund in less developed countries should, of course, not exceed amounts which the countries in question could economically absorb at the relatively low rates of interest which the Fund would be able to charge. Such investments would not be part of the Fund's own liquid reserves; they would be a means to the creation of liquidity in the hands of national monetary authorities, with beneficial side effects on the provision of resources for economic development.

Any long-term investment by the Fund in the less developed countries should presumably be carried out as far as possible through existing intermediaries, such as the IBRD and the IDA, though neither the terms and conditions of the investments nor even the investment criteria need be precisely those at present applied by either of these institutions. While the technique here discussed has some resemblance to the 'Stamp Plan',[27] there is no suggestion that the investments should be in any way tied to imports from such countries as are willing to accept additional claims on the Fund, nor is it suggested that those claims should necessarily take the form of transferable certificates rather than, for example, gold tranche positions.

The technique of investment (and disinvestment) has certain advantages over that of changes in the liberality or severity of drawing policies as a means of bringing about such temporary variations in the amount of liquidity as may be useful in counteracting cyclical fluctuations in the industrial world. Temporary changes in the amount of unconditional liquidity, such as may be called for by alterations in the condition of the foreign exchange markets, are likely to be evoked, through variations in the demand

[27] See the article by Maxwell Stamp in *Moorgate and Wall Street*, Spring 1961.

for drawings, even with constant drawing policies. Where some positive anticyclical action is called for, however, drawing policies are likely to prove too inflexible, and open market policies more effective. Investments for this purpose could be of a short-term though renewable character, and would normally be made predominantly in the industrial countries.

Long-term investment in central reserve countries might also be an appropriate means of counteracting any sudden and substantial decline in official holdings of reserve currencies. These investments should be on long term to cover the possibility that the decline might be a permanent one, but there could be arrangements for withdrawing the investments if official holdings of the currencies in question should recover.

WAYS OF ENSURING THE FUND'S ABILITY TO PROVIDE
INTERNATIONAL LIQUIDITY

The Fund provides its members with international liquidity through its readiness to provide financing, in the form of drawings or of repayment of the Fund's own indebtedness. But such financing involves the provision of currencies other than that of the country that is being financed. The Fund cannot carry out this financing unless it has access, preferably assured access, to the currencies that it requires. Moreover, as we have seen, acts of financing by the Fund, whether in the form of drawings, repayments or investment, give rise to claims on the part of the countries whose currencies are used— claims which are generally themselves of a liquid character. The Fund must have assurance that those of its members that are in a strong balance-of-payments position will be willing to accumulate and hold such claims, and will not compel it to withhold or withdraw financing from countries that need it. The Fund cannot create international liquidity, any more than a domestic banking system can create domestic liquidity, unless its members (customers) are willing to hold additional liquidity in the form of claims upon it. These are aspects of the Fund's problem of obtaining sufficient resources to enable it to discharge its functions properly.

Apart from repurchases (i.e. repayments of drawings)—which of course restore its power to extend new drawings but do not enable it to increase the net amount of drawings outstanding—the Fund has two main ways of replenishing its resources, and thus of ensuring

147

that it can continue to expand world liquidity, viz., increases in quotas and borrowing arrangements.

Increases in quotas

Increases in quotas affect countries' liquidity in the manner discussed in an earlier section. They also provide the Fund with additional resources consisting of gold and 'drawable' currencies, the former to the amount of 25 per cent of all quota increases, and the latter to the amount of 75 per cent of the additions to quotas of countries whose currencies are, at any given time, usable for drawings. The addition to the Fund's holdings of gold and drawable currencies is intended to maintain the Fund's liquidity, i.e. to enable it to honour the enhanced drawing facilities that accompany the quota increases without the necessity of paying out the currencies of countries that are in a weak balance-of-payments position or reserve position and might thus be embarrassed by the drawing. In the short run, before countries have had time to use their new drawing facilities, a rise in quotas will necessarily increase the Fund's liquidity. In the long run, however, if the increase in quotas is matched by a corresponding proportionate increase in the demand, and need, for drawings, the additional resources provided by an all-round increase in quotas will only suffice to enable the Fund to maintain its original degree of liquidity. Thus, if the original country distribution of quotas, relative to the distribution of potential payments surpluses and deficits, was such that the resources of the Fund had to be supplemented by borrowing arrangements with certain countries, and if the distribution of potential surpluses and deficits remains unchanged, a quota increase as described above will normally have to be supplemented by a proportionate increase in the borrowing arrangements. Only insofar as the increase in quotas outstrips the increase in the demand, and need, for drawings will it be possible for the Fund to reduce its reliance on such arrangements.

Borrowing arrangements

Under Article VII, Section 2, the Fund can borrow a member's currency from that member or (with the consent of both parties) from another source, whenever 'it deems such action appropriate to replenish its holdings of any member's currency'. Such borrowing may affect the liquidity of members directly, but much more important is its effect, or the effect of the arrangements under which it is carried on, on the liquidity or resources of the Fund itself.

The nature of the borrowing arrangements will determine:

(1) the nature of the resources made available to the Fund;
(2) the conditions governing repayment and the other characteristics of the instruments of Fund indebtedness; and
(3) the conditions under which the resources are made available to the Fund.

As regards (1), the proviso from Article VII, Section 2, quoted above, would seem to confine the currencies that might be borrowed to those suitable for being drawn from the Fund, though the Fund's need for the currencies in question does not necessarily have to be immediate.

As regards (2), countries acquiring claims on the Fund by lending to it might be able to require the Fund to convert these, on demand, into currencies or gold; or the claims might be repayable at fixed dates but (like gold tranche drawing rights) convertible into foreign currencies whenever required to meet payments difficulties experienced by the lending country; or convertible in some proportion to the decline in that country's other reserves; or repayable only on maturity. The duration of the claims might be short or long. They might be transferable generally, as between central banks, or not at all. They might be interest-bearing or otherwise.

The precise degree of liquidity to be accorded to a claim on the Fund arising out of an act of borrowing is thus variable, and should depend on the effect that the Fund wishes to exercise on world liquidity. In practice, it might be difficult to induce lending members to be content with a lesser degree of liquidity than that afforded by a gold tranche position in the Fund unless substantial interest were paid. On the other hand, it would be important for the Fund's own liquidity that lenders collectively should not be in a position to encash too high a proportion of their claims on the Fund at any one time. Any system of deposits withdrawable (i.e. convertible into currency or gold) on demand would leave the Fund exposed to the possibility of 'runs' that might deprive it of the power to maintain or expand world liquidity when this was required. It would, therefore, seem necessary that repayment of the Fund's indebtedness on the initiative of the creditor should be confined to situations in which the

149

creditor was able to represent that its balance of payments created a need for such repayment. The precise degree of liquidity that could safely be given to instruments of the Fund's indebtedness would depend in part, as will be shown, on the nature of the access to resources conferred on the Fund by the borrowing arrangements.

In discussions of international liquidity, emphasis is often laid on direct transferability among countries as an important attribute that would enhance the liquidity of claims on the Fund arising out of Fund indebtedness. Any value such transferability might have for the holders of such claims would depend on the willingness of other countries to accept transfers. Such willingness could certainly not be relied on in the absence of definite arrangements whereby countries would agree to accept transference of such claims up to specific amounts. These arrangements, in turn, would be likely to be at the expense of undertakings to provide resources directly to the Fund. Countries might even insist that claims on the Fund transferred to them be counted against any lines of credit which they might be extending to the Fund. The system is therefore not one which would provide additional facilities for Fund members at no cost to the Fund's resources. The fact that the transferee would be, by definition, a willing holder of claims on the Fund would be an advantage, but direct transfers, if bilaterally arranged, might conflict with those general understandings regarding an equitable distribution of liquid claims on the Fund which would probably be necessary if the Fund was to supply unconditional liquidity on a large scale. If lenders' rights to encash Fund indebtedness to meet any payments difficulties were made sufficiently automatic—in conformity with suggestions made earlier for further increasing the automatism of drawings in the gold tranche—the attractions of direct transferability might well become negligible.

It should be noted that if, as appears likely, the degree of liquidity attaching to instruments of Fund indebtedness were not very different from that attaching to gold tranche positions, an act of borrowing by the Fund, taken by itself, would be likely to have only a minor effect on countries' external liquidity. A member lending its own currency would probably be a country with a gold tranche position. The rise in the Fund's holdings of its currency would involve a decline in that position, to offset which the country would acquire a claim on the Fund of a degree of liquidity comparable to that afforded by a gold tranche position.[28] Conceivably the claim on the Fund, having the legal form of an asset, would be deemed by the member to be more worthy of inclusion in its reserves than any kind of drawing right. The real gain in liquidity would, however, be slight or negligible. Again, if a member lent to the Fund gold or the currency of another member, the lending member would acquire a highly liquid claim on the Fund but would suffer a corresponding loss in its reserves. A country whose currency was lent to the Fund by another member would suffer a decline in its Fund position, probably a gold tranche position, but its other reserves might benefit from the reduced supply of its currency in the international exchange market. However, if the act of lending to the Fund involved a decline in the holding of foreign exchange reserves, the net effect would be to reduce international liquidity.

The real significance of an act of borrowing is that it would increase the Fund's resources without having much direct or immediate effect on members' liquidity. (In this respect it contrasts with a quota increase, which, as we have seen, would not only increase Fund resources but also immediately enhance members' conditional liquidity in the form of drawing facilities in the credit tranches.) However, as soon as the Fund used the resources it had borrowed, whether for additional drawings or investment, a net increase in international liquidity of the sort described in earlier pages would occur.

As regards (3), resources might be made available to the Fund

(a) in the form of deposits made on the initiative of the lender, though on conditions laid down by the Fund and possibly subject to quantitative limits established by the Fund;

(b) under lines of credit, calls on which could be on the Fund's initiative subject to conditions agreed in the credit arrangement; or

(c) as the outcome of an agreed rule of a more or less automatic statistical character.

---

[28] It might conceivably be possible to assign currency borrowed by the Fund in advance of use to some reserve account which would not count as normal holdings and would therefore leave unimpaired the drawing facilities of the lending member. Any such reserve holding would, however, in the terminology of this paper, rank as investment, as defined above, and the increase in unconditional liquidity associated with this transaction would result from this 'investment' rather than from the borrowing as such.

The Fund could not, at present, accept deposits entirely at the will of the lender and in any currency that the lender chose to deposit. It could accept only currencies potentially needed for drawings, and then only if the country whose currency was deposited consented. However, the Fund could reasonably declare its willingness to accept deposits in any currency of which its holdings fell below a certain low percentage of quota (say, 25 per cent or 20 per cent), provided that the deposits were made by or with the consent of the country whose currency was deposited. Interest rates could be such as to make such deposits attractive. While depositors might hesitate to incur the loss involved in depositing at par strong currencies standing at a premium in the market, they might hope to recoup this loss by drawing premium currencies at par when the time came to withdraw their deposits. One attraction of this technique would be that, since the deposits would be made on the initiative of the depositor, no negotiation would be necessary between the lender and the Fund.

On the other hand, the system of voluntary deposits would seem to leave the Fund dangerously exposed to net withdrawals of its resources. This would be true even if the right to withdraw were confined to countries with a payments need, for there would be no assurance that surplus countries would necessarily be induced by the mere attraction of the interest paid, the gold guarantee, etc., to add to their deposits at a time when deficit countries were being compelled by payments difficulties to withdraw theirs. If deposits were encashable on demand, the situation would be even more precarious, since a general nervousness on world exchange markets, or a lack of confidence regarding the Fund's own liquidity, might lead to a net withdrawal of deposits just at the time when the Fund was anxious to extend itself in assisting member countries.

Lines of credit could be established by the Fund with individual lenders or, as in the General Arrangements to Borrow, with a group of lenders. The line of credit would have one very important advantage over the mere acceptance of deposits, in that it would ensure the Fund of access to additional resources for the lifetime of the stand-by arrangement. Voluntary deposits, once they had been withdrawn (e.g. to meet a payments deficit of the creditor) might not be reconstituted if the interest paid was not attractive or if the Fund's own liquidity was suspect. In the line-of-credit technique a similar difficulty would arise only when the credit arrangement lapsed and had to be renewed.

It might, moreover, be possible to have permanent credit arrangements or lines of credit which, like subscriptions, would give the Fund a permanent increase in reserves.

The nature of the tension between a lending country's right to secure payment of its loan at need, and the Fund's right to draw on the line of credit at *its* need, is broadly analogous to that described earlier as existing between a member's right to draw on a gold tranche position and the Fund's right to sell the member's currency and thus to increase or restore that gold tranche position. Some conventional rule is required to determine to what extent the Fund should draw on any given country's line of credit. The rule might be, for example, that the Fund would borrow from any given country to whatever extent was required to prevent its holdings of that country's currency from falling below some (low) percentage of its quota. The Fund's policy with respect to currencies to be drawn and used in repurchase would be determined so as to secure an equitable distribution of net IMF positions among creditor countries, including in the concept of net IMF positions not only gold tranche positions but also amounts lent to the Fund. Lending countries incurring payments deficits would be expected to take advance repayment of their loans before drawing their gold tranche positions below the aforesaid percentage of quota.

A good example of the third technique mentioned above, whereby countries would lend to the Fund amounts determined by some statistical criterion, would be an arrangement under which many or all Fund members would hold claims on the Fund in some proportion to, or as a function of, their total gold and exchange reserves. These claims would be acquired by depositing gold or currencies needed by the Fund. This would provide for a long-term growth in Fund resources *pari passu* with the growth of official reserves and, if used to finance an expansion in investment by the Fund, or in drawings relative to quotas, would make possible a long-term growth in the liquidity provided by the Fund. Such an arrangement would, however, make great demands on the willingness of countries to undertake important commitments—though not necessarily sacrifices —for an international end. Moreover, a once-for-all commitment would not suffice. If, as is probable, it became necessary, in order to secure a higher proportionate rate of expansion of world liquidity than that of monetary gold stocks, to raise periodically the proportion of reserves held in the form of claims on the Fund, a new agreement would be called for on the occasion of each increase.

One disadvantage of a simple system under which countries would hold a proportion of their reserves in the form of Fund deposits would be that, especially when that proportion was still small, they could use such deposits to cover only a small part of any payments deficits that they might have. This would make the holding of a deposit less attractive than the holding of a gold tranche drawing right, and might constitute a real hardship for the majority of countries whose own currencies would not be acceptable for deposit and who would therefore have to establish deposits at the expense of other reserves. The hardship would be greater if a part of the gold and foreign exchange holdings of the countries in question were pledged or otherwise unusable. A possible way round this difficulty might be a provision under which deposits with the Fund could be withdrawn *pari passu* with a decline in the depositor's other reserves and reconstituted *pari passu* with any recovery in these reserves until the required proportion was restored. Regulations might be required establishing priority between such reconstitution and repurchases of any drawings outstanding.

The three modes of Fund borrowing discussed above are merely illustrative. The borrowing instrument is very flexible. Many different combinations can be imagined. For example, the following system—involving a combination of the system of voluntary deposit with that of lending to the Fund in relation to a statistical criterion—might be of use for maintaining the level of international liquidity if that were threatened by some temporary or permanent decline in the propensity of monetary authorities to hold reserves in the form of foreign exchange, and if no adequate arrangements or understandings existed among these authorities with respect to the holding of reserve currencies.

The Fund would stand ready to receive deposits (i.e. to borrow) in reserve currencies held by monetary authorities to the extent that the latter wished to reduce their holdings thereof. Currencies thus acquired by the Fund would immediately be invested (i.e. held in a form apart from its ordinary currency holdings) in the countries whose currencies were deposited, and would thus leave unaffected the usual drawing facilities available to these countries. Such investments—which would, like other Fund investments, carry a gold

154

guarantee—would be amortized in gold or currency acceptable to the Fund over a lengthy period (e.g. twenty years), and would also be redeemable on demand in domestic currency at the Fund's request. If depositing countries should subsequently desire to increase their holdings of the currencies formerly deposited, they would be under obligation to do so in the first instance by withdrawing their deposits from the Fund, which would in turn encash its investments. As long as the transaction had not been reversed according to this procedure, the deposit, though convertible into needed currency if required to meet payments deficits of the depositor, would have to be reconstituted when the other reserves of the depositor increased (or possibly according to some repayments schedule).

The main effect of this arrangement would be to enable countries losing confidence in a reserve currency to substitute a gold-guaranteed claim on the Fund. If the loss of confidence should turn out to be permanent, the system would permit the euthanasia of the reserve currency in question, but this would not be assumed in advance to be inevitable. Instead, the fact that a temporary gold guarantee *could* be obtained whenever necessary would probably strengthen the desire to hold reserve currencies.

INTERRELATION BETWEEN THE FUND'S CREDIT POLICY
AND THE FORM IN WHICH RESOURCES ARE RAISED

The two main methods of expanding the Fund's resources, by increases in quotas and by borrowing arrangements, respectively, have consequences that differ in two respects. The first and obvious difference is that the former method implies that increases in countries' unconditional liquidity (in so far as achieved through the Fund) will take the form of quasi-automatic drawing rights, while the latter method implies that they will take the form of liabilities of the Fund. The second and more important difference is that increases in quotas are associated, while increases in borrowing arrangements are not, with increases in drawing facilities in the Fund. From these considerations it follows that any preferences between automatic drawing rights and Fund liabilities as the form in which unconditional liquidity created by the Fund should be held, or any preferences between increases in quotas and borrowing as the method whereby the resources of the Fund should be raised, will have implications for the extent to which drawing facilities can appropriately be provided, or investments appropriately acquired, relative to quotas.

For example, if it were desired to avoid the necessity for borrowing by the Fund, there would be a limit to the extent to which drawing policies could be liberalized, and/or drawing facilities extended to additional tranches, and/or investments expanded. All these acts would involve an expansion in the amount of credit extended by the Fund relative to the amount of quotas and thus relative to the resources in gold and drawable currencies provided by the subscriptions.

Again, if it were decided, in order to avoid the necessity for an immediate increase in quotas, that additional drawing facilities should be provided by the adoption of more liberal drawing policies, it should be realized that once this liberalization had had time to take full effect, it would increase the likelihood that recourse to borrowing would be necessary.

It was pointed out above that if it were desired that the growth in quasi-unconditional liquidity provided through the Fund should out-strip the growth in short-to-medium-term conditional drawing facilities, one of the ways of achieving this would be for the Fund to expand its holdings of investments relative to drawing facilities in the credit tranches. Such a development, however, would be likely, if carried far, to involve a necessity for borrowing by the Fund on a substantial scale.

If the extension of quasi-automatic drawing rights beyond the gold tranche, rather than investment, were the technique adopted for raising the Fund's contribution to unconditional liquidity relative to its contribution to conditional liquidity, the resultant dependence on borrowing arrangements would be considerably less. For example, suppose that quasi-automatic drawing rights were extended beyond the gold tranche by 250 units, while conditional drawing facilities in the credit tranches were maintained by an equal extension of the limit on total drawings. Precisely the same effect on the amounts of unconditional and conditional drawing facilities available to each country could have been achieved by a Fund investment to the amount of 250 units distributed among members in proportion to quotas and purchased with the currencies of the countries in which the investments were made. Drawings outstanding would increase under both procedures to a similar extent; but the investment method—to the extent that investments were made in countries whose currencies were drawable—would use up the Fund's stock of these currencies, and thus draw down the resources of the Fund, to a greater extent than would the method of extending automatic drawing facilities. If, as is likely, investments in the less developed countries were made not in their own currencies but in drawable currencies, the increase in unconditional liquidity resulting from the investments would be greater than has been assumed above; but so, *pro tanto*, would be the drain on the Fund's resources.

It does not follow from what has been said that pursuit of the investment path to the creation of international liquidity by the Fund necessarily involves undue reliance on borrowing. This could be avoided by means of suitable adjustments in drawing policies, in such a way that conditional drawing facilities were kept from rising proportionately while quotas were expanded to provide the resources necessary to finance the investment. However, in the past, drawing policies have not been very flexible, and such flexibility as there has been (since the first years of the Fund at any rate) has been mostly in the direction of liberalization.

CONCLUSION

It is reasonable to believe that there will be a need, as the years pass, for a gradual expansion in the amount of short-to-medium-term credit that is made available to monetary authorities conditionally on the adoption of policies directed toward the maintenance or restoration of equilibrium. Such conditional liquidity can suitably be provided by a gradual expansion of conditional drawing facilities in the Fund.

It is possible that the long-term upward trend in the liquid reserves of countries is inadequate and requires, or will require, to be reinforced by a similar or faster rate of growth of unconditional or near-unconditional liquidity in the form of quasi-automatic drawing rights and/or of indebtedness of the Fund with quasi-automatic repayment features.

Once it was decided what would be a desirable (long-run) rate of growth in the Fund's provision of conditional and quasi-unconditional liquidity, respectively, there would be a variety of ways— from an expositional standpoint an embarrassing variety of ways— in which this could be achieved.

157

For example, even if it were decided (1) that the Fund's borrowing arrangements should be confined to a given proportion of quotas, and (2) that an investment power should not be used, it would be possible to attain the desired expansion in the Fund's provision of conditional and quasi-unconditional liquidity by a suitable combination of (a) expansion of quotas, (b) adjustment, through drawing policies, in the proportion of conditional to quasi-automatic drawing facilities, and (c) adjustment, through drawing policies, in the proportion of total drawing facilities to quotas. In all probability, the proportion of conditional to quasi-unconditional drawing facilities and the proportion of total drawing facilities to quotas would both have to decline.

Again, if assumption (1), regarding borrowing, were retained, assumption (2) abandoned, and a new assumption (3) added, to the effect that no adjustment would be permitted in the proportion of conditional to quasi-automatic drawing facilities, then the desired result could be obtained by a combination of expansion of quotas, investment, and adjustment in the proportion of drawing facilities to quotas. In all probability, the proportion of investment holdings relative to quotas would have to rise, while that of drawing facilities relative to quotas would have to decline. As we have seen in the preceding section, this method would require a more severe curtailment of drawing rights relative to quotas than would the method considered in the preceding paragraph.

Finally, if it were impracticable for any reason for total drawing facilities to decline relative to quotas, it would no longer be possible to enforce any given upper limit on borrowing relative to quotas. This would be true whether the approach to the creation of unconditional liquidity was through the extension of quasi-automatic drawing facilities or through investment. Any such limit, however, would be more quickly reached if reliance were placed on investment than if it were placed on an expansion of quasi-automatic drawing facilities at the expense of conditional ones.

From what has been said, it would appear that the Fund could contribute to the long-term expansion in unconditional liquidity without necessarily engaging in more active investment. The same objective could be achieved with less resort to borrowing by an extension of quasi-automatic drawing rights beyond the gold tranche. On the other hand, investment would be a more selective way of expanding quasi-automatic drawing facilities, and the facilities in question would be less encumbered with (even nominal) repurchase obligations.

Insofar as the investment power was used for this purpose, there would be no reason why a proportion of the investment involved should not be directed toward the less developed countries.

In order to smooth out the growth in quotas, quota increases could take place in annual instalments.

The Fund's contribution to the long-term growth of unconditional liquidity could be slightly—but only slightly—enhanced if the accumulation of gold stocks that might otherwise result from quota increases was avoided by judicious purchases of needed currencies.

It would probably be necessary for the Fund to depend largely on borrowing to supplement its resources. Voluntary deposits would be an unreliable source of resources for the Fund. Lines of credit would be preferable, but should be kept as free as possible from restrictions that would hamper the Fund in the use of the resources received. One way to deal with long-term problems might be an arrangement in which each member normally held a proportion of its reserves in the form of deposits with the Fund, with provision for temporary withdrawal in times of need.

Cyclical or temporary variations in the desirable level of international liquidity may take place either because of variations in the instability of international payments or because of variations in the pressure of monetary demand for goods and services, or for both reasons. The first sort of change in the need for financing is likely to result in a change in the use of Fund drawing facilities and thus in an answering change in the supply of liquidity. In the second type of change, however, and even to some extent in the first, any responsiveness in the supply of liquidity is likely to be insufficient. In this event, there would be a case for varying either the amount of the Fund's investments or the liberality of its drawing policies. In view of the inflexibility of such policies, the former technique is likely to be the more practicable. This sort of variable investment should be short term and renewable and should be held mainly in industrial countries. The resources required to finance such temporary extensions of Fund credit might in some instances be provided by effecting increases in quotas (or increases in the proportion of reserves held in the form of deposits with the Fund) earlier than would otherwise be appropriate.

159

However, it would generally be appropriate to supplement the Fund's resources with borrowing arrangements of the stand-by type.

The third of the possible reasons, mentioned on page 124 above, why the Fund might have to take action in the field of international liquidity is that it might be necessary to offset the decline in liquidity that would ensue should there be any decline in countries' willingness to hold reserves in the form of foreign exchange. The most effective action open to the Fund in this contingency would appear to be the acquisition of long-term investments in reserve currencies, reversible if the willingness of countries to hold foreign exchange should recover. This, however, might create a temporary or permanent need by the Fund for additional resources. A scheme whereby such resources might, in the assumed circumstances, be raised by borrowing is described on page 149.

Chapter 6

Use and Acceptance of Reserve Claims*

In what follows, it is assumed that any reserve claims created by deliberate international decision will consist of claims held by the monetary authorities of countries on some international institution or agent. The claims may take the form either of liabilities of the institution or of rights to borrow from or to draw upon it. The use that countries can make of such claims in order to assist in financing their balance-of-payments deficits must always depend in the main on the willingness of other countries to accept transfer of the claims, either directly or via the institution, in exchange for gold or convertible currency.

VOLUNTARY ACCEPTANCE OF TRANSFER

In theory such willingness might be purely voluntary and based on the attractiveness of holding the claims. In practice, however, it would almost certainly have to be backstopped by the assumption, on the part of a sufficient number of countries, of definite legal obligations to accept transfer. If transfer were purely voluntary for the transferee as well as the transferor, the value of the claims in terms of gold and the principal currencies would not tend to remain at any particular parity but would fluctuate in response to changes in the rate of interest paid on the claims relative to that paid on other reserves, and to changes in speculative anticipations about the future values of the claims. In order to prevent such fluctuations in value—an unwelcome characteristic for a new reserve asset—claims could be transferred only at a fixed ratio to gold or currencies. The result of such price fixing on a free market, however, might be that in some circumstances the claims would find wide acceptance and could therefore be used without difficulty, while at other times, countries holding them would be unable to dispose of them at need.

* Reprinted, with slight alterations, from International Monetary Fund *Staff Papers*, Vol. XIII, No. 3, November 1966.

To avoid this result, it has been suggested that the right to transfer on a voluntary basis should be ensured by an obligation on the part of the issuing institution to convert the claims into gold or currency at fixed rates. Under this system, however, at times the claims might pass freely from country to country without conversion at the issuing institution, and at other times (especially if the liquidity of the issuing institution was itself in question) substantial conversions might take place. These conversions would force the institution to realize its assets or counterclaims, which might have the result of bringing about a net destruction of reserves at the very time when reserves were most required.[1] Moreover, the institution might not be able to avoid calling for the encashment of claims on countries whose own balance-of-payments positions were insufficiently secure, and this hazard to the debtors of the institution would tend to offset from the start the liquidity value of the reserve creation.

OBLIGATORY ACCEPTANCE OF TRANSFER AT PAR VIS-À-VIS DOMESTIC CURRENCY

An alternative system which suggests itself is one in which countries are both free to transfer claims and obliged to accept them to an indefinite extent. Such an obligation, however, is meaningless unless it specifies both what is to be provided in exchange for the claims and the rate at which the exchange is to take place. The obligation to purchase claims might be couched in terms of gold, own currency, or other convertible currency.

Under one variant of this system, transferees would accept reserve claims in exchange for their own currency at par. Profit considerations would impel transferors to purchase convertible currencies with the highest market values in relation to par, while considerations of convenience would impel them to purchase the currency most commonly used as a means of market intervention, namely U.S. dollars. The United States, as a special case, might have a balance-of-payments incentive to purchase the currencies of those countries

---

[1] In the General Account of the Fund such a reduction in the institution's claims on a member in the form of holdings of the member's currency would result in an increase in the member's drawing rights on the Fund, and these drawing rights, if in the gold tranche, would constitute reserve claims. In this case there would be transfer, albeit an indirect one, and no destruction, of reserves. In other institutional set-ups, however, the realization of the institution's assets would involve a net decline in country reserves.

most liable to convert dollar holdings into gold. Under such a system the circulation of reserve claims would be canalized in a somewhat arbitrary way. There would be a tendency for claims to flow to countries whose currencies were at a premium—which would not necessarily be those whose balances of payments were currently most favourable. There would be a second tendency for claims to flow to the United States and possibly back from the United States to the countries that were currently converting dollars into gold.

If the countries whose currencies were at a premium were anxious to avoid an accumulation of holdings of reserve claims at the expense of other types of reserves, they would have an incentive to reduce the premiums. If they did so, the effective range of currency variations within the permitted margins would tend to decline—a result which is probably far from desirable from the standpoint of the adjustment process.

Another transferability arrangement which, though less strongly biased, might be equally arbitrary in its effects would be one in which countries were both free to transfer reserve claims and obliged to accept transfer at par against U.S. dollars. Under this arrangement the transferor would have no particular profit incentive to direct claims towards any one country rather than any other. The convenience in transferring to the United States, though somewhat lessened by the fact that all transferees would provide dollars in exchange for claims, would remain and, since it would not be offset by profit considerations, would probably assume decisive importance. Claims would therefore tend to flow from all countries to the United States, which in turn would tend to transfer or retransfer claims to countries showing a propensity to convert dollars into gold. This system would have the merit of not interfering with the exchange rate policies of countries within the margins but, like the previous system, would impose upon the United States the responsibility for determining the circulation of the claims. To avoid the appearance of giving a special role to the United States, the transferee might be required to purchase claims in exchange for his own currency at a rate equivalent, on foreign exchange markets, to parity in terms of dollars, and to make this equivalence good by offering conversion facilities into dollars. Yet this requirement would not alter anything of substance in the system.

163

MORAL RESTRAINTS ON TRANSFER

Owing to the element of arbitrariness inherent in any system that combines free transferability of international reserve claims with an unlimited obligation to accept them, there is a danger that under such a system (a) reserve claims might be maldistributed relative to other forms of reserves, (b) countries might be asked to accept reserve claims in exchange for reserves of types usable for market intervention at times when, owing to balance-of-payments difficulty, they were tending to run short of those types of reserves, and (c) reserve claims might be transferred back and forth between countries with a velocity of circulation unflattering to their prestige.

The most important step towards securing a rational distribution of claims through transfer would be the acceptance of the principle that countries should not seek to transfer claims unless they had a balance-of-payments justification for doing so and were simultaneously utilizing at least some of their holdings of other reserves. There might even be an understanding as to the proportion of the decline in their reserves that countries should finance by reducing their holdings of claims. This does not mean that transfers need be subject to prior approval in the light of this criterion. It would suffice that, as for gold tranche drawings in the Fund, transferors should make a declaration of balance-of-payments need on the occasion of each transfer, or even that they should give a general undertaking of their intention to use the facility in the manner described above, with some provision for *ex post* review, if necessary. The main point is that transferors, while remaining as unhampered as possible in the immediate use of reserve claims, should not feel free to 'improve' the composition of their reserves by unloading the claims on other participants.

CREDITOR LIMITS

Although an undertaking as to the use of the facility just described would prevent abuse of the facility, it would not protect transferees against having to accumulate an inequitably high proportion of reserve claims in their reserves or to accept such claims at inconvenient times. Indeed, for certain countries the first of these difficulties would be intensified by the principle of use just enunciated. These are the countries that might find themselves, for quite arbitrary reasons, accumulating an unduly high proportion of reserve claims which they did not feel free to retransfer because their reserves as a whole were rising and their balance-of-payments position remained good.

One way suggested for meeting this difficulty is to set up quantitative limits on the reserve claims that countries would be obliged to accumulate as a result of the acceptance obligation. Since that obligation is in some sense a *quid pro quo* for the initial allocation of reserve claims to the different participating countries, it is usually suggested that creditor limits should be proportionate to the initial allocations in question. Clearly, if countries are to have reasonable assurance of being able to transfer their claims without an undue amount of negotiation, the sum of the holding limits must exceed substantially the amount of claims in existence. Thus, it is usually assumed that the limit for each country would have to be two or three times its cumulative allocation of reserve claims. Presumably countries would be free to accept transfer beyond their limits but would also be free to retransfer to other countries, until their holdings were down to the limits, without claiming or implying that they have any balance-of-payments need to do so. The plan might even go further and deny countries the right to refuse to accept transfer, leaving as the sole significance of the limits the freedom of any country attaining its limit to retransfer without any implication that it has a balance-of-payments need. Not much can be said, however, for having transfers that are immediately reversed; nor is it desirable to encourage countries to accept claims far beyond their creditor limits, then suddenly to unload the excess on other countries, perhaps because their attitude towards reserve claims has changed.

A theoretical possibility that would avoid giving a special position to any particular currency would be to make reserve claims transferable at par against gold. The great majority of countries, however, are unwilling to accept the convertibility of their own currencies directly into gold, and so would be most unlikely to agree to convert into gold any reserve claims which other countries might choose to transfer to them. Even if they were willing to do this, the ease of obtaining gold by such transfers and the need to hold gold in order to meet such transfers might cause an undue demand for gold at the expense of reserve-currency countries.

Notwithstanding holding limits such as those just discussed, countries whose reserves were low in relation to the amount of

165

claims allocated to them might run short of reserves in other forms before their holdings of claims had reached the prescribed multiple. This danger would be especially great if a large part of world reserves came to consist of reserve claims. It might be felt, therefore, that a country's obligation to accept transfer of reserve claims should cease when its holdings of reserves other than reserve claims fell to a given proportion of its total reserves, say, to one-half the proportion prevailing in the average participating country.

GUIDED TRANSFERABILITY

Even these two kinds of limits, however, might not satisfy potential transferees. They might want protection against having to accept reserve claims at times of payments difficulty, when acceptance, though followed by immediate retransfer, might be unwelcome, or against having to hold an inequitably high—or inequitably low—proportion of their reserves in the form of such claims. In this event, the only recourse would be to a form of transferability under some degree of collective guidance.

Such guidance might be either voluntary or compulsory. If compulsory, it might take the form either of rules which, though varied from time to time, left the transferor with considerable choice among potential transferees, or of more precise indications as to the direction of transfer. The provision of such guidance on a voluntary basis would seem to be a useful feature of any transferability scheme. Many transferors might be glad to avail themselves of such a facility, even if not obliged to do so, in order to escape the onus of deciding which other country was to accept more reserve claims at the expense of its reserves in other forms.

The general principles underlying such guidance would presumably be similar to those gradually elaborated in response to experience, with general approbation, in the Fund's policies on currencies to be drawn. Thus, countries would be encouraged to make any transfers to countries, other than those in balance-of-payments difficulties, whose holdings of reserve claims constituted a relatively low proportion of their total reserves, subject, however, to the above-mentioned limits on acceptance of transfer.

There is, of course, a certain tension in the system of guided transferability as described above between the existence of holding limits based on countries' relative degree of participation in the scheme and the principle of tending towards proportionality of reserve claims to other reserves. (An analogous tension is found also in the Fund's policies on currencies to be drawn, as between the reserves principle and the quota principle of distributing reserve positions in the Fund.) This tension is difficult to resolve. If transfers were guided so as to bring holdings of reserve claims by countries not in payments difficulty approximately into proportion with holding obligations, a country's actual holdings of such claims would not vary with its reserves until the country itself decided to transfer claims. On the other hand, if transfers were guided so as to effect a rough proportionality of reserve claims to other reserves, countries that had limited their participation in the scheme—and received relatively small allocations of reserve claims—would be denied the right to a corresponding limitation of their holding obligations.

A possible solution would be to dispense with fixed limits altogether, but to provide that transfers be guided so as to tend towards a distribution of reserve claims among countries not in balance-of-payments difficulty, based on some formula that takes account both of relative total reserves and relative degrees of participation in the scheme.

HOLDING RATIOS

Another approach to this whole problem dispenses both with creditor limits and with collective guidance of transfers and relies instead on some fixed proportionality between reserve claims and other types of reserves.

In one arrangement of this type, reserve claims and other forms of reserves would be exchanged between countries on fixed settlement dates in such a way as to restore a uniform proportion of such claims to the other types of reserves in question. Four variants of this arrangement are conceivable: claims may be held in a uniform proportion either to gold reserves or to total reserves and claims may or may not be transferable between settlement days. Proportionality to total reserves has the advantage that reserve claims would be transferred only *from* deficit countries and *to* surplus countries. Proportionality to gold alone would have the same result so far as countries' gold reserves and foreign exchange reserves moved up or down together. On the other hand, the linking together of gold holdings and holdings of reserve claims might somewhat affect the choice between holding gold and foreign exchange reserves. Transferability of claims between settlement dates would encourage a somewhat greater use of both reserve claims and gold than would otherwise occur.

Any system of transferability based on uniform holding ratios has the disadvantage, particularly in the early days of the scheme, that only a small proportion of any deficit could be financed by the transfer of reserve claims. For example, if the total amount of claims in existence was only 5 per cent of the total amount of gold, 95 per cent of any deficit financed by transfer of gold-*cum*-claims would in effect be financed by transfer of gold.

One variant of the proportionality rule offers more scope for choice in the composition of reserves. According to this plan, a country would be free to transfer claims only if the proportion of claims to gold in its reserves—or of claims to gold and foreign exchange—was higher than in the average country. Similarly, it would be obliged to accept transfer only if these proportions were lower than in the average country. A balance-of-payments deficit would tend to put countries in the former position, and a surplus to put them in the latter position. A country in balance-of-payments difficulty, however, might still have to accept claims in transfer, thus intensifying the decline in its other reserves, if, at the outset of its payments difficulty, it happened to have a relatively low proportion of claims in its reserves.

TRANSFER RATIOS

It is sometimes suggested that instead of linking the holding of reserve claims to the holding of gold, the transfer of these claims should be linked to the transfer of gold—or of gold and foreign exchange—in some fixed proportion. This proportion could diverge substantially from that of the average ratio of claims to gold—or of claims to gold and foreign exchange—in reserves. For example, reserve claims might move in a 50:50 ratio with gold. This system would permit a greater use of claims from the very beginning of the scheme than would a holding ratio system, though less than would a system under which claims were transferable by themselves.

The principal merit of the transfer ratio is that even if the transfer of claims-*cum*-gold, or claims-*cum*-other reserves, was as ill-directed or arbitrary—for the reasons discussed above (pp. 162–3)—as the transfer of reserve claims alone would be, the danger of transferees' having to accept claims while their other reserves were falling would be reduced. For this reason, and because a 50:50 package would probably be more willingly accepted than reserve claims alone, less need might be felt for creditor limits or for guidance of transfers. Since, however, this danger would be merely reduced and not eliminated, it is not clear that these safeguards could be entirely dispensed with.

There are, however, considerable technical difficulties in transfer ratio systems. Assuming that the obligation to receive transfer is at par—whether against transferee currency or dollars—the incentive to transfer reserve claims and the willingness to receive them will vary according to the market value of the other elements in the package—gold or foreign exchange or both as the case may be. If the transferor can transfer either gold or foreign exchange along with reserve claims, the composition of the package will also vary with market prices. This effect could be avoided only by allowing the transferee to vary the price at which he accepts transfer of the reserve claims according to the market value of the other elements in the package.

Special problems arise where reserve units need be accepted only when accompanied by gold. As the value of transferable reserve claims grows, countries normally holding little gold in their reserves might tend to convert foreign exchange into gold in order to get the wherewithal to utilize their claims. Also, if the United States exercised its right to transfer reserve claims-*cum*-gold, it might appear to be offering less than full gold convertibility for the U.S. dollar.

It is sometimes argued in favour of the transfer ratio that it would partly offset the decline in balance-of-payments discipline that would otherwise result from the creation of reserve claims. It might indeed have some effect of this sort, at least in the initial stages, when the claims still had to win acceptance as 'hard' reserves. However, since the main purpose of creating additional reserves is to increase the sense of balance-of-payments ease in the world, it is difficult to see the purpose of this offset. If the balance-of-payments constraint on policy is generally too weak rather than too strong, there seems little point in creating the reserves at all. In any event, reluctance to part with reserve claims could always be enhanced, if desired, by raising the rate of interest paid on them.

169

None of the systems based on proportionality to reserves, whether in the form of holding ratios or transfer ratios, makes allowance for the possibility that countries may wish to limit their participation in the reserve creation scheme and, therefore, to limit their obligation to hold reserve claims, compared with their share in the reserves (or the gold reserves) of all participants, even if this means limiting their participation in the initial distribution of new reserves.

CONCLUDING REMARKS

From what has been said, it will be clear that use and acceptance of reserve claims are intimately connected. Absolute freedom of use, i.e. of transfer, in the hands of the transferor risks making the acceptance obligations of the transferees excessively burdensome. Complete protection of the transferees, through narrow creditor limits or rigid proportionality arrangements, risks impairing the usefulness of the reserve claims to the transferor. A system of guided transferability holds the balance more evenly between transferor and transferee.

Chapter 7

Towards Assessing the Need for International Reserves*

Over the past few years, increasing attention has focussed on the question of deliberate creation of international reserves. No aspect of this question has presented greater difficulties, both theoretical and practical, than that of assessing the world's 'need' for such reserves.

In a paper published in 1961, I tried to develop a systematic approach to the problem.[1] This approach, which might be termed a teleological one, has won a measure of acceptance in official documents. Unlike the principal alternative approaches, it does not ask what amount of reserves each country would like to have, or what amount it would require in order to be able to follow desirable policies, and then add up the results to get a world total. Instead, it asks what would be the *effects* on world economic welfare—given the probable reactions of governments, central banks, and individuals—of increasing total reserves or rates of reserve growth, the increases being distributed among countries in some specified way.

On this approach the world's 'need' for reserves or for reserve growth is determined at the point where the effects of further reserve increments on world economic welfare cease to be positive and begin to become negative. (Some, including the author, would assess the effect on economic welfare by taking account of effects not only on real income but also on income distribution, both within and between countries.) Such an approach, though traditional in welfare economics, is open to the charge of being 'dictatorial'. Instead of accepting the preferences of governments, it seeks to evaluate them in the light of ultimate criteria. In any event, consensus between governments is unattainable, and the dictatorial judgments of economists may help to provide the basis for a reasonable compromise.

* Reprinted, with editing, from Essays in International Finance No. 58 (Feb. 1967), International Finance Section, Department of Economics, Princeton University.

[1] 'International Liquidity: Ends and Means', reproduced at Chapter 4 above.

Reserve changes generally exercise their effects on world real income through national monetary and fiscal policies, such as those affecting imports, capital exports, and exchange rates. There are some exceptions to this general rule. For example, such changes may act on the minds of private individuals by inspiring a greater or lesser degree of confidence in exchange stability. But even in this instance—and granting that hot-money movements have a direct impact on economic life—the ultimate effects on real income are largely mediated through national policies. However, as is explained later, if reserve changes as such act through national policies, the processes through which reserves come into existence or are acquired by countries may act more directly on the level of monetary demand.

CRITERIA FOR OPTIMIZATION

Other things being equal, the higher the level of a country's reserves and the better its prospects of increasing them in the future, the more the country will be inclined to adopt policies that, *inter alia*, worsen its balance of payments.

Thus, higher reserves will encourage a country to adopt more expansionary monetary and fiscal policies, relax restrictions on imports or even promote them, relax promotion of exports or even restrict them, relax restrictions on capital exports, restrict capital imports, be more willing to provide capital exports and aid in untied form, be more generous in the provision of foreign aid, or be less willing to devalue and more willing to revalue the rate of exchange.

The effect of a widespread increase in reserves on balance-of-payments equilibrium is ambiguous. Both the countries tending towards surplus and those tending towards deficit will be encouraged to expand demand, liberalize external expenditures, and compete less actively for external receipts. However, unless the distribution of new reserves is deliberately confined to countries in balance-of-payments surplus, stronger effects may be expected in deficit countries than in surplus countries, with the result that open payments imbalances will tend, on the whole, to increase. In other words, countries will have more extensive recourse to official compensatory or balance-of-payments financing, including the use of reserves.

The desirability of a particular change in reserves depends partly on whether the countries most likely to be affected are suffering from inadequate or excessive demand pressure, whether the degree of balance-of-payments restriction being applied to trade and capital movements offers scope for significant liberalization if reserves are increased, whether more or less recourse to official compensatory financing is appropriate, and whether more stability or more adjustment of exchange rates is required. It also depends, of course, on the relative effects that reserve changes may be expected to have on all these variables.

On further reflection, I consider that my 1961 paper treated desirable exchange rate behaviour too much as an ultimate objective, and paid too little attention to the desirability, other things being equal, of promoting balance in external payments, and thus minimizing recourse to official compensatory financing. The use of such financing, I would now maintain, provides prima facie evidence of a distortion of international capital flows. Although it is preferable, up to a point, to the kinds of misallocation of resources that in some situations may provide the only practicable alternatives—namely, those associated with trade restrictions, unemployment, price inflation, etc.—the distortion of capital flows through official compensatory financing is, nevertheless, a disadvantage to be taken into account. (The welfare loss involved in official compensatory financing may not be negligible. Prima facie, assuming free capital movements and good judgment on the part of capitalists, it would be measured by the amount of compensatory financing *times* approximately half the change in the differential between home and foreign interest rates that would be required to induce private financing to take the place of official.)

Broadly speaking, and making the type of value judgments that economists usually make, I would say that reserves and reserve growth ought to be increased to the point at which beneficial effects in the form of higher employment and reduction of impediments to international transactions are outweighed by untoward effects in the form of inflation and recourse to official compensatory financing.

RESERVE NEEDS AND THE ADJUSTMENT PROCESS

It is sometimes argued that international reserve regulation is to be judged by its contribution towards improving the process of balance-of-payments adjustment. From what has been said, it should be clear that this emphasis on payments adjustment, though not wrong, only pushes the question one stage further back. What is a good or a

173

better adjustment process must itself be judged by criteria of the kind just discussed. For example, the array of policy propensities in the various countries that might add up to a good adjustment process in a time of general burgeoning of demand might not be conducive to a good adjustment process in generally depressed conditions. The emphasis on the adjustment process may also be dangerous if it leads to the conclusion that the supply of reserves should be brought closer to what would be needed if that process were more or less perfect. For if the adjustment process were perfect —and this involves near perfection in domestic financial policies— the use of reserves (and in a sense the need for them) would be small. (The optimal level of reserves would be indeterminate above a low level, since reserves above that level would have no effect on policies.) Yet with the world as it is, a reduction in the use of reserves might well entail a net worsening of the adjustment process in the form of increased resort to restrictions or to unemployment in deficit countries.

There is a closely related half truth, which is quite popular nowadays, to the effect that an improvement in the adjustment process would necessarily reduce the 'need' for—in the sense of the use of— reserves. In fact, however, it all depends on what the improvement is. More effective incomes policies (better adjusted to the balance-of-payments situation), more flexible exchange rate policies, and demand policies that react more quickly to incipient inflationary or deflationary tendencies would all doubtless reduce the use of reserves. But less ready resort to restrictions on trade and capital movement, though it might also count as an improvement in the adjustment process, would probably intensify the use of reserves.

This being said, however, it is highly desirable that efforts to improve the supply of world reserves should be accompanied by efforts to improve the adjustment process in other ways. The fact that reserve creation has to take account of many different objectives means that it cannot pursue any of them effectively. For example, a stimulus to world-reserve growth now might well have good results in some countries and in some respects and bad results in other countries and in other respects. Thus, it might encourage some relaxation of restrictions on imports and capital exports in the United Kingdom and the United States, as well as a more generous flow of economic aid from industrial countries in general, while leading, on the other hand, to excessive inflationary pressures in deficit and surplus countries alike, and necessitating an excessive flow of official compensatory financing from continental Europe to the reserve-centre countries. This dilemma arises from the fact that the instruments available to national authorities for regulating the balance of payments are either too few or are not being so used in the various countries as to permit the simultaneous achievement of domestic and international objectives. Anything that can be done to enhance international control over national adjustment processes— to enforce the 'rules of the game'—will simplify the task of inter-national-reserve management.

The adjustment process is governed in some measure by the Articles of Agreement of the Fund and by the General Agreement on Tariffs and Trade. Attempts are now being made to improve the operation of this process, as between the principal industrial countries, through exchange of information, mutual consultation, and the informal adoption of 'rules of the game' within the framework of the Organization for Economic Co-operation and Development. It is, however, very difficult to secure effective co-operative action of this kind without some sort of financial sanction. By long odds, the most effective method of improving the adjustment process—at any rate insofar as countries in payments deficit are concerned—would be for a much higher proportion of international liquidity than at present to take a form, such as drawing facilities in the credit tranches of the Fund, that could be used only on condition that appropriate policies were adopted. It is a tacit presupposition of the current enquiry into deliberate reserve creation, however, that countries are unwilling either to accept an increasing reliance on conditional liquidity for themselves or to provide the financial resources that would enable other countries to satisfy a markedly higher proportion of their liquidity needs in this form.

RESERVE STOCKS AND RESERVE GROWTH

So far, I have referred rather vaguely to the need for reserves, for reserve growth, for increases in reserves, etc. The time has come to distinguish more clearly between stocks and growth rates of reserves. In considering how they will act on those instruments of policy that exercise a significant effect upon the balance of payments, the authorities of a country will be influenced, *inter alia*, by the extent to which their minds are at ease with respect to the balance of payments. This degree of balance-of-payments ease, in turn, is affected by both the stock and the rate of growth of the country's reserves. A high reserve stock and a high rate of growth of reserves are, from this standpoint, substitutes for each other. More precisely, the higher a country's reserve stock, the lower the rate of growth of reserves—and the higher the rate of growth of its reserves, the lower the reserve stock—that will be required to create in the mind of its authorities a given degree of balance-of-payments ease. This is easily understood. The sense of balance-of-payments ease has to do with the confidence of the authorities in their ability to meet payments deficits. Now, the higher the reserve stock, the greater is the country's ability to meet current and future deficits. On the other hand, the faster the current rise in reserves, the smaller such deficits are likely to be in the immediate future and the higher reserves are likely to be in the further future to meet such deficits as may then occur.

All this, of course, represents a considerable oversimplification. The degree of balance-of-payments ease engendered by a given rate of reserve growth—and hence the rate of substitution between reserve stocks and reserve growth—depends on such circumstances as

(1) how long the reserve growth is expected to persist (which, in turn, depends on how it comes about);

(2) the extent to which the growth of reserves is associated with a growth of liquid external liabilities;

(3) the extent to which reserve growth is associated with transactions that are 'above the line' in the balance-of-payments accounts of the country in question—i.e. are included in its balance-of-payments surplus or deducted from its deficit—rather than among the financing items.

Less account is taken of changes in the rate of reserve growth if they are considered essentially temporary than if they are considered enduring, if they are accompanied by liquid liabilities than if they are not so accompanied, and possibly if they are conventionally ranked 'below the line' rather than above it. The bearing of liquid liabilities in particular is difficult to determine. They are perhaps best considered as equivalent to negative reserves—and a rise in liquid liabilities as equivalent to a fall in reserves—but only to the extent of a fraction of their value. This fraction itself, however, varies according to the country's balance-of-payments strength: the stronger the country's balance-of-payments position, the more closely the fraction approaches zero. (Reserve stocks, likewise, will be less productive of balance-of-payments ease if they are accompanied by stocks of liquid external liabilities. However, even if the ratio of liquid liabilities to reserves were the same for stocks as for growth, it would not follow that the rate of substitution between reserve stocks and reserve growth would remain unaffected by the height of that ratio.)

To complicate matters further, a growth in liquid liabilities to official holders abroad, if it results from and helps to finance a payments deficit, may be taken as evidence that the country can expect to be able to finance future deficits in the same way. This expectation, so long as it lasts, is itself a substitute for reserves or reserve growth, and as such a source of balance-of-payments strength.

In addition to the distinctions mentioned above, reserve growth, quite apart from its effect on the degree of balance-of-payments ease and hence on balance-of-payments policies, may apply a direct stimulus to demand pressure in the country in which it occurs which will be greater

(4) the more it accrues through transactions that tend to add to the money supply, and

(5) the more it accrues through current account transactions which directly affect the level of incomes.

These distinctions assume considerable importance when we come to consider how the rate at which it is appropriate to create reserves by deliberate international action may be affected by the form in which they are created and by the proportions in which they are initially distributed among countries.

Let us for the moment assume, however, that any changes in reserve growth that may take place in a given country, other than those brought about by changes in its own policies, exercise no direct influence on its income or money stock, that they appear 'below the line', i.e. as financing items, in its balance of payments, and that they are expected to dwindle at a given proportionate rate over time. We can then derive certain propositions about the time shape of optimal reserve growth which, though highly abstract, have a certain practical relevance.

RESERVE STOCK, RESERVE GROWTH, AND BALANCE-OF-
PAYMENTS EASE IN AN INDIVIDUAL COUNTRY

First, let us look at the static relationship between reserve stock and
reserve growth in a particular country, as illustrated in Figure 7.1, in
the form of an indifference map, derived from the preference function
of the authorities. In this, reserves are measured along the y-axis,

FIGURE 7.1

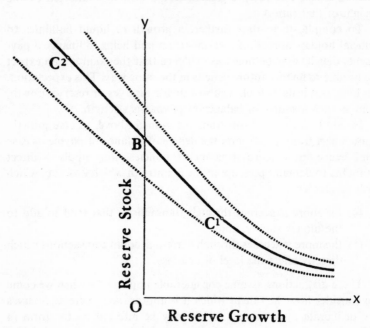

and reserve growth along the x-axis, while the various contours
represent degrees of balance-of-payments ease. The relationship
between x and y is assumed to be linear over the greater part of the
map, as would seem to be natural if, for example, any changes in the
current reserve growth would be expected to dwindle at a given
proportionate rate over time. However, there is also assumed to be
some minimum level below which reserves must not fall if confidence
is to be preserved, and all the indifference contours tend to the
horizontal as they approach that level. Provided that substitution of
reserves for reserve growth, or vice versa, does not affect the degree

178

of attainment of domestic goals associated with any given set of national policies, each indifference contour, representing a given degree of balance-of-payments ease, will be associated with a different set of policies affecting the balance of payments. The degree of balance-of-payments ease rises northwestwards on the chart, and if reserve acquisition is costless, or costs no more than the interest earned on reserve holdings, the increase in balance-of-payments ease will bring an increase in satisfaction to the authorities.

FIGURE 7.2

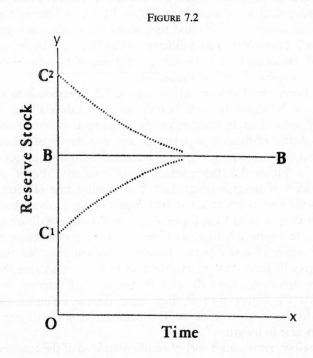

There is no 'desired' degree of payments ease, short of infinity; beyond a certain point, though, increasing ease may become a matter of indifference.

Now let us bring in the passage of time. If circumstances both inside and outside the country are sufficiently static, the country's indifference map, relating reserves and reserve growth, will remain constant through time. Each indifference contour will also continue

179

to be associated with the same set of balance-of-payments policies. For each contour (that is, for each degree of balance-of-payments ease, or each set of balance-of-payments policies), it will then be possible to draw a family of paths illustrating how the country's reserves would have to develop from any given starting point in order to avoid disturbing these policies. (This is a *required* not an *actual* development of reserves—the meaning is not that constant policies would tend to bring about this development, but that the development is necessary if the policies are to remain constant.) This development is represented in Figure 7.2, where reserve stock is measured along the y-axis and time along the x-axis. Each path in Figure 7.2 corresponds to a different initial level of reserves, and the whole set of paths corresponds to only one of the contours— say, the solidly-lined one—in Figure 7.1.

If the reserve level at time zero in Figure 7.2 corresponds to the point at which the solidly-lined contour cuts the y-axis in Figure 7.1 (point B), no change in reserves will be required to maintain over time the degree of balance-of-payments ease and the set of policies which that contour represents; the path starting from that level of reserves in Figure 7.2, therefore, remains horizontal. From any starting level of reserves lower than B, a positive rate of reserve change will be necessary to attain that degree of ease; this is shown by the position of point C_1 in Figure 7.1, or by the slope of the dotted line at C_1 in Figure 7.2. In order to permit the maintenance of the specified degree of ease, reserves must rise through time, but their rate of growth must decline, as shown in Figure 7.2, so that they move asymptotically towards level B. Similarly, if reserves start from level C_2, higher than B, they must decline asymptotically towards level B in order to permit the maintenance of the degree of payments ease in question.[2]

B, therefore, represents a sort of equilibrium level of the country's reserves in relation to a particular degree of balance-of-payments ease, that is, the level towards which its reserves must tend if this degree of ease is to be maintained indefinitely. We might call this an 'equilibrium level of required reserves'.

Now let us turn to the more interesting case in which, as time passes, the country, in order to maintain a given degree of balance-of-payments ease, requires either more reserves or a higher rate

[2] See Appendix, p. 193.

of reserve growth or both. (In a dynamic situation, maintenance of a given degree of balance-of-payments ease will lead to the maintenance of unchanged policies only if with such policies the degree of attainment of domestic policy targets also remains unchanged.) Reserve needs in this sense might rise either because of a rising propensity on the part of the authorities to worry about the balance of payments or because of a tendency for potential balance-of-payments deficits to increase in size, for example, because of a

FIGURE 7.3

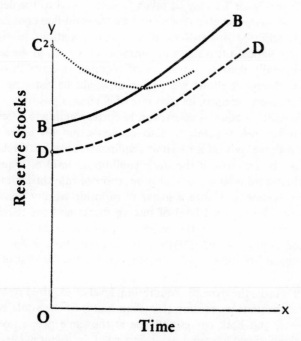

continuing growth in the value of international transactions. In either case, the contours in Figure 7.1 corresponding to given degrees of balance-of-payments ease will move upwards, as time passes, at a rate corresponding to the growth in the need for reserves; in the latter case, in addition, the contours are likely, at any point of time, to be at a higher level than would otherwise be the case, on account of *anticipations* of rising potential imbalances.

Under the new circumstances, the various paths representing the manner in which reserve stocks, starting from different levels at the base date, would have to move in order to maintain a given degree of balance-of-payments ease, will still, if reserve needs grow in some steady and systematic way, tend to converge on an equilibrium reserve path. In Figure 7.3, the growth of reserve needs is defined by the curve BB, which is the locus of the reserve levels that would be required at different points of time to achieve the given degree of balance-of-payments ease *at a zero rate of reserve change*. This may be called the curve of the 'static equilibrium level of required reserves'. (All curves in Figure 7.3 may be taken to correspond to the degree of balance-of-payments ease represented by the solid-line contour in Figure 7.1, adjusted upwards to allow for anticipations of rising potential imbalances.) It is not a required-reserves *path*, in the sense of a conceptually feasible movement of required reserves through time, since, though it shows what reserves would be required at a zero rate of reserve change, its own rate of change is positive.

Now the various required-reserves paths corresponding to different levels of initial reserves will tend to converge, not on this static equilibrium curve, but on a dynamic required-reserves path related to it. Thus, for example, if the static equilibrium level of required reserves rises steadily at a constant proportionate rate through time (and if we assume as before a linear relationship at any point of time between the required level of reserve stocks and the required rate of growth of reserves), the various required-reserves paths will tend to converge on a line (DD) which lies below the BB line, and whose distance from the x-axis is a constant fraction of that of the BB line.

In other words, the dynamic equilibrium level of required reserves will bear a constant proportion (less than unity) to the static equilibrium level, and both curves will rise at the same proportionate rate. In these circumstances, as is indicated in Figure 7.3, any required-reserves path that starts from a point C_2 above the static equilibrium level of required reserves will decline through time until it intersects the static equilibrium path, and will thereafter rise, at an accelerating rate, until as it converges on the dynamic equilibrium path it approximates the proportionate rate of growth of the latter. It is an interesting question whether the dynamic level of required reserves, corresponding to any given degree of payments ease, will be higher or lower at any point of time if potential imbalances are rising, and are expected to rise, than if they are constant and are expected to remain so. In the former event, the dynamic equilibrium level will be below the static equilibrium level, whereas in the latter event the two will coincide. On the other hand, in the former event, owing to anticipation of rising potential imbalances, the static level of required reserves will be higher than in the latter event.[3]

This model has, I think, some relation to a well-known reality. Assume a country whose reserves are declining but which (like the United States in the early 1950s) can maintain a considerable degree of balance-of-payments ease because its reserve stock is high relative to the static equilibrium level of reserves that is required to maintain that degree of ease. Such a country is likely to find later on that it has to check the decline in its reserves and, still later, to accumulate reserves if it is to maintain the same degree of ease. If it does not do so, its balance-of-payments position will deteriorate, not only because its reserves decline, but because the static equilibrium level of required reserves increases. (The situation in the United States has been complicated by the existence and growth of liquid external liabilities, which count to some extent as offsets to reserves, and by the existence—and dwindling—of a potentiality for financing a part of its deficits by a further accumulation of such liabilities, which, as mentioned earlier, is a kind of reserve substitute.)

WORLD RESERVE STOCKS AND OPTIMAL RESERVE GROWTH

Thus far, I have spoken of the bearing of a country's reserves and rate of reserve growth on its sense of balance-of-payments ease, and on its policies as they are affected thereby. The next step is to extend the analysis, with the necessary adaptations, to the world as a whole, and to see how far it can be used in the definition and measurement of the need for reserves or for reserve growth.

Broadly speaking—with a number of qualifications discussed below—the types of relationships described above as existing between the reserve levels and rates of reserve increase of individual countries, with respect to their effect on the balance-of-payments policies of these countries, will also obtain between aggregate reserve levels and rates of aggregate reserve increase of groups of countries. Subject to still further qualifications, we may even say

[3] See Appendix, p. 193.

that the sort of relationship that exists between 'required' and actual stocks and rates of increase of reserves in a single country will also obtain between optimal and actual stocks and rates of increase of aggregate reserves in a group of countries. In particular, the optimal level of aggregate reserves will tend to vary inversely, in any given circumstances, with the actual rate of growth of these reserves, and the optimal rate of growth of aggregate reserves will tend to vary inversely with the actual level of these reserves. It is time to decide on which of these optima to focus our attention; since sudden, once-for-all changes in the level of aggregate reserves are rare, it is undoubtedly more convenient to focus on the optimal rate of change of reserves as affected by the existing levels of reserves. This procedure represents an important departure from the way in which the reserve-needs problem has until recently been viewed, a departure which owes a good deal to the pioneering work of Mr Høst-Madsen of the IMF.[4]

Again, just as the effects of reserve growth in an individual country will vary according to the nature of the transactions by which reserves are increased, so the effects of a given rate of reserve growth in the world as a whole will vary according to the nature of the transactions or procedures whereby world reserves are increased. As is pointed out on page 191 below, that part of the growth in world reserves which results from additions to official holdings of foreign exchange is likely to have a weaker expansionary effect than that resulting from gold dishoarding, while the reserve growth resulting from gold production is the most expansionary of all.

EFFECT OF DISTRIBUTION OF RESERVES ON RESERVE
GROWTH AND OPTIMAL RESERVE GROWTH

The first set of qualifications we have to make in drawing an analogy between the required rate of growth of reserves of an individual country and the optimal rate of aggregate reserve growth of a group of countries arises from a consideration of the intercountry distribution of reserve growth and of reserves.

---

[4] Cf. Poul Høst-Madsen, 'Asymmetries Between Balance-of-Payments Surpluses and Deficits', Appendix, *Staff Papers*, Vol. IX, 1962, pp. 182–200, at p. 198. See also the trenchant paper by Milton Gilbert, *Problems of the International Monetary System*, Essays in International Finance No. 53 (Princeton, New Jersey, 1966). Mr Gilbert lays great, perhaps excessive, emphasis on the importance of reserve growth as compared with reserve stocks.

Basically (given the average degree of balance-of-payments ease prevailing among countries), the greater the disparity among countries with respect to balance-of-payments ease and difficulty, the higher is likely to be the optimal rate of growth in aggregate reserves. Such disparity may be greater than usual at any given time because payments imbalances between countries are larger than usual, because reserves are more than usually maldistributed in relation to potential payments fluctuations, or because actual payments imbalances are more than usually maldistributed in relation to the distribution of reserves—in other words, because to an unusual extent it is the countries with small reserves rather than those with large reserves that are tending to have deficits. Now, if we start from a position in which all countries have much the same degree of payments ease, and if we then shift reserve stocks or payments balances so that one country is better off and another worse off, the first country is not likely to liberalize trade and capital movements as much as the second will restrict them, nor is the first country as likely to expand demand as is the second to contract it. For these reasons, greater disparity in payments ease creates a case for increasing the rate of reserve growth and adding to ease all round. There are two main counter-arguments to this. One arises from the distortion of capital flows involved in reserve use and other forms of official balance-of-payments financing. An increase in payments disequilibria, such as would probably result from a stepping-up in the rate of growth of aggregate reserves, would increase the amount of such financing and such distortion. Again, if an increase in disequilibria called for the adjustment of exchange rates, a higher rate of growth of reserves might tend to delay the adjustment. These arguments, which partly overlap, can claim some validity only if the imbalances are of a long-term character and if their cure is to be sought in exchange depreciation in deficit countries. If they are short-term or of a type that should be arrested by action on the part of surplus countries, the arguments lose much of their force.

Distributive considerations enter into the estimation of optimal reserve growth in another way. Any additions made to world reserves by deliberate action must be distributed somehow between countries. Even if the initial recipients of these reserves are few, the reserves will tend sooner or later to be diffused throughout the generality of countries as a result of adaptations in balance-of-payments policies. The strength and character of the effects, however, will depend to some extent on the initial distribution of reserve additions.

Broadly speaking, the more the distribution of newly created reserves favours countries in balance-of-payments difficulties and countries where demand and imports can be easily expanded—notably the less developed countries—the more powerful will be the expansionary effects that reserve creation will have on demand and trade. Indeed, after a time lag, even the countries that do not participate in the initial distribution may well experience stronger expansionary effects than if they had received reserves directly, for they will earn the reserves through the balance of payments, which directly affects money supply, and possibly through the trade balance, which directly affects income as well.

A concentration of newly created reserves on countries that are in payments difficulties would tend to perpetuate payments disequilibria and increase the distortion of capital flows. A concentration of newly created reserves in less developed countries would also tend to produce a movement of funds that would be unjustified by market criteria, though it might well be justified by social criteria when account is taken of externalities and of the facts of international income distribution.

FACTORS AFFECTING OPTIMAL RESERVE GROWTH

In considering the path of optimal reserves through time, one has to take account of changes in four main groups of factors:

(1) As the value of international transactions grows, the normal magnitude of potential payments imbalances may be expected to grow also—other things being equal—at the same proportionate rate. Any increase in the relative importance of the more volatile types of international transactions, such as capital movements, might be expected to raise the level of potential imbalances relative to the value of international transactions. Any once-for-all increase in the relative level of potential payments imbalances, in turn, would tend to give rise to a temporary increase in the optimal rate of reserve growth.

(2) Among countries with similar propensities to react to given degrees of balance-of-payments ease, one would expect to find a

186

gradual drift towards equality in the degree of ease, a circumstance which would tend to reduce the need for reserve growth. However, all sorts of disturbing factors—military, social, cyclical—together with the disturbance created by the delayed and 'lumpy' character of exchange rate adjustment under the par-value system, give rise to erratic and short- to medium-run changes in such distribution.

(3) Cyclical and longer-run changes in autonomous demand pressures can bring about very large changes in the optimal level of reserve growth.

(4) Finally, and importantly, changes can occur in the attitudes of national authorities towards balance-of-payments goals as compared with domestic goals, and towards different techniques of bringing about balance-of-payments adjustment. To take an easy case, the lower the rate of reserve growth (given the level of reserves relative to international transactions) at which countries were prepared to allow balance-of-payments considerations a given degree of weight relative to domestic goals, the lower would be the optimal rate of reserve growth. A special example of this relationship would occur in a country which desired to keep a given proportion of reserves as backing for its domestic money supply and in which the money supply grew more slowly than its international transactions. More common, and more difficult to assess in terms of the effects on optimal reserve growth, are cases in which countries alter their preferences between different techniques of balance-of-payments adjustment. In such cases, the concept of 'degree of balance-of-payments ease' loses any semblance of precision.

QUANTIFICATION OF NEED FOR RESERVE GROWTH

It is clearly no easy matter to derive a quantitative estimate of needed reserve growth over a given period from the conceptual framework we have elaborated. In the first place, any such estimate must rest on value judgments as to the relative importance of different economic objectives—price stability, full employment, exchange rate stability, freedom of trade, freedom of capital movements, and the like; still worse, it involves value judgments as to the relative importance of welfare changes in different countries. Again, it is extremely difficult to derive from the rather tumultuous experience with balances of payments of the past three or four decades any quantitative relationships between reserve changes of various kinds and the behaviour of national governments, or even between the actions of governments and their effects at home and abroad.

On the other hand, if we are to formulate any arrangement for deliberately supplementing or damping down the rate of reserve growth, we must find some method of arriving at a numerical estimate. How is it to be done?

First of all, payments imbalances vary so much from year to year that it seems pretty hopeless to try to arrive at any estimate of needed reserve growth for periods of less than four or five years at a time. This limitation is mitigated by two considerations: (1) the organizational problem of getting international agreement on any estimate of need is such that decisions could in any case be made only at fairly lengthy intervals; (2) short-term variations in the need for reserves are reflected to some extent in the demand for balance-of-payments credit in the form of drawings from the Fund, use of swaps, etc., and such variations in the demand for balance-of-payments credit lead not only to desirable redistribution of reserves but also to responsive—and on the whole desirable—variations in their over-all supply.

Secondly, it helps to pose the quantitative question in terms of the need for reserve growth rather than the need for reserve stocks. The two are, of course, interconnected, but even if the level of reserves were well above the dynamic optimal equilibrium level, it seems unlikely that the optimal rate of aggregate reserve growth would be less than zero. Catastrophes such as wars and general devaluations aside, reserve levels seldom get very far out of line. This is because an excessive rate of reserve growth, by promoting inflation and price increases, is likely to result in an increase in the level of prices, in the magnitude of payments imbalances, and hence in the optimal equilibrium level of reserves.

Thirdly, in seeking to determine an optimal rate of reserve growth, there is some advantage in pursuing two different approaches and seeing to what extent they confirm each other. One approach is global, the other starts by considering individual countries or groups of countries.

Global approach

First the global approach. If we had at our disposal empirically tested propositions about the probable economic effects of increases

188

in the rate of reserve growth *plus* a reliable projection of the state of the international economy at the prospective rate of reserve increase, we could decide, in accordance with some given value system, whether and to what extent that rate of reserve increase should be supplemented. In practice, one has to fall back on an inferior method involving comparison between the prospective period and one or several base periods. The base period should have certain qualities. It should be a period in which the over-all degree of balance-of-payments ease appears to have been fairly satisfactory—meaning, not that it was satisfactory in every country, but that a higher rate of reserve growth would have done about as much harm (through increasing unrequited transfers of real resources, delaying exchange rate adjustments, and intensifying inflationary pressures) as it would have done good (through mitigating restrictions and expanding employment and economic activity). The period should also be as recent as possible and should comprise a reasonable number of years. The proportionate rate of reserve growth in this period will then serve as the starting point of the calculation. This reserve growth should be measured gross, but with an allowance— on a fractional basis, as explained in an earlier section of this essay— for any growth in liquid external liabilities.

Next, we must adjust the growth of reserves in the base period to allow for changes in reserve stocks since that period; this adjustment should be expressed as a proportion of some factor, such as the volume of international trade, which serves as a measure of potential payments deficits, and to allow for changes in reserve distribution. Unfortunately, we cannot derive from experience any very plausible estimates of the trade-off between reserves and reserve growth as to their effects on balance-of-payments ease. Perhaps one has to content oneself with some guess at the marginal rate of substitution between the two, such as that a decline of $5x$ in the stock of reserves, relative to trade, would have to be offset by an excess of x in the annual growth of reserves, relative to trade. Quantification of the effect of a change in reserve distribution is even more difficult.

Finally, we must allow, in theory, for the effect on optimal reserve growth of changes in official attitudes towards different types of policy. In practice, however, it is doubtful whether needed reserve growth has on balance been greatly affected by changes that have taken place in recent years. Most of these, such as increased willingness to resort to restrictions, particularly capital restrictions, and reduced willingness to adjust demand pressures to the balance-of-payments situation, tend on the whole to raise the optimal rate of reserve growth. On the other hand, such effect as 'multilateral surveillance' may have in inducing deficit countries to correct inflationary pressures and surplus countries to correct deflationary pressures at an early stage would tend to reduce the need for reserves (or reserve growth). The same would probably be true of any enhanced flexibility of exchange rates that might result from the currently popular advocacy of wider margins.

Individual-country approach

The second approach to the estimation of world needs for reserve growth begins by asking *for each country* the following question: Given the actual level of reserves, what rate of reserve growth would produce the 'best' effects on policy as to the goals of full employment, price stability, and liberalization of international transactions, etc.? This 'best' is judged more from an international than from a national standpoint. Restrictions on external transactions, for example, are evaluated for their effects on world real income rather than on national real income. (On the other hand, it is difficult, in practice, to decide to what extent the demand policies of each country should be expected to contribute towards the stimulation, or damping down, of demand pressures abroad; and, in practice, one would be content with a rate of reserve growth that would remove any constraints on domestic full-employment policy while avoiding any stimulus to domestic inflation.) After these figures are estimated for each country, they can be aggregated, subject to an adjustment to be mentioned below, to provide an estimate of the global optimal rate of reserve growth.

The estimation of these national optimal rates of growth involves the same sort of considerations as have been mentioned above in connection with global estimation, but, since we may expect to find more consistency in the behaviour of the authorities of individual countries than of heterogeneous groups, each member of which is exposed to very different rates of reserve growth at any given time, the coefficients necessary to the making of these estimates may be somewhat easier to arrive at. However, some of this greater ease in the initial stages of the estimation is bought at the price of difficulty in the final stage—when the national optimal rates of growth have to be combined into a global estimate. For reasons analogous to those already indicated in discussing the bearing of inequalities of balance-of-payments ease on the amount of optimal reserve growth, the optimal rate of growth of aggregate reserves will usually be greater than the sum of the national optima. Imbalances of international payments of greater or lesser magnitude are inevitable, and the countries whose payments balances are in deficit (or at less than their optimal surplus) are likely to react more vigorously to this discrepancy—and in ways probably harmful to economic welfare—than are countries whose payments surpluses exceed their national optima. To what extent world reserve growth should be raised above the figure arrived at by adding together the optimal rates of growth of the individual countries, in order to mitigate these deficit-country reactions, is very difficult to determine. Even if no such adjustment is made, however, the 'national' approach to the estimation of needed reserve growth in the world has the merit of providing a somewhat less unreliable estimate of the *minimum* needs for such growth.

NEED FOR SUPPLEMENTARY RESERVES

The practical purpose of estimating optimal reserve growth is to know by how much, if at all, the rate of growth of reserves from existing sources should be supplemented by deliberate reserve creation. There are really two questions here. How should the planned supplementation of reserve growth vary with differences in the prospective growth of existing types of reserves? And to what extent should year-to-year supplementation vary with deviations of actual from prospective growth in existing types of reserves?

In answering both questions, we must take account of differences in the 'effectiveness' of different types of reserve creation, existing and new. Thus, the part of reserve growth generated by gold production exercises the most powerful effect, since it not only tends to expand the stock of money and the cash reserves of deposit banks but also enters into the income stream from the very moment of its creation. The negative contribution to reserve growth that results from gold hoarding (or the positive contribution that results from dishoarding) is less powerful, since it does not affect the income stream, but it does affect the supply of money and the reserves of the

191

banking system. The part of reserve growth generated by additions to currency reserves and accruing in the first instance to reserve centres exercises a still less powerful effect. Not only is it offset by a corresponding increase in the liquid liabilities of the reserve centre, but it enters below the line in the balance of payments, has no effect on the income stream, and little, if any, on the money supply. Reserve growth generated by a growth in reserve positions in the Fund resulting from an expansion in drawings outstanding in the conditional tranches falls somewhere between that generated by gold production and that generated by increases in official holdings of foreign currencies. Like the last, it is accompanied by a growth in liabilities, but the liabilities are medium-term. Moreover, the reserves created accrue in the first instance to drawing countries that usually need to spend them at once. Subsequent recipients earn them in the relatively expansionary form of additional exports or an improved capital account.

Similar considerations arise as to the type of reserve increase that is likely to be associated with deliberate reserve creation. Deliberately created reserves, unless they are put into circulation through an investment institution such as the World Bank, are likely to make their first appearance as a financing item rather than as earned reserves, though they are unlikely to be associated with a corresponding increase in the liquid liabilities of the countries to which they are initially distributed. Newly created reserves, though not entering from the start into the income stream, might nevertheless exercise almost as strong an effect on the world economy as would an addition to gold production if they were directed in the first instance towards countries in balance-of-payments difficulty or towards less developed countries avid of investment capital. In both of these cases, the recipient countries would be likely to increase their balance-of-payments deficits with little delay to nearly the full extent of the additional reserves they have received, thus exercising a strong expansionary influence on other countries.

Any plan for supplementing reserves should take into account the prospective growth of all forms of existing reserves, with proper allowance for degrees of effectiveness of different forms of reserve growth.

It appears reasonable to ignore deviations of actual from expected reserve growth if these deviations result from short-term variations in the growth of Fund reserve positions, as these deviations may be considered to correspond to variations in the need for such growth. Other types of variation, however—e.g. those due to variations in gold hoarding or in the holding of foreign exchange reserves—should probably be offset by variations in deliberate reserve creation. For reasons already explained, the quantitative degree of offsetting required would differ in the two cases. It is also arguable that since both types of variation are liable to affect reserves of particular countries—in the second case, obviously, reserve-currency countries —any offsetting variations in reserve creation should be of a special type, likewise affecting the reserves of particular countries, rather than the normal type of deliberate reserve creation, which would be spread over a wide range of participating countries.

Appendix

Let y_t be the level of required reserves at time t, and

$\bar{y}_t$ be the value of y_t for which $\dfrac{dy_t}{dt} = 0$.

Let each contour on Figure 7.1 be represented, over its linear portion, by the equation

$$\frac{dy_t}{dt} = -a(y_t - \bar{y}_t), \qquad \text{(i)}$$

where $-a$ is a negative constant representing the slope of the contour.

Now Figure 7.2 is based on the assumption that the relationship in equation (i) remains valid through time and that

$$\bar{y}_t = b$$

where b is a constant.

Then $\qquad \dfrac{dy_t}{dt} = -a(y_t - b)$ and

$\therefore \qquad y_t = b + Ae^{-at},$

where $A \ (= y_0 - b)$ is an arbitrary constant representing the amount by which the initial value of y_t exceeds the equilibrium value.

As $\qquad t \to \infty,$

$$y_t \to b = \bar{y}_t.$$

Figure 7.3 also is based on the assumption that equation (i) remains valid through time but that (as represented in Figure 7.3 by the BB curve),

$$\bar{y}_t = ce^{ft}$$

where $c = \bar{y}_0$ is a constant and also f is a constant.

Then

$$\frac{dy_t}{dt} = ace^{ft} - ay_t$$

and

$$y_t = \frac{ac}{a+f}e^{ft} + Be^{-at},$$

where $B\left(= y_0 - \frac{a}{a+f}\bar{y}_0 \right)$ is an arbitrary constant (represented in Figure 7.3 by the excess of OC² over OD).

In Figure 7.3 $\frac{ac}{a+f}e^{ft}$ is represented by the DD curve which, if f is positive, lies below the BB curve.

As

$$t \to \infty,$$

$$y_t \to \frac{ac}{a+f}e^{ft}.$$

Part Three

Balance-of-Payments Policy and
the Adjustment Process

Chapter 8

Exchange Depreciation, Financial Policy and the Domestic Price Level*

The present essay constitutes the first part of a study designed to show the order of magnitude of the increases in domestic prices that will result, on specified assumptions regarding the relevant foreign trade elasticities and propensities, from exchange depreciation accompanied by appropriate financial policies. Exchange devaluation may be used to improve the balance of payments or to permit a relaxation of import restrictions. Only the former use is considered here. It is assumed here that exchange depreciation is accompanied by a financial policy that leaves unchanged the level of aggregate employment. For the type of depreciation examined, such a policy is taken to be compatible with the maintenance of stability in the prices of home trade goods (i.e. goods that neither are exportable nor compete with imports), while the prices of import and export goods will rise.

Several hypothetical cases (in all of which exports and imports are assumed to be initially in balance) are defined by assigning sets of numerical values to the relevant coefficients (Table 8.1). Illustrations are then given of the price effects that will result in these cases from (1) an exchange depreciation of 10 per cent and (2) a depreciation leading to an improvement in the balance of trade equivalent to 5 per cent of national output (Table 8.2). For some of the cases, the extent to which the price level may be expected to rise after adjustments have been made to indirect taxes for the purpose of restoring budgetary equilibrium is indicated (Table 8.8). Finally, the effect on the price level of a defined tendency for wage rates to rise in response to, though to lesser extent than, increases in the cost of living is illustrated (Table 8.9). In general, it appears that, if an appropriate financial policy is pursued, and if a wage-price spiral can be prevented, price increases are likely to be fairly moderate relative to

* Reprinted, with editing, from International Monetary Fund *Staff Papers*, Vol. VI, No. 2, April 1958.

the improvement achieved in the balance of trade, although considerable differences exist in this respect between different cases.

Consideration is also given to the magnitude of the disinflationary effort that will be required to implement the financial policy defined as appropriate. It is shown that domestic expenditure will usually, though not always, have to be reduced below its initial level (Table 8.3), and that in all the cases examined official action tending to curtail expenditure by substantial amounts will be necessary (Table 8.4). It is argued that only a relatively minor part of this curtailment should fall on public and private consumption (Table 8.5); most of it should fall on public and private investment. A broad indication—on very uncertain assumptions—of the very considerable extent to which the money supply might have to be reduced is given for certain cases (Table 8.7).

Nature of the Problem and Assumptions

Countries with over-valued currencies are sometimes deterred from making appropriate adjustments in their exchange rates by the fear that depreciation might necessitate a substantial increase in prices on the domestic market, and that this, in turn, through its reaction on the cost of living, might provoke an upward spiral of wages and prices. The object of this paper is to inquire how far, on various assumptions, such fears may be justified. However, in order to treat the question fruitfully, it is necessary to give it a somewhat circumscribed interpretation. Undoubtedly, if exchange depreciation is not accompanied by appropriate financial policies, or if money wages move in a rigid proportion to the cost of living, domestic prices may in some cases rise *pari passu* with the domestic prices of foreign currencies, thereby stultifying the depreciation as a means of improving the balance of payments. But it is as unlikely as it is undesirable that the monetary authorities of the devaluing country should remain passive in the face of the monetary and financial consequences of depreciation, and it would be tedious to examine the effects of depreciation under all the conceivable permutations and combinations of domestic policy. Moreover, the price effects arising out of the existence of a link between money wages and the cost of living are dependent on the price effects that would emerge in the absence of this link; they are more conveniently discussed at a later stage in this essay. What will be attempted here, therefore, is to indicate

(1) the price effects that may be expected, in the absence of a link between wages and the cost of living, if appropriate financial policies are pursued,
(2) the nature and scope of the policies that may be required, and
(3) additional complications introduced by any dependence of wages on the cost of living.

The answer to (1) will be affected crucially by the degree of flexibility displayed by wages (and other factor prices) in response to changes in demand and supply. If wages were sufficiently flexible, a proper financial policy might be one that maintained the stability of the domestic price level by bringing about such adjustment in the prices of domestic factors and products as might be required to offset the price changes directly associated with the devaluation, i.e. those affecting import and export goods. In this case, of course, the effect of the devaluation on the general level of prices would, by definition, be nil. A still higher degree of factor price flexibility would, of course, do away with the need for an exchange rate adjustment; any necessary alignment of domestic and foreign cost and income levels could then be brought about exclusively through financial policy's acting on the domestic price level.

In reality, wages usually show considerable flexibility in an upward direction and some flexibility in a downward direction. Under normal circumstances, in most countries, however, they are too 'sticky' to permit a reduction of any size to be brought about through demand pressure without a disproportionate sacrifice of employment and output. It is true that if, prior to an exchange depreciation, prices have been rising fairly rapidly and wages lagging behind, so that profit margins are abnormally high, it may often be possible, by curtailing monetary demand, to slow down or arrest the inflation and to prevent wages—and, even more so, domestic product prices—from rising as much as they would otherwise have done, and that this can be done without giving rise, in the process, to any excessive amount of unemployment. But it is probably illogical to assume both that a financial policy of this sort would *not* be applied in the absence of devaluation and that it *would* be applied after a devaluation. It would therefore appear prudent to assume that, while the wages of any sector of the labour force for which there is an increasing demand are likely to rise, the wages of any sector of the labour force for which there is a declining demand are for practical purposes rigid, save where a substantial increase in unemployment is allowed to emerge.

A proper financial policy is conceived, in general terms, as one that allows no substantial increase in unemployment and, subject to this, prevents any unnecessary increase in prices. That is to say, the level of domestic demand will be kept as low as is compatible with an avoidance of substantial unemployment in those sectors of industry which are disfavoured by depreciation, after account is taken of the transfer of labour to sectors favoured by depreciation. The wider the range of industries relatively disfavoured by demand, the smaller will be the increase in aggregate money demand for the country's products that will be necessary to prevent an increase in unemployment. Since, in the cases discussed in this essay, the relatively disfavoured sectors usually constitute a much larger proportion of total output than the relatively favoured sectors, the assumption is made that a proper financial policy involves the avoidance of any increase in unemployment as a result of depreciation.

The type of exchange depreciation considered in the present essay is one that is not accompanied by any changes in the *ad valorem* level of import duties or in the severity[1] of import restrictions. Also, only uniform exchange rates are considered.

An attempt is made to calculate the magnitude of the effects on prices that would be expected from the type of depreciation which is being examined, under various assumptions as to the magnitude of certain basic parameters, viz.,

(1) the proportionate importance in the economy of sectors of output and demand that are particularly involved in foreign trade,
(2) the elasticities of demand and supply for foreign trade goods with respect to (a) prices and (b) aggregate domestic expenditure.

For convenience, it is assumed that in the devaluing country—which we may term country A—three clearly demarcated types of

---

[1] The severity of import restrictions can be measured by the amount of the *ad valorem* import duty that would have an equally restrictive effect.

goods exist: export goods, import goods, and home trade goods. Export goods consist of goods actually exported (in volume q_{x1}) and of similar goods absorbed in A (q_{x2}). Import goods consist of goods actually imported (q_{m1}) and import-competing goods produced in A (q_{m2}). All export goods, whether consumed abroad or at home, have the same price in A (p_x); so have all import goods, whether produced abroad or at home (p_m); and so have all home trade goods (p_h).

The volume of A's exports is equal to A's output, *less* absorption, of export goods. The former is regarded as depending on the price of export goods relative to that of home trade goods in A; the latter, as depending both on this price ratio and on the level of aggregate domestic expenditure (S) deflated by the price of home trade goods in A. (Note that domestic expenditure is defined to include expenditure on imports and to exclude export receipts.)

Thus the volume of A's exports is taken as dependent on the price ratio and on deflated home expenditure. Similarly, the volume of A's imports is taken as dependent on the price of imports, relative to that of home trade goods, and on home expenditure, deflated by the price of home trade goods. These relationships give rise to four of the parameters used in this study: ϵ_a, the elasticity of A's *net* supply of export goods with respect to the export price ratio; λ_x, the elasticity of A's demand for export goods with respect to deflated home expenditure; η_a, the elasticity of A's net demand for imports with respect to the import price ratio; and λ_m, the elasticity of A's demand for import goods with respect to deflated home expenditure. It is not found necessary in this paper to split up the elasticities of A's net demand for imports and net supply of exports into their component elasticities of demand for and supply of import goods and export goods, respectively.

The net demand in the outside world (non-A) for A's exports is regarded as determined solely by the world market price, in non-A currency, of A's exports: the assumption is that any responsive changes in non-A's own prices or expenditures are proportionately so small as to be negligible. Similarly, non-A's net supply of A's imports is treated as a function of the world market price, in non-A-currency, of A's imports. (The world market price of A's exports is assumed to be equivalent to the price in A; the world market price of A's imports, however, will differ from the price in A to the extent of

201

any import duties or any windfall profits arising from import restriction in A.) These relationships give rise to two elasticities: η_b, the price elasticity of non-A's net demand for A's exports, and ϵ_b, the price elasticity of non-A's net supply of A's imports.

In this study we have arbitrarily assumed different sets of numerical values for the parameters $p_x q_{x1}$, $p_x q_{x2}$, $p_m q_{m1}$, $p_m q_{m2}$, $p_h q_h$, η_a, η_b, ϵ_a, ϵ_b, λ_x, and λ_m, and we have calculated the price effects of a given devaluation for each set of parameter values. Some of the numerical values have been chosen in such a way as to illustrate the influence of the different parameters, and some in such a way as to reproduce the circumstances of different sorts of countries. In reality, of course, the economic system takes time to react to disturbing factors. The values that can realistically be assigned to these parameters for any particular country will be a function of the reaction time allowed. We have, in fact, had in mind a reaction time of one to two years and have therefore been exploring the 'medium-term' effects of depreciation. But the formula evolved can easily be used to calculate either short-term or long-term effects, if suitable values are assigned to the coefficients.

A more troublesome difficulty is that it cannot be assumed that any values assigned to the parameters will hold true irrespective of the nature of the disturbance. In particular, if we are starting from full employment it cannot be assumed that demand and supply elasticities with respect to price will be the same for price increases as for price declines. But since in this essay we are concerned solely with price increases, the problem is not of importance here.

Price Effects of Exchange Depreciation Prior to Fiscal Adjustments

The effects on the internal price level of an exchange depreciation in country A which is not accompanied by any change in the *ad valorem* level of any import restriction will now be considered.[2] It is assumed that there are no export restrictions or subsidies and, for the time being, that no changes in indirect taxation accompany depreciation. Since, in the absence of unemployment, no decline will take place in domestic wage rates in any major sector of industry,

[2] That is, the *ad valorem* level of import duties, if these constitute the effective limitation on imports, or the *ad valorem* equivalent of quantitative restrictions, if these constitute the effective limitation.

depreciation is likely to be accompanied by some increase in A's over-all cost of absorption (i.e. the price level of goods domestically consumed or invested), owing to a rise in the domestic currency price of both import and export goods. The domestic price of import goods will rise because the foreign currency price at which other countries supply them cannot be expected to fall to the full extent of the devaluation and because the home supply of import substitutes is not completely elastic; and the price of export goods will rise because the cheapening of their foreign currency price will bring about an increase in foreign demand for A's exports impinging on a not completely elastic supply.

It is assumed that the price of home trade goods remains constant. This seems to be reasonably compatible with our assumption regarding financial policy, which is that total domestic demand will be controlled so as to prevent the emergence of any excess demand for labour in the home trade sector as labour is attracted from that sector to the foreign trade sector. Such a policy may well result in a slight net increase in wages even in the home trade sector; but since aggregate expenditure on home trade goods will have declined, there may be an associated decline in profit margins which will enable product prices to remain constant.

Although the prices of foreign trade goods will rise, they will not rise to the full extent of the devaluation. This is because

(1) the decline in the demand for imports, which may be expected (in the absence of an increase in domestic expenditure) to result from their increased domestic price, will tend to bring down their supply price abroad in foreign currency, and

(2) the increased supply of exports resulting from the rise in the domestic price will cause some fall in their foreign-currency demand price.

Broadly speaking, the extent to which an exchange depreciation of a given magnitude will raise the price of export goods will depend on the extent to which a decline in the foreign-currency price evokes an additional net demand for such goods abroad, the extent to which a rise in the A-currency price evokes an additional net supply of such goods in A, and the extent to which any change in aggregate expenditure in A results in a change in home absorption of such goods. In other words, it will depend on the elasticity, with respect to

203

ESSAYS IN INTERNATIONAL ECONOMICS

price, of net demand abroad (η_b) and of net supply in A (ϵ_a), and on the marginal propensity to buy export goods in A ($q_{x2}\lambda_x$). Similarly, the extent to which a given depreciation will raise the price of import goods will depend on the price elasticities of net supply abroad (ϵ_b) and of net demand in A (η_a) and on the marginal propensity to buy import goods in A ($q_m\lambda_m$).[3] Since the prices of A's import goods and export goods will increase as a result of the depreciation, while the price of home market goods will remain constant, the extent of the rise in A's cost of absorption will be the greater, the greater is the share of import goods and export goods, relative to home market goods, in A's total absorption.

As far as price elasticities are concerned, the rise in A's price level will be the smaller, the lower the elasticities abroad (η_b and ϵ_b) and the higher the elasticities at home (η_a and ϵ_a). High values of η_b and ϵ_b mean that a big increase in the net demand for A's exports, and a big reduction in the net supply of A's imports, will be generated abroad in response to any decline in their respective prices in terms of foreign currency, and this will naturally tend to raise the prices of export and import goods in A. Low elasticities abroad mean that this price-raising effect will be relatively weak. High elasticities at home mean that any increase in the price of export or import goods—consequent on a rise in the foreign net demand for them—will lead to a big increase in domestic supply and a big decline in domestic demand for these goods, which naturally tends to limit the rise in their price.

The elasticity of the net supply of exports in A will be the greater, the greater are (1) the elasticities both of A's output and of its absorption of export goods and (2) the proportion of its output of these goods that is absorbed at home. The elasticity of A's net demand for imports will be the greater, the greater are (1) the respective elasticities both of its output and of its absorption of import goods and (2) the proportion of its absorption of such goods that it produces at home. The analogous propositions hold true of the outside world in its trade with A.

Since the outside world (non-A) will normally be much larger economically than A, the ratio of absorption to output for any foreign trade product will normally be nearer to unity in non-A

---

[3] Since p_h, the price of home trade goods, is assumed to remain constant, it drops out of the definition of the various foreign trade elasticities in A. Thus η_a and ϵ_a become straightforward elasticities with respect to p_m and p_x respectively, λ_x and λ_m likewise resolve into elasticities with respect to money expenditure in A. q_m is short for $q_{m1}+q_{m2}$.

than in A. Mainly for this reason, the foreign trade elasticities will normally be greater in non-A than in A; and when A's exchange rate depreciates, the average price of foreign trade goods in A will normally rise by more than half as much as the price of foreign currencies in A. Since, however, supply elasticities with respect to price are usually higher, save in the short run, than the corresponding demand elasticities for the product in question, and since the former tend to play a greater part, relative to the latter, in determining export than in determining import elasticities, there is a general tendency for export elasticities to be higher than import elasticities. From this it follows that export prices in A will normally rise less than import prices and may often rise less than half as much as the prices of foreign currencies in A. It would be expected that the larger the devaluing country, A, the higher would be its foreign trade elasticities, relative to those of the outside world, and the smaller the increase in prices of its foreign trade goods relative to the extent of the depreciation.

As regards the elasticities of domestic demand for, and supply of, export and import goods, the elasticities of demand will vary with the extent to which individuals and firms are prepared, in their pattern of absorption, to replace these goods by home trade goods, as the prices of the former rise; such substitution will be the greater, the greater is the similarity between foreign trade and home trade goods. The elasticities of home output of export and of import goods will be the greater, the greater is the mobility of labour and other resources as between home trade industries, on the one hand, and those producing exportable and import-competing goods, on the other.

The influence exercised by the marginal propensities to purchase import and export goods out of home expenditure will make itself felt only to the extent that the pursuance of a proper financial policy requires some change in the aggregate level of home expenditure as exchange depreciation brings about an improvement in the balance of trade.

A distinction has to be drawn between the level of home expenditure in real and in money terms. If a country embarks on devaluation from an initial position of full employment, the observance of a proper financial policy is bound to require a significant reduction of home expenditure in real terms. Real home expenditure (absorption) is limited to that portion of real output *plus* real imports that is not

205

used for export. Since, under the conditions assumed here, devaluation cannot increase the volume of output, and since, if it is not completely nullified by a rise in domestic prices, it will entail an increase in real exports and a decline in real imports, there must be a corresponding decline in real absorption or home expenditure. Failure to bring about such a decline will lead to such a rise in domestic costs and prices as to frustrate the purpose of the devaluation.

Transposed into terms of money values, however, the argument is less straightforward. True, the value of home expenditure must, by definition, be equal to the value of output *plus* the value of imports *less* the value of exports. Again, exchange depreciation will normally —though not necessarily—lead to an increase in the value of exports *less* the value of imports, so that, if a proper financial policy had required that the value of output should remain constant, home expenditure would have had to fall by an amount equal to the increase in the value of exports *less* the value of imports.

For the value of output to remain constant, however, expenditure on home trade goods would have to decline to the full extent of the rise in the value of output of export goods and import-competing goods. This is more than is called for by a proper financial policy. Since wages in all trades are assumed to be inflexible in a downward direction, and since there is something less than full mobility of labour between home trade industries, on the one hand, and export and import-substitute industries, on the other, it follows that a decline in expenditure on home trade goods, even if balanced by an equivalent increase in demand for other products, is likely to give rise to unemployment. Some rise in the value of output will therefore be appropriate, and home expenditure will not be curtailed to the full extent of the improvement in the balance of trade. Indeed, if the foreign trade elasticities in A (η_a and ϵ_a) are too low, the rise of export and import prices may not only entail a rise, rather than a fall, in the proportion of home expenditure directed to foreign trade goods; it may even divert more of A's expenditure from home trade to foreign trade goods than it will attract resources from the home trade to the foreign trade industries. If this occurs, it will be necessary to increase rather than reduce home expenditure, thus further pushing up prices in the foreign trade sector.[4]

---

[4] This will happen if $q_{m1}\eta_a + \dfrac{dp_x}{dp_m} q_{x1}\epsilon_a < q_m + \dfrac{dp_x}{dp_m} q_{x2}$.

In most cases, however, it will be possible, without creating undue unemployment, to reduce home expenditure sufficiently to moderate significantly the pressure of demand and the rise in prices in the foreign trade sector. The reduction will be the greater, the higher are (1) the foreign trade elasticities in A and non-A, (2) the expenditure elasticities of demand for import and export goods in A, and (3) the proportionate importance of import and export goods in A's domestic absorption. These are also conditions that normally tend to increase the effect of a given devaluation in improving the balance of trade.

It is not clear that a relatively large foreign trade sector in A will contribute to keeping down the rise in prices of import and export goods resulting from a given devaluation; while it will enhance the moderating effect of any decline in home expenditure, it will also tend to reduce A's price elasticities. But whatever may be the effect on the price of foreign trade goods, the effect on A's general price level, or cost of absorption, is unambiguous and important. Given the rise in the price of import and export goods, it is clear that the greater the share of these goods in total absorption, the greater will be the rise in the general price level.

The financial measures required to bring about an appropriate adjustment of domestic expenditure may include some adjustment in the rates of taxation on consumption or investment. A consideration of the price effects resulting from such adjustments will be postponed until financial policies have been considered.

The manner in which the various factors discussed above—other than the fiscal repercussions just mentioned—combine to determine the proportionate increase in the general price level associated with a given proportionate depreciation of the rate of exchange is described in algebraic terms in Part I and Part II(a) of the Appendix. Strictly speaking, the formula applies only to infinitesimally slight devaluations, but when the foreign trade elasticities are interpreted as arc-rather than point-elasticities, it gives an approximation to the correct results for moderate devaluations.

Nine cases are defined in Table 8.1, each characterized by a different combination of numerical values for the relevant parameters in A and non-A. For each case, the effect that an exchange depreciation of 10 per cent would have on prices of foreign trade goods, on the cost of absorption, and on the balance of trade are shown in

Table 8.2. The meanings of the various symbols used in these tables are set forth below; the brief description given here of the elasticities is to be interpreted in the light of the fuller definitions given above.

η_a: price elasticity of net demand for imports in A

ϵ_a: price elasticity of net supply of exports in A

η_b: price elasticity of net demand for A's exports in non-A

ϵ_b: price elasticity of net supply of A's imports in non-A

λ_m: expenditure elasticity of demand for import goods in A

λ_x: expenditure elasticity of demand for export goods in A

$p_m q_{m1}$: initial ratio of value of imports at home market prices to value of tota output in A

$p_x q_{x1}$: initial ratio of value of exports at home market prices to value of total output in A

$p_m q_{m2}$: initial ratio of value of output of import goods at home market prices to value of total output in A

$p_x q_{x2}$: initial ratio of value of expenditure on export goods at home market prices to value of total output in A

$p_h q_h$: initial ratio of value of output of home trade goods at home market prices to value of total output in A

S: initial ratio of value of total expenditure to value of total output in A

Δp_m: percentage increase in the price of import goods in A

Δp_x: percentage increase in the price of export goods in A

ΔP: percentage increase in the cost of absorption in A

ΔB: increase in A's trade balance at world market prices[5] as a percentage of initial level of value of total output

$\dfrac{dP}{dB}$: percentage rate at which A's cost of absorption rises as its balance of trade (as a percentage of value of output) improves

t: ratio of the internal to the external price of import goods in A ($= 1 + ad\ valorem$ equivalent of any import restriction in A)

TABLE 8.1. *Numerical Values Assigned to Parameters in Various Cases*

	Cases										
	1	2	3	4	5	6	7	8	9	10	11
η_a	1	1	·5	1	1	1	1	·5	·5	1·5	1·5
ϵ_a	4	4	4	2	4	4	4	5	4	3	2
η_b	3	3	3	3	·5	3	3	2	2·5	3	5
ϵ_b	8	8	8	8	8	4	8	4	6	10	15
λ_m	1	1·5	1	1	1	1	1	1	1	1	1
λ_x	1	1·5	1	1	1	1	1	1	1	1	1
$p_m q_{m1}$	·3	·3	·3	·3	·3	·3	·45	·15	·6	·15	·6
$p_x q_{x1}$	·2	·2	·2	·2	·2	·2	·3	·1	·4	·1	·4
$p_m q_{m2}$	·1	·1	·1	·1	·1	·1	·15	·05	·1	·1	·1
$p_x q_{x2}$	·1	·1	·1	·1	·1	·1	·15	·2	·2	·1	·05
$p_h q_h$	·6	·6	·6	·6	·6	·6	·4	·65	·3	·7	·45
S	1·1	1·1	1·1	1·1	1·1	1·1	1·15	1·05	1·2	1·05	1·2

[5] Strictly speaking, the equivalent in A's currency of the increase in the foreign currency value of A's trade balance.

The first seven cases are defined so as to illustrate the direction and magnitude of the influence that the individual parameters exercise, in the event of exchange depreciation of the type under investigation, on prices, the balance of trade, etc. Case 1 is taken as the standard of comparison, and other cases differ from it only with respect to a single parameter or group of parameters. The parameter or group of parameters from which the numerical value in any particular case diverges from that of case 1 is indicated by italics.

Cases 1, 8, 9, 10, and 11 are supposed to be more or less realistic typical country cases: case 8 is a large, and case 9 a small, industrial country; case 10 a large, and case 11 a small, primary producing country; case 1 may be regarded as an 'average' country. The choice of elasticities has been based on the following assumptions:

(1) Large countries tend to have higher foreign trade elasticities at home (η_a and ϵ_a) and tend to encounter lower foreign trade elasticities abroad (η_b and ϵ_b) than do small countries of the same type.

(2) Industrial countries tend to have a more elastic export supply than do primary producing countries of the same size; this is linked to the fact that home consumption of exportable goods tends to be more important in industrial than in primary producing countries.

(3) The demand for imports tends to be less elastic for industrial countries than for primary producing countries because of the higher proportion of necessary food and raw materials.

(4) Industrial countries tend to encounter a less elastic world demand for their exports than is encountered by primary producing countries; although the products of the industrial countries are of a less necessary type, they are more specialized and less easily substitutable for those of competing countries.

(5) Industrial countries tend to encounter a less elastic world supply of their imports than do primary producing countries, because both the supply and the demand for primary products abroad tend to be less elastic than for industrial goods.

In choosing the elasticities, some account—but not too much— has been taken of such estimates of these elasticities as have been

209

calculated for particular countries by econometric methods. For export supply elasticities (ϵ_a and ϵ_b), such estimates are almost entirely lacking. Estimates for import demand elasticities (η_a and η_b) are available, but good reason exists for believing them to be highly uncertain and, in most cases, too low.

TABLE 8.2. *Effects of Simple Exchange Depreciation on Prices and the Balance of Trade of the Depreciating Country*

	Effects of a 10 Per Cent Depreciation				
Case	Δp_x	Δp_m	ΔP	ΔB (per cent of value of output; $t = 1 \cdot 5$)	Percentage Rise in P Associated with an Improvement in Trade Balance Equal to 5 Per Cent of Value of Output ($t = 1 \cdot 5$)
		(in per cent)			
1	4·05	8·4	3·4	5·3	3·25
2	3·7	7·7	3·15	6·6	2·38
3	4·2	9·2	3·7	3·7	5·10
4	5·85	8·7	3·7	4·05	4·54
5	1·1	8·9	3·3	1·1	15·66
6	4·0	7·1	2·9	5·3	2·76
7	3·8	7·85	4·6	9·5	2·41
8	3·0	9·0	2·3	1·2	9·42
9	3·5	8·3	5·4	8·6	3·16
10	4·8	8·5	2·5	2·6	4·72
11	6·9	8·0	5·0	17·6	1·41

On the basis of the numerical values assigned to the parameters under the respective cases in Table 8.1, calculations have been made of the percentage changes in the prices of exports (p_x) and imports (p_m), the general price level or cost of absorption (P), and the balance of trade (B) that will result from a 10 per cent exchange depreciation in country A.[6] The last has been calculated on the assumption of a degree of import restriction equivalent to an *ad valorem* import duty of 50 per cent. Since the initial ratio of the value of imports at home market prices to the value of exports in all cases equals 1·5, this implies that in all cases imports and exports at world market prices are assumed to be initially in balance.

Consider, first, cases 1 to 7. In consonance with the foregoing argument, the price level is seen to rise somewhat more steeply where, as in cases 3 and 4, the foreign trade elasticities in A are low,

[6] For details of these calculations, see Appendix, Part I, Part II(a) and Part II(b).

and to rise somewhat less where, as in case 2, the expenditure elasticities in A are high, or where, as in cases 5 and 6, the foreign trade elasticities in non-A are low. The fact that the price rise in case 5 is almost as great as in case 1 is because the decline in domestic expenditure (S) in case 5 is much smaller than in case 1 so that the smaller rise in p_x is nearly offset by the greater rise in p_m. The most substantial price rise of all occurs in case 7, where it is due to the relatively large importance of foreign trade in the economy as a whole.

In regard to the special cases 8–11, the most important factor in determining the degree of price rise is clearly the size of the foreign trade sector—which varies inversely with the size of the country, but tends to be larger in industrial than in primary producing countries of a given size. This accounts for the relatively large price increases in 9 and 11 and the relatively small increases in 8 and 10. The increases in p_x are, as would be expected, greater for small countries 9 and 11 than for large countries 8 and 10, and greater for primary producers 10 and 11 than for industrial countries 8 and 9. More surprising are the results for import price: p_m rises more in the industrial than in the primary producing countries, and more in the large than in the small countries. The reason p_m is shown as rising more in case 8 than in case 10, and in case 9 than in case 11, despite that fact that the foreign supply is assumed to be more elastic for the industrial imports of cases 10 and 11 than for the primary product imports of cases 8 and 9, is that the price elasticity of demand for imports is also assumed to be higher in the former than in the latter pair of cases. The reason p_m rises more in case 8 than in case 9, and in case 10 than in case 11, is not connected with the size of the price elasticities at all; these would tend to lead to the opposite results. The reason lies in the fact that the proportionate decline in home expenditure is very much less, and in addition the proportion of this decline in expenditure that falls on foreign trade goods is much less, in the large countries with a relatively small foreign trade sector (cases 8 and 10) than in cases 9 and 11.

Thus far, we have been concerned with the effect on prices of an exchange depreciation of a given magnitude. Fundamentally, however, what is important to governments in considering the advisability of an exchange rate adjustment is something else, namely, the effect on prices of whatever exchange depreciation is required to bring about a given improvement in the balance of payments in terms of foreign currency. When considered from this new angle, the relative price-raising effects of exchange depreciation in the different cases change quite appreciably.

Consider, first, the degree of improvement in A's trade balance,[7] measured relative to the value of A's output, that results, in the different cases, from a given percentage depreciation. The balance-of-trade effect of depreciation depends to some extent on the intensity of import restriction applied in A (even though, by the basic hypothesis in this paper, the severity of the restriction remains unchanged as the exchange rate falls). In Table 8.2, the degree of restriction has been assumed to be equivalent to an *ad valorem* import duty of 50 per cent. As will be seen from Table 8.2, the balance-of-trade effects vary far more widely, as between the various cases, than do the price effects. Over the range of parameter values considered here, the improvement in the balance of trade tends to be the greater, the higher are A's own foreign trade elasticities (including the expenditure elasticities of demand for foreign trade goods), and also the higher is the elasticity of net import demand in non-A. Where, as in many of the cases, A's net import elasticity (η_a) is unity, variations in non-A's net export elasticity have little effect on the balance of trade; but where, as in cases 3, 8, and 9, η_a is less than unity, the improvement in the balance will be the greater, the less elastic is non-A's net export elasticity. But the main factor in determining the effect on the balance of trade, measured as a proportion of the value of output, is simply the relative importance of the foreign trade sectors. This factor operates powerfully in cases 7, 9, and 11. The particularly small improvement in the balance of trade in case 5 is due to the low elasticity of net demand for A's exports abroad; and the particularly large improvement in case 11 is due to the combination of high foreign trade ratios and particularly high levels of η_a, η_b, and ϵ_b. An improvement in the trade balance amounting to 18 per cent of the value of output seems an extraordinary effect to achieve from a 10 per cent devaluation. It has to be borne in mind, however, that if an improvement of this order were brought about it would be extremely difficult to carry out a financial policy sufficiently disinflationary to fulfil the assumptions of the model by keeping the

[7] Strictly speaking, the A-currency equivalent of the improvement in the foreign-currency trade balance.

price level of home trade goods from rising. On the other hand, it should seldom be necessary to achieve an improvement of this order, and a country of this type should be able to rectify every normal disequilibrium with a relatively slight exchange depreciation.

As will be seen from the last column of Table 8.2, the proportionate rise of the cost of absorption associated with a given improvement in the trade balance is much less affected by the relative importance of the foreign trade sectors than is either the balance-of-trade effect or the price effect of depreciation, taken separately. As can be seen by comparing case 7 with case 1, however, high foreign trade ratios, being associated with high marginal propensities to buy foreign trade goods, tend somewhat to reduce the rise in P; a similar result is seen in case 2, where the expenditure elasticities of demand for foreign trade goods are high. The greatest price rise of all occurs in case 5, because of the low value of the elasticity of net demand abroad for A's exports. A low elasticity of net demand for imports in A (case 3) also makes for a high price rise, as does a low elasticity of net supply abroad for A's imports (case 4). The substantial price rise in case 8 (the large industrial country) is due to the low elasticities of net demand for imports both in A and in non-A. However, such a country may not often require a correction of its trade balance as large as 5 per cent of the value of its output. The very small price rise in case 11 is due to its high elasticities of net demand for imports in A and in non-A and to its high foreign trade ratios. In general, save in case 5, the price increases seem quite moderate in relation to the improvements in the balance of trade.

Financial Policies Required

If the price level is to rise as little, and the balance of trade is to improve as much, with a given devaluation, as indicated above, the aggregate level of domestic absorption will have to be so adjusted as to maintain constant prices and full employment without excess demand in the home trade goods industries. By definition, domestic expenditure, or the value of domestic absorption, is necessarily equal to the value of output *less* the balance of trade, all the component elements being valued at domestic prices, either net or gross of expenditure taxes. But the balance of trade at domestic prices consists of the balance of trade at world prices *less* the excess of the domestic over the world market value of imports.[8] It follows that the domestic expenditure (net of expenditure taxes) should decline with devaluation by the amount by which the balance of trade in domestic currency, at world market prices, tends to improve,[9] *plus* the amount by which the excess of the domestic over the world market value of imports tends to decline, *less* the amount by which the value of output, at factor cost, tends to rise, *when equilibrium as described above is maintained in the home trade goods industries.*

The magnitude of the appropriate changes in A's expenditure, the value of output, and the excess of the domestic over the world market value of imports associated with (1) a 10 per cent depreciation and (2) a depreciation resulting in a 5 per cent improvement in the trade balance, respectively, are shown for various selected cases in Table 8.3.[10]

Let ΔV stand for the percentage change in the value of output at factor cost,

ΔS for the change in domestic expenditure (net of tax) as a percentage of the initial value of output,

ΔR for the change in the excess of the domestic over the world market value of imports (expressed as a percentage of the value of output), and

ΔB, as in Table 8.2, for the change in the balance of trade at world market prices. (Since exports and imports are assumed to be, initially, of equal value, ΔB can stand, indifferently, for the domestic-currency equivalent of the change in the balance of trade in foreign currency or for the change in the balance of trade in domestic currency.)

It will be seen that the appropriate level of domestic expenditure declines in all cases, save case 8. The increase in expenditure in this case is associated with the comparatively low elasticities of foreign net demand for A's exports and of A's net demand for imports, and

[8] Here the domestic value of imports is based on the domestic price before payment of any expenditure taxes but after payment of any import taxes.

[9] See Appendix, Part II(b), equation (xxx).

[10] The basic formulas underlying this calculation are found in the Appendix, Part II(a), (b), (c) and (d).

with the resulting small influence of depreciation on the trade balance. The rise in export prices is so small that not enough labour is attracted from industries producing home trade goods to compensate for the switch in demand from these industries to pay for higher priced imports. At the other extreme, the decline in domestic expenditure required for a 10 per cent depreciation in case 11 is enormous—18 per cent of the value of national output; this is

TABLE 8.3. *Appropriate Changes in Value of Output and in Domestic Expenditure Associated with Exchange Depreciation*

(Expressed in percentage of the value of output)

Case	Resulting from a 10 Per Cent Depreciation				Resulting from a Depreciation that Improves the Balance of Trade by 5 Per Cent of the Value of Output		
	$-\Delta B$	ΔV	ΔR	ΔS	ΔV	ΔR	ΔS
	$t = 1 \cdot 5$						
1	$-5 \cdot 3$	$2 \cdot 05$	$-0 \cdot 4$	$-3 \cdot 7$	$1 \cdot 95$	$-0 \cdot 4$	$-3 \cdot 5$
8	$-1 \cdot 2$	$1 \cdot 3$	$0 \cdot 25$	$0 \cdot 4$	$5 \cdot 5$	$1 \cdot 0$	$1 \cdot 6$
9	$-8 \cdot 6$	$2 \cdot 9$	$-0 \cdot 3$	$-6 \cdot 05$	$1 \cdot 7$	$-0 \cdot 2$	$-3 \cdot 5$
10	$-2 \cdot 6$	$1 \cdot 8$	$-0 \cdot 3$	$-1 \cdot 1$	$3 \cdot 4$	$-0 \cdot 6$	$-2 \cdot 1$
11	$-17 \cdot 6$	$3 \cdot 9$	$-4 \cdot 3$	$-18 \cdot 0$	$1 \cdot 1$	$-1 \cdot 2$	$-5 \cdot 0$

associated with a very large improvement in the balance of trade and a considerable decline in the value of imports which, since the *ad valorem* severity of import restriction is constant, reduces the excess of the domestic over the world market value of imports. A decline in expenditure of this magnitude might well be impossible to achieve in practice. On the other hand, a 10 per cent depreciation may very well be unnecessary in such a case. As will be seen from the right hand side of the table, the decline in S required in connection with a given improvement in the balance of trade is not much greater in case 11 than in other cases.

The extent of the disinflation to be carried out by official action in the event of exchange depreciation, however, is not measured by the required decline in domestic expenditure alone; it must, in addition, suffice to counteract any increase in expenditure that may naturally tend to arise from the improvement in the balance of trade and the increase in national income associated with the exchange depreciation.

In order to indicate the order of magnitude of the disinflationary effort that may be required in typical cases, an illustrative calculation is made below for case 1 on the assumption of a depreciation of 10 per cent and on stated assumptions regarding the magnitude of the relevant structural coefficients. These coefficients are chosen to fit the basic assumption that, initially, some 75 per cent of total absorption consists of private consumption, 15 per cent of public consumption, and 10 per cent of (net) investment. (All the following figures are expressed in percentages of the value of national output.)

(1) The required decline in domestic expenditure, net of consumption and investment taxes, (S), is 3·66.

(2) If indirect taxes on consumption and investment are assumed to amount to 8 per cent, the required decline in domestic expenditure at market prices is 3·95.

(3) Assume that half the margin between the domestic and the world price of imports accrues to importers as 'windfall gains', that the transfer of interest on the national debt from government to individuals amounts to 5, and that all industry is in private hands. Then private incomes initially amount to 110. Assume that the income tax takes 8 per cent of this income, leaving a post-tax income of 101·2, of which 12 per cent is saved. Private consumption at market prices is thus, initially, 89·1. The rise in the cost of absorption, owing to devaluation, is 3·42 per cent. Therefore, if private consumption were to remain unchanged in real terms, it would have to increase in money terms by 3·05.

However, we shall assume that there is a marginal propensity to consume of 0·6, so that real private consumption declines by 60 per cent of the decline in real private incomes. Now the fall in the purchasing power of private incomes is 3·46;[11] but money incomes rise by 1·83,[12] which, less income tax, amounts to 1·68. Therefore, real private incomes fall by 1·78. If 60 per cent of this is subtracted from real private consumption, private consumption in money terms will rise by 1·98.[13]

(4) There appears to be no good reason why the remaining constituents in absorption—government absorption of goods and

[11] 3·42 per cent of 101·2.

[12] $\Delta V - \Delta R/2 = 2·05 - 0·22.$

[13] 3·05 − 1·07.

services and private investment—should not tend, in the first instance, to remain unchanged in real terms. For government absorption it is convenient to assume this as a starting point for estimating the degree of final disinflation that may be necessary. Moreover, since it is assumed that the volume of output is not affected by the devaluation and that the average price of output rises almost as much as the cost of investment goods, it seems plausible that the tendency, at constant interest rates, would be to maintain an unchanged volume of private investment. Since aggregate domestic expenditure at market prices was initially 118·9[14] and private consumption was assumed above to be 89·1, the remaining categories of expenditure accounted together for 29·7. If these tend to remain constant in real terms, money expenditure on these items will tend to rise by 1·02.

(5) When the results of (3) and (4) are added together, domestic expenditure will tend to rise by some 3·00. When this is added to the required decline in expenditure given in (2) above, it appears that official action would be required to curtail domestic expenditure by some 6·95 at market prices. For the purpose of making a comparison with national output at factor cost, this should be netted of indirect taxes; when this is done, the curtailment required amounts to some 6·44 per cent of the value of national output.

It should be noted that the inflationary gap that has to be bridged by official action lies between the amount of the target improvement in the balance of trade (some 5·3 per cent of the value of output) and the amount of the required decline in real absorption (some 7·4 per cent of the value of output). This is no accident. The amount by which the required decline in real absorption exceeds the target improvement in the balance of trade corresponds to the decline in real national income.[15] The amount by which the required decline

---

[14] 108 per cent of 110.

[15] The statement is unambiguous and strictly true only when the trade balance is initially equal to zero. When the initial trade balance is positive (negative) the effect of exchange depreciation on the balance of trade in domestic currency will be more (less) positive than the equivalent in domestic currency of the effect on the balance of trade in foreign currency. The required decline in real absorption will exceed the decline in real income by an amount intermediate between the domestic-currency equivalent of the improvement in the balance of trade in foreign currency and the improvement in the balance of trade in domestic currency. See Appendix, Part II(f), equations (xxx), (xxxvi) and (xxxvii).

in real absorption exceeds the inflationary gap corresponds to the fall in real consumption resulting from the decline in real national income; and the amount by which the inflationary gap exceeds the target improvement in the balance of trade corresponds to the decline in real national savings resulting from the decline in real national income.

TABLE 8.4. *Curtailment of Domestic Expenditure (Net of Tax) to be Brought About by Official Policy*

(In per cent of value of output at factor cost; $t = 1 \cdot 5$)

Case	Resulting from a 10 Per Cent Depreciation	Resulting from a Depreciation that Improves the Balance of Trade by 5 Per Cent of the Value of Output
1	6·4	6·1
8	1·5	6·3
9	10·7	6·2
10	3·2	6·1
11	21·9	6·2

Table 8.4 shows the extent of the curtailment of expenditure to be brought about by official action for the cases presented in Table 8.3, on assumptions as to tax rates, transfer incomes, and consumption ratios that are similar to those made above for case 1.

For the various cases, it is clear that the differences in the extent of the deflationary effort required on the part of the authorities in connection with a 10 per cent devaluation are largely associated with differences in the size of the improvement achieved in the balance of trade; for a given improvement in the latter, much the same effort is required in all cases (see Table 8.4, column 2). The slightly greater effort required to achieve a given improvement in the trade balance in case 8 is due to the big loss of real income arising out of a deterioration in the terms of trade; this is only partly offset by the relatively small loss of real income from the reduction of already restricted imports[16] and the relatively large spontaneous reduction

---

[16] The adverse effects exercised by exchange depreciation on real national income arise, as can be seen from the Appendix, Part II(f), equation (xxxviii), from two factors: (1) a deterioration in the terms of trade, and (2) a decline in the volume of imports, the adverse influence of the latter being weighted by the margin between the domestic and the world market price of imports.

in real consumption. In case 11, there is very little deterioration in the terms of trade; there is, however, a substantial loss of real income from a decline in restricted imports and, since half of this falls, in the first instance, on state rather than private income, the spontaneous decline in real consumption is relatively small.

How much of the required curtailment of expenditure should fall on consumption and how much on investment? How much of the needed disinflation should be carried out by budgetary, and how much by monetary, policy? These questions are interrelated, for the view that is taken as to the appropriate change in public saving—the excess of current account receipts over current account expenditures in the public sector—will largely determine the answer to the first question, as well as affect the answer to the second.

Prima facie, there seems no very good reason why devaluation should affect the proportion of national income devoted to public saving. Although some important qualifications to this principle will be admitted later, let us adopt it for the present, with the additional simplifying assumption that the proportion of public saving deemed appropriate in country A is zero and that a state of zero public saving—a balanced budget on current account—prevails in the pre-devaluation situation. On these assumptions, most of the required curtailment of expenditure will fall on investment. The position may, once more, be illustrated from case 1.

With A's exchange rate depreciating by 10 per cent, the budgetary implications are as follows:

(1) The decline in target domestic expenditure (prior to indirect taxation) amounts to 3·66. At a tax rate of 8 per cent, the corresponding fall in the yield of general indirect taxation will be 0·29. The yield of import taxation will decline by 0·22.[17] Target private income, however, will rise by 1·83; and at an 8 per cent tax rate, the income tax yield will increase by 0·15. Altogether, the tax revenue corresponding to target levels of consumption and private income will fall by 0·36.

(2) Initially, the tax revenue was 38·0, of which 8·8[18] was from general indirect taxation, 8·8[19] from indirect taxation on expenditure, and 5 from import duties; 5 was paid out in interest transfers, leaving

[17] 0·5 times ΔR.
[18] 0·8 times 110.
[19] 0·8 times 110.

17·6 available to be spent on public consumption at market prices. With the rise in the cost of absorption, public expenditure for an unchanged volume of public consumption at market prices would therefore be 0·60.[20]

(3) From (1) and (2), the excess of public consumption over tax revenues corresponding to target levels of national income and expenditure would appear to be 0·96.

(4) Assume that real public consumption should be reduced in the same proportion as private. Since a reduction of 1·07 in real private consumption has been assumed above (page 216), the corresponding reduction in public consumption is 0·21.

(5) In order to restore a balanced budget on current account, the remaining gap of 0·75 will have to be eliminated by additional taxes and reductions in public consumption. In order to maintain proportionality between reductions in private and public consumption—and since only 60 per cent of any fall in private incomes will result in a fall in private consumption—it will be necessary to cut public consumption by a further 0·09 and to increase taxation by some 0·66.

(6) If the budget is balanced in this way, public consumption at market prices will have been curtailed by 0·30 and private consumption by 0·40,[21] making 0·70 in all. On a net-of-tax basis, this is equivalent to 0·65, against a total required curtailment of expenditure of 6·44. The remaining curtailment of expenditure, amounting to 5·79 per cent of the national output, will have to come from public or private investment.

(7) For an exchange depreciation that will lead to an improvement in the trade balance equal to 5 per cent of the value of output, the required curtailment of investment expenditure would be 5·49.

The results of similar calculations made for all the cases appearing in Table 8.4 are shown in Table 8·5.

The table shows certain variations among cases as to the extent to which mere restoration of budgetary balance will curtail consumption expenditure for a devaluation of a given balance-of-trade effect. In case 8 this curtailment is relatively small, because the tendency towards a budget deficit arising from the decline in import and

[20] 3·42 per cent of 17·6.
[21] 0·6 *times* 0·66.

220

expenditure taxes is relatively small; this again is due to the relatively low level of η_b, the elasticity of foreign demand for A's exports. On the other hand, the curtailment achieved by budgetary policy in case 11 is relatively large because of the relatively powerful tendency towards a decline in import and absorption taxes, owing to the high import demand elasticities abroad and at home and the high marginal propensity to import.

TABLE 8.5. *Curtailment of Various Classes of Domestic Expenditure (Net of Tax) to be Brought About by Official Policy*

(In per cent of value of output at factor cost)

Case	Resulting from a 10 Per Cent Depreciation		Resulting from a Depreciation that Improves the Balance of Trade by 5 Per Cent of the Value of Output	
	Consumption	Investment	Consumption	Investment
1	0·65	5·8	0·6	5·5
8	0·1	1·45	0·35	5·95
9	1·0	9·7	0·55	5·65
10	0·35	2·9	0·65	5·45
11	2·6	19·3	0·75	5·45

In all cases, much the largest part of the required curtailment of expenditure falls on investment. It should be remembered, however, that, from the standpoint of national wealth, the cut in home investment is largely compensated by the increased rate of accumulation—or reduced rate of loss—of net claims on the outside world and/or of metallic reserves, associated with the improvement in the balance of trade.

The proposition that much the greater part of the required curtailment of absorption should fall on investment is open to certain important qualifications, both of principle and of practice:

(1) The illustrative figures given in Table 8.5 are calculated on the assumption of unchanged interest rates. But for the required reduction in investment to be carried out, it will be necessary to raise interest rates, or, more precisely, to increase the scarcity of investible funds. This development may well evoke some increase in private savings and may even be held to justify an increase in the level of

public savings, if any. To this extent an additional part—which is not, however, likely to be very large—of the burden of contraction will be transferred from investment to consumption.

(2) More important in practice is that, if an over-rapid contraction of investment should seem likely to give rise to undue unemployment in capital goods industries—which may not be the industries particularly stimulated by the devaluation—there may be a case for temporarily raising the level of public savings by raising taxes and so spreading over a wider industrial front the deflationary pressure involved in the decline in home absorption. The importance of this point will be appreciated when it is recalled that, in the foregoing discussion, it has been assumed that the amount of investment prior to the depreciation amounted to no more than 10·5–12 per cent, according to the case in question, of the value of national output. Thus, what is called for by Table 8.5, in the event of a depreciation that improves the balance of trade by 5 per cent of the value of output, is approximately a cutting in half of the pre-existing volume of investment. On the other hand, the need for a decline in home absorption will manifest itself only gradually as the devaluation gradually takes effect on the balance of trade.

(3) Finally, allowance has to be made for irrationality in the savings policy of governments. Although the level of public savings or dissavings should logically be determined in relation to national income, the level of private savings, and the scarcity of capital, it may often in fact be influenced by the possibility which an external deficit provides of obtaining real resources from abroad and thus financing a budget deficit without inflationary consequences. To the extent that the improvement in the balance of trade brought about through depreciation threatens to create an inflationary situation, governments may be disposed to increase public saving more than has been assumed in the foregoing discussion. Where, however, simultaneous but mutually independent decisions are taken to reduce an external deficit by depreciation and to cut a budget deficit deemed excessive in relation to national income, it would be wrong to impute to depreciation the cut in consumption involved in the latter decision.

If, nevertheless, we continue to assume, despite the foregoing considerations, that the curtailment of home absorption is to take the form, predominantly, of a curtailment of investment, its implementation will lie primarily in the sphere of monetary and credit policy rather than of budgetary policy. In countries where a large sector of investment is under the control of the public authorities, the state should be able by direct measures to influence the level of investment. Fiscal policy may be adjusted to reduce the incentive to invest. But, in the main, the task of influencing the level of private investment, and to a lesser extent public enterprise investment, is likely to fall on monetary policy, in the broad sense that includes government policy with respect to the composition of the national debt.

The object of monetary policy should be to keep the volume of money in circulation—including checking accounts and with due allowance for the existing volume of various types of quasi-money—at a level which will so raise the price and scarcity of investible funds that the volume of investment will be curtailed to the extent required. This is likely, in most cases, to call for a considerable non-recurrent reduction in the supply of money and a considerable permanent reduction in the rate of expansion of bank credit to domestic borrowers.

The need for money for transactions purposes may be assumed to depend primarily on the level of the value of output and, to a lesser extent, on that of domestic money expenditure. As we have already seen from Table 8.3, the value of output in A will usually rise somewhat because of the rise in the prices of import and export goods, although, because of weighting considerations, the proportionate increase in the value of output will not be precisely the same as the proportionate increase in the cost of absorption. On the other hand, since the improvement in the balance of trade (at domestic prices)[22] is larger than the rise in the value of output, the appropriate level of domestic expenditure will usually fall. It is probable that the transactions demand for money is influenced much more by the value of output than by domestic expenditure, since the need for business balances arises mainly from the flow of current account transactions, and the need for private balances from the flow of personal incomes rather than of consumption expenditure. An average of the changes in the volume of output and in domestic expenditure, in which the

[22] That is, the improvement, in A-currency, in the balance of trade *less* the excess of the home market over the world market value of imports.

223

weight of the former is three times that of the latter, is given in Table 8.6 for the cases dealt with in Tables 8.3 to 8.5.

The figures given in Table 8.6 give a rough impression of the changes in the money supply that would be appropriate in the event of depreciation if no changes were to occur in the velocity of circulation of money. In truth, however, the velocity of circulation is likely to increase substantially as the increased scarcity of investible funds, necessary to induce the required curtailment of investment indicated in Table 8.5, induces firms and individuals to make a more economical use of money balances; it follows that the supply of money should be curtailed to a corresponding extent.

TABLE 8.6. *Weighted Mean* $[\frac{1}{4}(3\Delta O + \Delta S)]$ *of the Appropriate Changes in Value of Output and in Domestic Expenditure Associated with Exchange Depreciation*

(Expressed in per cent of value of output; $t = 1\cdot5$)

Case	Resulting from a 10 Per Cent Depreciation	Resulting from a Depreciation that Improves the Balance of Trade by 5 Per Cent of the Value of Output
1	0·6	0·6
8	1·1	4·5
9	0·7	0·4
10	1·1	2·0
11	−1·6	−0·4

Let x stand for the proportional increase in the scarcity of investible funds (as measured by some composite rate of interest) that tends to bring about a unit proportional decline in real investment (assuming the effect on consumption to be negligible) when real output remains unchanged; and let y stand for the proportional increase in the velocity of circulation that tends to result from a unit proportional increase in the rate of interest. Then a given proportional decline in investment will be associated with a proportional increase, xy times as great as itself, in velocity. But the proportional increase in velocity is, by definition, the excess of the proportional increase in the value of transactions (however defined) over the proportional increase in the money supply. It follows that the proportional decline in the money supply that is required can be measured by xy *times* the proportional target decline in investment *less* the proportional target increase in the value of transactions—as shown in Table 8.6.

But what is x? And what is y? Unfortunately, the available evidence as to the magnitude of these coefficients in typical cases shows a wide range of variation. Thus, an empirical study of the response of velocity to variations in interest rates in a number of countries at different periods shows values for y (the interest elasticity of demand for money) which range from 0·1 for the United States in the 1930s to 3·9 for the Netherlands in post-war years.[23] Most of the more reliable results, however, show an elasticity of less than 2, especially in industrial countries. While y would be expected to rise as the rate of interest (r) itself approaches zero, there is no reason to expect any systematic relationship between y and r for normal variations of r, and none is visible in the data.

About $1/x$, the (negative) elasticity of investment with respect to the rate of interest, even less is known than about y. A series of estimates for various countries relating to the inter-war period and the period before World War I show that a 1 per cent variation in long-term interest rates tends to bring about a variation in gross investment (or other series related thereto), ranging from -56 per cent to zero.[24] The form of the calculation implies (as is probably true) that the elasticity of investment with respect to interest will tend to increase as the interest rate rises. If interest rates are assumed to be of the order of 5 per cent, this elasticity shows a range of variation similar to that already shown for the elasticity of velocity with respect to the rate of interest. On the assumption that in the average country net investment might be about half as great as gross investment, these calculations would suggest a value of $xy = \frac{1}{2}$ as a reasonable central assumption for illustrative purposes. However, there is some reason to believe that the market rate of interest constitutes a less adequate measure of the scarcity of funds from the standpoint of investors than from the standpoint of money holders and that the true value of $1/x$ is somewhat higher than has been assumed.

However, even if a value of $xy = \frac{1}{4}$ is assumed, substantial reductions in the money supply would still have to accompany

[23] From an unpublished study by William H. White.

[24] See J. Tinbergen, *Statistical Testing of Business Cycle Theories: A Method and its Application to Investment Activity* (League of Nations, Geneva, 1939).

exchange depreciation, in order to hold investment and absorption down to the appropriate levels.

The proportion of investment to the value of output implicit in the calculations underlying Tables 8.5 and 8.6 is some 11 per cent in case 1, 10·5 per cent in cases 8 and 10, and 12 per cent in cases 9 and 11. From this and the data given in Table 8.6, the percentage decline in the money supply that is required in each case to bring about a curtailment of investment of the magnitude shown in Table 8.5, on the assumption that $xy = \frac{1}{4}$, can be calculated; the results are given in Table 8.7.

TABLE 8.7. *Percentage Reduction in Money Supply Required on Certain Assumptions*

Case	In Connection with a 10 Per Cent Depreciation	In Connection with a Depreciation that Improves the Balance of Trade by 5 Per Cent of the Value of Output
1	12·6	11·9
8	2·3	9·7
9	19·5	11·4
10	5·8	11·0
11	41·8	11·8

The fact that part of investment is under govenment control and can be curtailed directly does not necessarily imply that the contraction in the money supply should be any less severe. If the initial magnitude of public investment relative to private investment was correct, the reduction in public investment should, ideally, be no greater than would result in a rational private economy from the increased scarcity of investible funds. In order to obtain the appropriate reduction in private investment, interest rates will therefore have to be raised—and the money supply reduced—to much the same extent, whatever the relative magnitude of the private and public sectors. On the other hand if, to avoid structural unemployment or for some other reason, part of the curtailment which would otherwise fall on investment is applied to consumption, by raising taxes or reducing public expenditure, the degree of monetary contraction required will be correspondingly reduced.

The contraction in the supply of money will have to be achieved by a non-recurrent contraction in bank credit to the domestic economy. In addition, in order to keep the amount of money at its new lower level, it will be necessary to bring about a permanent reduction in the pre-devaluation rate of domestic credit expansion. For the devaluation will tend to improve the balance of payments, both on current and on capital account, and hence to diminish the rate of loss of foreign assets by the banking system. If the volume of money is to remain the same, there must be a corresponding decline in the rate of accumulation of domestic assets. The improvement in the balance of payments, the effect of which on the volume of money is to be offset by domestic credit policy, will be greater, and may be much greater, than the improvement in the balance of trade, discussed above. For the flow of capital between A and the rest of the world is likely to shift in A's favour as a result of the depreciation, both because of the rise in the price and scarcity of investible funds in A and because of the weakening or disappearance of any pessimistic anticipations that may have existed initially regarding the future movements of A's exchange rate.

In view of the very great uncertainties regarding (1) the degree of monetary contraction necessary in order to effect a given curtailment of investment and (2) the effect of devaluation on the international flow of capital, it will usually be undesirable to fix in advance any hard and fast targets for the reduction in the money supply, or for the reduction of bank credit to domestic borrowers. Some tentative fixing of targets may well be helpful to illustrate the magnitude of the problem, but in practice it would seem best to look directly to the ultimate objective of preserving or restoring a correct level of demand pressure in the industries producing home trade goods and to turn the screw of credit contraction to whatever point is necessary to achieve this objective.

Mention was made above (see (5), page 220) of an increase in taxation, amounting to 0·66 of the value of output, that would be appropriate in case 1 as a contribution towards meeting the budgetary deficit brought about by declines in revenue and increases in expenditure arising out of a 10 per cent exchange depreciation. To some extent, the additional revenue will doubtless be raised in the form of indirect taxation on domestic absorption: indeed, since the effect of the depreciation, and the accompanying financial policy, is to increase the revenue from direct taxation, and to lower the revenue from indirect taxation, it might well be deemed appropriate to raise all the additional revenue by indirect taxes. If import duties are raised (from the 25 per cent assumed in the above calculations), the only effect will be to curtail the fortuitous incomes of the possessors of import licences; to the extent that expenditure taxes are increased, however, price levels (cost of absorption) will be raised above those indicated in Table 8.2. The magnitude of the additional taxation required, expressed as a percentage of domestic expenditure, and the total amount of the price increase occasioned by an exchange depreciation, assuming that half the additional revenue is raised from expenditure taxes, are shown in Table 8.8, for selected cases.

TABLE 8.8. *Additional Tax Revenue Required (in Per Cent of Domestic Expenditure ΔT_r) and Percentage Rise in Cost of Absorption (ΔP), Associated with Exchange Depreciation When Half the Additional Tax Revenue is Raised by Taxation on Domestic Expenditure*

Case	10 Per Cent Depreciation		Depreciation that Improves the Balance of Trade by 5 Per Cent of the Value of Output	
	ΔT_r	ΔP	ΔT_r	ΔP
1	0·60	3·7	0·57	3·5
8	—	2·3	—	9·4
9	0·74	5·8	0·43	3·4
10	0·34	2·7	0·64	5·0
11	2·67	6·3	0·76	1·8

Only in case 11 does the tax adjustment that is required to preserve a balanced budget significantly affect the increase in the general level of prices. Perhaps the main significance of these adjustments is slightly to mitigate the advantages enjoyed by a country with high foreign trade elasticities in being able to secure a big improvement in its balance of trade with a small rise in prices.

Linking of Wages to Cost of Living

The price increases mentioned in preceding sections of this essay have been calculated on the assumption that wage rates are unresponsive to change in the cost of living. Virtual wage stability was assumed in the industries producing home trade goods,[25] and wages in industries producing foreign trade goods were implicitly assumed to rise only to the extent required to attract labour from the home trade goods industries without its causing substantial unemployment in the latter.

If, however, wages rise generally in response to the increase in the cost of living, increases additional to those discussed thus far will clearly take place in A's product prices and cost of absorption. The latter, however, will not rise to the full extent of the rise in wages; only the prices of home trade goods will rise to this extent, the increase in the prices of foreign trade goods being damped down through the influence of demand and supply in non-A. The effect of the general rise in A's wages on the prices of foreign trade goods relative to home trade goods will be the same as the effect of an exchange appreciation of equal magnitude.

Thus, if a depreciation of x per cent leads to an initial price rise of xy per cent, which leads to a wage rise of xyz per cent, there will be a secondary price rise of approximately $xyz(1-y)$ per cent. This again, through its repercussion on wages, will lead to a tertiary price rise of $xyz^2(1-y)^2$, and so on indefinitely. However, if $z(1-y)$ is positive and less than unity, the price increments will be successively smaller and the aggregate price rise will amount to $xy/1-z(1-y)$ per cent. This price increase will be the higher, the nearer either y or z is to unity, but it will never be greater than the depreciation itself. To take an example: if a 10 per cent depreciation ($x = 0.1$) leads to an initial price rise of 4 per cent ($y = 0.4$), and if a 4 per cent price rise leads to a 2 per cent rise in wages ($z = 0.5$), the ultimate price increase will be approximately 5·7 per cent.

Since an increase in wage rates exercises an effect on the balance of trade similar to that of exchange appreciation, any repercussions of price changes on wage rates, such as those described above, will tend to reduce the improvement in the balance of trade (in terms of foreign currency) that will result from a given exchange depreciation. Therefore, in order to attain a given improvement in the balance of trade, a larger exchange depreciation will be necessary, and the enhancement which the connection between wages and the cost of

[25] Strictly speaking, a slight rise in wages even in these industries may have been implicitly assumed—large enough to keep prices of home trade goods from falling as the scale of operation in these industries is reduced.

229

living gives to the price increase resulting from exchange deprecia-tion will be greater for a depreciation yielding a given improvement in the balance of trade than it will be for an exchange depreciation of given magnitude.

The formula for the price rise associated with a depreciation yielding a given improvement in the balance of trade is somewhat simpler than that for the price rise associated with a given

TABLE 8.9. *Effect of Exchange Depreciation on the Cost of Absorption before and after Allowances for Wage Reactions* $(z = 0 \cdot 5)$

Case	Effect of a 10 Per Cent Depreciation		Effect of a Depreciation that Improves the Balance of Trade by 5 Per Cent of the Value of Output	
	Before wage reactions	After wage reactions	Before wage reactions	After wage reactions
1	3·7	5·4	3·5	7·1
8	2·3	3·7	9·4	18·8
9	5·8	7·3	3·4	6·7
10	2·7	4·2	5·0	10·1
11	6·3	7·7	1·8	3·6

depreciation, viz., $xy/(1-z)$. To secure a given improvement in the balance of trade, a given decline in real wages is necessary; and if, for example, money wages are raised by four-fifths of any rise in prices ($z = 0 \cdot 8$), prices will have to rise 5 times as much as they would otherwise have done.

Table 8·9 illustrates the ultimate price increases to be expected for the various cases examined in Table 8·8, on the assumption of: (1) an initial price increase (including the price increase resulting from the adjustment of indirect taxation) as shown in that table, and (2) a 50 per cent response of wages to increases in the cost of absorption ($z = 0 \cdot 5$).

It is noteworthy that, for a given exchange depreciation, the extent to which the mechanism of the wage spiral multiplies the initial price increase is the greater, the smaller is that initial increase; this mechanism therefore tends to equalize price increases in different cases. For a depreciation leading to a given improvement in the balance of trade, this multiplier is not only much larger than that for a given exchange depreciation, but it is uniform and equal to what it would be in a closed economy.

Appendix

Part I

Let q_{x1} stand for the volume of A's exports,

q_{x2} for the volume of A's absorption of export goods,

q_{m1} for the volume of A's imports,

q_{m2} for the volume of A's output of import goods,

q_h for the volume of A's output (or absorption) of home trade goods,

$q_m \equiv q_{m1} + q_{m2}$ and $q_x \equiv q_{x1} + q_{x2}$,

p_x stand for the home market price, in A-currency, of A's export goods,

p_m for the home market price, in A-currency, of A's import goods,

p_h for the home market price, in A-currency, of A's home trade goods,

$S\ [\equiv q_m p_m + q_{x2} p_x + q_h p_h]$ for A's domestic expenditure,

t for the ratio of p_m to the world market price, in A-currency, of A's import goods,

c for the price of A-currency in terms of non-A-currency.

A's export supply function be

$$q_{x1} = f_1\left(\frac{p_x}{p_h}, \frac{S}{p_h}\right),\tag{i}$$

A's import demand function be

$$q_{m1} = f_2\left(\frac{p_m}{p_h}, \frac{S}{p_h}\right),\tag{ii}$$

non-A's export supply function be

$$q_{m1} = f_3\left(\frac{p_m c}{t}\right),\tag{iii}$$

231

non-A's import demand function be

$$q_{x1} = f_4(p_x c). \tag{iv}$$

With reference to equation (i), let

$$\epsilon_a \left[\equiv \frac{\delta q_{z1}}{\delta(p_x p_h^{-1})} \cdot \frac{p_x}{p_h q_{x1}} \right] \tag{v}$$

stand for the price elasticity of A's net supply of export goods, and

$$\lambda_x \left[\equiv -\frac{\delta q_{x1}}{\delta(S p_h^{-1})} \cdot \frac{S}{p_h q_{x2}} \right] \tag{vi}$$

stand for the elasticity, with respect to domestic expenditure, of A's demand for export goods.

With reference to equation (ii), let

$$\eta_a \left[\equiv -\frac{\delta q_{m1}}{\delta(p_m p_h^{-1})} \cdot \frac{p_m}{p_h q_{m1}} \right] \tag{vii}$$

stand for the (negative) price elasticity of A's net demand for import goods, and

$$\lambda_m \left[\equiv -\frac{\delta q_{m1}}{\delta(S p_h^{-1})} \cdot \frac{S}{p_h q_{m.}} \right] \tag{viii}$$

stand for the elasticity, with respect to domestic expenditure, of A's demand for import goods.

With reference to equation (iii), let

$$\epsilon_b \left[\equiv \frac{\delta q_m^{1}}{\delta(p_m c t^{-1})} \cdot \frac{p_m c}{t q_{m1}} \right] \tag{ix}$$

stand for the price elasticity of non-A's net supply of A's imports.

With reference to equation (iv), let

$$\eta_b \left[\equiv -\frac{\delta q_{x1}}{\delta(p_x c)} \cdot \frac{p_x c}{q_{x1}} \right] \tag{x}$$

stand for the (negative) price elasticity of non-A's net demand for A's exports.

Now p_h is assumed to be constant, i.e. $\dfrac{dp_h}{dc} = 0$.

Then, from equations (i), (v), and (vi),

$$\frac{dq_{x1}}{dc} = q_{x1} p_x^{-1} \epsilon_a \frac{dp_x}{dc} - q_{x2} S^{-1} \lambda_x \frac{dS}{dc}. \tag{xi}$$

From (iv) and (x),

$$\frac{dq_{x1}}{dc} = -q_{x1}p_x^{-1}c^{-1}\eta_b\left(c\frac{dp_x}{dc}+p_x\right). \tag{xii}$$

From (ii), (vii), and (viii),

$$\frac{dq_{m1}}{dc} = -q_{m1}p_m^{-1}\eta_a\frac{dp_m}{dc}+q_mS^{-1}\lambda_m\frac{dS}{dc}. \tag{xiii}$$

From (iii) and (ix),

$$\frac{dq_{m1}}{dc} = q_{m1}p_m^{-}c^{1-1}\epsilon_b\left(c\frac{dp_m}{dc}+p_m-p_mct^{-1}\frac{dt}{dc}\right). \tag{xiv}$$

From (xi) and xii),

$$-\frac{dp_x}{dc} = \frac{q_{x1}p_xc^{-1}\eta_b-q_{x2}p_xS^{-1}\lambda_x\dfrac{dS}{dc}}{q_{x1}(\epsilon_a+\eta_b)}. \tag{xv}$$

From (xiii) and (xiv),

$$-\frac{dp_m}{dc} = \frac{q_{m1}p_mc^{-1}\epsilon_b\left(1-t^{-1}\dfrac{dt}{dc}\right)-q_mp_mS^{-1}\lambda_m\dfrac{dS}{dc}}{q_{m1}(\epsilon_b+\eta_a)}. \tag{xvi}$$

Now, by definition,

$$\frac{dS}{dc} = \frac{d(p_mq_m)}{dc}+\frac{d(p_xq_{x2})}{dc}+\frac{d(p_hq_h)}{dc}. \tag{xvii}$$

It is assumed that any reserves drawn from the production of home trade goods will be employed elsewhere at equally valuable work, i.e. that

$$p_h\frac{dq_h}{dc} = -p_x\left(\frac{dq_{x1}}{dc}+\frac{dq_{x2}}{dc}\right)-p_m\frac{dq_{m2}}{dc}. \tag{xviii}$$

Then, since $\dfrac{dp_h}{dc} = 0$,

$$\frac{dS}{dc} = p_m\frac{dq_{m1}}{dc}-p_x\frac{dq_{x1}}{dc}+q_m\frac{dp_m}{dc}+q_{x2}\frac{dp_x}{dc}. \tag{xix}$$

233

From (xi), (xiii), and (xix),

$$\frac{dS}{dc} = \frac{S\left[\frac{dp_m}{dc}(q_m - q_{m1}\eta_a) + \frac{dp_x}{dc}(q_{x2} - q_{x1}\epsilon_a)\right]}{S - p_m\lambda_m q_m - p_x\lambda_x q_{x2}}. \tag{xx}$$

Let units be so chosen that, in the initial position, $p_x = p_m = c = 1$.

Then, from (xv) and (xx),

$$-\frac{dp_x}{dc} = \frac{q_{x1}\eta_b(S - q_m\lambda_m - q_{x2}\lambda_x) - q_{x2}\lambda_x(q_m - q_{m1}\eta_a)\dfrac{dp_m}{dc}}{q_{x1}(\epsilon_a - \eta_b)(S - q_m\lambda_m - q_{x2}\lambda_x) - q_{x2}\lambda_x(q_{x2} - q_{x1}\epsilon_a)} \tag{xxi}$$

and from (xvi) and (xx),

$$-\frac{dp_m}{dc} = \frac{q_{m1}\epsilon_b(S - q_m\lambda_m - q_{x2}\lambda_x)\left(1 - t^{-1}\dfrac{dt}{dc}\right) - q_m\lambda_m(q_{x2} - q_{x1}\epsilon_a)\dfrac{dp_x}{dc}}{q_{m1}(\epsilon_b + \eta_a)(S - q_m\lambda_m - q_{x1}\lambda_x) - q_m\lambda_m(q_m - q_{m2}\eta_a)}. \tag{xxii}$$

Let $f \equiv q_{x2}\lambda_x(q_m - q_{m1}\eta_a)$

$g \equiv q_{x1}\eta_b(S - q_m\lambda_m - q_{x2}\lambda_x)$

$h \equiv q_{x1}(\epsilon_a + \eta_b)(S - q_m\lambda_m - q_{x2}\lambda_x) - q_{x2}\lambda_x(q_{x2} - q_{m1}\epsilon_a)$

$f' \equiv q_m\lambda_m(q_{x2} - q_{x1}\epsilon_a)$

$g' \equiv q_{m1}\epsilon_b(S - q_m\lambda_m - q_{x2}\lambda_x)$

$h' \equiv q_{m1}(\epsilon_b + \eta_a)(S - q_m\lambda_m - q_{x2}\lambda_x) - q_m\lambda_m(q_m - q_{m1}\eta_a).$

Then, from (xxi),

$$-\frac{dp_x}{dc} = \frac{g - f\dfrac{dp_m}{dc}}{h} \tag{xxiii}$$

and from (xxii),

$$-\frac{dp_m}{dc} = \frac{g'\left(1 - t^{-1}\dfrac{dt}{dc}\right) - f'\dfrac{dp_x}{dc}}{h'}. \tag{xxiv}$$

Since t is constant, i.e. $\dfrac{dt}{dc} = 0$, $\therefore$ from (xxiii) and (xxiv),

$$-\frac{dp_x}{dc} = \frac{gh' - fg'}{hh' - ff'} \qquad \text{(xxv)}$$

and
$$-\frac{dp_m}{dc} = \frac{g'h + f'g}{hh' - ff'}. \qquad \text{(xxvi)}$$

Part II

(a) Let P stand for the cost of absorption.

Then, by definition, and since $\dfrac{dp_h}{dc} = 0$,

$$\frac{dP}{dc} = \frac{q_m \dfrac{dp_m}{dc} + q_{x2} \dfrac{dp_x}{dc}}{q_m + q_{x2} + q_h}. \qquad \text{(xxvii)}$$

(b) Let $B \; [\equiv c(q_{x1}p_x - t^{-1}q_{m1}p_m)]$ stand for A's balance of trade in non-A-currency, and $B_h \; [\equiv q_{x1}p_x - t^{-1}q_{m1}p_m]$ for A's balance of trade in A-currency.

Then, since $p_x = p_m = c = 1$, and $\dfrac{dt}{dc} = 0$,

$$\frac{dB_h}{dc} = q_{x1}\frac{dp_x}{dc} + \frac{dq_x}{dc} - t^{-1}q_{m1}\frac{dp_m}{dc} - t^{-1}\frac{dq_m}{dc}, \qquad \text{(xxviii)}$$

$\therefore$ from (xxii), (xxiv), and (xxviii),

$$\frac{dB_h}{dc} = q_{x1}(1 - \eta_b)\frac{dp_x}{dc} - q_{m1}t^{-1}(1 + \epsilon_b)\frac{dp_m}{dc} - q_{x1}\eta_b - t^{-1}q_{m1}\epsilon_b \qquad \text{(xxix)}$$

and
$$\frac{dB}{dc} = \frac{dB_h}{dc} + B_h. \qquad \text{(xxx)}$$

(c) Let $V \; [\equiv p_x q_x + p_m q_{m2} + p_h q_h]$ stand for the value of output.

Then, from (xviii), and since $\dfrac{dp_h}{dc} = 0$,

$$\frac{dV}{dc} = q_x \frac{dp_x}{dc} + q_{m2}\frac{dp_m}{dc}. \qquad \text{(xxxi)}$$

(d) Let $R\,[\equiv q_{m1}p_m(1-t^{-1})]$ stand for the excess of the home market over the world market value of imports.

Then, from (xiv), since $\dfrac{dt}{dc}=0$,

$$\frac{dR}{dc}=q_{m1}(1-t^{-1})\left[(\epsilon_b+1)\frac{dp_m}{dc}+\epsilon_b\right].\qquad\text{(xxxii)}$$

(e) Let S_r stand for real absorption.

Then, by definition, $\dfrac{dS_r}{dc}=p_m\dfrac{dq_m}{dc}+p_x\dfrac{dq_{x2}}{dc}+p_h\dfrac{dq_h}{dc}$,

$\therefore$ from (xviii),

$$\frac{dS_r}{dc}=\frac{dq_{m1}}{dc}-\frac{dq_{x1}}{dc}\qquad\text{(xxxiii)}$$

$\therefore$ from (xxix),

$$\frac{dS_r}{dc}=-\frac{dB_h}{dc}+\left(q_{x1}\frac{dp_x}{dc}-q_{m1}t^{-1}\frac{dp_m}{dc}\right)+(1-t^{-1})\frac{dq_{m1}}{dc}.\qquad\text{(xxxiv)}$$

(f) Let $Y[\equiv V+R]$ stand for national income and $Y_r\left[\equiv\dfrac{Y}{P}\right]$ for real national income. Now,

$$Y=B_h+S\qquad\text{(xxxv)}$$

$\therefore$
$$Y_r=\frac{B_h}{P}+S_r,$$

and
$$\frac{dY_r}{dc}=\frac{dS_r}{dc}+\frac{dB_h}{dc}-B_h\frac{dP}{dc}.\qquad\text{(xxxvi)}$$

From (xxx), since $c=1$,

$$\frac{dY_r}{dc}=\frac{dS_r}{dc}+\frac{dB}{dc}-B\left(1+\frac{dP}{dc}\right).\qquad\text{(xxxvii)}$$

From (xxxiv),

$$\frac{dY_r}{dc}=\left(q_{x1}\frac{dp_x}{dc}-q_{m1}t^{-1}\frac{dp_m}{dc}\right)+(1-t^{-1})\frac{dq_{m1}}{dc}-B\frac{dP}{dc}.\qquad\text{(xxxviii)}$$

Chapter 9

Domestic Financial Policies under Fixed and under Floating Exchange Rates*

The bearing of exchange rate systems on the relative effectiveness of monetary policy on the one hand, and of budgetary policy on the other, as techniques for influencing the level of monetary demand for domestic output, is not always kept in mind when such systems are compared. This essay attempts to show that the expansionary effect of a given increase in money supply will always be greater if the country has a floating exchange rate than if it has a fixed rate. By contrast, it is uncertain whether the expansionary effect on the demand for domestic output of a given increase in budgetary expenditure or a given reduction in tax rates will be greater or less with a floating than with a fixed rate. In all but extreme cases, the stimulus to monetary demand arising from an increase in money supply will be greater, relative to that arising from an expansionary change in budgetary policy, with a floating than with a fixed rate of exchange.

THE MODEL

Assume a simple Keynesian model[1] in which:

(a) taxation and private income after tax both vary directly with national income,

(b) private expenditure (on consumption and investment) varies directly with income after taxation[2] and inversely with the interest rate,

(c) the interest rate varies directly with the income-velocity of circulation of money (the ratio of national income to the stock of money),

* Reprinted, with editing, from International Monetary Fund *Staff Papers*, Vol. IX, No. 3, Nov. 1962.

[1] See Appendix (pp. 245–8) for a mathematical formulation.

[2] It is assumed that the private marginal propensity to spend will always be less than unity with respect to income before tax.

8

(d) the balance of trade (exports *less* imports of goods and services) varies inversely with domestic expenditure[3] and directly with the domestic currency value of foreign exchange, and

(e) the balance of payments on capital account varies directly with the rate of interest.

All magnitudes are expressed in domestic wage units, and wages are assumed to remain constant in domestic currency. No account is taken of any changes in the propensity to spend that may result from real income changes associated with changes in the terms of trade. No account is taken, initially, of the effect of exchange speculation on capital movements.

EFFECTS OF AN EXPANSIONARY SHIFT IN BUDGETARY POLICY
Compare, first, the effects of an expansionary shift in budgetary policy brought about by an increase in public expenditure, without any change in tax rates, under (a) a fixed exchange rate system and (b) a floating exchange rate system, respectively. (A decline in taxation, resulting from a reduction in tax rates, would have effects on expenditure, income, and the balance of payments similar to, though less powerful than, those resulting from an equal increase in public expenditure. No essential feature of the ensuing analysis would be altered if it had been concerned with the former rather than the latter type of budgetary expansion.)

Under fixed exchange rates, an increase in public expenditure will give rise to an increase in income which will be associated—if the economy was previously under-employed—with increases in employment and output.[4] The increase in expenditure will lead to a deterioration in the balance of payments on current account, owing, notably, to a rise in imports. The increase in expenditure and income will also enhance tax revenues, though not to such an extent as to equal the initial increase in public expenditure.[5]

[3] It is assumed that the marginal propensity for the balance of trade to decline as expenditure increases is less than unity.

[4] Since the marginal propensity to spend out of income is less than unity and since a fraction of each round of expenditure leaks abroad in additional net imports, the increase in income and expenditure will be limited, though possibly large. See Appendix, paragraphs 3 and 4.

[5] The rise in tax revenue could exceed the initial rise in government expenditure only if the marginal propensity to spend out of private income after tax were substantially greater than unity. See Appendix, paragraph 5.

In order to isolate the effect of a change in budgetary policy, it is necessary to assume that monetary policy remains, in some sense, unchanged. In this essay, that is taken to mean that the stock of money is held constant.[6] To keep the money stock constant while the increase in government expenditure is pushing up incomes will necessitate economy in the use of money which is possible only if the interest rate is raised or allowed to rise. The rise in interest, in turn, will result in (a) a check to the increase in expenditure and income, though some increase will remain,[7] and (b) a favourable shift in the balance of payments on capital account, i.e. a decline in capital exports and/or an increase in capital imports.

Since the increase in public expenditure provokes an unfavourable shift in the current balance and a favourable shift in the capital balance, it is uncertain whether the balance of payments as a whole will deteriorate or improve. It is the more likely to deteriorate, and the less likely to improve, the greater are the increase in the value of imports and the adverse effect on the value of exports as domestic expenditure increases, the less sensitive is the rate of interest to changes in money income and hence in the velocity of circulation, and the less sensitive are capital movements to changes in the rate of interest.[8]

To the extent that the increase in public expenditure gives rise to an improvement or a deterioration, respectively, in the balance of payments, the maintenance of a constant stock of money will call for a decline or an increase, respectively, in the rate of expansion of bank credit. More important is the fact that, if the policy of budgetary expansion results in a deterioration of the balance of payments, shortage of reserves may ultimately compel the authorities to abandon the policy and to renounce the associated expansion in income and employment.[9]

[6] The only clear-cut alternative would appear to be that of defining constancy of monetary policy as the maintenance of a constant rate of interest. In 'Flexible Exchange Rates and Employment Policy', *Canadian Journal of Economics and Political Science*, November 1961, R. A. Mundell has compared the effects of monetary policy (defined as interest policy), fiscal policy, and commercial policy in a flexible exchange rate system and a fixed exchange rate system, respectively.

[7] It is uncertain whether private expenditure, stimulated by the rise in income and depressed by the rise in interest, will increase or decrease. But expenditure as a whole, like income, will increase, except where income velocity is entirely inelastic. See Appendix, paragraphs 6 and 7. In this extreme case, not only expenditure but also income and the balance of trade will remain unchanged.

[8] See Appendix, paragraph 8.

[9] It is assumed not only that the exchange rate will remain fixed but that there will be no resort to restrictions on international transactions.

Suppose, now, that the increase in public expenditure takes place in a country where the balance of payments is kept in equilibrium through exchange rate adjustments. Then, if the parameters of our model—notably the sensitivity of capital movements to changes in the rate of interest—are such that a rise in public expenditure would have resulted, with a fixed exchange rate system, in a deterioration in the balance of payments, it will result, with a floating rate system, in a depreciation of the exchange rate, which will mitigate the deterioration in the trade balance. (This will, in general, be no more than a mitigation since some net deterioration of the trade balance, as compared with the situation before the rise in public expenditure, must remain to offset the improvement in the capital balance.) To the extent that the current balance is restored, there will be an increase—over and above that discussed above—in expenditure, income, and output. In other words, the stimulus to income, output, and employment resulting from a given increase in public expenditure will be greater with a floating exchange rate than with a fixed exchange rate.[10] If capital movements were entirely insensitive to the rise in the rate of interest, the exchange rate would depreciate to whatever extent was necessary to completely restore the trade balance, and the stimulus to income and output would be of the same order as would have occurred in a closed economy.

On the other hand, if a rise in public expenditure would, with a fixed exchange rate, have effected an improvement in the balance of payments, it will, with a floating rate, lead to an exchange appreciation; and, to the extent that appreciation intensifies the deterioration in the trade balance, the net stimulus to income, output, and employment will be less than in an open economy with a fixed rate.[11] At first sight, the case in which a rise in government expenditure produces an exchange appreciation would appear to be an academic *curiosum* without practical significance. However, as is shown in a paper prepared by Mr R. R. Rhomberg, expounding an econometric model of the Canadian economy,[12] the responsiveness of international capital movements to changes in interest rates, and the responsiveness of interest rates to changes in money national

[10] See Appendix, paragraph 10.
[11] Ibid.
[12] R. R. Rhomberg, 'A Model of the Canadian Economy Under Fixed and Fluctuating Exchange Rates', *Journal of Political Economy*, Vol. LXXII, No. 1, February 1964, pp. 1–31.

income, have probably been sufficiently great in that country over a large part of the post-war period, relative to the marginal propensity to import, for a rise in government expenditure at a constant money stock to have tended to produce just such a result.

It is of interest to note that, if the flow of capital between the country whose public expenditure increases and the outside world were infinitely elastic with respect to the interest rate, the appreciation of the exchange rate resulting from the inflow of capital would bring about a net deterioration in the current balance of payments large enough to offset completely the stimulating effect of the budget deterioration on national income. National income would not increase at all, and the interest rate would remain at the original level.[13]

EFFECTS OF AN INCREASE IN THE STOCK OF MONEY

Now, let us compare the effects on income, output, and employment of increasing the stock of money (a) with fixed exchange rates and (b) with floating exchange rates, respectively.

An increase in the stock of money will entail a decline in the velocity of circulation and lead to a reduction in the rate of interest which will stimulate an increase in private expenditure on investment and consumption, both directly and via the Keynesian multiplier. The rise in expenditure will be associated, as before, with a (smaller) increase in income and output[14] and a deterioration in the balance of payments on current account.[15] The rise in income will moderate the decline in the rate of interest but not to the point of eliminating it; otherwise, neither investment nor income could increase.[16] Since the monetary expansion, even after the rise in expenditure and income, lowers the interest rate, some deterioration will tend to occur in the balance of payments on capital account. In the case of a monetary expansion, therefore, by contrast with that of an increase in public

---

[13] See Appendix, paragraph 11. A high sensitivity of the interest rate to changes in velocity of circulation, i.e. a low elasticity of velocity with respect to the interest rate, while it makes for a favourable balance-of-payments response to government spending, and while it therefore tends to make the income response smaller under floating than under fixed exchange rates, also tends to reduce the magnitude of that response under both exchange systems. If the velocity of circulation was completely inelastic, a change in government expenditure would have no net effect on income under either exchange system.

[14] See Appendix, paragraph 12.

[15] See Appendix, paragraph 13.

[16] See Appendix, paragraph 14.

expenditure, a deterioration in the balance of payments as a whole is bound to occur in all circumstances. It follows that the monetary expansion, and the associated expansion of income and output, could only be sustained indefinitely to the extent that in their absence the balance of payments would have been favourable.

It is easy to see that a monetary expansion must always exercise a more powerful effect on income and output when there is a freely floating rate of exchange than when the exchange rate is fixed. The initial tendency towards an adverse shift in the balance of payments will cause a depreciation of the exchange rate to whatever extent may be necessary to keep external transactions as a whole in balance. The favourable influence of the exchange depreciation on the trade balance must come to outweigh the adverse influence of the increase in income to whatever extent may be necessary to produce a net improvement in that balance equal to the deterioration in the capital balance. The stimulus afforded by the depreciation to the trade balance will also act, both directly and via the multiplier, as a stimulus to income, raising it above the level that would have prevailed with a fixed exchange rate.[17]

The expansive effect of a given increase in the stock of money under the floating exchange rate system will be the greater, the greater the responsiveness of the international capital flow to movements in the rate of interest. If there were no responsiveness whatever, the exchange rate would depreciate to the point at which, despite the monetary expansion, no change occurred in the current balance of payments. Income would expand to the same extent as in a closed economy. On the other hand, if the capital flow were infinitely elastic with respect to the interest rate, the exchange rate would depreciate to the point at which the balance of trade became so favourable, and income increased so much, that the rate of interest remained at its original level. This implies that money income would increase by the same percentage as the stock of money.[18]

RELATIVE EFFECTS OF THE TWO KINDS OF FINANCIAL POLICY
It remains to show that the effect on income and output of a given monetary expansion relative to that of a given budgetary expansion

[17] See Appendix, paragraphs 15 and 16. However, in the extreme case where velocity of circulation is completely inelastic, money income will rise proportionately to the money stock under either exchange system. See Appendix, paragraph 17.
[18] See Appendix, paragraph 18.

will never be less, and will generally be greater, under a floating exchange rate than under a fixed rate, even where budgetary expansion has a tendency to cause a depreciation of the exchange value of the currency.[19] The simplest way to demonstrate this is to compare an increase in the monetary stock (Policy A) and an increase in public expenditure (Policy B) such that, under a fixed exchange rate, the two policies have equal effects in the aggregate on income, output, and employment, and to show that, under a floating rate, the effect of Policy A will never be less, and will in general be greater, than that of Policy B.

Since we have supposed that under a fixed exchange rate the two policies have the same aggregate effect on income and output, they will bring about approximately the same adverse shift in the balance of trade.[20] Since, with incomes the same under the two policies, the money stock will be greater and the velocity of circulation less under Policy A than under Policy B, the rate of interest will be less under the former than under the latter policy. If capital movements were totally insensitive to changes in the interest rate, the two policies would, under a fixed exchange rate, have the same effects on the balance of payments as a whole; and under a floating rate, they would require an equal exchange depreciation to restore external equilibrium. The consequent restoration of the trade balance and the associated further stimulus to income would be the same for the two policies. However, if capital movements respond in any degree to interest changes, the two policies will have different effects. Since Policy A reduces, and Policy B raises, the rate of interest, Policy A under a fixed exchange rate will occasion a more unfavourable capital balance than Policy B. It follows that under a floating rate, Policy A will require, to restore payments equilibrium, a deeper exchange depreciation, and will consequently bring about a greater improvement in the trade balance, and a greater stimulus to income and output, than Policy B.[21] The superiority of Policy A over Policy B as a means of increasing income and output depends notably, as we have seen, on the sensitivity of international capital

---

[19] To put the same thing in other words, the effect under a floating rate relative to the effect under a fixed rate will never be greater, and will generally be less, for budgetary expansion than for monetary expansion.

[20] We have to neglect, as unknown, any effects on trade of the difference in the composition of expenditure under the two policies.

[21] See Appendix, paragraph 19.

movements to changes in the rate of interest. At zero sensitivity, there is nothing to choose between the two policies. If the sensitivity is infinite, the level of income resulting from Policy A will exceed that resulting from Policy B in much the same proportion as the money stock under A exceeds that under B.

The nature of the exchange regime has an important bearing not only on the relative effectiveness in influencing income and output of the two types of financial policy—monetary policy and budgetary policy—but also on their relative practicability or sustainability. Thus, under a fixed exchange rate—except to the extent that the external accounts were originally in surplus—monetary expansion can be sustained only as long as reserves hold out, while budgetary expansion, if capital movements are sufficiently sensitive to interest rates, may be sustained indefinitely.[22] Under a floating exchange rate, on the other hand, not only is monetary expansion, while it lasts, likely to generate more additional income than budgetary expansion, relative to what would happen under a fixed exchange rate, but both types of policies can be sustained indefinitely, so far as the balance-of-payments situation is concerned.

THE EXCHANGE SPECULATIVE ELEMENT IN CAPITAL MOVEMENTS

The foregoing argument has generally assumed the absence of exchange speculation. Under a floating exchange rate, the influence of exchange speculation on the effectiveness of fiscal and monetary policies will vary according to whether the speculation is equilibrating or disequilibrating. If it is equilibrating—as was generally the case, for example, in Canada in the 1950s—it will tend to mitigate the exchange rate variations resulting from variations in internal financial policy, whether that policy is budgetary or monetary in character. However, since the greater relative effectiveness which a floating rate gives to monetary policy, compared with budgetary

---

[22] It should be noted, however, that the responsiveness of capital movements to interest rate changes is made up of two components: a relocation of existing capital and a shift in the location of the placement of new savings. Since the former component is non-recurrent and the latter recurrent in character, it is probable that the sensitivity of capital movements to interest changes will be greater in the short run than in the long run. Consequently, the difference between the two policies with respect to effectiveness and sustainability is also likely to be less in the long run than in the short.

policy, is attributable to the stronger influence that the former exercises on exchange rates, it is to be expected that equilibrating speculation, by damping down exchange rate effects, will tend to reduce the difference in effectiveness between the two kinds of policy. Disequilibrating speculation on the other hand, by exaggerating exchange rate variations, will tend to accentuate this difference in effectiveness.[23]

Appendix

1. Let Y stand for national income,
   T for taxation,
   N for private income,
   X for private expenditure,
   S for public expenditure,
   Z for total expenditure,
   B for exports *less* imports,
   M for stock of money,
   V for income velocity,
   R for rate of interest,
   C for net capital import, and
   F for domestic-currency value of foreign currency.

2. Then

$$Y \equiv X + S + B.$$
$$Z \equiv X + S.$$
$$V \equiv \frac{Y}{M}.$$
$$N \equiv Y - T.$$

$T = T(Y).$ $\qquad$ $1 > T_y > 0.$

$X = X(N,R).$ $\qquad$ $X_r < 0,$ $\qquad$ $1 > X_n(1 - T_y) > 0.$

$R = R(V).$ $\qquad$ $R_v > 0.$

$B = B(Z,F).$ $\qquad$ $1 > -B_z > 0.$ $\qquad$ $B_f > 0.$

$C = C(R).$

---

[23] Exchange speculation has a bearing not only on the relative effectiveness but also on the practicability and sustainability of the two policies. Under exchange rates that are fixed and are expected to remain so, exchange speculation would be absent. But if confidence in the fixed rate were less than complete, the fear of arousing disequilibrating movements of capital would tend to limit the magnitude and duration of the expansionary financial policies, particularly of monetary policy, the effect of which on the balance of payments is in any case the more adverse than that of budgetary policy.

3. Let $\left(\dfrac{dY}{dS}\right)_{00}$ signify $\dfrac{dY}{dS}$ under fixed exchange rates when $dF = 0$ and $dM = 0$,

and $\left(\dfrac{dR}{dS}\right)_{00}$, $\left(\dfrac{dT}{dS}\right)_{00}$, $\left(\dfrac{dC}{dS}\right)_{00}$, $\left(\dfrac{dB}{dS}\right)_{00}$, $\left(\dfrac{dC}{dR}\right)_{00}$, $\left(\dfrac{dB}{dR}\right)_{00}$

be analogously defined.

Then $\left(\dfrac{dY}{dS}\right)_{00} = \dfrac{1 + B_z}{1 - (1 + B_z)\left[X_n(1 - T_y) + \dfrac{X_r R_v}{M}\right]}.$

4. Since $1 > -B_z > 0,$
$\qquad 1 > X_n(1 - T_y) > 0,$
and $\quad X_r < 0,$

$\therefore \left(\dfrac{dY}{dS}\right)_{00} > 0.$

5. For the same reasons,

$\left(\dfrac{dT}{dS}\right)_{00} = \dfrac{T_y(1 + B_z)}{1 - (1 + B_z)\left[X_n(1 - T_y) + \dfrac{X_r R_v}{M}\right]} < 1.$

6. $\left(\dfrac{dX}{dS}\right)_{00} = \dfrac{1}{\dfrac{1}{(1 + B_z)\left(X_n(1 - T_y) + \dfrac{X_r R_v}{M}\right)} - 1} \gtrless 0,$

as $X_n(1 - T_y) + \dfrac{X_r R_v}{M} \gtrless 0.$

7. $\left(\dfrac{dZ}{dS}\right)_{00} = \dfrac{1}{1 - (1 + B_z) X_n(1 - T_y) + \dfrac{X_r R_v}{M}} > 0.$

8. $\left(\dfrac{dR}{dS}\right)_{00} = \dfrac{R_v}{M}\left(\dfrac{dY}{dS}\right)_{00} > 0.$

$\left(\dfrac{dC}{dS}\right)_{00} + \left(\dfrac{dB}{dS}\right)_{00} = \left(\dfrac{dR}{dS}\right)_{00}\left[\left(\dfrac{dC}{dR}\right)_{00} + \left(\dfrac{dB}{dR}\right)_{00}\right]$

$$= C_r + \frac{MB_z}{R_v(1+B_z)} \gtrless 0,$$

as $\dfrac{C_r R_y}{M} \gtrless \dfrac{-B_z}{1+B_z}$.

9. Let $\left(\dfrac{dY}{dS}\right)_{10}$ signify $\dfrac{dY}{dS}$ under floating exchange rates, when $dB + dC = 0$ and $dM = 0$.

Then $\left(\dfrac{dY}{dS}\right)_{10} = \dfrac{1}{1 - X_n(1-T_y) - (X_r - C_r)\dfrac{R_v}{M}} > 0.$

10. $\left(\dfrac{dY}{dS}\right)_{10} \gtrless \left(\dfrac{dY}{dS}\right)_{00}$ as $\dfrac{-B_z}{1+B_z} \gtrless \dfrac{C_r R_v}{M},$

i.e. as $\left(\dfrac{dC}{dS}\right)_{00} + \left(\dfrac{dB}{dS}\right)_{00} \lessgtr 0.$

11. As $C_r \to \infty$,

$$\left(\dfrac{dY}{dS}\right)_{01} \to \dfrac{1}{\infty} \to 0.$$

12. Let $\left(\dfrac{dY}{dM}\right)_{01} = \dfrac{dY}{dM}$ at fixed exchange rates when $dF = 0$ and $dS = 0,$

and $\left(\dfrac{dR}{dM}\right)_{01}, \left(\dfrac{dC}{dM}\right)_{01}, \left(\dfrac{dB}{dM}\right)_{01}$ be analogously defined.

$$\left(\dfrac{dY}{dM}\right)_{01} = \dfrac{-X_r R_v Y}{M^2}\left[\dfrac{1}{\dfrac{1}{B_z+1} - X_n(1-T_y) - \dfrac{X_r R_v}{M}}\right].$$

13. $\left(\dfrac{dB}{dM}\right)_{01} + \left(\dfrac{dC}{dM}\right)_{01} = \dfrac{B_z}{1+B_z}\left(\dfrac{dY}{dM}\right)_{01} + C_r\left(\dfrac{dR}{dM}\right)_{01} < 0.$

14. $\left(\dfrac{dR}{dM}\right)_{01} = \dfrac{-R_v Y}{M^2}\left[\dfrac{1 - X_n(B_z+1)(1-T_y)}{1 - (B_z+1)X_n(1-T_y) + \dfrac{X_r R_v}{M}}\right] < 0.$

247

15. Let $\left(\dfrac{dY}{dM}\right)_{11} = \dfrac{dY}{dM}$ under floating exchange rates, when

$dB + dC = 0$ and $dS = 0$.

Then

$$\left(\frac{dY}{dM}\right)_{11} = \frac{R_v Y(C_r - X_r)}{M^2}\left[\frac{1}{1 - X_n(1 - T_y) + \dfrac{R_v(C_r - X_r)}{M}}\right] > 0.$$

16. $\left(\dfrac{dY}{dM}\right)_{11} - \left(\dfrac{dY}{dM}\right)_{01}$

$$= \frac{R_v Y}{M^2}\left[\frac{C_r - X_r}{1 - X_n(1 - T_y) + \dfrac{R_v}{M}(C_r - X_r)} + \frac{X_r}{\dfrac{1}{B_z + 1} - X_n(1 - T_y) - \dfrac{X_r R_v}{M}}\right]$$

$> 0.$

17. As $R_v \to \infty$,

$$\left(\frac{dY}{dM}\right)_{01} \to \frac{Y}{M}$$

and $\left(\dfrac{dY}{dM}\right)_{11} \to \dfrac{Y}{M}.$

18. As $C_r \to \infty$,

$$\left(\frac{dY}{dM}\right)_{11} \to \frac{C_r R_v Y}{M C_r R_v} = \frac{Y}{M}.$$

19. Let $k = \dfrac{\left(\dfrac{dY}{dS}\right)_{00}}{\left(\dfrac{dY}{dM}\right)_{01}} = \dfrac{M^2}{-X_r R_v Y}.$

Then $\dfrac{\left(\dfrac{dY}{dS}\right)_{10}}{\left(\dfrac{dY}{dM}\right)_{11}} = \dfrac{M^2}{(C_r - X_r)R_v Y} < k,$

unless $X_r = -\infty$ or $R_v = \infty$.

Chapter 10
Official Intervention on the Forward Exchange Market*

Interest in the problems of official intervention in forward exchange markets has received impetus from recent changes of practice on the part of the U.S. monetary authorities. In March 1961, the U.S. Treasury intervened for the first time on the exchange markets in support of the forward dollar; and since February 1962, the Federal Reserve System has concluded a number of swap arrangements with other central banks.[1] In view of these developments, it appears timely to consider what, in theory, are the short-run and long-run effects of official transactions in forward exchange, and under what circumstances such transactions are likely to serve a useful purpose. Tentative answers are given in this essay to such questions as the following: Should intervention be 'limited' in extent and/or duration, and, if so, in what sense, and why? In what sort of payments situation is official support of the forward exchange rate appropriate? Need it be confined to meeting 'speculative' attacks?

The approach in this essay is a simplified one.[2] The purpose is to provide a straightforward account of the theory of intervention and to use it to discuss the problems just raised. To do this, a new classification of the forces determining the forward rate is developed: the rate must be such as to equalize the Net Speculative Position (defined as the sum of the net assets—spot or forward—of residents of country A in other currencies *less* the sum of the net assets—spot

---

* Reprinted, with slight amendment, from the paper of the same name by J. Marcus Fleming and Robert A. Mundell, International Monetary Fund *Staff Papers*, Vol. XI, No. 1, March 1964.

[1] Charles A. Coombs, 'Treasury and Federal Reserve Foreign Exchange Operations', *Federal Reserve Bulletin*, September 1963, pp. 1216–23, and Board of Governors of the Federal Reserve System, Press Release, October 31, 1963.

[2] For a mathematical exposition of the interrelationships determining forward exchange rates under more general assumptions, see S. C. Tsiang, 'The Theory of Forward Exchange and Effects of Government Intervention on the Forward Exchange Market', *Staff Papers*, Vol. VII, 1959–60, pp. 75–106. See also William H. White, 'Interest Rate Differences, Forward Exchange Mechanism, and Scope for Short-term Capital Movements', *Staff Papers*, Vol. X, 1963, pp. 485–503.

or forward—of residents of other countries in A's currency) and the Net Loan Position (defined as the sum of the net lending of residents of A to residents of other countries). This presentation is believed to have certain expositional merits.

DETERMINATION OF EQUILIBRIUM

To simplify the analysis, complications arising from the multiplicity of foreign currencies are ignored: official intervention is thought of as taking place on the forward market for the domestic currency versus 'foreign currencies in general', which, for convenience, will generally be referred to as though they constituted a single currency.

It is further assumed, initially, that spot rates are rigidly fixed. Finally, the complications arising from the variety of maturity dates of forward exchange contracts are left out of account; all forward contracts are treated as if they had the same maturity, and all forward rates as if they were only a single rate.

The forward exchange market may be conveniently treated in terms of stocks rather than of flows; that is, the forward exchange rate is taken as reconciling the desires of market participants with respect to the holding—rather than the changing—of forward exchange positions. In every forward exchange contract, each of the contracting parties holds a forward asset in one currency and a forward liability in another currency. Forward exchange positions are forward positions (assets or liabilities) in currencies other than that of the country of which the holder is a resident. Spot exchange positions are assets or liabilities, other than forward positions, in currencies other than that of a country of which the holder is a resident.

If a resident of country A lends to a resident of country non-A, either the A resident acquires an asset in non-A-currency, or the non-A resident acquires a liability in A-currency; in either case, there will not only be an increase in the net lending of the A resident to the non-A resident but also an increase in the net exchange position of the A resident *less* the net exchange position of the non-A resident. On the other hand, if an A resident concludes a forward exchange contract with a non-A resident, the net forward exchange position (positive or negative) acquired by the A resident in non-A-currency will be balanced by an equal net forward exchange position acquired by the non-A resident in A-currency; there will not only be no change in net lending between residents of the two areas, but also no change in the net exchange position of A residents *less* the net exchange position of non-A residents. It follows that the sum of the net assets (spot or forward) of A residents in non-A-currency *less* the sum of the net assets (spot or forward) of non-A residents in A-currency, which may be termed the Net Speculative Position (NSP) of country A, is necessarily equal to the sum of the net lending of A residents to non-A residents, which may be termed the Net Loan Position (NLP) of country A. It is convenient to exclude foreign exchange held in official reserves both from the NSP and from the NLP of the reserve-holding country, but neither from the NSP nor the NLP of the country whose currency is held.

While these Net Positions are necessarily equal *ex post*, they are not necessarily equal *ex ante*. The desire to lend abroad is not necessarily matched individually or collectively by the desire to hold a foreign currency. A decision to borrow or lend abroad is, in principle at least, different from a decision to undertake an exchange risk. Let us assume that, where neither the lender nor the borrower wishes to bear the foreign exchange risk that is necessarily involved in the loan, the party that takes the risk in the first instance seeks to cover it by concluding a forward exchange contract. In this event, there will be a net demand in the forward market for A-currency in terms of non-A-currency, or vice versa, and the forward exchange rate will move until the equilibrium of the market is restored and the desired NSP equals the desired NLP.[3]

The manner in which, given the spot exchange rate, the forward exchange rate serves to bring about equality between the desired NSP and the desired NLP is illustrated in Figure 10.1. In that figure, the balance of claims (which can be regarded, *ex post*, either as the NLP or the NSP) is measured on the horizontal axis, while the forward exchange rate is measured on the vertical axis. Both NLP and NSP are considered from the standpoint of country A. The forward rate represents the forward price of A-currency in terms of non-A-currency. The curves are drawn on the assumption that the spot rate of exchange, the anticipated future spot rates of exchange, and

---

[3] A change in the forward exchange rate is not, in fact, the only way in which an *ex ante* disequilibrium between NSP and NLP manifests itself. In the absence of a forward exchange market, such a disequilibrium would manifest itself in a change in the interest rate at which A residents lend to non-A residents (or vice-versa) in A-currency, compared with that at which they lend in non-A-currency.

the rates of interest in A and non-A are not affected by changes in the forward exchange rate.

As the diagram shows, country A's NLP slopes negatively, and its NSP positively, with respect to the forward price of its currency. (Strictly speaking, while the NSP varies directly with the outright forward rate, the NLP varies inversely with the forward premium, i.e. the excess of the forward value of A's currency over its spot value. But with the spot exchange rate fixed, this is equivalent to saying that it varies, inversely, with the forward rate.) It is easy to

FIGURE 10.1

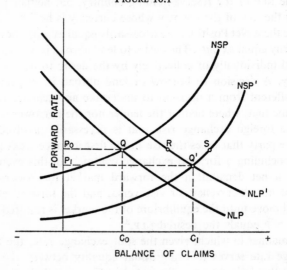

BALANCE OF CLAIMS

see why the NLP schedule, as a function of the forward rate, slopes negatively. The higher the forward rate (and hence the greater the forward premium on A-currency), the cheaper it is for non-A lenders or A borrowers (whoever is bearing the exchange risk) to cover that exchange risk by a forward contract. The higher the forward rate, the greater will be the incentive for non-A residents to lend to A residents on a covered basis, and the amount of such lending will tend to increase. For analogous reasons, the cost of covered lending from A residents to non-A residents will increase, and the amount of such lending will tend to diminish. Moreover, the changes in loan positions need not take the form of changes in

252

covered exchange positions; they may take the form of switches between spot positions (positive or negative) and forward positions of the same sign. For example, a rise in the forward exchange rate will tend to induce A residents with positive spot positions in non-A-currency to switch to forward positions, and non-A residents with positive forward positions in A-currency to switch to spot positions.

There is another way in which a rise in the forward rate will reduce the NLP. Such a rise will lead to an increase in the cost of covering, and hedging, the foreign exchange risk involved in A's exports and a decline in the cost of covering, and hedging, the risk involved in A's imports. (We use the term 'covering' to mean offsetting by a forward contract the exchange risk involved in any trade credit that extends over the period from the date when owner-ship passes to the date of payment; we use 'hedging' to mean a similar offsetting of the exchange risk involved in the export contract over the period from the date of contract to the date when ownership passes.) In so far as this results in a decline in A's exports and a rise in A's imports, which in turn involves a decline in A's covered trade credit to non-A and a rise in non-A's covered trade credit to A, there will be a decline in the NLP other than that already taken into account.

The NSP schedule normally has a positive slope. On the assumption that changes in the forward rate have no effect on expectations regarding future spot rates, a rise in the forward rate (i.e. in the forward price of A-currency in terms of non-A-currency) will induce an increase in the net positions of A residents in non-A-currency and a decline in the net positions of non-A residents in A-currency. Residents of A will have an incentive to increase their forward positions in non-A-currency, whether or not they have negative spot positions in non-A-currency which they can cover by so doing; analogously, non-A residents will reduce their forward holdings of A-currency even though this may involve leaving spot positions uncovered or other risks unhedged. To some extent, as we have seen, these shifts in forward positions will be matched by corres-ponding shifts in the opposite direction in spot positions. Spot positions, however, involving as they do the opportunity cost of tying up funds in a particular use, are not perfect substitutes for forward positions, and a change in the forward rate, i.e. in the price of forward positions, will involve a net change in the sum of spot and forward positions taken together, i.e. a change in the NSP.

In so far as the rise in the forward rate worsens the trade balance, it is likely not merely, as we have seen, to reduce the NLP by reducing the balance of covered trade credits but also to raise the NSP by reducing the hedging of the currency risks associated with export contracts (prior to the time of actual export) and increasing the hedging of currency risks associated with import contracts.

Equilibrium between the NSP and the NLP is determined at the point Q, common to both schedules, where the market is willing to maintain the Net Speculative Position implied by the desired Net Loan Position. The equilibrium point determines both the equilibrium forward rate (P_0) and the equilibrium balance of claims (C_0).

Suppose now that there is a rise in the expected exchange value of foreign currencies in terms of the domestic currency. This will lead to a tendency toward an uncovered capital movement, expressed in a shift of both the NSP and the NLP schedules to the right by an equal amount (assumed to be QR). But, in addition, there will be a tendency toward increased speculation in the forward market, expressed in a further shift in the NSP schedule which has no counterpart in the NLP schedule. At the original forward rate (P_0) the increase in spot speculation is QR and the increase in forward speculation RS. The NLP line, therefore, shifts to the right, by QR, to NLP', while the NSP line shifts to the right, by $QR + RS = QS$, to NSP'. At the original forward rate, therefore, there is an excess of the NSP over the NLP, which is equivalent to an excess supply of the domestic currency for forward delivery. The forward exchange rate then falls until the NSP is reduced and the NLP is increased to the point where the two are again equal. The new equilibrium is at Q', where the new schedules intersect. At Q', the forward rate (P_1) is lower, and the balance of claims of residents on nonresidents (C_1) has increased.

The results of changes in other variables are easily discovered. An increase in interest rates at home relative to those abroad will tend to stimulate an inward capital movement because of the higher return both on a covered and on an uncovered basis. The tendency towards an uncovered capital movement will be reflected in a shift of both the NLP and the NSP curves by equal amounts, but the tendency to a shift in covered arbitrage will involve a further shift of the NLP schedule to the left. The result will be a decline both in the forward exchange rate and in the balance of claims.

COUNTERPART OF INTERVENTION

Official intervention in the forward exchange market can be analysed by regarding the authorities either as part of the market or as distinct from it. If the NSP is defined exclusive of official intervention, then the new equilibrium requires, not equality of the NSP and NLP, but a difference between the two equal to the amount of the intervention itself. On the other hand, if the government position is included as part of the market, government purchases or sales of forward currency represent a change in speculation. We shall adopt the latter alternative.

Let us continue to assume, initially, that neither the official intervention itself nor the associated change in the forward rate has any effect on expectations with regard to the future course of the exchange rate. Now consider the effect of forward intervention by A's government in support of A's currency, i.e. a purchase of A's currency forward. The NSP schedule as a whole will move to the left by the amount of the official intervention; the slope of that schedule will not alter, nor will the NLP schedule be affected in any way. The forward purchases of domestic currency by the authorities will create an excess demand for A's currency, i.e. a tendency for the NSP to fall short of the NLP, which can be relieved only by an increase in price. The forward rate will therefore rise until the NLP has fallen and the NSP has risen, along their respective schedules, sufficiently to restore equality between the two. To put it another way, the rate must rise until the private market is willing to supply (against foreign currency) the extra amount of forward domestic currency demanded by the authorities.

The effect of the intervention is illustrated by Figure 10.2. Starting from an initial equilibrium at Q, government intervention to the amount $G = SQ$ (in the form of forward sales of foreign currency in exchange for domestic currency) gives rise to a new NSP curve (NSP') which yields a new equilibrium at Q'. The counterpart of the official intervention can then be seen to be ST and TQ, the former representing an increase in private net speculation against (or a reduction in private net speculation in favour of) the domestic currency, and the latter a reduction in net claims (or an increase in net liabilities) of domestic residents *vis-à-vis* residents abroad.

FIGURE 10.2

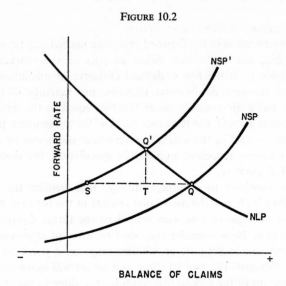

BALANCE OF CLAIMS

It will be noticed that the inflow of funds arising from the intervention is necessarily less than the amount of the intervention. Moreover, the more inelastic is the NLP line (i.e. the less the international mobility of funds) and the more elastic is the NSP line (i.e. the more assured are people's anticipations about future exchange rates and the greater is their willingness to speculate on them), the less will be the ratio of the inflow of funds to the amount of the intervention.[4]

---

[4] The ratio of the funds attracted to the amount of the intervention is uniquely determined by the elasticities of the NLP and NSP schedules. Specifically, the change in claims (C) as a fraction of a (small) government intervention (G) in support of the home currency is as follows:

$$\frac{C}{G} = \frac{-\eta_L}{\eta_L - \eta_S}$$

where η_L and η_S are, respectively, the elasticities of the NLP and NSP schedules. Since $\eta_S > 0$ and $\eta_L < 0$, an increase in G (intervention in support of the home currency) reduces C. But it is easily seen that the reduction in the balance of claims is always less than the amount of the intervention; $\frac{C}{G}$ is always a (negative) fraction.

256

'SWAP' TRANSACTIONS AND EXTRA-MARKET TRANSACTIONS

We have dealt with official intervention in the forward exchange market as if it took the form exclusively of outright forward transactions unaccompanied by any spot transaction. In fact, forward intervention may take the form of 'swap' transactions which involve simultaneous operation in the spot and forward markets so as to leave the Net Speculative Position of the authorities unchanged. Thus, a forward sale of foreign (and a forward purchase of domestic) currency would be accompanied by a spot purchase of foreign (and a spot sale of domestic) currency.

As long as we adhere to the assumption that spot exchange rates are rigidly fixed, the 'spot' element of the swap will have no effect on the forward rate, which will be affected, in the manner described above, exclusively by the forward element in the transaction. The effect of the 'spot' element will depend on the mechanism through which the spot rate is held constant. For example, assume that the spot rate for A-currency in terms of non-A-currencies is held constant by direct intervention of the authorities in A on the foreign exchange market. If these authorities were to undertake a swap transaction, selling non-A-currencies forward and buying them spot, they would immediately be obliged, in order to stabilize the rate, to sell these currencies spot for A-currency, thus rendering the spot element in the swap null and void. This is what would normally happen in the case of 'swap' transactions by the monetary authorities of countries other than the United States. In the special case of the United States, however, it is more realistic to assume that the spot rate is held constant by the foreign authorities who, however, could call upon the U.S. authorities to convert dollars into gold at a fixed rate. The effect of the U.S. spot purchase of foreign currencies then would be partly to reduce U.S. official holdings of gold and partly to increase foreign official holdings of dollars. It would, however, have no effect either on the forward rate or on the balance of payments on official settlements account. These would be affected exclusively by the forward sale.

Official swap transactions are frequently undertaken not on the open market but by direct arrangement with foreign monetary authorities or with commercial banks. Such operations are likely to differ from swaps on the open market in that they exercise a greater

257

influence on the Net Loan Position, and little, if any, influence on the forward rate or on the private Net Speculative Position.

In the case of direct intercentral bank or intergovernmental transactions where the foreign authorities refrain from passing on the swap to commercial banks or other private parties, there is no reason why the forward rate or the private Net Speculative Position should be influenced at all. Suppose that the authorities of country A sell foreign currencies forward and buy them spot through transactions with the authorities of other countries. The loan position of the foreign authorities will be affected directly by the transaction, and the NLP curve will shift to the left by an amount equal to the intervention by the authorities in country A. The speculative position of the foreign authorities will not be directly affected by the transaction itself, but the NSP curve will shift to the left by the same amount as the NLP curve because of the change in the speculative position of the authorities in A. Indirectly, however, a part of the inflow of official funds brought about by the transaction may be offset if the foreign authorities are induced by the swap transaction to reduce their uncovered reserve holdings in A-currency below the level at which they would otherwise have maintained them.

Even if the foreign authorities pass on the swap to their commercial banks by direct negotiation at a forward rate (and premium over spot) more favourable than the rate prevailing in the market, they may be able to ensure that the balances in A-currency thus acquired by the commercial banks on a covered basis are largely additional to those they would otherwise have held and covered at the market rate. If they were completely 'additional', there would be a leftward shift in A's NLP curve precisely equal to the amount of the swaps. However, unless the foreign banks would otherwise have held no A-currency on a covered basis, it is unlikely that this condition would be fulfilled and it would be difficult to avoid some decline in the amount of these holdings covered through the market. In this event the leftward shift in the NLP curve will be less than that of the NSP curve. If the foreign commercial banks make no addition to their holdings of A-currency and in effect pass on the swaps to the market —as they may have a pecuniary incentive to do—there will be no leftward shift of the NLP curve at all.

BALANCE-OF-PAYMENTS EFFECTS

In considering the effects on the balance of payments of official intervention of the sort under discussion, we must distinguish non-recurrent ('stock') effects from continuous ('flow') effects. Both types take time—say, a number of months—to manifest themselves fully, a fact which tends to blur the distinction between them. For sharpness of analysis, however, we shall assume that the 'stock' effects occur almost instantaneously.

The principal kinds of 'stock' effects arise from once-for-all readjustments of asset and liability positions:

(a) To the extent that the official sales of forward exchange evoke a fall in the NLP, i.e. an inflow of foreign funds or a repatriation of domestic funds on a covered basis, there will be, at fixed exchange rates, a corresponding rise in gross reserves.

(b) On the other hand, the forward exchange liabilities acquired by the authorities may themselves be regarded as weakening the external liquidity of the country, as would any other short-term liability to foreign holders.

Now, as we have seen, in the case of market intervention the increase in official forward exchange liabilities must always exceed the induced net inward capital movement by an amount equal to the induced increase in private (forward) exchange speculation. The increase in gross reserves will therefore fall short of the increase in official forward exchange liabilities. Under our present assumption of fixed speculative anticipation, however, this fact has no importance from the standpoint of external liquidity. There would be an enhanced danger of a future drain on reserves only to the extent that there was an enhanced danger of a future outflow of funds on a covered basis. This danger, in turn, would arise only with respect to that part of the counterpart of the official intervention which consisted in an influx of funds on a covered basis, i.e. a decline in the NLP; and that part of the counterpart has been fully matched by an increase in reserves.

Moreover, on the assumption that the authorities are willing to renew their forward liabilities on maturity, such a withdrawal of funds on a covered basis would be likely to occur only if there were a loss of confidence in the willingness or ability of the authorities to fulfil these renewed contracts—a situation that seems remote.

259

For the reasons mentioned above, the portion of the official forward exchange liabilities that serves as counterpart to the adverse forward speculation induced by the rise in the forward exchange value of the domestic currency gives rise to little or no objective liquidity risk. If the proportions in which the official intervention evoked an addition to the unofficial Net Speculative Position and a diminution in the Net Loan Position, respectively, were exactly known, the proportion of official forward liabilities taken up by adverse speculation could simply be ignored. Since, however, the proportion is not exactly known, the authorities are likely to regard their reserve needs as enhanced by some fraction of their forward liabilities, irrespective of whether these in fact correspond to additional unofficial speculation or to inward capital movements. It therefore becomes important that the proportion of induced capital movement to induced speculation should, in fact, be as large as possible.

The 'recurrent' or 'flow' effects on the balance of payments of official support of the domestic currency in the forward market fall into three main categories:

(1) To the extent that domestic and foreign merchants carrying on the foreign trade of the country concerned are accustomed to cover on the forward market the exchange risks incidental to such trade, the appreciation of the forward value of the currency resulting from official support will tend to raise the price of exports to the foreign importer and lower the price of imports to the domestic importer. This will bring about a fall in exports and a rise in imports which, with normal foreign trade elasticities, will involve a deterioration in the balance of payments on current account.

(2) To the extent that the support of the forward exchange rate involves a decline in the NLP—and on the assumption that interest rates at home and abroad are kept constant—there will be a decline in receipt of interest from abroad and/or an increase in payments of interest to foreigners.

(3) The fact that forward exchange rates diverge from the spot rates as they ultimately turn out to be at the date of maturity of the forward contracts gives rise to profits and losses, some of which may enter into the balance of payments. To the extent that the sale of forward exchange by the authorities evokes additional purchases—whether by way of speculation or covered interest arbitrage—on the

part of foreigners, rather than residents, the balance of payments will show a gain or a loss, depending on whether the forward value of the domestic currency at the supported level is below or above the spot value. Again if, apart from the official purchases, residents have a positive (negative) net position in foreign currencies on forward account,[5] the rise in the forward value of the domestic currency will bring about an improvement (deterioration) in the balance of payments on current account equal to the extent of the appreciation (expressed as an annual rate) *times* the net forward position.

Of the adverse effects on the current balance resulting from official support of the forward exchange value of the domestic currency, the effect on the balance of trade (category 1, above) is likely to be more important than the interest cost (category 2). Take the United States as an example: Suppose that an appreciation by 1 per cent a year of the forward dollar and forward dollar margin *vis-à-vis* all foreign currencies would evoke a once-for-all inward flow of foreign and U.S. funds (decline in the NLP) of the order of $500 million, and that an appreciation of spot and forward dollars by 1 per cent would reduce exports by $2\frac{1}{2}$ per cent of $20 billion, i.e. $500 million a year, and increase imports by 1 per cent of $15 billion, i.e. $150 million a year, or $650 million a year in all. However, since an appreciation of 1 per cent a year on a three-month forward contract represents an absolute appreciation of only $\frac{1}{4}$ per cent, this last figure is cut to $160 million. Moreover, if we assume that only 60 per cent of U.S. trade is covered by forward contracts, the adverse effect on the U.S. balance of trade would be reduced to something like $100 million.

Even $100 million a year, however, is a considerable payments loss to incur in addition to the interest cost of, say, $20 million on an inward movement of arbitrage funds of the order of $500 million.[6]

---

[5] This implies that foreign residents would have had a corresponding negative (positive) net position in domestic currency on forward account.

[6] From the standpoint of real national income, the two figures are on a very different footing. The loss of $20 million in interest is a net loss to the country even if full employment is preserved—though it may be 'worthwhile' if the $500 million inflow of funds is added to the real capital of the country. The $100 million loss on the trade balance may involve no loss at all in real income if employment is preserved by a corresponding addition to domestic expenditure. Indeed, there may be a net gain from the improved terms of trade. However, both the $20 million and the $100 million are apt to generate declines in income and employment which may intensify the real loss involved. In most cases in which official intervention on the forward market in support of the domestic currency arises, a decline in competitiveness on world markets would be unwelcome.

EFFECT ON SPECULATIVE ANTICIPATIONS

We must now reconsider the assumption, earlier adopted, that official support of the forward exchange value of the currency has no effect on expectations as to the future course of the spot rate. The precise effect on such expectations is uncertain; there are possible effects in both directions. Much depends on the situation, and particularly on what is generally believed to be the extent of official intervention. In so far as those participating in foreign exchange markets are ignorant of the fact or extent of official support operations, the impression given by the appreciation of the forward rate itself that other people are feeling less bearish about the currency is likely to impose a more optimistic view about the future spot value of the supported currency. Knowledge by some of the potential operators that the authorities are supporting the forward market will likewise tend to encourage bullishness in so far as it is interpreted as evidence of official determination to defend the currency and of official willingness to continue to have resort to this particular technique of increasing reserves. On the other hand, knowledge of the past accumulation of official forward liabilities as such will have a bearish or pessimistic influence, and the intervention as such may be interpreted as a sign of weakness. In considering the relative strength of these influences, it should be borne in mind that many of those whose expectations concerning rates are important (i.e. many potential 'speculators') are not market operators at all, but traders, who are likely to be more influenced by visible criteria, such as reserve movements, than by changes in official forward exchange liabilities, data on which are not published and the magnitude of which is unknown. Danger would arise only if the market were to assign an undeserved importance to that part of the official forward liabilities that corresponds to the induced adverse speculation, or if the total magnitude of forward liabilities were to be exaggerated by rumour.

On the whole, it appears that official support of the forward market is more likely to enhance than to reduce confidence in the future spot rate of the currency in question, particularly in the short run, and provided that the operations are not believed to be too large. The restoration of confidence will, of course, be merely temporary if the underlying deficit persists.

In so far as official support of the forward market leads to more bullish expectations regarding the future spot rate, causing a shift in spot speculation, both the NLP and the NSP curves will lie further to the left than in Figure 10.2; and insofar as official support affects forward speculation, it will result in a further shift to the left in the NSP' curve. The reduction in the balance of claims (the favourable capital movement) will thus be greater, and the forward rate higher, than in Figure 10.2.

In so far as the official support of the forward market leads to less bullish, or more bearish, anticipations about the spot rate, the NLP curve will lie to the right and the NSP' curve still further to the right, of the corresponding curves in Figure 10.2. Even if the effect on forward speculation is insufficient to outweigh the initial official intervention, and the forward rate therefore rises above the initial position, the effect on spot speculation may be such that the balance of claims actually increases (i.e. the net effect on capital is unfavourable).

OFFICIAL FORWARD SUPPORT WITH FLOATING SPOT RATES

We have thus far been assuming that spot exchange rates are fixed by official action. In the context of the sort of arrangements that prevail in the world for keeping exchange rates in the vicinity of par values, this is equivalent to assuming that the balance of spot market transactions is such as to hold the spot exchange value of the domestic currency at rates which evoke the stabilizing intervention of domestic or foreign monetary authorities. At any one time, this is likely to be true of the spot exchange rates relative to some foreign currencies but not relative to others.

If the spot value of the domestic currency is not at an official buying or selling point, the effect of official support of the currency on the forward market will be different from what has been described. The consequences of forward intervention under a floating spot rate system would take too long to describe fully here. The following summary treatment is impressionistic rather than precise. The tendency, which exists when the spot rate is fixed, for the rise in the forward value of the currency to evoke a decline in the NLP will operate, under a floating spot rate, to promote a rise in the spot value of the currency. Thus, the effect of supporting the forward rate will be to raise both forward and spot rates of exchange.

If it is assumed that any short-run effect of the rise in the spot rate on the balance of current payments is of negligible proportions, the rise in the spot rate must, in fact, be sufficient to choke off entirely the tendency towards a decline in the NLP that results from the rise in the forward rate. This is accomplished in two ways: the rise in the spot value of the currency (given that anticipations regarding future spot rates remain the same) evokes adverse spot speculation; and the inward shift in covered interest arbitrage is reduced because the decline in the forward discount on the currency that results from official forward support is less with a floating than with a fixed spot rate. This effect on covered interest arbitrage means that the forward rate will have to rise more, relative to the expected spot rate, with a floating than with a fixed spot rate in order to evoke the addition to forward speculation required to equilibrate the forward market. In the end, the entire negative official speculative position in forward exchange will be balanced by an increase in private forward speculation.

Even if the spot value of the currency is free to appreciate only over a narrow range, the effect of this freedom will be to reduce the benefit which the country's gross reserves will derive from the favourable effect on capital movements. Any inward arbitrage will be at least partially offset by outward uncovered capital movements, unless, indeed, the rise in the spot rate has the effect of raising the anticipated future level of the spot rate.

CONCLUSIONS

Official support of the foreign exchange value of a currency is in some respects analogous to official borrowing from abroad, on a short-term but renewable basis, in foreign currency or accompanied by a foreign exchange guarantee. From the standpoint of the country that seeks to attract funds from abroad, such intervention in the forward exchange market differs from direct official borrowing chiefly in that it is less conspicuous, and engages less fully and less openly the credit of the authorities; on the other hand, it tends, in a way which may be unwelcome, to worsen the trade balance. From the standpoint of the lending countries, it has the characteristic, in contrast to intergovernmental or intercentral bank loans, of attracting private funds and thus reducing the liquidity of the commercial banking system. Quite apart from these comparative advantages or disadvantages of the technique, a country's readiness to have recourse to such operations makes available a source of external liquidity which, though not large, is for the most part additional to those otherwise available. From what has been said it is clear that the most appropriate use of the technique will be to meet a temporary deficit which, if successfully financed, would be likely to be followed, within a period of time measured in months rather than years, by a corresponding surplus.

A good example would be an outflow of funds caused by a temporary loss of confidence in a currency that was basically sound, in the sense that in the long run it could be satisfactorily maintained without devaluation, though there might be some temporary weakness in the basic balance of payments. Such an outflow of funds—provoked, say, by some political event or by a misunderstanding of the policy intentions of the government—would be not only temporary but inherently reversible. While it lasted, it would probably be associated with a discount in the forward exchange value of the currency, which would be giving a temporary stimulus to the balance of trade. In these circumstances, official support of the forward market would offset the effect on reserves of the outflow of funds; the eventual reflux of these funds would enable the authorities to shed their forward liabilities; in the meantime, a large part of the speculative outflow could be prevented without raising the forward rate above the spot rate, i.e. without exchange loss to the authorities or even, probably, to the country. The stimulus to the balance of trade afforded by the forward discount would be removed; in certain circumstances, however, this may not be undesirable.

The next most promising occasion for applying the policy of forward support would be to deal with a short-term capital outflow stimulated by a relative decline in a country's interest rates, likely to be followed at some not too distant date by a reflux attributable to a relative increase in the interest rates. Such a situation might arise if a country whose balance of payments was in fundamental equilibrium was suffering from a recession when other countries were prosperous.

In this case, if there were no concurrent loss of confidence in the currency, the outflow of funds, though draining the country's reserves, would lead to an appreciation in the forward value of the currency, given the fact that at least part of the outflow was on a covered basis. Official support of the forward value of the currency, by reducing or even reversing the outflow of covered interest arbitrage, would reduce or check the over-all capital outflow. If, however, as might be the case, such support should create or accentuate a forward premium on the currency, the authorities would incur losses from their forward operations, partly to the benefit of foreign participants on the forward market. The substantial rise to be expected in the forward premium would, of course, have an adverse effect on the foreign balance, which might be unwelcome from a cyclical standpoint though it would probably merely involve a diminution in the improvement that would otherwise have occurred as a result of the recession.

Such use of forward support to counteract interest-motivated capital movements is unlikely to be as successful as in the case previously considered. In the first place, there will always be un-certainty concerning when the tide of capital movements will turn and whether it will turn to the full extent. The period over which intervention would have to be maintained might have to be long. Secondly, since no one would credit the possibility of revaluation in the circumstances envisaged, the rise in the forward premium would evoke a large amount of adverse forward speculation. This means that considerable intervention would have to be undertaken, and large losses incurred, in order to achieve a given effect on the movement of capital.

A temporary deficit in the current balance of payments that was due to some such event as a harvest failure would not constitute a good occasion for the application of the technique of forward support. The current account deficit resulting from this cause, while it would be temporary, would not be succeeded by any subsequent surplus in the balance of payments. The deficit in question could be offset, as far as the effect on reserves is concerned, by an influx of capital brought about by forward exchange support; but since there would be no ensuing surplus, the official debit position on forward exchange would have to be renewed indefinitely. This, as we have seen, involves some deterioration in the current balance as a consequence of the appreciation of the forward exchange rate. In any event, a permanent debit position on forward exchange would constitute a permanent weakness in the reserve position, so that it would be preferable that such a contingency should be met by long-term borrowing.

The only situation in which a case might be made for forward exchange support operations to meet a current deficit would be one in which it appeared probable that the current deficit would, within a reasonable time, be replaced by a surplus without the necessity for resorting to devaluation. If the turn-around in the current balance could be achieved only by devaluation, it would be preferable that the forward support not be undertaken until after devaluation has taken place—otherwise the authorities would incur a loss as a result of their operations, part of which would accrue in the form of windfall gains to non-residents.

Chapter 11

Guidelines for Balance-of-Payments Adjustment under the Par-Value System*

INTRODUCTION

The policies that countries may adopt in dealing with imbalances of payments are to some extent regulated by the provisions of inter-governmental agreements. For example, the Articles of Agreement of the International Monetary Fund limit the freedom of action of member countries with respect to changes in par values (exchange rates), the imposition of exchange restrictions on current transactions, the adoption of multiple-currency practices, and so forth, while the General Agreement on Tariffs and Trade limits the freedom of action of the contracting parties with respect to tariffs, import restrictions, export subsidies, and the like.

This framework of legal obligations, however, is far from sufficient to ensure that the self-regarding actions of countries in dealing with their payments problems will mesh together into a satisfactory system of mutual accommodation and adjustment calculated to promote on a world-wide scale the objectives of high employment and real income, development of productive resources, and expansion of international trade set forth, for example, in the Purposes of the Fund. International organizations, both world-wide and regional, therefore, carry out many activities, other than administering a legal code, to assist their members in solving their payments problems. Thus the financial assistance provided by the Fund and, to a lesser extent, by the European Fund and the Bank for International Settlements, assists countries in meeting temporary payments deficits and so makes it possible for them to avoid resort to measures such as restriction of international transactions, excessive devaluation, or undue deflation that would be destructive of national or international prosperity, while pursuing sounder, if slower, methods of restoring equilibrium. In the case of the Fund, at any rate, such assistance is often made conditional on the adoption of

* Reprinted from Essays in International Finance No. 67 (International Finance Section, Department of Economics, Princeton University, May 1968).

268

satisfactory adjustment policies. Finally, a number of international agencies, notably the Fund and the Organization for Economic Co-operation and Development, regularly advise their members on the policies that appear to be required in the prevailing circumstances to maintain or restore internal and external equilibrium, and occasionally make statements of general application regarding the types of policies which they favour.

While the prescriptions offered by international bodies such as the Fund and the OECD to their member countries are doubtless imbued with the philosophy characteristic of the organization in question, they are for the most part tailor-made to fit the concrete circumstances of particular cases, and cannot be entirely free from the defects of the 'ad hoc'. It has, therefore, sometimes been felt that they might gain in consistency and stability if made in the light of an explicit 'code of good behaviour' with respect to balance-of-payments adjustment somewhat more detailed and comprehensive than any that could be derived from the present framework of international legal obligations in this sphere.

One or two attempts to formulate such a code were made during the lifetime of the OEEC, but much the most comprehensive and fully worked-out formulation to date is that contained in the pioneering Report on the Balance-of-Payments Adjustment Process recently prepared by Working Party No. 3 of the Economic Policy Committee of the OECD (Organization for Economic Co-operation and Development, Paris, August 1966).

The present essay is intended to explore the possibility of elaborating a code more precise and, in a way, more ambitious than the guidelines set forth by the intergovernmental OECD Working Party. The system outlined below, like that of Working Party No. 3, is based upon the existing legal foundations provided by the Articles of the Fund and the provisions of the GATT. No new international agreements are envisaged and no new invasions of sovereignty proposed. Nevertheless, it may very well be that some of the suggestions made below would put a greater strain on the willingness of countries to co-operate internationally than is likely to prove practicable. It has seemed to me that there was much to be learned at the present stage from a presentation of the full implications for international co-operation of a whole-hearted attempt to make the present system work well, and I have therefore refrained from any premature application of the 'art of the possible'.

EARLIER ADJUSTMENT SYSTEMS

Before outlining a code of balance-of-payments adjustment designed to meet present day conditions, it may be useful to mention two main systems of policy in this area that have in the past found favour with many economists. These might be described for convenience as pre-Keynesian and Keynesian, respectively.

The pre-Keynesian or gold standard view is that the exchange value of currencies should be fixed in terms of gold and of each other, that budgets should be balanced (with perhaps a small Sinking Fund to absorb the public indebtedness accumulated in previous wars), and that monetary policy should be aimed primarily at maintaining and restoring balance in international payments, in the short run through its effect on capital movements and, in the longer run, through its effect on domestic expenditure and prices. The aims of preserving full employment and ensuring optimal growth would not be served directly by these policy instruments, at least in their over-all aspects, but would be safeguarded by the presumed flexibility of wages and prices—in conjunction with a low or negative elasticity of price expectations—and by the propensity to save in the private sector.

What is here called the 'Keynesian view' is really the view of the later Keynes, as synthesized from scattered evidences—for example, by Ragnar Nurkse.[1] This is that fiscal and monetary policy should be applied in a mutually reinforcing manner, with a view to securing full employment without inflation, while the needs of the balance of payments should be met initially by the use of reserves (supplemented as desired by controls over capital flows, compensatory credits, official intervention in the forward exchange market, and so forth) and then by temporary import restrictions and by exchange rate adjustment. This view was based on four assumptions:

(1) that wages and prices are too sticky in a downward direction to enable a gold standard or fixed exchange system to work successfully,

(2) that reasonably full employment is normally possible without inflation,

[1] Cf. *Conditions of International Monetary Equilibrium*, Essays in International Finance No. 4 (Princeton University, 1945) and 'Domestic and International Equilibrium', in Seymour Harris, ed., *The New Economics* (Knopf, New York, 1947).

(3) that monetary policy itself is too feeble or chancy an instrument to secure internal stability without the supplementation of budgetary deficits or surpluses, and

(4) that private international capital flows are undesirable if they are of a disequilibrating character, i.e. if they are such as to intensify rather than relieve balance-of-payments difficulties.

The ideas regarding the international adjustment mechanism that are built into the provisions of the Fund's Articles of Agreement and of the GATT are largely based on this Keynesian view, modified by a more conservative tendency originating in the U.S. Administration, which laid greater emphasis on the importance of exchange rate stability and on the avoidance of restrictions on current transactions, particularly restrictions of a discriminatory kind.

The last two decades have witnessed some weakening of the Keynesian presuppositions but no emergence of a stable post-Keynesian orthodox view. First came a phase in which, behind a protective wall of discriminatory restrictions and with the help of substantial devaluations, trade was liberalized, originally on a bilateral, subsequently on a regional basis. There followed a euphoric phase, based partly on the emergence of a temporarily favourable structure of international payments, partly on the realization that in post-war conditions price inflation was more of a danger than massive unemployment. In this phase a conservative reaction took place towards a gold-standard-like system, in which changes in exchange rates would be regarded as but a remote possibility and demand policies would be geared primarily to the state of the balance of payments. There was even a short-lived enthusiasm for the complete liberalization of capital flows.

With the recrudescence of payments problems in the later 1950s, came a bifurcation or trifurcation of thinking on the process of balance-of-payments adjustment. First, an academic revolt against the par-value system of Bretton Woods sought to achieve or preserve the freedom of international transactions through a general adoption of a flexible or floating rate of exchange. This school of thought, which probably predominates in academic circles, has more recently trimmed its sails somewhat towards an advocacy of a par-value system with wide exchange rate margins, or of a par value—the 'crawling peg'—that would gradually but continuously vary in

271

response to payments conditions. Bankers and officials, however, together with a proportion of the academic community, still adhere by and large to the Bretton Woods system of adjustment, albeit with a recognition that the adjustment process needs to be improved. Within this consensus, one school lays greater emphasis on the need for the provision of an adequate volume of official compensatory financing, including if necessary the deliberate creation of a reserve asset supplementary to traditional reserves, to provide adequate time for underlying adjustments. Another school lays more emphasis on the need for a speedier adjustment process, to be achieved by means that are not always clearly specified but appear at any rate to involve greater control over private capital movements. Both schools give at least lip service to an idea, propagated partly in official, partly in academic circles in the last five years, according to which monetary policy would be directed primarily towards influencing the international movement of capital in such a way as to rectify the balance of payments (even if this had excessive or undesirable effects on internal demand), while fiscal policy would be directed primarily towards attaining target levels of internal demand (even if this meant moving in the 'wrong' direction from the standpoint of the balance of payments).

There has been an impressive corpus of first-rate *analytical* work on international trade and payments, including, in the case of Professor J. E. Meade in particular, minute analyses of the effects of alternative balance-of-payments policies. Nevertheless, attempts by academic economists to set forth a coherent *normative* system, based on the legal framework of the Fund and GATT for the adjustment of different sorts of imbalances in international payments, were almost entirely lacking from 1947, when Nurkse wrote the articles previously mentioned, to 1966, when Professors Fellner, Machlup, Triffin and eleven other economists wrote a book entitled *Maintaining and Restoring Balance in International Payments*. It is significant that the initiative to call the meetings, for which the papers in the book were prepared, was taken by some of the officials participating in Working Party No. 3 of the OECD. Perhaps the reluctance of academics to venture on their own initiative into the code-building terrain is an indication of the foolhardy nature of the enterprise. The writer of the present essay has derived considerable stimulus from this volume, particularly from the three comprehensive papers by the named authors and from a short, but pithy, paper by Professor James Tobin, on 'Adjustment Responsibilities of Surplus and Deficit Countries'.

FEATURES OF THE PROPOSED SYSTEM

It is convenient to mention at this point some of the general features of the system of adjustment outlined below. In the first place, being, as already indicated, consistent with the Articles of Agreement of the Fund, it is based on the assumption that exchange rates (par values) should be adjusted only to correct fundamental disequilibria (i.e. long-term imbalances that cannot be corrected by aggregate demand policy in a reasonable time without an excessive degree of unemployment or inflationary pressure). Subject to this constraint, the merits of which will not be argued in this essay, the object of the code will be, as far as practicable, to maximize economic welfare.

The problem of adjustment is approached on a country-by-country basis. Each country is expected to take action with respect to its own balance-of-payments situation without making its actions conditional on actions by other countries. While each country's payments surplus or deficit is, of course, related to the surpluses and deficits of all other countries, it seldom reflects the deficit or surplus of any single other country or small number of other countries, and if each country waits for others to save it the trouble of taking action, adjustment is likely to be long delayed.

There may be appropriate partial exceptions to this individualistic approach in the case of disequilibria affecting very large countries or countries that are heavily dependent on the economy of a single other country. In general, however, it is the only approach that is practicable for world organizations like the Fund, or even organizations of more limited membership like the OECD, to adopt as a general rule. This does not mean that account should not be taken of probable developments in the rest of the world in assessing the probable direction of, and hence the appropriate prescriptions to remedy, the disequilibrium of any given country. Nor does it mean that countries, in dealing with their own payments imbalances and domestic goals, are free to ignore the interests and objectives of other countries. What it does mean, as we shall see, is that the necessary element of international co-operation is sought to be provided through general prescriptions regarding the types of policies that are commendable

273

in different types of disequilibrium situations affecting individual countries, and through collective judgments as to the extent to which these situations prevail in particular instances, rather than through specific prescriptions for co-ordinated action by a number of countries.

Broadly speaking, symmetry is maintained in the treatment of 'surplus' and 'deficit' countries. Countries are expected to take action roughly commensurate with the magnitude and character of their respective imbalances, whether these be positive or negative. As has been pointed out by Professor Fritz Machlup in the volume previously referred to, the methods of adjustment open to surplus countries, especially in the sphere of demand policy, capital restrictions, and trade restrictions, are generally less costly in terms of economic welfare than those open to deficit countries, and on this criterion it might be appropriate that the main responsibility for adjustment should lie with surplus countries. However, as the same author has also indicated, imbalances are more often caused by bad policies on the part of deficit than of surplus countries. To avoid ill effects on incentives, it therefore seems best to try to assign responsibilities for adjustment to both classes of countries. It is sometimes argued that the international community is so much less able to bring pressure to bear on surplus than on deficit countries that it is unrealistic to call on the former to make any sacrifice of domestic objectives. From a less cynical standpoint, however, the difficulty of applying sanctions to surplus countries would make it seem all the more necessary that the responsibilities of these countries should be clearly stated, and the moral pressure on them vigorously applied.

The prescriptions contained in the code of behaviour are determined by the characteristics of the over-all balance of payments and not by the composition of that balance with respect to current and capital account transactions, except insofar as that composition may affect the 'time shape' of imbalances—their reversible, temporary, or persistent character. By contrast with what is recommended by the Report of Working Party No. 3, it is not here proposed that account be taken of countries' targets for their balances of payments on current account. As between countries that are free from restrictions on international transactions (and from undue unemployment) imposed or incurred on balance-of-payments grounds, the prospect of a persistent over-all payments deficit, for example, will be taken as prima facie evidence that the current account balance, if negative, should become less so, and if positive, should become more so, irrespective of whether that balance exceeds or falls short of any national target. The underlying assumption here is that over any long period of years voluntary flows of funds are likely to provide a better indication of the appropriate flow of real capital—as distinct from aid—than are politically determined national targets—which are, moreover, certain to be mutually incompatible.

Since the system proposed contains a variety of methods both of financing imbalances and of removing them, it has considerable flexibility in adapting to the circumstances of particular countries. However, no attempt has been made to provide radically different codes of behaviour for different classes of countries. The system described is primarily designed to meet the needs of relatively stable countries, including, one hopes, all the industrial countries, and some of the less developed ones. This matter is touched upon again at a later point in this essay.

THE CODE OF ADJUSTMENT

In this section a par-value system of balance-of-payments adjustment is presented in outline form on the left side of the page. A commentary on various features of this system is provided in the notes appearing on the right side of the page opposite to the relevant sections of the text.

Text

(1) A country should be deemed to be in balance-of-payments deficit if it is:

(a) losing reserves[1] on a larger scale, or gaining them on a smaller scale, than corresponds to its share in world reserve growth,[2] or

(b) avoids this only by undertaking for balance-of-payments reasons one or more of the following measures:

Notes

[1] If there were no holding of reserve currencies by monetary authorities, it would be natural to measure changes in reserves on a gross basis. As things are, the question arises to what extent, if any, changes in liquid liabilities to foreign monetary authorities should be subtracted from changes in the gross reserves of reserve-currency countries. Such netting could be carried out on a 1:1 basis (each dollar of liabilities counting as negative reserves to the extent of one dollar), or it could be omitted altogether, or reserve changes could be calculated on a semi-gross basis (for example, each dollar of liabilities counting as negative reserves to the extent of 50 cents). Whatever procedure was adopted for reserve

Text

(i) official borrowing;

(ii) promoting an 'artificially' favourable net international flow of capital by one or other of the methods described at (13) below;

(iii) providing abnormally restricted aid to foreign countries;

(iv) restricting imports;

(v) subsidizing exports; or

(vi) maintaining a level of aggregate demand that is less than is optimal[3] from the standpoint of its effect on price inflation and unemployment.

(2) A country should be deemed to be in balance-of-payments surplus if it is:

(a) gaining reserves on a larger

Notes

countries would have to be adopted also in calculating aggregate reserve changes. The argument for complete netting is that any accumulation of liabilities to foreign monetary authorities, even if not solicited by the reserve centre in question, represents financing of a compensatory character rather than a capital inflow that is justified by its effect on world productivity. Unless offset by an accumulation of reserves by the reserve centre—which is equivalent to an outflow of official compensatory financing—it therefore signifies prima facie an imbalance which, if persistent, should be corrected. The main argument for a less-than-complete netting of such liabilities is that in the present state of uncertainty regarding the adequacy of deliberate reserve creation the world cannot do without the supplement to reserves arising from the accumulation of currency reserves. Nor can that supplement be distributed suitably throughout the world unless the reserve centres have, over the long run, some—though not an equivalent—payments deficit on a net official basis.

[2] The object of asking countries to take account of the growth of world reserves in deciding what to regard as equilibrium is to try to prevent too many countries from adopting restrictive measures to meet payments deficits when the total amount of world reserves is falling or is rising too slowly, and to prevent too many countries from adopting expansionary measures when world reserves are rising too fast. It would, of course, be simpler to allow countries to base their balance-of-payments policies on a more 'natural' definition of equilibrium and to influence their behaviour by adjusting the net sum of payments surpluses through an appropriate amount of deliberate reserve creation. However, until an internationally agreed system of deliberate reserve creation exists and is in satisfactory operation countries must be asked to adapt their balance-of-payments targets to the actual growth of world reserves.

[3] By the 'optimal' level of aggregate demand for any country at any time is meant either one compatible with the

Text

scale, or losing them on a smaller scale, than corresponds to its share in the growth of world reserves, or

(b) avoiding this only by undertaking for balance-of-payments reasons one or more of the following measures:

  (i) official lending;
  (ii) promoting an 'artificially' unfavourable net flow of capital;
  (iii) providing abnormally expanded aid to foreign countries;
  (iv) subsidizing imports;
  (v) restricting exports; or
  (vi) maintaining a level of aggregate demand that is more than is optimal from the standpoint of its effect on price inflation and unemployment.

(3) A country should be deemed to be in chronic deficit if the conditions described at (1) above are expected to prevail, in the absence of measures of adjustment, over the average of the ensuing five years.[4]

(4) A country should be deemed to be in chronic surplus if the conditions described at (2) above are expected to prevail, in the absence of measures of adjustment, over the average of the ensuing five years.[4]

Notes

'normal' relationship between unemployment and price increase described below at (7), *Alternative A,* or one compatible with the 'national' norm described at (7), *Alternative B.*

[4] The condition for a chronic deficit or surplus should be deemed to be satisfied if an actual deficit or surplus exists, and is not clearly likely to disappear within the next two or three years. It is, however, possible for a country to be in chronic deficit and actual (temporary) surplus, or in chronic surplus and actual (temporary) deficit.

Text

(5) Any country that is in chronic surplus, and does not have a weak liquidity position,[5] should be urged to remove not only balance-of-payments restrictions of all sorts but also, to a degree commensurate with its surplus, any other restrictions on imports and capital exports that are contrary to the interests of the international community.[6]

(6) Any country that has an appreciable[7] chronic deficit, and does not have a relatively strong liquidity position,[8] should pursue such a combination of aggregate demand policy and incomes policy as is likely to result in stable prices. Any country that is in approximate payments balance should pursue such a combination of aggregate demand policy and incomes policy as is likely to result in slightly rising prices. Any country that has an appreciable chronic surplus, and does not have a relatively weak liquidity position, should pursue such a combination of aggregate demand policy and incomes policy as is likely to result in moderately rising prices.[9]

Notes

[5] The strength of a country's liquidity position depends primarily on the level of its gross reserves relative to its international transactions with an allowance (on less than a 1:1 basis) for liquid liabilities, and an allowance for access to balance-of-payments financing. It should be noted that a reserve-centre country that is maintaining balance on the basis of a definition that involves a full netting of reserves for liquid liabilities to official holders, may nevertheless be improving its liquidity position, since only a partial netting of such liabilities may be required to sustain its external liquidity. On the other hand, it may be suffering a deterioration in external liquidity if balance is maintained only thanks to an accumulation of liquid liabilities to private holders.

[6] If this is not strictly a part of the code of balance-of-payments adjustment, it is a useful extension of it.

[7] Payments balance, a state in which a country is neither in appreciable chronic deficit nor in appreciable chronic surplus, may be thought of as a band of some width rather than as a mere dividing line.

[8] Countries' adjustment policies should take account, not only of the nature and extent of their payments imbalances, whether explicit or suppressed, but also of their relative liquidity positions. Deficit countries with strong liquidity positions should not be pressed to adopt premature adjustment policies that might deny to other countries the reserves the latter may require to finance subsequent deficits. Similarly, surplus countries with very low reserves should not be pressed to adopt premature adjustment policies that would prevent them from accumulating the reserves they themselves may require to finance subsequent deficits. On the other hand, it is not suggested that countries in payments balance should adopt adjustment policies merely to acquire or merely to discard reserves, since this might involve too frequent reversals of relative price levels, and since there are other ways (for example, *ad hoc* international lending) of adjusting relative liquidity positions.

[9] The object of (6) is to ensure that policy instruments other than exchange-rate devaluation or revaluation are used,

Text   *Notes*

at least to some extent, to assist in bringing about such adjustments in the relative price levels of surplus and deficit countries as will promote balance in international payments without continued resort to restrictions or distortion of international trade and capital flows. In most cases, though admittedly not in all, this will mean that these countries should adopt price policies of the kind described in (6). The differential target rates of price-level increase for deficit and for surplus countries, respectively, through which the desired adjustment of relative price levels is to be brought about, must be fixed with reference to some norm at which countries in equilibrium are expected to aim. In determining this norm, and also the extent to which deficit and surplus countries can be expected to aim at rates of price increase respectively below and above this norm, it has to be borne in mind that:

(a) given the present strength of cost-push factors and incomes policies in relatively stable countries, most such countries find that some degree of price inflation in excess of zero is necessary to avoid what they would regard as excessive unemployment;

(b) that surplus countries are unlikely to tolerate rates of price increase, or deficit countries levels of unemployment much in excess of those corresponding to the compromise between price stability and full employment which they prefer on purely domestic grounds, merely in order to adjust payments imbalances. To illustrate the sort of figures that might be reasonable under present circumstances, anything from 0 to 2 per cent increase per annum in GNP deflator might be regarded as the degree of price stability to be expected of deficit countries, and anything from 2 to 4 per cent increase per annum as the range of price increase to be expected of surplus countries. The precise target ought, of course, to depend on the size of the chronic surplus or deficit. The rate of price increase of 2 per cent here suggested as normal for a country in a balanced payments position should be compared with the actual average rates of price increase in major industrial countries of 2·9 per cent in the quinquennium

(7) Alternative A

A view should be arrived at, possibly on the basis of informal international agreement, as to the

279

Text

relationship between percentage unemployment and rate of increase of price level that for an average stable country in a balanced payments position would represent a reasonable compromise between the objectives of full employment and price stability and, therefore, a reasonable target for policies affecting aggregate demand.[10] A country that is in chronic deficit (surplus) and does not have a strong (weak) liquidity position, should maintain a level of demand somewhat lower (higher) than is likely to be compatible with the maintenance of this 'normal' relationship.[11]

Alternative B

Each country should be asked to define the relationship between percentage unemployment and rate of price increase that it regards as the least unsatisfactory compromise from a purely domestic standpoint.[12] A country that is in chronic deficit (surplus), and that does not have a strong (weak) liquidity position, should maintain a level of aggregate demand somewhat lower (higher) than would be likely to be compatible with the maintenance of this nationally preferred relationship.

Notes

1955–60, and of 2·4 per cent in the quinquennium 1960–65.

[10] For any given country over any given short period, we may assume that the lower the unemployment, the higher will be the rate of price inflation. (This relationship is obviously connected with the so-called Phillips curve, relating unemployment and wage increase, which, in some countries at any rate, appears to be fairly stable over considerable periods, when allowance is made for cyclical factors.) For each possible curve relating unemployment and inflation (which may be termed the U/I curve) there will be a point representing the best or least bad compromise between full employment and price stability. The 'normal' relationship in (7) *Alternative A* may be thought of as the locus of such compromise points on different possible U/I curves. The more unfavourable the U/I curve, the higher will be *both* unemployment and inflation. The relationship in question might be a linear one, in which a low rate of unemployment is associated with a zero rate of price increase, and increments of unemployment are associated in a fixed ratio with increments in price inflation. For example, there might be some such scale as the following:

Percentage Unemployment	Percentage Rate of Increase of Prices per annum
1	0
2	1·5
3	3
4	4·5
5	6

Such a uniform standard relationship not only does some violence to national preferences as between full employment and price stability but would also require, for its full justification, that the possible U/I curves of different countries, or of a given country at different times, should have similar slopes. Despite the implausibility of this assumption, a normal relationship of this sort offers a less one-sided criterion for judging the appropriateness of demand policies than would *either* a normal level of unemployment, *or* a normal rate of price increase, taken alone.

Alternative C

Subject to (6) above, each country should be free to maintain aggregate demand at whatever level it prefers.[13]

Notes

While an objective standard, such as is provided by *Alternative A*, has the advantage of defining the obligations of countries more clearly, it may be impossible to get countries to agree on, or to acquiesce in, the application of such a standard. For this reason, *Alternatives B and C* are added.

[11] The appropriate degree of divergence from the 'normal' relationship would, of course, depend on the degree of payments imbalance in the country in question. It is sometimes thought to be unjustifiable to allow the level of unemployment to be increased for balance-of-payments reasons, on the grounds that unemployment is the costliest (in terms of real income) of all ways of correcting the balance of payments. This, however, is dubious, even in the short run, since in the vicinity of optimal employment an increase in unemployment may yield some gains in productivity and in allocation of labour to offset the direct loss in output. It is still more questionable, in the long run at least, if the choice is deemed to lie between unemployment and the imposition of restrictions on international transactions, since a temporary increase in unemployment may bring about a more permanent adjustment in national price levels, and reduce, for a long period, the need for restrictions.

[12] This is something of a half-way house between *Alternatives A* and *C*. It permits a more flexible adaptation of policies to current and anticipated situations than does *A*, corresponds more closely to national preferences, and puts less of a strain on willingness to co-operate in an international system. It might therefore be preferable to *A*, if only countries would keep their 'preferred' relationships constant through periods of balance-of-payments surplus and deficit. However, countries would doubtless insist on the right to change their minds about the relationship at least with the advent of every new government, so that some of the objectivity characteristic of *Alternative A* would be lost under *Alternative B*.

[13] *Alternative C* is introduced for the sake of completeness, but it amounts to renouncing the imposition of any

Text	Notes

(8) Countries should pursue more severe incomes policies when they are in appreciable chronic deficit and do not have a strong liquidity position than when they are in appreciable chronic surplus and do not have a weak liquidity position. If possible they should pursue incomes policies which, in conjunction with the demand policies under (7), are likely to eliminate the chronic imbalance.

obligation on countries to adjust their demand policies in the interest of balance in the foreign payments, and would be likely to put an impossible strain on incomes policies under *(8)*. The result might be either a failure to adjust, and a consequential necessity to revert to restrictions and distortions, over long periods, or a frequency of recourse to exchange rate adjustment difficult to reconcile with the assumptions of the par-value system.

(9) If a chronic disequilibrium is too great to be corrected within a reasonable period of time by the policies described at (6) to (8) above, it should be corrected by exchange rate adjustment.[14]

[14] A moot question is whether, when a country's rate of price increase remains stubbornly in excess of that compatible with balance in its foreign payments, the country should over-devalue (so as to become a surplus country) in expectation of a continuance of the inflationary tendency. Given the rate of inflation, this might be justifiable as reducing the average need for balance-of-payments restrictions over time, but the over-devaluation might itself stimulate the inflationary tendency.

(10) Any short-term imbalance, and any chronic imbalance in course of correction by the methods described above, should be financed through reserve movements and compensatory official financing, or suppressed through diversion of private capital flows, rather than suppressed through restriction of imports.[15]

[15] The preference here expressed for adjustment to meet short-term imbalances through the capital rather than through the current account does not derive from pure considerations of economic welfare. From that standpoint the contrary presumption prevails: that diversion of current and diversion of capital transactions (including reserve movements) should go together. The preference derives partly from the Articles of the Fund, which regard capital restrictions much more leniently than current restrictions, and partly from the consideration that restriction or diversion of current account transactions tend to undermine the structure of international agreements relating to trade and current payments, whereas no such structure exists in the case of capital transactions.

A difficult question is where in this scale of preferences to place export subsidization (for deficit countries) and export taxation (for surplus countries).

Text

Export subsidization may be positively beneficial from the standpoint of resource allocation, and may pave the way for a necessary exchange rate adjustment. However, it is contrary to the provisions of the GATT and is particularly likely to be resented by other countries and to evoke imitation or retaliation on the part of countries not in payments difficulty. Export taxation is open to the same objections on grounds of resource allocation as is import restriction, but is much less resented and less likely to endanger trade agreements.

It is not a matter of great moment, from the standpoint of resource allocation, to what extent payments imbalances are financed by reserve movements, financed by compensatory official capital flows, or diminished by diversion of private capital flows. In order to avoid disequilibrating exchange speculation, which would intensify the short-terms payments imbalance, however, it is prudent to limit the role of reserve movement to what the deficit country can clearly afford to sustain.

(11) Countries in deficit, unless their liquidity position is strong, should attempt to finance or diminish their deficits through compensatory official borrowing and inward diversion of private capital flows. If adequate official financing cannot be obtained on reasonable terms, and adequate diversion of private capital flows is impossible or cannot be brought about without undue distortions, and if the liquidity position is weak, such countries may apply restrictions, preferably in the form of surcharges, on imports and other current expenditures.

(12) Countries in surplus, unless their liquidity position is weak, should attempt to finance or diminish their surpluses, through compensatory official lending (including, if so required, lending to the Fund and other international

Text

financial agencies), debt repayment, and outward diversion of private capital flows. They may also tax or otherwise restrict exports.

(13) Diversion of private capital flows for balance-of-payments reasons should be achieved as far as possible through measures providing price incentives rather than through quantitative controls, 'voluntary' or otherwise. While there may be a case for discrimination by country,[16] there should be as little discrimination as possible by type of capital flow.[17] There are a number of ways by which a relatively non-discriminatory diversion of international capital flows can be brought about:

(a) Countries in payments deficit could tax purchases of assets by domestic from foreign residents and subsidize the sale of assets by domestic to foreign residents, while countries in payments surplus could tax the sale of assets by domestic to foreign residents and subsidize the purchase of assets by domestic from foreign residents.[18]

Notes

[16] There is a case, on balance-of-payments grounds, for countries that are diverting capital flows towards themselves to grant partial exemption from such measures to other countries that are also in balance-of-payments difficulty or that hold reserves and idle balances in currencies of countries in payments difficulty. On more general welfare grounds, there is a case for favouring capital flows to countries of low per capita income. On the other hand, even this kind of discrimination is subject to objections analogous to those discussed in the following note.

[17] There is a high degree of substitutability between different types of capital flow. If capitalists are induced, by measures such as those discussed at (13) (a), (b), and (c), to divert capital flows of a particular type, say short-term banking funds, from country A to country B, while analogous incentives to divert are not given in the case of another type of capital flow, say long-term bonds, the diversion of the first type of flow from A to B will be partly offset by a diversion of the second from B to A, which will become more profitable as a result of the first diversion. Such substitution not merely reduces the effect on the balance of payments of any given amount of diversion of the first type of flow; it also normally entails that any given net improvement in the balance of payments will be achieved at a lower level of real income than would otherwise be the case.

[18] The interest-equalization tax is a partial measure of this type but one that discriminates, not only by countries but by type of funds since it is not used to restrict American purchases of short-term assets or American direct investment abroad, nor is there a corresponding subsidization of sales of assets by domestic to foreign residents.

Official intervention in the forward exchange market, whereby monetary authorities take a credit position in the currency of a deficit country and a debit position in the currency of a surplus country may be regarded as a measure of the type described at (13)(a). However, it applies only to short-term

284

Text

(b) Countries in payments deficit could maintain abnormally low taxes on income from investment at home and relatively high taxes on income of domestic residents from investment abroad, while countries in payments surplus could maintain abnormally high taxes on income from investment at home and relatively low taxes on income of domestic residents from investment abroad.[19]

(c)(i) Countries in payments deficit could subsidize, and countries in payments surplus could tax, private-investment expenditure.

(ii) Countries in payments deficit could adopt a budgetary position involving either an artificially low rate of public saving or an artificially high rate of public investment or both, and countries in payments surplus could adopt a budgetary position involving either an artificially high rate of public saving or an artificially low rate of public investment or both.

Either (i) or (ii) above would enable interest rates to be higher in deficit countries, and lower in surplus countries, than would otherwise be possible without detriment to domestic targets for aggregate demand.[20]

Notes

capital flows of a commercial, banking, or speculative character.

One way of achieving the result described at (13)(a) would be for countries to have separate exchange rates for current and capital transactions, respectively. In the absence of official intervention, such 'floating' capital exchange rates would tend to choke off all net capital movements into or out of each country. However, monetary authorities would be expected to prevent their capital exchange rates from falling to a discount unless their countries were in payments deficit, and to prevent them from rising to a premium unless their countries were in payments surplus. This system, whatever its technical interest, could hardly be regarded as compatible with the Articles of Agreement of the Fund relating to exchange stability and multiple-currency practices.

[19] Ideally, taxes on investment income should be levied only by the country whose residents own the investments. In this event, the prescription would be for both deficit and surplus countries to discriminate, in taxing their respective nationals, in favour of investments in the former. Double-taxation arrangements, however, usually lead to investors' paying taxes at the rate of the country of investment or the investing country, whichever is the higher. Hence the rather mixed form of the prescription in the text.

[20] The policies described in (13)(c) constitute the fiscal/monetary mix in its 'static' form. Action under (13)(c)(i) is assumed to leave the budget balance at a normal level but to act on the private incentive to invest. Action under (13)(c) (ii), on the other hand, affects the magnitude of the surplus or deficit of the budget on a national income basis. The saving and investment levels achieved through (13)(c) may be described as 'artificial', in the sense that they do not correspond to what the saving and investing propensities of private individuals and public authorities would dictate at the interest rates required on balance-of-payments grounds and in the absence of preoccupations about maintaining a target level of aggregate demand. A deficit country in the sense of (1), if it does not

285

Text

Notes

restrict imports or divert capital movements in some other way, will be unable to reduce its deficit without undue unemployment unless it maintains artificially low savings or artificially high investment.

If the marginal propensities to import (or to reduce exports) associated with consumption expenditure and investment expenditure, respectively, are equal, the levels of savings and investment in a deficit country should be such as would result from the application of a domestic rate of interest common to both savings and investment, but lower than the rate at which the country must pay (or must forfeit) internationally in order to keep its external accounts in balance. This is what would result from a policy such as *(13)(a)*—and any combination of policies under *(13)(c)*, the results of which differ from those of *(13)(a)*, would be inferior to the latter. Since, in general, investment is believed to be more sensitive than saving to interest rates, it would seem that, under the conditions described, the bulk of the adjustment, quantitatively speaking, should fall on investment, public and private, rather than on saving. This would be less true, or not true at all, for countries where the marginal propensity to import (or reduce exports) is greater for investment than for consumption expenditure.

In maintaing artificially high, or artificially low, consumption and investment, a proper balance should, of course, be maintained between private and public consumption, and between private and public investment.

(14) If a country has sufficiently effective, and sufficiently flexible, instruments of the type of (13) (a) to be able to achieve its desired balance of payments (in the statistical sense), irrespective of the level of domestic interest rates,[21] *it can devote monetary as well as general fiscal instruments to the attainment of its*

[21] This implies that the country, if a deficit country in the sense of *(1)* above, for example, will be able to achieve a sufficiently large inward diversion of international capital flows to limit its statistical deficit to tolerate proportions.

Text

desired level of internal demand.

(15) If a country relies, at least at the margin, on the methods of (13)(c) for the attainment of its objectives with respect to the (statistical) balance of payments and the level of internal demand, the safest simple rule is to direct monetary policy towards the balance-of-payments objective and budgetary policy towards the internal demand objectives.[22]/[23]

Notes

[22] This is a dynamic approach to the fiscal/monetary mix envisaged at *(13)(c)*. Interest rates and scarcity of funds (proximately determined by monetary policy) should be such as to promote the level of capital transfers that is appropriate in relation to the balance-of-payments situation; fiscal policies should be such as, given these interest rates and that degree of scarcity of funds, will promote the level of demand appropriate in the light of *(7)*. Any measures that may be applied under *(13)(a)* or *(b)* will, of course, affect the level of domestic interest rates at which monetary policy under *(13)(c)* should aim. While fiscal policy should attempt to maintain a proper balance between public and private investment and between public and private consumption, it will not be possible for it, consistently with its demand objective, to avoid, in a country in payments deficit (surplus), promoting both an artificially high (low) level of investment, and an artificially low (high) level of savings, and it may have difficulty in avoiding other types of misallocation of resources. It is for this reason that countries that may have overcome their statistical deficits or surpluses by these means are nevertheless, in *(1)* and *(2)* of the Text, still considered to be in deficit or in surplus, respectively, and if their condition is chronic, are expected to apply the prescriptions of *(5)* and *(6)* of the Text.

[23] Both fiscal and monetary policies affect both internal demand and the balance of payments, but the former instrument has a comparatively larger influence on the former target; the latter instrument on the latter target. The pairing of instruments with targets, suggested in *(15)* of the Text, will, as Professor Mundell has shown, avoid any danger that the system may fail to converge on the two targets in question. However, this pairing will not always lead to the desired levels of the balance of payments and of internal demand by the shortest route. For example, if a country has a deficiency in demand and an undesired payments surplus, the 'mix' indicated by the formula in the text

287

Text   *Notes*

would be that of a more expansionary budget and lower interest rates. However, if the demand deficiency were small and the undesired payments surplus large, such a policy combination might lead to a state of excess demand, and the best mix would be a reduction of interest rates combined with a slightly less expansionary budget. On the other hand, if the demand deficiency were large and the payments deficit small, the best combination would probably be a more expansionary budget and a slight increase in interest rates.

COMPARISON WITH OTHER SYSTEMS OF ADJUSTMENT

The code of behaviour outlined above is basically 'orthodox'. It is pre-Keynesian in its assumption that the adjustment of chronic disequilibria should not be left to exchange rate policy alone but should be promoted, if only to a limited extent, by policies affecting aggregate demand. The more modern device of incomes policy (that is, price and wage policy) is, however, invoked to reinforce the classical adjustment process. The system is Keynesian, and in accordance with the spirit of Bretton Woods, in giving preference to compensatory official financing and diversion of capital flows over diversion or restriction of trade as an expedient for meeting temporary disequilibria, but is post-Keynesian in seeking to find more systematic and sophisticated ways of achieving such diversion than the crude device of quantitative capital controls. In this context, it gives a qualified support to modern ideas on the fiscal/monetary mix as among the ways, though not necessarily the best possible way, of achieving the diversion of capital flows. Finally, it treats chronic reliance on measures of restriction or diversion, whether in the sphere of trade or capital flows, as an indication of chronic disequilibrium, irrespective of whether or not a statistical imbalance persists.

The code presented here does not differ fundamentally from that which is adumbrated in the Report of Working Party No. 3 on the Balance of Payments Adjustment Process, though the official document is naturally less ambitious in respect of precision. There are, however, certain differences of emphasis. As regards the approach, I do not follow the Report in relating prescriptions to presumed causes of disequilibrium, such as 'inappropriate levels of internal demand, inappropriate international competitive positions, and excessive inflows or outflows of capital'. Such 'causes' are seen, on closer examination, to be merely ways of defining the situation in terms of the remedy that is required, which makes much of the subsequent argument tautological. On substance, the present essay, as compared with the Report, places rather more of the burden of adjustment on the surplus countries, looks rather more kindly on capital flows, which it considers can be defective as well as 'excessive', and is more explicit in regarding the persistence of measures restricting or diverting such flows, as well as any other distortions in the use of resources inspired by balance-of-payments considerations, as indices of a need for fundamental adjustment.

Between the system of adjustment presented in this essay and that in Tobin's chapter on the responsibilities of surplus and deficit countries, in *Maintaining and Restoring Balance in International Payments*, mentioned at page 273 above, there is an even more far-reaching measure of agreement, and differences are confined to matters of detail. Whereas Tobin suggests separate international norms for employment and growth (as well as prices), I suggest a norm for the relationship between the two. Whereas for me the persistence of payments imbalance would justify deviations from this norm, for Tobin it would justify rather a difference between obliging and permitting a country to approach his norms. Tobin does not envisage restrictions, even for capital transactions, as part of his system and, therefore, the application of such restrictions does not appear—as in the present work—as a criterion of need for fundamental adjustment. Finally, Tobin has the interesting concept that a country's obligation to provide financing should depend not only on whether or not it is in payments surplus but also on whether or not it is failing to carry out an obligation to expand demand. To me it seems safer to say that surplus countries should always be under an obligation to provide financing if in the judgment of an international body (such as the Fund), the policies of the deficit countries are such as to entitle them to receive financial assistance.

MODIFICATIONS OF PAR-VALUE ASSUMPTION

As was indicated above (page 273), the 'rules of the game' here set forth are based on the assumption that the par-value system, as at present applied under the Articles of Agreement of the IMF, is maintained. The rules that would be appropriate under a system of floating exchange rates are so different from those considered here as to be unsuitable for discussion in this essay. It may, however, be worth mentioning how the rules here developed might be affected by certain modifications of the par-value system that have been suggested in academic circles.

Thus, if the margins by which exchange rates are permitted to diverge from parity were extended substantially beyond the present limits,[2] it would be reasonable to expect countries in payments surplus to allow their rates to appreciate and those in payments deficit to allow their rates to depreciate within the margins, thus providing an incentive for equilibrating flows of private capital. Any tendency for exchange rates to remain over a substantial period of time near the upper limit would then be one of the indications of chronic surplus, and any tendency for them to remain near the lower limit an indication of chronic deficit, calling for the adoption of appropriate demand and incomes policies as set forth at points (6) to (8) of the 'Code of Adjustment'.

Again, if it were desired that par values, apart from any substantial changes that might be undertaken to correct fundamental disequilibria, could, as suggested by Professor Meade and others, be adjusted by microscopic amounts from month to month, such adjustment would presumably take its place as one of the measures to be adopted, along with appropriate demand and incomes policies, to deal with chronic surpluses or deficits. Such policies, while they might take some of the strain off price adjustments and render substantial exchange adjustments under point (9) of the Code less necessary, would presumably also in the short run increase the need for measures of the type discussed at point (13) to influence capital flows.

DISCRETIONARY ELEMENTS IN THE SYSTEM

Many of the criteria on which the prescriptions of the code presented above are based are imprecise and any agency attempting to apply them would have to exercise a wide discretion in determining, for example:

---

[2] Under Article IV, Section 3(i) of the IMF, exchange rates should not differ from parity by more than 1 per cent. A Fund decision under Article VIII, Section 3, however, permits members to maintain cross rates within 2 per cent of parity whenever these result from maintaining rates *vis-à-vis* a particular currency within margins of no more than 1 per cent of parity.

(a) how strong a country's liquidity position should be deemed to be;

(b) whether a country's deficit or surplus should be considered progressive, chronic, temporary, or reversible;

(c) to what extent a given chronic deficit or surplus calls for a departure from a country's preferred level of demand under *Alternative B* of point (7) of the Code, or from the 'normal' relationship between unemployment and price increase under *Alternative A*; or

(d) how far deficit countries should go in obtaining official balance-of-payments financing, or in diverting private capital flows inwards before having resort to current account restrictions, and how far surplus countries should go in making official financing available and diverting private capital flows outwards.

INTERNATIONAL ACTION REQUIRED TO IMPLEMENT OR
SUPPLEMENT THE SYSTEM

Some of the criteria to be applied under the system to countries in deficit or in surplus call for the establishment of certain basing points, which could best be done on the basis of explicit, though presumably informal, international agreement. This applies, for example, to:

(a) the expected rate of world reserve growth with reference to which countries would be classified as deficit or surplus countries under point (1) of the 'Code of Adjustment';

(b) the standard or normal relationship between unemployment and price increase with reference to which the appropriate aggregate demand policy of individual countries should be judged under *Alternative A* of point (7); and

(c) the standard or normal rate of price increase against which the achievement of individual countries would have to be measured under point (6).

In all these cases it should be noticed that the norms established would determine the appropriate behaviour of all countries, including not only those in substantial payments surplus or deficit but also those closer to equilibrium.

In addition, in so far as countries apply the technique of the fiscal/monetary mix, as described at points (13)(c) and (15) of the Code, to approach statistical balance in foreign payments, it will be advantageous to supplement national policies designed to affect interest rates in each country relative to others by international action to raise or lower the average level of such rates in the world as a whole.

Even if the general adoption by major countries of the system of policy described at point (*13*)(*c*) were to result in a structure of *relative* interest rates that brought about the desired pattern of international capital flows, it would not suffice to determine a satisfactory average *absolute* level of interest rates. It might result in a level of rates that made it difficult for fiscal policy in certain countries to prevent inflation or (more probably) rates that made it difficult in other countries to maintain full employment, or it might result in a level of rates that placed too much, or (more probably) too little of the burden of fiscal distortion required to reconcile domestic and international objectives on surplus as compared to deficit countries. In the former event, it could lead to too high, in the latter to too low an aggregate level of world savings. The object of international action to influence the average level of interest rates should be to enable monetary policy, as well as fiscal policy, to make some contribution to the stabilization of aggregate world demand, to distribute fairly, as between surplus and deficit countries, the burden of fiscal distortion required to balance the international accounts, and so far as possible to ensure that undersaving in deficit countries is balanced by oversaving in surplus countries.

With the possible exception of direct action to promote the observance of the 'code of behaviour' itself, the type of international action with the greatest potential bearing on the operation of the international adjustment process is probably that taken to control the supply of international liquidity, whether in the form of conditional credit facilities (for example, Fund quotas) or of unconditionally available reserves (for instance, the creation of Special Drawing Rights in the Fund).

The expansion of credit facilities whose availability is conditional on the adoption of appropriate adjustment policies is clearly favourable to the adoption of such policies, particularly by deficit countries. The supply of unconditional liquidity or reserves, however, is also relevant in this connection, since the higher the rate of reserve growth, the lower will be the statistical deficits of some countries, and the higher the statistical surpluses of others. Countries with payments surpluses in the sense of point (*2*) of the Code will have a greater incentive to apply the expansionary policies recommended for such countries; those with payments deficits in the sense of point (*1*) will have less incentive to carry out the adjustments recommended for them, but also less incentive to pursue other restrictive policies not recommended to them but tending to suppress their deficits.

The considerations relevant to international decisions to speed up or slow down the growth of reserves, which include, but are not confined to, their effect on the adjustment process, have been discussed at some length by me elsewhere,[3] and will not be repeated here.

APPLICABILITY TO LESS DEVELOPED COUNTRIES
It may be objected that the system of adjustment presented in this essay is not well adapted to the circumstances of less developed countries. It is true that various of its functions have been thought out with the more highly developed industrialized countries primarily in mind. Nevertheless, the objections that might be raised require a little probing to separate out those that are really valid from those that are only superficially so. For example, it may be argued that the supply of capital to such countries is too inelastic with respect to interest rates to permit capital-diverting measures of the type discussed at point (*13*) of the Code to be very effective, and that the financial institutions of such countries are not such as to permit the application of a fiscal/monetary mix of the type set forth at point (*15*). These objections are no doubt in large part valid, though with a *caveat* regarding the possibility of influencing the choice of local capitalists in less developed countries as between holding their funds abroad or at home. But, insofar as they are valid, they provide a case for placing greater reliance in less developed than in industrialized countries on the provision of official financing (for example, through the International Monetary Fund) as against diversion of private capital flows. They strengthen the case for having relatively high Fund quotas for less developed countries, but do not otherwise greatly affect the applicability to them of the adjustment system under discussion. More fundamental are the following objections relating to different, and in some respects

---

[3] E.g. Chapters 4 and 7 above.

contrasting, categories of less developed countries. There are some such countries with respect to which the basic Keynesian assumption regarding the (downward) inflexibility of wages and other supply prices does not as yet apply. Such countries may be best served by a system of fixed exchange rates ('gold standard') in which the level of aggregate demand is made to respond not only to chronic but even to temporary payments imbalances. There are other less developed countries in which, for one reason or another, inflationary pressures are so strong that any attempt to get them to conform (under point (6) of the Code) to a normal rate of price increase that would be acceptable to industrial countries must be regarded as hopeless. For such countries, the only recourse is a flexible, and depreciating, exchange rate. It seems probable, however, that the number of less developed countries falling into the first category will decline, and it is to be hoped that the number falling into the second category will decline likewise. In this event, the code of behaviour here set forth should become applicable, in its broad outlines, to an increasing proportion of less developed countries.

CONCLUDING REMARKS

The system of adjustment outlined above is an integrated one, and its various aspects are mutually interdependent. As has already been mentioned, if the provisions for adjustment of chronic imbalances were not operative, the provisions for interim financing and diversion of capital flows might cease to be appropriate. For example, if countries in chronic deficit will neither keep their prices stable nor devalue, they cannot expect to receive balance-of-payments financing on the scale envisaged. And if countries in chronic surplus will neither allow their prices to rise by a more than 'normal' amount nor revalue, they must be pressed to provide compensatory official financing on a greater scale than would otherwise be reasonable.

The system is, moreover, far from foolproof. Not only would it be extraordinarily difficult to get international agreement on the various norms referred to in the section on 'International Action Required to Implement or Supplement the System' above, but there are no very compelling incentives for individual surplus countries to take the actions appropriate to their situation. It is true that if deficit countries, making all appropriate efforts to adjust their prices, cannot obtain an adequate amount of interim financing they are free to adopt restrictions on capital and current account. These, however, have the effect of suppressing the deficits and removing the corresponding surpluses, thus leaving the erstwhile surplus countries with little or no apparent obligation to adjust or to provide financing. At this point three courses lie open:

(1) to make it clear that an obligation to provide financing via an appropriate international organization such as the Fund, in order to enable the latter to relieve the payments difficulties of other countries, lies not merely on countries in statistical payments surplus but on all countries not themselves in payments difficulty;

(2) to abandon the country-by-country approach, and to urge policies of adjustment on countries that *would be* in chronic surplus if the countries in chronic deficit had not been forced into restrictive measures; and

(3) to urge deficit countries to make greater use of the possibility of exchange rate adjustment. However, surplus countries, if they consult their collective interest, should welcome the type of code of behaviour that is outlined in this essay, since the burdens laid upon them by observance of the prescriptions of such a code would really be much less than those they might have to bear from the unregulated defensive actions of deficit countries.

Chapter 12

Dual Exchange Rates for Current and Capital Transactions: A Theoretical Examination*

INTRODUCTION

In a recent paper,[1] one of the writers mentioned that one way in which a non-discriminatory diversion of international capital flows for balance-of-payments reasons could be brought about 'would be for countries to have separate exchange rates for current and capital transactions, respectively. In the absence of official intervention ... "floating" capital exchange rates would tend to choke off all net capital movements into or out of each country. However, monetary authorities would be expected to prevent their capital exchange rates from falling to a discount unless their countries were in payments deficit, and to prevent them from rising to a premium unless their countries were in payments surplus. This system, whatever its technical interest, could hardly be regarded as compatible with the Articles of Agreement of the Fund relating to exchange stability and multiple-currency practices.'

While history shows no examples of a dual exchange rate system with complete segregation of current and capital transactions, there have been many cases in which most capital transfers (and some current transactions) have been carried on at free market rates more depreciated than those at which the bulk of current transactions took place. Such cases have occurred not only in less developed countries but also in such industrial countries as Belgium and the United Kingdom. And there has been at least one case—Switzerland in the early post-war period—in which capital transfers took place at free market rates higher than the par value applicable to trade transactions.

The aim of this essay is to consider what might be the results if a number of countries attempted a fairly complete segregation of international transactions on current and on capital account,

---

* A hitherto unpublished paper written in 1968. The mathematical appendix was prepared by Michael G. Kuczynski.

[1] Reprinted at Chapter 11 above, p. 268.

respectively, and, while maintaining exchange rates at par for current transactions, saw to it that capital transactions took place at separate exchange rates which, though responsive to supply and demand, might be subject to some degree of official intervention. This examination is carried out at a rather high level of abstraction, without prejudice to the legal status of such a practice under the Articles of Agreement of the Fund, and—though some indication is given as to how the segregation of markets might be implemented —without any very close attention being paid to the exchange control aspects of the system. The question it is sought to answer is, assuming that such a system could be brought into operation at all, what might its economic consequences be? The answer to this question depends to a large extent on the manner in which and the purpose for which the system would be applied, and these, in turn, are influenced by the principles, if any, on which it would be regulated internationally.

DUAL RATES IN A SINGLE COUNTRY

A. *Without intervention*

Let us assume, initially, that a floating exchange rate for capital transactions is introduced by a single country which is simultaneously keeping its rate for current transactions close to par, and that it is intended to prevent any net movement of capital into or out of the country.

If the country in question would have been a net exporter of capital had all transactions taken place at par, its floating rate for capital transactions (expressed in units of foreign currency per unit of domestic currency) will fall to a discount; if at uniform parity rates it would have been a net importer of capital, its capital rate will rise to a premium.

The segregation of the markets for current and capital transactions may be attempted in different ways. Probably the way that would permit the maximum freedom of transfer and arbitrage would be to establish two types of nonresident balances in the currency in question. If that currency were Etrurian francs, there would be, let us say, 'current francs' and 'capital francs'. Transfers would be freely permitted between current franc balances and between capital franc balances, but not from current franc balances to capital franc balances, or vice versa.

If the capital franc was at a discount, in the sense that its rate of exchange against foreign currencies was below that of the current franc, there would have to be regulations under which residents (other than dealers):

(a) could receive transfers from capital franc accounts or sell foreign exchange through the capital franc market only to an amount equivalent to their sale of capital assets in Etruria or abroad to nonresidents;

(b) could purchase from nonresidents capital assets in Etruria or abroad only through transfers from resident to capital franc accounts or in foreign exchange bought on the capital franc market;

(c) must obtain payment for exports, visible or invisible, either directly through transfers from current franc accounts or in foreign exchange which they must then sell on the current franc market; and

(d) could make transfers to current franc accounts, or purchase foreign exchange on the current franc market only to make payment for imports (visible or invisible).

These regulations would permit without hindrance transfers from current franc accounts to resident franc accounts and transfers from resident franc accounts to capital franc accounts.

If the capital franc was at a premium, there would have to be somewhat different regulations under which residents (other than dealers):

(α) must obtain payment for sales to nonresidents of capital assets in Etruria or abroad either through transfers from capital franc accounts or in foreign exchange;

(β) could make transfers to capital franc accounts only to make payment for capital assets in Etruria or abroad, and use foreign exchange purchased on the capital franc market only to make payment for such assets;

(γ) could receive transfers from current franc accounts or sell foreign exchange on the current franc market only to an amount equivalent to their exports, visible and invisible; and

(δ) must pay nonresidents for imports, visible or invisible, in current francs or in foreign exchange obtained on the current franc market.

These regulations would permit, without hindrance, transfers from capital franc accounts to resident accounts and transfers from resident accounts to current franc accounts.

If Etruria wished to segregate the markets for current and capital transactions in a manner that would be effective whether the capital franc was at a premium or a discount *vis-à-vis* the current franc, so as to provide for the case where the capital franc rate was liable to move from premium to discount or from discount to premium, it would have to apply regulations concerning the prescriptions and prohibitions contained in the two sets of regulations set forth above. This looks like a rather formidable set of controls. However, since there are only two classes of francs, current and capital, it might be possible to achieve the desired restrictions on one class of transactions through controls and restrictions applied solely to the other. In particular, if it were possible to ensure that all current transactions and only current transactions were paid for through the current franc market, it might be possible, without capital controls, to make all capital transactions and only capital transactions go through the capital franc market. Thus, enforcement of regulations (c), (d), (γ) and (δ) would, respectively, ensure the observation of regulations (a), (b), (α) and (β).

If, therefore, Etruria could impose effective controls on current transactions, it could achieve the required segregation of current and capital transactions whether the capital franc were at a premium or a discount by providing that:

(i) residents received transfers from current franc accounts or sold foreign exchange through the current franc market to an amount no less and no greater than the value of their exports, visible and invisible, and

(ii) residents made transfers to current franc accounts or purchased foreign exchange through the current franc market to an amount no less and no greater than the value of their imports, visible and invisible.

Banks and other foreign exchange dealers resident in Etruria would be allowed, unlike other residents, to hold assets in both current and capital francs. However, since, like other holders, they would not be allowed to make transfers between the two types of accounts, they would be unable to make a profit by buying foreign exchange for one type of franc and selling it for another. Moreover, their holdings of foreign exchange and of current francs would be allowed to vary only temporarily and within prescribed limits.

With these regulations in force, a nonresident holding current franc balances would be free only (a) to transfer them to other nonresidents without restriction, (b) to transfer them to resident accounts in connection with an export from Etruria, or (c) to purchase foreign exchange in the current account market. A nonresident holding capital franc balances would be formally free to transfer them to resident or nonresident accounts without restriction, but the controls over current transactions would ensure that in fact he transferred them either to other nonresidents without restriction or to resident accounts in connection with capital flows, or used them to acquire foreign exchange on the capital franc market.

As already indicated, 'exports' and 'imports' should be understood to include invisible as well as trade items. In particular, export receipts include receipts of interest and profits on assets held abroad, and receipts from foreign tourists in Etruria, while import payments include payment of interest and profits on foreign-owned assets in Etruria as well as Etrurian tourist expenditures abroad.

There are, of course, difficult—indeed insoluble—problems involved in enforcing the segregation of current and capital transactions. Thus increases and reductions in current franc balances held by nonresidents, though strictly speaking capital flows, would affect the demand for, and supply of, current francs. The same is true of increases or reductions in the amounts of international commercial credit extended in connection with Etrurian exports and imports ('leads' and 'lags') and also of variations in the amount of dealers' balances in foreign exchange acquired on the current franc market. In order to prevent profitable evasion of the segregation of the two markets arising out of direct investment and tied lending, it would be necessary to ensure that payments through the current franc market took place with respect to all profits of foreign-owned firms in Etruria and Etrurian firms abroad, and that any re-investment of such profits gave rise to payments through the capital franc market; and also that payments through the current franc market took place with respect to all trade transactions, even those between a parent firm and its subsidiary. Clearly, it would not be possible entirely to avoid evasion resulting from the under- or over-valuation of these and other current transactions. Even greater difficulties would arise in verifying the true value of tourist transactions, both outwards and inwards, and ensuring their settlement through the current franc market.

Problems of a different sort arise in the case of assets such as bills of exchange where interest is not paid explicitly as such but in the form of a difference between the price at maturity and the price at the time of issue. To deal with these it would be necessary to require that all realized capital appreciation on assets owned across the Etrurian frontier should give rise to the same obligation to make payments through the current franc market as would the receipt of interest on such assets.

While any country attempting to apply the system described above would have to content itself with a less than complete segregation of current and capital exchange transactions, it might not be impossible to achieve a reasonable measure of such segregation. In any event, for the remainder of this paper we shall examine what might be the consequences of such segregation, temporarily suspending any disbelief as to the possibility of applying it.

Both current francs and capital francs would be bought and sold on the relevant markets against foreign exchange. Arbitrage would eliminate any discrepancies between the rates for capital francs *vis-à-vis* the various foreign currencies and the prevailing exchange rates between these currencies; and the same would hold true for current francs. The Etrurian authorities would intervene in the usual way to stabilize within the usual limits the value of current francs in terms of dollars and hence of other currencies, while rates for the capital franc would fluctuate freely in response to demand and supply.

Any decline in the market value of the capital franc in terms of foreign exchange would tend to increase the profitability to foreigners of investing in Etruria since the earnings from any such investment would be transferable through the current franc market at par while the capital cost in foreign exchange of acquiring such an investment would decline. There would, therefore, be an increase in the amount of capital francs purchased and probably also in the amount of foreign exchange spent in the acquisition of such francs. Similarly any decline in the market value of the capital franc would tend to reduce the profitability to Etrurian residents of investing abroad. There would, therefore, be a decline in the amount of foreign exchange purchased on the capital franc market, and probably also in the amount of francs used for such purchases. Unless the elasticity of demand for foreign assets with respect to prices in Etruria and in the outside world, respectively, averaged less than one-half, it would always be possible to find some stable exchange rate that would clear the market for the capital franc.[2] In the absence of official intervention on the capital franc market, the rate would be such as to prevent a *net* movement of capital into or out of Etruria.

The price elasticity or responsiveness to price changes of the net demand of residents in one area for securities in another is rather a complex affair which depends on (a) the extent to which the residents in question will substitute securities in one area for securities in the other in the make-up of their portfolios as their relative prices change, together with the rate at which such substitution will be achieved through time, (b) the extent to which the residents in question will substitute securities in one area for securities in the other in the investment of a given volume of current savings as their relative prices change, and (c) any real income effects of changes in the price of foreign securities on the volume of savings. In the short run (a) is likely to be the most important element and should be sufficiently great to ensure the short-run stability of the capital exchange rate.

The fact that the capital exchange rate fluctuated freely with demand and supply would, however, affect the demand for Etrurian securities abroad, and foreign securities in Etruria in another way, namely by increasing the uncertainty of the future return on such securities insofar as the return relevant to the investment might involve a repatriation of capital that would have to be carried out at a future, and therefore unknown, rate of exchange on the capital franc market. This uncertainty might well tend to reduce the net demand for foreign securities in Etruria as well as the net demand for Etrurian securities abroad.

---

[2] Even if the average price elasticity of demand for foreign assets in the two areas averaged less than one-half, it might still be possible to achieve a stable market equilibrium provided that the supply elasticities in the two areas were less than infinite.

B. *With intervention*

It would be unnecessary, and somewhat irrational, for a country to operate the system, as we have assumed Etruria to do, in such a way as to prevent net capital movements, inwards or outwards. There is no particular virtue in the segregation of current and capital markets as such. On the other hand, in a world where chronic disequilibria are frequent, it is much more plausible that a country in balance-of-payments deficit should wish to employ such segregation as a means of reducing or eliminating its deficit by influencing capital transactions, thus minimizing or avoiding resort to currency devaluation or import restriction, curtailment of foreign aid or the tying of current or capital transactions to exports. Or that a surplus country should want to reduce or eliminate its surplus by acting on its capital account, thus minimizing or avoiding the need for currency revaluation, the taxation of exports, or other unpleasant steps affecting the current account. The accumulation of reserves associated with a surplus is really a form of capital export—a particularly unremunerative form—and it would seem more logical to discourage, to a moderate extent, *all* types of capital import and encourage *all* types of capital export than to concentrate the distortion on one particular variety.

If the Etrurian authorities were to take balance in over-all payments and receipts rather than balance on capital transactions as their criterion for determining the capital franc rate, they would be able to obtain the appropriate level for that rate only by intervening on the capital franc market, by buying or selling capital francs against foreign exchange. If the intervention of the authorities on the current franc market, as required to keep the current franc close to par, yielded a surplus of foreign exchange, they would sell that amount of foreign exchange on the capital franc market. Conversely, if their intervention on the current franc market resulted in a deficit, they would replenish their reserves by selling capital francs for foreign exchange. The capital franc rate would then settle at a premium or a discount from par according to whether Etruria would have had an over-all surplus or an over-all deficit (*not* a surplus or deficit on capital account) if all transactions had taken place at par.

This, of course, is not the only way in which the capital franc market could be manipulated to bring about an over-all balance. For example, if Etruria had a surplus on current account, instead of

303

buying capital francs with foreign exchange it could permit or compel certain outward capital transactions to take place through the current franc market, or certain inward current transactions through the capital franc market. This, however, would be discriminatory as between various types of capital transactions, or as between various types of current transactions, and therefore prima facie more uneconomic than the sale of foreign exchange on the capital franc market.

A sort of 'reverse transfer problem' would arise in connection with the system of floating capital exchange rates just described. The 'transfer problem' as originally posed concerned the difficulties that might occur in bringing about a change in the balance of payments on current account to correspond to an autonomous change in capital flows or in unilateral money transfers. The 'reverse transfer problem' or 'refinancing problem' concerns the difficulties that might arise, under a dual exchange rate system, in bringing about a change in capital flows to correspond to an autonomous change in the balance on current account. A country whose current account deficit was increasing might find that it had to carry out larger and larger proportionate depreciations in its capital exchange rate to obtain a given addition to the flow of foreign exchange accruing to its central reserves from intervention in the capital exchange market. There might even come a point at which any further depreciation would reduce rather than increase that flow.

In any precise exposition of this matter, account has to be taken of the complex character of the elasticity of net demand for foreign securities as set forth in page 302. For convenience, the relationship at (a) on that page may be assumed such that capitalists immediately adjust the target distribution of their portfolios to changes in relative security prices and cause the actual to approach the target distribution at a speed proportional to the discrepancy between the two. Under these conditions, any given decline in Etruria's capital exchange rate (assuming domestic security prices to remain unchanged in Etruria and abroad), would be likely to evoke increased net purchases of Etrurian securities by foreigners and reduced net purchases of foreign securities by Etrurians, starting at a relatively high level, as capitalists in Etruria and abroad adjusted their portfolios, but dwindling towards a level that corresponded to the change in the composition of placements of current savings in both areas. Assuming that the capital franc rate was initially in stable equilibrium, the decline in the rate would, even in the long run, enable Etruria to earn more, or lose less, foreign exchange through the capital franc market. Further depreciation in the capital franc rate would, of course, enable Etruria to earn additional foreign exchange through the capital franc market in the short, and even in the long run. However, there is some reason to expect that after a point these effects would become progressively weaker; desire to maintain a geographical diversification of asset holdings would make it harder merely by raising effective yields in Etruria relative to those abroad to induce either Etrurians to give up more of their remaining holdings of foreign assets or foreigners to invest still more capital in Etruria; in the latter case the cheapening of the capital franc rate would enable foreigners to continue to add to their purchases of Etrurian securities as these became cheaper after they had ceased to add to their expenditure of foreign exchange for this purpose. In other words, the long-run price elasticities of Etrurian demand for foreign securities and foreign demand for Etrurian securities might decline to a point where the capital exchange rate became unstable.

Even while the capital franc rate still retained long-run stability, the discrepancy between short- and long-run elasticities would ensure that any attempt to increase foreign exchange earnings through the capital franc market would lead to a *gradual* decline in the rate to a new level. Once the rate became unstable in the long run, however—though it might retain short-run stability—any such attempt would lead to an indefinite decline in the rate.

As soon as the floating capital exchange market was subject to official intervention, budgetary consequences would be apt to arise. Maintenance of a depreciated capital exchange rate is equivalent to applying a tax on capital exports and an equivalent subsidy on capital imports. If the capital exchange rate is above par, the tax is on capital imports and the subsidy on capital exports. Now, if the authorities were to support the capital exchange rate by injections of foreign exchange earned on the current exchange market, they would earn a net revenue in domestic currency so long as the capital exchange rate was below par but would suffer a net loss if the capital rate was above par. Correspondingly, if they depressed

305

the capital exchange rate in order to make the capital exchange market contribute to reserves, they would make a net profit so long as the capital rate remained above par but would suffer a net loss if that rate was below par. Such revenue considerations make it unlikely that the authorities would press their support of the capital exchange market far enough to eliminate a large payments surplus, and might limit the extent to which they acquired reserves through the capital market.

A question arises whether a country adversely affected by the depreciation of another country's capital exchange rate would be desirous of resisting or retaliating against such depreciation. The former country might well suffer a payments loss from the artificial encouragement to capital imports in the country whose capital rate was depreciated. However, it could not easily react to this in an effective way. It would be difficult to prevent either the decline of capital exports from the country of depreciated currency to the affected country or the diversion of third country capital exports away from the affected country towards the country of depreciated currency unless the affected country were to follow suit and institute a uniformly depreciated capital exchange rate on its own. Even the movement of funds from the affected country to the country of depreciated currency would be hard to control since any special discriminatory measures might be evaded by a detour through third countries.

DUAL RATES IN SEVERAL COUNTRIES

Suppose that two or more countries wished to practice a dual rate system. For the currency of each country practising that system, there would now be four classes of rates: (i) current-current rates, (ii) current-capital rates; (iii) capital-current rates, and (iv) capital-capital rates. In each of these hypothetical rates the adjective before the hyphen indicates the type of balance in the currency of the country in question, and the adjective after the hyphen the type of balance in the currency of the other country participating in the transaction. Undifferentiated balances, in currencies where there is no dual rate, are classed as current balances. To take account of the likely possibility that different dual rate countries would not define current and capital transactions in quite the same way, and to avoid the necessity for burdensome co-ordination between them, it would suffice if each of the dual rate countries would prescribe that (a) exports must, and only exports could, be sold for current balances in its currency or for foreign exchange to be repatriated through the current-current, or current-capital exchange market, while (b) imports must, and only imports could, be paid for in current balances in its own currency or in foreign exchange obtained through the current-current, or current-capital exchange markets. Any transaction between the dual rate countries that was classed as current in one country and capital in the other would be subject to a current-capital rate (from the standpoint of the first country), which would also be a capital-current rate (from the standpoint of the second). 'Foreign exchange' here refers to any type of balances in foreign currency. Dealers would be strictly limited in their power to vary their positions with respect to current balances either in domestic or in foreign currency. Arbitrage through the foreign exchange markets would bring into conformity the exchange rates for: current balances in any one currency against current balances in any other; capital balances in any one currency against capital balances in any other; capital balances in any one currency against current balances in any other; and capital balances in any currency against current balances in the same currency. As a result, for example, any resident of country A (a country with a capital-current rate[3] at 90 per cent of par) that wanted to buy an asset in country B (a country with a capital-current rate at 120 per cent of par) would have to pay $120/100$ *times* $100/90$, i.e. $1\frac{1}{3}$ units of his currency to obtain 1 unit of the currency of the country of investment.

Monetary authorities would presumably keep their foreign exchange reserves in the form of current balances, or undifferentiated balances, and intervention by a monetary authority on its own capital exchange markets would presumably take the form of buying or selling such balances for capital balances in its own currency. However, if a country of reserve currency should also maintain a dual exchange rate system, it might find it convenient to intervene on its own capital exchange market by buying or selling current balances in its own currency for capital balances in the same currency.

---

[3] Since it is assumed that all current-current rates are kept at par by official intervention, we can speak (in the singular) of *the* capital-current rate of any currency.

A GENERALIZED SYSTEM OF DUAL EXCHANGE RATES[4]

The peculiarities of the system stand out most clearly if it is assumed —quite unrealistically—that it is adopted by all countries. How, in these circumstances, would the structure of capital-current and capital-capital rates be determined? In an n-country world there would be n^2 capital-current rates (including the rates of exchange between capital and current balances in each currency), $n(n-1)/2$ current-current rates and $n(n-1)/2$ capital-capital rates. Assuming that the current-current rates would be exogenously determined by well-known factors, including official intervention, then it is only necessary to determine, by the relationships to be discussed, n independent rates among the remainder, e.g. the $(n-1)$ rates of exchange between capital balances in non-U.S. currencies and capital balances in dollars *plus* the rate of exchange between capital dollars and current dollars. All other rates would then be determined by arbitrage.

These n unknown rates are determined by reference to the various relationships that exist between capital-capital rates and capital-current rates on the one hand, and net private demands and official demands[5] for capital balances, on the other. The fact that there are n currencies, for each of which there is a net private and an official demand for capital balances, raises the number of unknowns to $3n$.

Consider, first, the net private demand for capital balances in each currency. Other things (including the return on capital in each country expressed in domestic currency) being equal, this will depend on the structure of capital-capital exchange rates. This yields $(n-1)$ independent net demand equations *plus* one equation stating that (since the purchase of capital balances in one country is matched by the sale of capital balances in another) the aggregate value of net private demands for capital balances in all currencies, when priced at the exchange rates relevant to any given numeraire, is equal to zero.[6]

---

[4] Some of the points made in this section are developed and exemplified in the Appendix.

[5] In the definition of 'net private demand' and of 'official demand' for capital balances, any supply of such balances counts as a negative demand.

[6] This is strictly true only on the assumption that all countries apply the same definitions of current and capital transactions when segregating the markets. Private transactions deemed 'current' in one country and 'capital' in another would, like acts of official intervention, directly affect rates on the current-capital markets. To take them into account here would further complicate the analysis.

It should be noted, for later reference, that the amounts of these private net capital flows are assumed to depend entirely on the capital-capital rates, i.e. on the *relative* rather than the *absolute* level of the capital-current exchange rates. It is clear that the effective rate of interest which a resident in one country could earn on an investment in any other country would depend entirely on the capital-capital rate between the two countries and not at all on the absolute level of their capital-current rates. Thus, in the example given in the previous section, if country A had had a capital-current rate of 180 instead of 90, and country B a capital-current rate of 240 instead of 120, any resident of country A wanting to invest in B would still have had to pay $1\frac{1}{3}$ units of A-currency to obtain 1 unit of B-currency for the purpose of investment.

The official demand for capital balances in any currency, on the other hand, i.e. the demand arising from official sales of current balances through the capital-current exchange market, will be related, and probably inversely related, to the capital-current exchange rate of the country in question. This is because the smaller the premium or the larger the discount of a country's capital-current rate in relation to par the less will be the domestic-currency loss, or the greater the domestic-currency profit accruing to the monetary authorities as a result of any sale of current balances through the capital-current exchange market, and the less will be the profit or the greater the loss of any purchase of current balances through that market. These relationships supply us with n additional equations.

The n equations still required are supplied by the condition that the sum of the net private demand, and the official demand, for capital balances in each currency must be equal to zero in order that the markets may be cleared.

These market-clearing equations, taken in conjunction with the equation stating that the aggregate value of the private net demands for capital balances in the various currencies is equal to zero, have an important corollary, namely that the aggregate net value of official demands for capital balances, when priced at the exchange rates relevant to any given numeraire, is equal to zero; it follows that net official sales of current balances through the capital-current markets must sum to zero. This condition, which is a natural consequence of the segregation of capital and current exchange markets, defines an important requirement which the relationships governing official demands for capital balances must meet if the system is not to be self-contradictory.

These relationships are of vital importance to the system as a whole. It is only through them that the capital-current exchange rates, as distinct from the capital-capital rates, are determined at all. If there were no official intervention on the capital-current markets, the requirement, imposed by the market-balance equations, that the net demand for capital balances in each currency should equal zero, would suffice to determine the $(n-1)$ independent capital-capital rates of exchange. Since current-current exchange rates are fixed at par, all capital-current rates would have to rise or fall *en bloc*, but there would be nothing to determine where the general level of such rates would be. Again, if the amount of reserves which some countries wish to acquire, relative to the amount which other countries are willing to lose through intervention on the capital-current exchange markets, declines too little as capital-current rates decline, and rises too little as they rise, there may be no point at which these two amounts become equal. There may, therefore, be no equilibrium level for capital-current rates in general, which may fall indefinitely if some countries are trying to acquire more current balances by capital market intervention than others are willing to sell, or rise indefinitely in the opposite case.

While this would scarcely be likely to occur even in a completely generalized dual rate system, the general level of capital-current rates—as distinct from the structure of capital-capital rates—would be likely to be very unstable as a result of the thinness of the capital-current exchange markets. Apart from such slight and temporary accommodation as might be possible for shifts in the working current balances of dealers and others, a monetary authority desiring to acquire current balances by selling capital balances in its own currency would have to wait until the whole structure of capital-current rates had declined to a point at which other monetary authorities were prepared to sell more—or buy less—current balances on the capital-current markets. In practice, all official exchanges of current for capital balances would probably be routed through the capital-current market for some central currency. Thus, if the U.K. authorities wished to sell capital sterling for current dollars, they would do so by first selling capital sterling for capital dollars, then selling capital dollars for current dollars; and if the German authorities wished to sell current dollars for capital deutsche mark, they would first sell current dollars for capital dollars, then sell capital dollars for capital deutsche mark. Even so, the market for current dollars versus capital dollars could scarcely be a broad and steady one.

It should be noted that any increase in a country's propensity to acquire current balances through the capital-current market would tend both (a) to depress the capital-capital exchange rates for the currency of that country, and (b) to lower the general level of capital-current rates. Again, any change in private capital movements which brought about changes in the capital-capital rates might tend to affect the general level of capital-current rates also, because of differences in what might be called the 'elasticities of intervention' of different national authorities with respect to changes in their respective capital-current rates.

The foregoing examination of a situation of generalized adoption of capital exchange rates is, of course, of merely academic interest. In the far more probable case in which such rates were adopted by some countries only while others maintained uniform exchange rates for all transactions, the general level of capital-current exchange rates in the currencies of dual rate countries would be 'anchored' by the fact that the uniform rate countries in effect pegged their own capital-current rates at par. This means that the uniform rate countries would lose reserves to, or gain reserves from, the dual rate countries on account of capital transactions according as, at the anchored level of capital-current rates, the latter chose in the aggregate to buy or to sell current balances net through intervention in the capital-current exchange markets.

PROS AND CONS OF THE SYSTEM

To the extent that the segregation of capital and current transactions could be made effective, the adoption of a dual exchange rate system of the type described, by one or a number of countries, would be likely, provided that it was used defensively and not aggressively to promote equilibrating and to mitigate disequilibrating capital flows.

It is, of course, possible, unless steps were taken to prevent aggressive official intervention on capital exchange markets, that the system might become the instrument of a scramble for reserves. The same is true of any other policy that affects the balance of payments, such as import restriction or depreciation of current exchange rates, but the danger might appear to be particularly great in the present case. Competitive depreciation of capital exchange rates, of course, would not affect trade or current account transactions, but it might be used to draw reserves out of countries that did not themselves operate a dual rate, or that maintained their capital exchange rates at a fixed level. The remedy in this case, as in the case of the other types of balance-of-payments policies mentioned above, would be to adopt rules of international good behaviour in the operation of a dual exchange rate system. Besides providing that capital exchange rates should not be applicable to current transactions, such rules might provide, for example, that a country would be prohibited from forcing or permitting its capital-current exchange rate to fall to a discount whenever it was in surplus in its over-all balance of payments. (There would probably be no necessity for making the corresponding rule forbidding deficit countries to force or permit their capital-current exchange rates to rise to a premium, as there would be little motive—except possibly a fiscal one—for countries to act in this way.)

Assuming the dual exchange rate system to be operated in an equilibrating way, the question remains whether the equilibrium which it tends to promote would be a desirable one. To some extent it would doubtless take the place of other techniques for influencing capital flows in an equilibrating sense and from this standpoint it would have certain advantages. Since its effect could be spread evenly over almost all types of capital flows, it would avoid some of the anomalies and extreme distortions likely to result from *ad hoc* restrictions, or incentives, affecting particular types of capital flow—measures, the effectiveness of which is frequently reduced by offsetting repercussions or types of capital flow not directly affected by the measures in question. A widespread adoption of dual rates would tend to bring about discrimination on balance-of-payments grounds as between countries of destination of each country's capital exports; it would not, however, take account of any other reasons there might be for preferring one form of capital export to another or one country of investment to another. As compared with the technique of manipulating capital movements

312

through interest-rate (monetary) policy, while offsetting demand repercussions through fiscal policy, the dual rate system would probably be less subject to parliamentary hazards, would avoid undesired repercussions on public saving, and would lead to fewer anomalies in the relationship between public and private investment. Finally, as compared to the use of reserves or compensatory official financing, it would avoid automatic inflationary effects in surplus countries and deflationary effects in deficit countries—which might be a good or a bad thing according to circumstances—and might also make for a more rational distribution of investment in both sets of countries; though this could be disputed.

To some extent, the operation of a dual rate system would substitute not for other forms of distortion of the capital account, but for adjustment of the current account. Insofar as this meant that deficit countries were enabled to avoid the necessity for resorting to a restriction or subsidization of foreign trade that might endanger the structure of international agreements in this field, it should probably be put down to the credit of the dual rate system, though from an economic standpoint the disadvantages of distorted capital flows has to be weighed against the advantage of freer trade. Insofar as the effect was to delay the adjustments in price levels and exchange rates that would otherwise have taken place, the balance of advantage would be a much more doubtful one. By giving more time for fundamental adjustments in the current balance, the system might permit the avoidance of substantial unemployment or strong inflationary pressure. On the other hand, it might promote the continuance of currency over-valuation or perverse demand policies that would have to be put right sooner or later. In any event, like other policies affecting capital flows, it would involve an excessive flow of capital towards deficit countries. A particularly unfortunate aspect of this maldistribution is that since the attraction of capital towards a deficit country would depend in some measure on its fiscal ability to subsidize the sale of capital balances of its currency for foreign exchange and on its ability to pay on all net capital imported the abnormally high real interest rate involved in a depreciated capital rate, the bulk of the diversion of capital involved would be towards richer countries rather than towards less developed countries in payments difficulty.

What has been said above takes account neither of the costs of applying an elaborate system of exchange controls over current transactions, nor of the inevitable imperfections and loopholes characteristic of such controls. The greater the divergence between the exchange rates applicable to current and capital transactions respectively, the more profitable it would become to make current payments, outwards or inwards as the case may be, through the capital exchange markets, with the result that certain types of invisible or less easily traceable exports or imports would be encouraged, without economic justification, relative to visible or more easily traceable ones. Moreover, to the extent that the existence of, or changes in, premia or discounts in the capital exchange rates led to anticipations of changes in current exchange rates, they might result in speculative capital flows of those types (leads and lags, withdrawals of current account balances, etc.) that, owing to imperfections in the controls, could not be prevented from passing through the current exchange markets. It seems unlikely, however, that the disturbing repercussions of such speculative flows on the resources of the country concerned would be as great as if the tendencies causing the changes in capital exchange premia and discounts had operated on the current exchange market and thus directly affected reserves. It should be noted that insofar as speculative capital transfers evoked by the fluctuations in the capital exchange rate flowed through the capital exchange market, they would have no effect on reserves and would probably tend in the main to stabilize the capital exchange rate.

DISCRIMINATORY 'REGIONAL' SYSTEMS

Suppose that there is a group of countries that maintain free (unrestricted) capital flows as between themselves but operate *vis-à-vis* the rest of the world dual rate systems designed to keep each of them in over-all payments balance.

It is conceivable that such a system could be implemented with less exchange control than if the countries in question had maintained non-discriminatory national dual rate systems. Each member of the group would establish a third category of external balances in their currencies in addition to capital balances and current balances, viz., balances held by residents of other members of the group. Transfers between the accounts of national residents and 'group' accounts in any member currency would be made freely. No transfers would be

314

allowed between current balances, or capital balances, on the one hand, and these 'group' balances, on the other, but the exchange rates of group balances in the different member currencies would be kept in the vicinity of par by official intervention.

The maintenance of 'freedom' of capital movements at par within the group would be likely to have certain effects on capital flows in general even in the special case in which, under a regime of non-discriminatory capital exchange rates, the capital-capital exchange rates would have been at par between all the members of the group. Suppose, for example, that for all members of the group capital-current exchange rates would have been at a discount of 20 per cent and capital-capital rates within the group would, therefore, have been at par. Some members of the group would have been exporting capital net to others and earning foreign exchange thereby to the amount of, say, $100 million. After the institution of 'group' balances, assuming for the moment that capital exchange rates vis-à-vis the outside world remained at a 20 per cent discount, there would be no reason for any change in capital flows. Net capital flows between group members would be the same as before, but net capital exporters would now earn not $100 million but $125 million of foreign exchange from the net capital importers. This would make the former less eager, and the latter more eager, than before to earn foreign exchange through capital transactions with the outside world. As a result of this change in the propensity to intervene in the capital exchange markets, the capital exchange rates of the former countries would probably appreciate, and those of the latter depreciate, making the capital balance of the former with the outside world less favourable and that of the latter more favourable.

Such repercussions, however, would be relatively minor. In the more general case in which, under non-discriminatory national capital exchange rates, some members of the group would have smaller discounts or larger premia than others in their capital exchange rates, so that the capital-capital rates within the group would diverge from par, the general effect of the introduction of freedom of capital movements within the group at par would be to give rise to increased capital flows from members whose capital exchange rates were relatively depreciated to those whose rates were relatively appreciated. As a result, the former class of members would lose reserves which they would seek to recoup through

315

intervention in the markets for capital transactions with third countries; while the latter class of members could be less acquisitive of reserves in their interventions in their own capital exchange markets with third countries. The capital-current rates of the former would consequently fall, while the rates of the latter would rise, thus evoking a more favourable net flow of capital as between the former class of member countries and outside countries and a less favourable flow as between the second class of member countries and third countries. Thus, quite apart from any effects operating through the interest rates of member countries—and indeed there need be no such effects—the increased flow of capital from one class of members to another would be offset by repercussions on the flows of both classes *vis-à-vis* non-member countries. Since the current account balance of payments of both classes of members would remain unchanged, the total net capital flows of both classes of members would likewise remain unchanged in real terms. All that would happen would be an elaborate reshuffling of ownership as between different categories of members and the outside world. Those members that would attract additional capital funds from other members as a result of putting intra-group capital movements on a par-value basis would get worse 'terms of trade' for their intra-group capital transactions but better terms for their transactions with the outside world, and the contrary would be the case for the other members.

Insofar as this reshuffling of capital flows had any substantive effect at all, e.g. because of the association of ownership with know-how, or because of the different 'tastes' with respect to investment of capitalists in different countries, the effect, resulting as it would from a non-functional type of discrimination, would be likely to be uneconomic. It would not even promote a higher degree of economic integration as between group members, since if more funds would be flowing from low capital rate members to high capital rate members, less would be flowing from the latter to the former.

The best that can be said in favour of the arrangement is that it might be less unfavourable to fundamental adjustment than purely national dual rate systems. For if the freedom of intra-group capital flows forced the deficit countries of the group to depreciate their capital rates still further than under non-discriminatory dual rates, the increased marginal fiscal cost of subsidizing capital inflows might lead them to look more kindly on monetary or exchange policies that would increase their competitiveness and improve their current accounts.

Appendix
by Michael G. Kuczynski

A Generalized System of Capital Exchange Rates

It is intended to demonstrate here how, in a system in which all n countries had adopted dual exchange rates to separate capital from current transactions, the prices of capital balances of different currencies would be determined, both in terms of each other and in terms of current balances. It is assumed that current transactions are exogenously determined, and, in particular, that the prices of current balances of different currencies in terms of each other are known.

Let a_{ij} be the price of one unit of capital balances of i-currency in terms of capital balances of j-currency,

b_{ij} the price of one unit of capital balances of i-currency in terms of current balances of j-currency, and

c_{ij} the price of one unit of current balances of i-currency in terms of current balances of j-currency.

It may be noted in passing that, by definition, $a_{ii} = c_{ii} = 1$ for any i.

By assumption all c_{ij} are known (all but $(n-1)$ of them are in fact determined either by definition, as above, or by arbitrage); the problem is thus to determine the $n(n-1)$ remaining a_{ij}, and all the b_{ij}, of which there are n^2. It is the case, however, that once the values of any n of these unknowns have been determined, consistency in the configuration of prices implies unique values for the remaining $2n(n-1)$ unknowns. In other words, given the values of any n of the unknown prices, the values of the remainder are uniquely determined by arbitrage. This may readily be shown as follows.

317

At all times consistency in the configuration of prices requires that for any i, j and k

$$a_{ij}a_{jk} = a_{ik} \tag{i}$$
$$a_{ij}b_{ji} = b_{ii} \tag{ii}$$

and
$$b_{ii}c_{ij} = b_{ij}. \tag{iii}$$

Suppose that the n given unknowns are a_{1j} for $j = 2, \ldots n$, and b_{11}. If a_{1j} is given for any j then a_{j1} is implied (the first relation above yields $a_{ij}a_{ji} = 1$ when $k = i$, a result which is in any case evident from the definition of a_{ij}). Then, knowing for any j and k both a_{j1} and a_{1k}, we know a_{jk} for any j and k, because $a_{j1}a_{1k} = a_{jk}$ by the first relation.

As regards the b_{ij}, we have $a_{1j}b_{j1} = b_{11}$ from the second relation, so that we know b_{j1} for any j. We also have $b_{jj}c_{j1} = b_{j1}$ from the third relation, so that, given the prices of current balances of different currencies in terms of each other, we know b_{jj} for any j. Consequently b_{ij} is determined for any i and j, since $a_{ji}b_{ij} = b_{jj}$ from the second relation, and we have seen that a_{ji} is determined for any i and j.

It has thus been demonstrated that, given a_{1j} for $j = 2, \ldots n$ and b_{11}, all other a_{ij} and b_{ij} are uniquely implied by the arbitrage conditions (i) to (iii); and it can readily be seen that a similar result would hold whatever the n unknowns given at the outset are. It will therefore be sufficient in what follows to show that n of the $(2n^2 - n)$ prices for different types of currency balances can be determined, and leave the rest to be implied by the arbitrage conditions. For expository convenience it will be assumed that a_{1j} for $j = 2, \ldots n$ and b_{11} are the n prices to be determined.

It will be shown that conditions of net demand, both private and official, for capital balances of different currencies can be envisaged so as to determine n such prices. Private and official demands are considered in turn, and then the conditions under which they are reconciled in the various markets for capital balances.

NET PRIVATE DEMAND FOR CAPITAL BALANCES

It is assumed that, for the purposes of this exercise, yields on capital assets are given and invariable in terms of local currency. Let δ_{ij} be the number of units of capital balances of j-currency demanded by private holders of capital balances of i-currency (δ_{ii} can be thought of as equal to zero). Under the circumstances δ_{ij} can be expected to bear an inverse relation to the price a_{ji} of capital balances of j-currency in terms of i-currency, or a direct relation to the price a_{ij} of capital balances of i-currency in terms of j-currency (since $a_{ij}a_{ji} = 1$). In addition, δ_{ij} can of course be expected to depend upon the prices a_{ki} of capital balances of all other k-currencies as well ($k \neq j$). The disregard of these other prices at this stage does not, however, involve any loss of generality in the formulation of net private demand for capital balances, presently to be set out.

Total gross private demand for capital balances of i-currency then amounts to $\sum_{j=1}^{n} \delta_{ji}$ units of i-currency, or $\sum_{j=1}^{n} \delta_{ji}a_{i1}$ equivalents of 1-currency (any one of the n currencies may be chosen as numeraire). Total gross private supply of capital balances of i-currency, which is the sum of i-currency holders' demands for capital balances of other currencies, amounts to $\sum_{j=1}^{n} \delta_{ij}a_{j1}$ equivalents of 1-currency. Thus total net private demand for capital balances of i-currency may be expressed as $\sum_{j=1}^{n} (\delta_{ji}a_{i1} - \delta_{ij}a_{j1})$ equivalents of 1-currency. From this expression it can be seen that net private demands for capital balances of any currency are such that their sum over all currencies, when expressed in terms of one currency, is equal to zero: that is, it may be readily verified that

$$\sum_{i=1}^{n} \sum_{j=1}^{n} (\delta_{ji}a_{i1} - \delta_{ij}a_{j1}) = 0.$$

Any reformulation of the total net private demands for capital balances of individual currencies, such as is now set out, has to be such as to conform to this result for their aggregate.

Expressed in units of i-currency, instead of 1-currency, total net private demand for capital balances of i-currency amounts to $\sum_{j=1}^{n} (\delta_{ji}a_{i1} - \delta_{ij}a_{j1})\,a_{1i}$, that is, to $\sum_{j=1}^{n} (\delta_{ji} - \delta_{ij}a_{ji})$. It has been noted that δ_{ji} can be expected to be directly related to a_{ji}, and δ_{ij} to a_{ij}. If it is now assumed that these relationships are best expressed in their linear form (such as $\delta_{ij} = A'_{ij} + B'_{ij}a_{ij}$), total net private

319

demand for capital balances of i-currency may be rewritten, in units of i-currency, as

$$\alpha_i = \sum_{j=1}^{n} A_{ji} a_{ji} \qquad \text{(iv)}$$

where the A_{ji} are coefficients that depend upon the A'_{ij} and B'_{ij} (thus $A_{ii} = \sum_{j=1}^{n} (A'_{ji} + B'_{ij})$, and $A_{ji} = A'_{ij} + B'_{ji}$ for $i \neq j$). The coefficient A_{ji} is equal to $\dfrac{\partial \alpha_i}{\partial a_{ji}}$, that is to say, it is a fraction whose numerator is the change in net private demand for capital balances of i-currency induced by a change in the price of capital balances of j-currency in terms of capital balances of i-currency, all other prices remaining equal, and whose denominator is the change in the price of capital balances of j-currency in terms of capital balances of i-currency. It is assumed that these coefficients are known; they can normally be expected to be positive, though the constant term A_{ii} might not be.

It has been seen that, when each is expressed in terms of the same common currency, the net private demands for capital balances of all currencies must sum to zero; that is,

$$\sum_{i=1}^{n} \alpha_i a_{i1} = 0. \qquad \text{(v)}$$

This constraint implies that only $(n-1)$ net private demands of the form (iv) may be written down independently, while the nth must be deduced from (v).

NET OFFICIAL DEMAND FOR CAPITAL BALANCES

In order to acquire one unit of capital balances of i-currency, the i-monetary authorities must sell b_{ij} units of current balances of j-currency, while in order to acquire b_{ij} units of current balances of j-currency they must sell $b_{ij} c_{ji}$ units of their own i-currency. Thus in purchasing one unit of their currency on the market for capital balances the i-monetary authorities incur a profit (or loss, when negative) of $(1 - b_{ij} c_{ji})$ units of i-currency, that is, of $(1 - b_{ii})$ units of i-currency.

It is supposed that, in this system, the broad intention of the monetary authorities in their intervention on the market for capital balances is to dispose of any net accumulation of current balances due to a surplus on current account, or recover any net loss due to a deficit. The important element in this supposition is not the precise equality of intervention to the current account balance: it is, for instance, quite conceivable that under certain circumstances monetary authorities might wish to increase their holdings of current balances over time, by selling somewhat less than their surpluses on current account, and buying somewhat more than their deficits. Such behaviour would involve only a very minor modification in the following argument. What is important is rather that, in their intervention on the market for capital balances, monetary authorities are supposed to have an intention which is independent of the prices of capital balances (and so determined outside the system considered here), whether it be to intervene to the precise extent of the current account balance—as it is here supposed—or in some other way. The execution of such an intention, it is then further supposed, is qualified by a desire to check the local currency profits or losses arising from intervention. If the situation is such that one unit of capital balances of i-currency exchanges for one unit of its current balances, the i-monetary authorities incur neither profits nor losses in intervention ($b_{ii} = 1$), and if they intervene to the precise extent of the current account balance, their net purchases of capital balances of i-currency equal their net accumulation of current balances.

Let C_i be the equivalent in units of 1-currency of the i-monetary authorities' net accumulation of current balances (it is positive for a surplus and negative for a deficit). If the modification in the authorities' behaviour due to local currency profits or losses is temporarily disregarded, their net demand for capital balances of their own i-currency will be equal to the equivalent of C_i in units of capital balances of i-currency, that is $\dfrac{C_i c_{ii}}{b_{ii}}$ (if the authorities do not intervene to the precise extent of the current account balance some other exogenously determined parameter may be substituted for C_i). Then the most straightforward way to account for any modification in this net demand due to local currency profits or losses is to add on a term which depends on those profits or losses and which is nevertheless such as to keep net official demand equal to the current account when the country's capital balances are at par

321

with its current balances. It will be readily verified that the following expression for β_i—the i-monetary authorities' net demand for capital balances of i-currency, expressed in units of i-currency—fulfils these conditions, though doubtless other forms might do just as well.[7]

$$\beta_i = \frac{C_i c_{1i}}{b_{ii}} + \frac{D_i}{b_{ii}} (1 - b_{ii}). \tag{vi}$$

D_i is here some positive parameter peculiar to the i-monetary authorities, a measure of the importance that they attach to checking the local currency profits or losses incurred in intervention. D_i is likely to depend upon the absolute size of C_i. It is clear that when capital balances of i-currency are at par with current balances ($b_{ii} = 1$) net official demand is equal to the net accumulation of current balances, expressed of course in units of i-currency. When capital balances of i-currency are at a discount *vis-à-vis* current balances ($b_{ii} < 1$), net official demand for capital balances of i-currency will exceed net accumulated current balances, due regard being taken of sign: thus if there is a current account surplus the authorities' purchases of capital balances will exceed the surplus, whereas with a deficit their sales of capital balances will fall short of the deficit. When capital balances of i-currency are instead at a premium *vis-à-vis* current balances ($b_{ii} > 1$), net official demand for capital balances of i-currency will fall short of net accumulated current balances, again taking sign into account: thus if there is a current account surplus the authorities' purchases of capital balances will fall short of the surplus, whereas with a deficit their sales of capital balances will exceed the deficit.

DETERMINACY OF THE SYSTEM'S SOLUTION

The prices for capital balances of each currency, both in terms of other capital balances and in terms of current balances, are such as to clear each market. Thus total net demand, both private and official, for capital balances of i-currency must be zero, and we have the n equations

$$\alpha_i + \beta_i = 0. \tag{vii}$$

These n equations close the system which already comprises the $(n-1)$ equations of net private demand for capital balances of the first $(n-1)$ currencies,

[7] For instance, $\log \beta_i = \log C_i + \log c_{1i} - D_i \log b_{ii}$.

$$\alpha_i = \sum_{j=1}^{n} A_{ji} a_{ji} \tag{iv}$$

together with the one equation expressing the fact that net private demands for capital balances of all currencies sum to zero when all are reckoned in the same currency,

$$\sum_{i=1}^{n} \alpha_i a_{i1} = 0 \tag{v}$$

and the n equations of net official demand for capital balances of each currency,

$$\beta_i = \frac{C_i c_{1i}}{b_{ii}} + \frac{D_i}{b_{ii}} (1 - b_{ii}). \tag{vi}$$

The coefficients A_{ji} and D_i specify the reactions of private holders and monetary authorities respectively to different configurations in the prices for capital balances. Like C_i and c_{1i}, these behavioural coefficients are taken as given and external to the system. The system has then been expressed in $3n$ linear equations (the equations of net official demand are linear in $1/b_{ii}$) and inspection reveals that these $3n$ equations are linearly independent. They comprise $3n$ unknowns (the n net private demands α_i, the n net official demands β_i, the $(n-1)$ prices a_{1j} of capital balances of 1-currency in terms of capital balances of the other currencies, and the one price b_{11} of capital balances of 1-currency in terms of current balances of 1-currency: it has been shown that determination of these a_{1j} and b_{11} implies unique values for all other a_{ij} and b_{ij}, either through arbitrage or by definition). The system can therefore be solved to yield unique values for all unknowns, and, in particular, for the prices of capital balances of all the various currencies, both in terms of each other and in terms of current balances.

Two observations are worth making with regard to this system. In the first place, (v) and (vii) taken together imply that

$$\sum_{i=1}^{n} \beta_i a_{i1} = 0$$

so that, like net private demands, net official demands for capital balances sum to zero when all are reckoned in terms of the same currency. It follows that net official sales of current balances, again all reckoned in terms of the same currency, must also sum to zero.

This important condition leads to the second observation. If, instead of conforming to (vi), some i-monetary authorities determine their sales of current balances of other currencies (i.e. their demand β_i for capital balances of their own i-currency) without reference to the price b_{ii} of capital balances of i-currency in terms of current balances of i-currency (so that, in effect, $D_i = 0$), then only $(n-1)$ monetary authorities may do so. Thus, if the system is always to be consistent, the intervention of the nth monetary authorities cannot also be exogenously determined.

SOLVING THE SYSTEM IN THE TWO COUNTRY CASE

The determination of the prices of capital balances is illustrated here for a system comprising only two countries (it is assumed, as before, that there are no other countries outside the system).

In accordance with the preceding exposition we may write down the following six equations:

Net private demand for capital balances of 1-currency,

$$\alpha_1 = A_{11} + A_{21}a_{21}. \tag{viii}$$

Net private demand for capital balances of all currencies,

$$\alpha_1 + \alpha_2 a_{21} = 0. \tag{ix}$$

Net official demand for capital balances of 1-currency,

$$\beta_1 = \frac{C_1}{b_{11}} + \frac{D_1}{b_{11}}\,(1 - b_{11}), \tag{x-a}$$

and of 2-currency,

$$\beta_2 = \frac{C_2 c_{12}}{b_{22}} + \frac{D_2}{b_{22}}\,(1 - b_{22}). \tag{x-b}$$

Finally, clearing in the market for capital balances of 1-currency,

$$\alpha_1 + \beta_1 = 0 \tag{xi-a}$$

and in the market for capital balances of 2-currency,

$$\alpha_2 + \beta_2 = 0. \tag{xi-b}$$

The arbitrage condition $b_{22} = a_{21}b_{11}c_{12}$ can be used to substitute for b_{22} in equation (x-b), and the system then yields the following solution:

$$b_{11} = \frac{(C_1 + D_1)\,D_2 + (C_1 + C_2 + D_1 + D_2 c_{21})\,A_{21}}{D_1 D_2 + (D_1 + D_2)\,A_{21} - D_2 A_{11}}$$

and
$$a_{21} = \frac{C_1 + C_2 + D_1 + D_2 c_{21}}{b_{11} D_2} - \frac{D_1 + D_2.}{D_2}$$

These solutions may be simplified by noting that, in the two country case, one country's accumulation of current balances is the other's loss, and consequently $C_1 + C_2 = 0$. Certain assumptions may introduce further simplifications. For instance, if it is supposed that one unit of current balances of 1-currency is worth one unit of current balances of 2-currency ($c_{21} = 1$), and that, quite plausibly, the authorities' behaviour is such that in each country D_i is equal to the absolute value of C_i, the current account balance, the solutions become

$$b_{11} = \frac{2CA_{21}}{C^2 + CA_{21} - CA_{11}}$$

and
$$a_{21} = \frac{C^2 - CA_{11}}{CA_{21}}$$

where C is the current account balance common to both countries, positive for one and negative for the other. It has been noted above that A_{11} need not in practice be a positive coefficient.

Chapter 13

Wider Margins of Exchange Rate Variation*

This essay examines the probable effects, merits and demerits, of a widening in the margins above and below parity within which members of the International Monetary Fund are obliged to maintain exchange rates for spot transactions.

PRESENT MARGINS

At the present time variations in relative exchange rates are kept within relatively narrow limits by arrangements under which countries other than the United States maintain the value of their currencies within a certain margin of parity relative either to the U.S. dollar or to some other currency that in turn is pegged to the dollar. While the Articles of Agreement obligate each member to keep the exchange rates prevailing in its own territory between its currency and those of other members within 1 per cent of parity, the Fund does not object to exchange rates within 2 per cent of parity provided such rates result from the maintenance of exchange margins of no more than 1 per cent for a convertible currency. In practice, most industrial countries keep the value of their currencies within approximately ¾ per cent of parity *vis-à-vis* the dollar, and therefore within 1½ per cent of parity *vis-à-vis* other currencies.

PROVISIONAL ASSUMPTIONS

Proposals for widening exchange margins, or for a 'wider band' as it is sometimes called, vary in character according as they envisage that the principal countries should determine their mutual exchange rates by buying and selling gold within appropriate margins of parity, or that the system of pegging on the dollar or other reserve currencies should be retained as at present (though within wider

* A hitherto unpublished paper, written in 1969.

margins of variation), and in the latter case according to whether the United States should continue to exchange gold for dollars within narrow margins or should also widen its gold points.

In the present essay, at least initially, it is assumed:

(a) that countries would continue to control the value of their currencies through buying and selling reserve currencies and that the widening of the margins within which relative exchange rates may vary would be brought about through a widening of the margins on either side of parity within which countries peg their exchange rates on U.S. dollars;

(b) that the United States would continue to exchange gold for dollars with monetary authorities within the present margins;

(c) that countries would continue, as at present, to be entitled to change the par value of their currencies in order to correct a fundamental disequilibrium; and

(d) that countries would refrain from making any aggressive use of these margins, in that they would neither force their dollar exchange rates down at times when their balances of payments were favourable and they were gaining reserves, nor force their exchange rates up when their balances were adverse and they were losing reserves.

Assumptions (a) to (c) define the type of widening of exchange margins that appears least unlikely to be adopted and therefore most relevant to discuss. Assumption (d) is at this stage a mere behavioural supposition and may require to be buttressed by institutional arrangements to make it plausible. The effects of removing any or all of these assumptions will be examined later in the essay.

In order to give concreteness to the notion of wider exchange margins, it will be assumed that countries would be 'allowed' to buy and sell U.S. dollars within a range of 5 per cent above and below parity. It follows from this assumption that a currency whose dollar exchange rate was at its upper limit would stand at a premium of 10 per cent *vis-à-vis* one whose dollar rate was at its lower limit, and that the relative values of any two currencies other than the dollar could theoretically vary over time as much as 20 per cent.

EFFECTS OF A WIDENING OF MARGINS
(a) *Short-term capital flows*

It is convenient, in considering the possible effects of a widening of margins of the type described above, to begin by assuming that the changes in exchange rates made possible by the wider margins would not affect the use countries made of other policy instruments, and then in the light of these effects to consider the policy changes likely to be associated with the adoption of wider margins.

The effects which a widening of margins would have on short-term international capital flows depend primarily on the effects which it would have on expectations regarding future exchange rate movements and these, in turn, on its effects on the movement of actual rates.

To take the last element in this interrelated complex first, it seems safe to say that with wider margins as defined above, any given payments deficit[1] arising in a country where exchange rates stood at par would tend to bring about a larger exchange depreciation, and any surplus a larger appreciation, than with the present margins. The extent of this magnification of exchange rate variation would depend on (a) the extent to which the widening of the permitted margins led to a widening of the points at which the monetary authorities of the country in question actually intervened on the exchange market to limit swings in the rate, and (b) the extent to which the movements in the rate elicited equilibrating speculation, in the manner described below.

The widening of exchange margins, involving as it would both in anticipation and in fact greater variation in exchange rates, would be likely to affect exchange rate expectations in two main ways:[2] (i) by widening the range of uncertainty as to future rates, and (ii) by giving rise to many more occasions in which a substantial movement of rates in one direction or the other appeared probable.

The effect of uncertainty as such would be to make financing and trading firms and individuals more reluctant to take uncovered positions (spot or forward) in foreign currency even when there

---

[1] The payments and surpluses referred to in this section are intended to be measured exclusive of the equilibrating or disequilibrating shifts to short-term capital flows that are under discussion.

[2] There is a third probable effect, viz., an increase in the diversity of expectations as to future exchange rates. Some implications of this will be mentioned later in this essay.

appeared to be a probability of gain. The existence of a forward exchange market would take the risk out of individual international placements of short-term funds. Unwillingness to take uncovered positions would, however, tend to reduce the volume of net international flows of short-term funds in response to differences in interest rates, or to anticipated exchange appreciations or depreciations of given probable magnitude, particularly where that magnitude was not very large. It would also, in all probability, reduce the variability of net short-term flows with respect to changes in relative interest rates or changes in expected movements in exchange rates. However, because of the factor mentioned at (ii) above, net flows of short-term speculative capital, despite the inhibiting effect of uncertainty, might be no less with wider than with narrow margins. The important question is whether and in what circumstances the existence of wider margins would be likely to make speculative capital flows more strongly equilibrating (less strongly disequilibrating) or less strongly equilibrating (more strongly disequilibrating) than under the present narrow margins. By 'equilibrating' capital flows are meant, in this context, those that tend to reduce, and by 'disequilibrating' capital flows those that tend to increase, the movement of monetary reserves from country to country.

With wider margins, a payments deficit of given size would probably give rise to a larger decline in actual exchange rates and also to a larger decline in expected exchange rates than with narrow margins. For the latter decline there are two reasons: (i) even if, thanks to official intervention, actual exchange rates did not move at all, the widening of margins would increase the possibility that rates might be allowed to decline in future; and (ii) the decline in actual rates would probably aggravate the decline in expected rates. Whether, in these circumstances, the widening of margins would exercise an equilibrating or a disequilibrating influence on capital flows depends primarily on whether its effect on the decline in expected exchange rates would be less or greater than its effect on the decline in actual exchange rates. Thus, if with present exchange margins, a payments deficit of given size would produce a $\frac{1}{2}$ per cent decline in actual exchange rates and a $\frac{1}{4}$ per cent decline in the exchange rates expected to prevail over the ensuing twelve months, while with wider margins it would produce a 4 per cent decline in actual exchange rates and only a 2 per cent decline in expected exchange rates, the prospect of a

2 per cent appreciation under wider margins would probably provide a more powerful magnet for short-term funds than would the prospect of a mere $\frac{1}{4}$ per cent appreciation under present margins. If, on the other hand, with wider margins the decline in the actual rate had been as little as 2 per cent and that in the expected rate as much as 3 per cent, the prospect of a further depreciation of 1 per cent would clearly have encouraged an outflow of funds.

Which of these outcomes is to be expected is likely to depend, in the main, on the extent to which monetary authorities are prepared to allow actual exchange rates to vary within the margins. To take one extreme, if the monetary authorities of the country experiencing a payments deficit refused to allow the exchange rate in practice to fall to any greater discount from parity under wider margins than they would under narrow margins, the fact that the potential depreciation (short of an adjustment of par values) was greater in the former case would probably ensure that the deficit brought about a greater fall in the expected exchange rate and evoked more adverse speculation and more strongly disequilibrating capital flows under wider than under narrow margins.

At the other extreme, if the authorities allowed the exchange rate to fall freely to the extent necessary or until it reached the vicinity of the lower limit permitted by the wider margins, and if they took care to maintain reasonable stability of prices and demand pressure in the country in question, capital flows would almost certainly be more equilibrating or less disequilibrating than under narrow margins. If the disequilibrium was considered to be temporary, expected exchange rates might diverge very little from par, so that if a deficit moved the actual rate to the lower limit, equilibrating capital flows would be much more profitable with wider than with narrow margins. If the disequilibrium was of uncertain duration but was not expected to give rise to a change in par values under either system of margins, wider margins would still give rise to expectations relatively favourable to equilibrating capital flows— though to a lesser extent than in the previous case—since once the exchange rate had reached its limit it would not be expected to decline further while its potentiality for appreciation would be much greater with wider than with narrow margins. Even if the disequilibrium was considered to be permanent and so large as to necessitate a reduction in par value under either system of margins, the decline in exchange rates permitted by these margins, though it would not evoke equilibrating speculation, would probably mitigate the disequilibrating speculation that would have occurred with narrow margins. This is because the existence of wider margins would permit the actual exchange rate, before any change in par value had taken place, to fall closer to the anticipated equilibrium rate than would otherwise be possible.

Two circumstances in which wider margins without premature intervention might reasonably be expected to exercise a disequilibrating effect on capital flows would be (a) if a decline in the actual exchange rate within the wider margins was expected to give rise to a more than proportionate increase in domestic prices, and thus to a decline in the anticipated long-term equilibrium exchange rate greater than that in the actual rate, or (b) if a deficit was expected to give rise to an adjustment of par values under wider margins but *not* under narrow margins. It is argued below that the adoption of wider margins might indeed lead to more frequent devaluations, but some such devaluations might take place after rather than during times of pressure on the exchanges; the situation envisaged at (b) above would surely be less frequent than situations in which devaluation would either be likely both under wider and under narrow margins or likely under narrow margins but avoidable under wider ones.

What has been said about the equilibrating or disequilibrating effects of wider margins in circumstances of payments deficit and exchange depreciation applies, *mutatis mutandis*, to situations of payments surplus and exchange appreciation also. The term 'expected exchange rates' in the foregoing should not be taken to imply that all participants in exchange markets hold unanimously a firm expectation as to future exchange rates. It signifies merely a sort of average market expectation as to the rate that is most likely to prevail over the period relevant to short-term capital flows (e.g. up to six months). The exchange rate expectations in question may act on capital flows either directly or *via* their effect on forward exchange speculation and covered interest arbitrage. This distinction, of which too much is often made, is of secondary importance.

To sum up, it would appear that a widening of exchange rate margins, provided that it is not nullified in practice by premature intervention on the part of the monetary authorities in question and provided that it is not offset by changes in domestic price levels relative to those abroad, would be likely to exercise an equilibrating effect on private short-term capital flows. This does not mean that under wider margins such capital flows would be of an equilibrating character; in some circumstances they might merely be less disequilibrating than they would have been under the present narrow margins.

It should not be thought that the equilibrating influence of wider margins would operate only in the immediate proximity of the upper and lower limits. In Canada, during the period of the floating rate, when of course no such limits existed, there is evidence that quarterly changes in exchange rates tended to be associated with equilibrating short-term capital flows.[3] The presence of limits to the permitted fluctuation of exchange rates could only add to the strength of the equilibrating tendencies evoked by any given degree of actual fluctuation.

(b) *Effects on long-term capital flows*
While the precise timing of international flows of long-term funds (particularly in outstanding securities) may not be entirely unaffected by the equilibrating influences that we have been discussing, the more important question, so far as long-term capital movements are concerned, is whether the mobility of such funds is likely to be reduced by increased uncertainty as to the return (in domestic currency) on funds invested abroad. Since, as Keynes pointed out, the exchange risk in long-term lending cannot be covered by forward contracts, the risk element in question might affect gross capital flows, inwards and outwards, in each country, and not merely, as in the case of short-term lending, the net flow in one or the other direction. The importance of this factor, however, can easily be exaggerated, for the following reasons.

Where direct or equity investment is concerned it is by no means clear that the real current net yield to the investor of capital held abroad would become any more uncertain because of the variability of the exchange rates at which that yield was convertible into the

[3] See, for example, R. R. Rhomberg, 'A Model of the Canadian Economy under Fixed and Fluctuating Exchange Rates', *Journal of Political Economy*, Vol. LXXII, No. 1, February 1964, pp. 11–12. After 1955 the association was much less close than before, largely because interest rates and monetary conditions in relation to those in the United States were frequently such as to evoke disequilibrating flows.

investor's currency. Insofar as the yield of the investment depends on the level of profits in the country of investment, the flexibility in exchange rates permitted by wider margins in that country might make it easier to maintain the stability of these profits and investment yields in domestic currency, and this might counterbalance any increased uncertainty as regards the rate. Even where long-term fixed interest investments are concerned, uncertainty as to the return might not be much greater under a regime of wider margins than under the present regime of narrow margins, since the parities themselves are always liable to adjustment in the longer run. The enhancement of uncertainty would arise primarily in the case of medium-term credit or in cases where the duration of the investment, though too great to permit hedging through the forward exchange market, was intended to be limited; here uncertainty as to the future exchange rates at which capital could be repatriated would enhance uncertainty as to the return on the investment as a whole.

(c) *Effects on current account*

In addition to its effects on capital flows, a widening of exchange margins would have implications for balances of payments on current account. In the preceding section, mention has already been made of possible effects on the stability of the real yield on capital held abroad. So far as the trade balance is concerned, it is useful to draw a distinction between the international trade repercussions of temporary movements in stocks (inventories) and more basic shifts in trade flows.

Movements in the stocks of internationally traded goods and associated commodities can have a strong effect on the trade balance. In particular, increases in stocks of importable goods, or goods produced with the aid of importable materials, will create a demand for additional imports, while increases in stocks of exportable goods or of goods entering into the production of exportable goods will tend to reduce the volume and probably the value of exports.

The level of stocks held is influenced, *inter alia*, by speculative considerations, i.e. by anticipation of price increases or price declines, and these price anticipations, in turn, are affected by exchange rate movements in two different and, in some cases, contradictory ways. Thus, the prices of internationally traded goods will be expected to rise (and the level of such stocks will therefore increase) (a) if exchange rates are expected to fall, or (b) if exchange rates have already fallen but the effects of the fall on the prices of the goods in question have not yet worked themselves out.

To the extent that price anticipations are influenced by exchange rate anticipations, a widening of exchange margins would tend to have trade effects that reinforce the effects on capital flows already discussed. That is, the stock-induced trade effects would be generally equilibrating provided that exchange rates were allowed to move freely within the wider margins and provided that internal conditions were sufficiently stable to ensure that a decline in actual exchange rates did not lead to an equivalent decline in expected exchange rates. Under these conditions, a decline in exchange rates would tend to evoke more favourable anticipations as to the future movement of rates and, provided that prices were expected to adjust themselves to rates with a short time lag, would tend to evoke a reduction in the stocks of internationally traded goods with an associated reduction in imports or increase in exports.

However, to the extent that price anticipations were influenced by recent past changes in exchange rates, the price effects of which had not yet been passed on by intermediaries to the ultimate purchaser, a decline in exchange rates, even though exercising a favourable effect on exchange rate anticipations, might nevertheless lead to the anticipation of price increases rather than declines and hence to an increase in the stocks of intermediaries and consumers and a deterioration in the balance of trade.

It is difficult to gauge the probable relative strength of these two contradictory tendencies in speculative stocking. The experience of the United Kingdom during the year following the devaluation of November 1967 suggests that in countries where price increases are passed on rather slowly through the stages of production the perverse effect could be uncomfortably strong. On the other hand, this effect would be reversed when the higher priced imports reached intermediaries and consumers, and at that point the equilibrating effect arising from improved exchange rate anticipations would prevail.

As regards basic trade flows, if one abstracts from temporary effects of speculative stock changes, the effects of exchange rate movements (within the wider margins) in response to payments deficits or surpluses might differ not only in degree but even in sign

334

according to the amount of time that had elapsed since the movement in question. Within the first six months of an exchange appreciation or depreciation, or even longer, the effects on the basic current account balances of payments are likely to be disequilibrating or neutral; later, if the movement itself was not reversed, and if domestic demand and price policies aiming at stability were reasonably effective, the effects are fairly certain to be equilibrating.

The reason for this is that the (disequilibrating) effects of exchange rate movements on the relative prices of imports and exports tend to manifest themselves more quickly than the (equilibrating) effects on the quantities traded. The extent of the discrepancy between immediate and longer-run effects would depend to some extent on whether in the absence of the movement in exchange rates the shares of the countries concerned in domestic and foreign markets would have been stable or otherwise. Where a movement in rates tended to prevent or reduce, rather than to induce, a general change in the competitiveness of a country's foreign trade industries, its equilibrating effect on trade quantities and hence on the balance of payments might be less delayed.

The extent of the improvement in the balance of trade that can be brought about, in the long run, by a change in relative cost levels—and hence by a movement in exchange rates that is not offset by a contrary movement in domestic prices—is likely to be the greater the lower are the costs of transport and the lower are the effective barriers to international trade. In present day conditions—as contrasted with those that prevailed from the 1920s to the mid-1950s—the relevant trade elasticities are probably higher than was formerly the case, and this is one reason why devaluations or revaluations of 5 to 15 per cent are frequently considered to be all that is necessary to correct the disequilibria of individual industrial countries with quite substantial over-all payments imbalances. For example, the long-term price elasticity of foreign demand for the exports of an industrial country might be of the order of $2\frac{1}{2}$ and the price elasticity of domestic demand for imports (including materials and foodstuffs) approximately unity.[4] In this case, a devaluation of

4 Junz and Rhomberg, on the basis of their statistical results for all industrial countries, concluded that: 'price elasticities of demand for exports of manufactures of individual supplying countries may be rather higher than was previously supposed. An elasticity of -2 is often used as a rule-of-thumb when it is necessary to make quantitative assumptions about the effects of relative price changes of individual

5 per cent that was offset by no more than one third by repercussions on domestic costs would yield in the long run an increase of 5 per cent in the dollar value of its exports and a decrease, say, of 3½ per cent in the dollar value of its imports. It is clear that any improvement of this order in trade flows, *plus* a possibly significant gain on current invisibles, in conjunction with the appropriate adjustment in domestic expenditure, could correct quite a substantial payments deficit.[5]

From the foregoing treatment of basic trade flows, two conclusions can be drawn:

(1) Inventory movements apart, the effect of temporary exchange rate movements on the current balance might be neutral or even disequilibrating.

(2) Exchange rate movements of the magnitude that would be feasible with margins of 5 per cent without a change in par values

---

countries' exports. With regard to exports of manufactures by industrial countries to industrial markets, the findings of this study suggest that, in a longer-run context, a value for the price elasticity in the range of -3 to -5 may be a more appropriate assumption.' (H. B. Junz and R. R. Rhomberg, 'Prices and Export Performance of Industrial Countries, 1953–63', International Monetary Fund *Staff Papers*, Vol. XII, No. 2, July 1965, p. 259.)

Kreinin examined the same problems as Junz and Rhomberg only using data on manufacturers' exports disaggregated by types of manufactures. Because of limitations of price data for these subgroups, he used cross-sectional regressions for 1955–57. He found the following elasticities for all countries combined (p. 513):

Chemicals	$-1 \cdot 6$
Machinery and transportation equipment	$-1 \cdot 7$
Other manufactures	$-4 \cdot 5$
All manufactures	$-2 \cdot 6$

Kreinen points out that: 'these are short-run estimates (three years), and would undoubtedly be much larger if a longer time period were allowed to elapse. Thus, the elasticity of $-2 \cdot 6$, obtained for all manufactures, is not inconsistent with' the figures of Junz and Rhomberg presented above (p. 514). (Mordechai Kreinin, 'Price Elasticity in International Trade', *The Review of Economics and Statistics*, Vol. 49, No. 4, November 1967, pp. 510–16.)

On the import side, Rhomberg and Boissonneault obtained implicit elasticities of $-1 \cdot 0$ for Western European imports from the United States and of $-1 \cdot 3$ for United States imports from Western Europe. (See 'Effects of Income and Price Changes on the U.S. Balance of Payments', *I.M.F. Staff Papers*, Vol. XI, p. 66.) Kreinin used quarterly data on U.S. imports for 1954–64 to estimate an import demand equation for each of five commodity groupings and for total imports. His price variable was the ratio of import prices to the domestic wholesale price index. Real GNP was also used as an explanatory variable. He found a price elasticity of demand for imports (all commodities) of $-1 \cdot 1$.

[5] Some improvement in the long-term capital account is also to be expected on account of the rise in interest rates that will be required if domestic investment is to be sufficiently curtailed to make room for the improvement in the current balance.

might be far from negligible in their longer-run effects on the current balance. Admittedly, to complete an exchange rate adjustment of the order usually called for to correct a fundamental disequilibrium might require a shift in par values, and to restore scope for exchange rate fluctuations to deal with temporary disequilibria, after a definitive shift in the rate to the vicinity of one or other of the limits, would certainly require a change in par values. Even in these cases, however, it would often be possible, prior to such a change, for the rate to move, within the margins, much closer to its equilibrium level.

(d) *Effects on the stability of demand and activity in general and in the foreign trade industries*
A widening of the margin, to the extent that the exchange rate was in fact allowed to vary within the wider band, might affect the stability of demand and output both in the economy as a whole and in the exporting and import-competing industries in particular. The effects in question would depend on the nature of the forces giving rise to the variations in the rate and also on the domestic policies pursued. At this point we are still examining the effects of changes on the exchange rate within the wider margins on the assumption that such changes are not offset by changes in other domestic policies. It is in any case unrealistic to suppose that such offsetting can ever be complete.

Where the movement in the exchange rate was caused by (a) a change in the severity of foreign competition with the country's industries, (b) a demand switch as between the products of the foreign trade industries of the country in question and the products of competing industries abroad, or (c) a change in aggregate demand abroad, the effect of the movement would be to minimize disturbance both to aggregate demand and output in the country and to demand and output in its foreign trade industries. Where the causal factor was a demand shift affecting the product of some particular exporting or import-competing industry, the movement in the rate would affect the demand for the products of other such industries. Some disturbance to other industries would, of course, be inevitable in this case whatever happened to exchange rates if a policy of stabilizing aggregate demand was followed.

Where the cause of the movement in the exchange rate was a

change in the international flow of capital, the effect of the movement in the rate would be to change the demand for and output of the country's foreign trade goods. If the change in the capital flow was closely associated with a corresponding change in investment expenditure in the country, the movement in the rate would tend to prevent a change in aggregate demand for the country's products. If not, it would tend to alter aggregate demand.

Where the cause of the movement in the exchange rate was a change in aggregate expenditure in the country in question and where such change had no repercussions on capital flows, a rise (fall) in expenditure would produce a fall (rise) in the rate. This would intensify the change in aggregate demand for the country's products, and would also intensify the change in monetary demand for the products of the foreign trade industries. The effect on output in these industries is more doubtful. Thus, if domestic inflation produced a fall in the exchange rate the consequential rise in demand for the products of these industries might well enable them to avoid a decline in output which would otherwise have resulted from a diversion of resources to production for the home market. Where, as has been happening more and more often in recent years, an increase (reduction) in domestic expenditure promoted a substantial influx (efflux) of capital, the exchange rate might rise (fall), thus tending to stabilize aggregate demand to an even greater extent than would have taken place under a fixed exchange rate regime. The effect on the output of foreign trade goods would, however, be destabilizing.

From what has been said, it will be seen that any fluctuations in exchange rates made possible by the widening of margins would tend to stabilize demand and output in some cases and to destabilize it in others, and that their effect on demand and output for foreign trade goods would probably be less often stabilizing, or more often destabilizing, than their effect on aggregate demand and output.

It has to be borne in mind that effective demand, and still more output and employment in foreign trade industries, tend to react to changes in exchange rates only gradually. (This is why the effect of devaluation on the trade balance is often neutral or negative and a positive effect takes time to develop.) Therefore, very short-term fluctuations in rates, e.g. those reversed within the year, would be unlikely to have much destabilizing effect.

EFFECTS OF WIDER MARGINS ON NON-EXCHANGE POLICIES

Thus far, it has been assumed that the widening of exchange margins would have no repercussions on other policies of the countries concerned, though it would, of course, inevitably affect the extent to which they would have to allow their external reserves to rise or fall in the course of defending their exchange parities. This assumption, however, is unrealistic and must now be removed. Insofar as movements of exchange rates within the wider margins tend to reduce disequilibria in the balance of payments as a whole, they may be expected to reduce or eliminate the need for applying other policy instruments in such a way as to reduce these disequilibria.

That wider margins, to the extent that they are effectively utilized, would reduce the need to relate monetary (interest rate) policy to the requirements of the balance of payments, and would thus enable it to be directed to a greater extent to the preservation of internal economic stability, is a point that was emphasized by Keynes in his pre-war advocacy of this arrangement. This has a double aspect: disequilibria arising in the balance of payments would no longer—or only to a lesser extent—necessitate domestically disturbing monetary policies; and changes in monetary policies required to meet incipient changes in domestic situations need no longer—or only to a lesser extent—be inhibited out of regard for their effect on the balance of payments. As an illustration of the second aspect, suppose a recession of output and employment to take place for reasons unconnected with the balance of payments. With fixed exchange rates and narrow margins a decline in interest rates undertaken to combat the recession might lead to an outflow of funds and of reserves that would compel the abandonment of the policy. (This argument assumes either that capital is highly mobile internationally or that the decline in demand associated with the recession has comparatively little effect on imports.) With wider margins the reduction in interest rates would bring about a decline in exchange rates that would offset the effect on capital flows, thus permitting the expansionary monetary policy to continue.

What is said above regarding the increased independence which wider margins would confer on monetary policy applies much less forcibly to fiscal policy regarded as an instrument for the control of demand. Broadly speaking, the first, but not the second of the two aspects of independence described above, holds true in the case of

339

fiscal policy. However, the institution of wider margins would be relevant to the use of fiscal policy also.

Nowadays it is increasingly recognized that fiscal policy has to be considered in conjunction with monetary policy with a view to the maximum reconciliation of external and internal economic goals. Thus, under the present par-value system it may be possible and appropriate, in the short run at any rate, to reconcile the objectives of external equilibrium and an adequate level of internal demand by directing interest rate policy primarily with a view to external equilibrium and fiscal policy primarily with a view to internal demand objectives. The reason for this division of labour lies in the powerful effect exercised by interest policy on international capital flows. To the extent that the achievement of external equilibrium can be entrusted to a flexible exchange rate, however, the situation as regards the mix of fiscal and monetary policies is completely changed.[6] While exchange rate variability enhances the impact of both instruments on internal demand, the enhancement is considerably greater in the case of monetary (interest rate) policy, whose special influence on capital flows is reflected back, via the exchange rate, upon the balance of trade and hence on incomes. It, therefore, becomes possible for monetary policy to take over from fiscal policy much more of the burden of attaining aggregate demand objectives, releasing the latter instrument for the pursuit of other domestic objectives such as the maintenance of an appropriate growth rate and various social goods which might otherwise have had to be sacrificed.

The foregoing argument, however, requires qualification inasmuch as:

(a) the variability of the exchange rate is subject to limits (albeit wider ones) and to the possibility of official intervention on the exchange market within the margins, and

(b) the authorities may be reluctant to see changes in domestic consumption or investment offset by changes in the trade balance, i.e. to see changes in home market industries offset by changes in foreign trade industries; or they may simply dislike to see exchange

<hr>

[6] See R. A. Mundell, 'Flexible Exchange Rates and Employment Policy', *Canadian Journal of Economics and Political Science*, November 1961, pp. 509–17, and J. M. Fleming, 'Domestic Financial Policies under Fixed and under Floating Exchange Rates', reproduced at Chapter 9 above.

rates alter in response to what may turn out to be cyclical developments.

Insofar as it has equilibrating tendencies, the widening of exchange margins may be expected also to lessen recourse to payments restrictions on trade and payments and to take the place of other methods of manipulating capital flows, such as capital restrictions, interest equalization taxes, investment subsidies, and the like. As regards official intervention on the forward exchange market, however, it should be noted that wider margins, though rendering such intervention less necessary, might also serve to increase its effectiveness when it was employed. This is because the greater uncertainty about the exchange rate created by wider margins would probably reduce the amount of private forward speculation evoked by a change in the forward rate, and therefore increase the equilibrating effect on capital flows of any given amount of official intervention in the forward market.[7]

Wider margins would favour a prompter adaptation of exchange rates to small and gradual changes in the long-term equilibrium rate. Moreover, since anticipated adjustments of par values under wider margins would be less closely associated with anticipated changes in actual rates and would therefore generate less disequilibrating speculation than under narrow margins, willingness to contemplate more frequent, though smaller, changes in par values would probably be increased. For both of these reasons, countries' incentives to counter changes in competitiveness by measures acting on aggregate demand as well as by restrictions affecting the current account would probably be weakened, and it seems likely that relative price levels and exchange rates would undergo greater changes, even in the long run, under wider than under narrow margins.

This conclusion, viz., that wider margins would favour the adjustment to chronic disequilibria through exchange rate adjustments rather than through price level adjustments achieved through demand policy, might be challenged on the following grounds. The

[7] Of any given amount of official forward purchases, part will be offset by private speculative forward sales, and part by private forward sales covering private spot purchases, both evoked by the rise in the forward rate. Uncertainty as to the future exchange rate would increase the riskiness of speculative positions and probably reduce the amount of private speculative forward sales that would be induced by a given rise in the forward rate.

existence of wider margins by permitting changes in actual exchange rates without changes in par values would in many cases make it *possible* to resist par-value changes when this might otherwise be impossible, or to postpone them much longer than would otherwise be possible. In some cases the forces making for the emergence of fundamental disequilibria might, given time, reverse themselves. In other cases, where this did not happen, the breathing space given by the wider margins might give the authorities of the country concerned time to check and reverse the tendencies to disequilibria through an appropriate, and not too costly, demand policy.

There is no doubt that wider margins would make it *possible* for countries, if they so desired, to have fewer par-value changes. On the other hand, since they would also reduce the urgency of the need for corrective demand policies and would also make par-value changes less cataclysmic, it is in my opinion likely that the frequency of such changes would in fact be increased.

GENERAL APPRAISAL

Summing up the effects thus far analysed, one would expect that wider margins, provided that they were not stultified by premature intervention on the part of the monetary authorities and were not offset by movements in domestic prices and costs, would exercise an equilibrating effect on capital flows and possibly also on the current balance in the event of short-term disequilibria that were recognized to be such. Disequilibria might be judged to be temporary either because of their intrinsic nature or because the country in question was known to be attached to the maintenance of its par value and to be likely to apply corrective demand and price policies whenever incipient longer-term disequilibria tended to move its actual rate towards one or other of the limits.

Where the country in question was thought unlikely to apply such corrective action to incipient disequilibria, or thought likely to adjust its par value if its actual rate remained for some time at one or other of the limits of variation, wider margins of this order would be less certain to exercise an equilibrating effect in the short run on the balance of payments as a whole.

The experience of countries with freely fluctuating rates both in the 1920s and in the post-war period shows that some exchange rate can always be found to equilibrate a country's balance of payments, but that if price inflation is allowed to take hold, capital flows will be disequilibrating, exchange rate movements will outrun the movement of relative price levels, and the equilibration will be achieved through a current account surplus which will intensify the inflation.[8] On the other hand, where internal stability is preserved, at least to a degree comparable with that of competing countries, speculative capital flows will be equilibrating[9] and the fluctuation in exchange rates may take place within limits little, if at all, wider than those resulting from the margins envisaged here. For example, after 1921, when price levels had been somewhat stabilized following the post-war slump to 1925 when the gold standard was restored, the dollar value of the freely floating pound sterling never diverged from its average rate over the period by more than 6·3 per cent. The Netherlands guilder likewise remained within 5·4 per cent and the Swiss franc within 6·9 per cent of their respective average dollar values over the same period, though in these cases there was a certain amount of official intervention. The performance of the Canadian dollar, which floated with only slight stabilizing official intervention from 1950 to 1962, is even more remarkable. From mid-1952 to mid-1961 the dollar rate never diverged by more than 2·7 per cent from its average value. Admittedly this was only possible for the period after 1957 because the Canadian authorities were willing to tolerate a level of unemployment that was comparable to, and even higher than, that prevailing in the United States; but even if a more active anticyclical policy had been pursued, and a mix of policies adopted more suitable to the circumstances of a floating rate, while the trend value of the Canadian dollar would certainly have declined somewhat after 1957 there is no reason to think that its short-term fluctuations round that trend would have been much enhanced.

The short-term equilibrating effect on capital flows which wider margins may be expected to exercise under suitable conditions cannot

---

[8] The classic example of this was provided by France in the 1920s. See Ragnar Nurkse, 'International Currency Experience' (League of Nations).

[9] In the early 1920s, in the three countries mentioned below in the text, speculation was usually unimportant or equilibrating. At times, however, disequilibrating speculation à la hausse developed owing to anticipations of a return to pre-war parities. Cf. S. C. Tsiang, 'Fluctuating Exchange Rates in Countries with Relatively Stable Economies', International Monetary Fund *Staff Papers*, October 1959, and R. Z. Aliber, 'Speculation in the Foreign Exchanges: The European Experience', *Yale Economic Essays*, Vol. 2, No. 1, 1962.

be said to be clearly preferable from the standpoint of resource allocation to certain other forms of compensatory financing, e.g. the use of reserves or intergovernmental credits, or certain general methods of influencing private capital flows. But reserves may run out, balance-of-payments assistance be difficult to obtain, and other general methods of influencing capital flows (such as an appropriate mix of fiscal and monetary policies) be difficult to apply in practice. As compared with partial restrictions on certain capital flows, or as compared with restrictions on trade and economic activity, the harnessing of equilibrating speculation, so far as this can be done through wider margins (possibly supplemented by official forward exchange rate intervention) appears clearly preferable.

In certain circumstances, as has been indicated, exchange rate fluctuations arising from temporary influences on the balance of payments would tend to have disturbing effects on the stability of aggregate demand and activity, and on the stability of the foreign trade industries. In other circumstances the opposite would be true. The fact that greater exchange flexibility, to the extent made possible by wider margins, would increase the freedom and effectiveness of domestic financial policies aiming at stabilization should go far to mitigate the tendency of rate flexibility to 'contain', and therefore intensify, inflationary or deflationary pressures originating internally, and to ensure that the over-all effect of such flexibility on internal stability in the face of possible shocks of all kinds is predominantly a favourable one. However, a distinction has to be drawn between countries where the authorities are and those where they are not reasonably efficient in demand management. The former might be assisted, the latter hampered, by a flexible rate and to a lesser extent by wider margins in their attempts to maintain internal stability.

As regards the stability of the foreign trade industries, the successful pursuit of a stabilizing demand management policy would remove one sort of instability but might add another. Thus a domestic slump, uncorrected by official policy, might reduce imports, drive up the exchange rate, and reduce demand for exports. An incipient domestic slump, nipped in the bud by an expansionary monetary policy, might provoke an outflow of capital, depress the rate, and *increase* demand for exports. However, to the extent that exchange rate flexibility enables countries to dispense with the use of import restrictions and similar devices applied for balance-of-payments reasons, it will remove causes of instability in foreign trade industries that would otherwise have existed. For example, in the event of a decline in foreign demand for a country's exports, it is more conducive to stability in the foreign trade industries to meet this by a decline in the exchange rate than by the application of import restrictions which would stimulate import-competing trades while leaving export trades depressed. In the matter of the effect of exchange flexibility on the stability of the foreign trade industries, therefore, it remains difficult to strike a balance between the pros and the cons.

It is sometimes argued that exchange rate flexibility, within widened margins, or without limits of any kind, would be likely to reduce the volume of international trade. It is difficult to find much warrant for this thesis in economic logic or in historical experience. So far as individual trade transactions financed by short-term credit are concerned, exchange risk can normally be avoided by importers or exporters through the use of forward exchange markets, the commissions charged on such markets being negligible as a barrier to international trade. Of course, forward exchange premia and discounts would often be wider than at present. But these, while they discourage trade in particular directions, encourage it in the opposite directions with no necessary effect on the over-all volume. Only to the extent that foreign exchange dealers themselves assume exchange risks in the course of their operations, e.g. through discrepancies in the respective time distributions of claims and of obligations in particular currencies, might there be a tendency to an increase in percentage commissions, and any such tendency might be outweighed by the substantial increase that is to be expected in the turnover of financial transactions.[10] It was in the period of fluctuating exchange rates of the early 1920s that the forward exchange markets first developed on a large scale.

Not all the exchange risks involved in individual trade transactions can be covered in the forward market. Even where transactions financed by short-term credit are concerned, difficulties may arise in connection with the making or evaluation of price quotations or the

[10] There are two reasons for this: the greater uncertainty as to future rates increases the desire of traders and others to cover and hedge exchange risks on the forward market; and the increased divergency of expectations as to future rates gives rise to apparent opportunities for profitable contracts on the forward markets.

covering of exchange risk where deliveries and dates of payment are delayed or uncertain. Particularly in the capital goods industries, where exports are typically financed by medium-term credits that cannot be covered for exchange risk on the forward market, uncertainty as to future rates must be an element tending to discourage trade.

The exchange risks involved in investment in export industries cannot, of course, be covered on the forward market. In this connection, it is important to bear in mind (a) what has been said above regarding the mixed effects of exchange rate variability on the stability of demand in the foreign trade industries, and (b) (where long-term investment is concerned) the point that uncertainty as to exchange rates in the further future may not be much greater under wider margins than under the present par-value system.

One may perhaps conclude from all this that the exchange flexibility permitted by wider margins would probably increase, if only slightly, the uncertainties and therefore the cost involved in exportation, particularly for capital goods. Even so, any adverse effect on the value of international transactions might well be outweighed if countries are enabled by this flexibility to have less recourse to restrictions on imports, tourism, etc.

It is in facilitating a smooth and timely adjustment of exchange rates to longer-term disequilibria and thus of avoiding the application over periods of years of restrictions on international transactions and deviations from the demand policies appropriate to domestic conditions, that the device of wider margins could, in my opinion, perform its most important function.[11] The adjustment of rates to incipient long-term disequilibria could take place within the margins, without waiting for a par-value adjustment to which the monetary authorities, for political and psychological, as well as for economic reasons, might be slow to resolve themselves. Such a more continuous type of adaptation would, over the delayed and discontinuous movements in rates that would be necessary under a regime of narrow margins, have the advantages of (a) limiting the anticipatory capital flight that would have occurred in the latter case, and (b) making an earlier start with the necessary process of

---

[11] Neglect of this aspect—the bearing of rate movements within wider margins on the ease of par-value adjustments—is responsible for what I would consider the unduly negative verdict on the wider margin device passed by many economists generally favourable to exchange rate flexibility.

correcting the balance of payments on current account. The initial phase of any such adjustment may have a perverse or disequilibrating effect on the balance of payments on current account; but this phase would have to be gone through, sooner or later, whether the adjustment was prompt or delayed. If, as is not unlikely, the 'defusing' of par-value alterations of their traumatic character led to their becoming more frequent and smaller in amount, the greater part of the exchange rate adaptation to basic disequilibria might take place within the margins, with changes in par values tending to ratify adjustments that had already occurred rather than to initiate further adjustments. Once the requisite adaptation of exchange rates, or a major part of it, had been accomplished within the margins, the psychological obstacles to an appropriate change in parities would probably be greatly reduced. The example of the deutsche mark revaluation of October 1969, which was preceded and facilitated politically by a period of nominally floating exchange rates, is instructive in this regard.

If, however, it is true that the most important changes in exchange rates under wider margins might occur through changes in the position of the actual rates relative to par within the margins rather than as an immediate consequence of changes in par values, great importance both from a national and an international standpoint would attach to the rules governing national intervention in exchange markets within the permitted range of variation, and to this subject we now turn.

RULES GOVERNING OFFICIAL INTERVENTION WITHIN WIDER MARGINS

Any introduction of wider exchange margins would have to be accompanied by the adoption of rules and conventions with a greater or lesser degree of legal force regarding the behaviour of monetary authorities with respect to official intervention within the margins.

On page 327 above, it was assumed as a necessary basic rule that monetary authorities would be prohibited from intervening aggressively in the market by forcing down their exchange rates at a time when their reserves were rising, and forcing them up at a time when their reserves were falling. The object of such a rule would be to prevent a country from either exporting unemployment and sustaining demand through competitive devaluation, or manufacturing an excuse for the imposition of import restrictions through competitive revaluation. This rule falls into two parts, which may not be of equal importance.

The prohibition of aggressive intervention might be objected to on the ground that it would prevent monetary authorities from 'squeezing' short-term speculators. This objection seems of insufficient weight to warrant a departure from the rule. Longer-term speculation that tended to drive the actual exchange rate further from the equilibrium rate would probably prove unprofitable in any case.

A much more important objection is that countries belonging to groups, such as the sterling area, the EEC, etc. might wish to maintain fixed rates *vis-à-vis* each other while retaining some of the benefits of wider margins in their transactions with outside countries. Even in this case the non-aggression rule could still be applied to the group as a whole. Members of the group could keep their relative rates in line through some of them acquiring the currencies of others, settling with each other in gold or dollars, or extending mutual credit, as they chose; they would, however, be expected not to acquire external reserves,[12] save from each other, when their rates, moving together, were rising in terms of dollars, and not to sell external reserves, save to each other, when their rates were falling in terms of dollars.

A further reason for departing from the non-aggression rule might arise in the case of countries whose reserves were either very high or very low. A country with very low reserves might reasonably be allowed to depreciate its rate of exchange within the margins even though it was accumulating reserves up to a prescribed rate, while a country with very high reserves might reasonably be allowed to appreciate its rate of exchange within the margins even though it was losing reserves up to a prescribed rate. Exemptions of this kind from the rule might be granted by *ad hoc* decision of the Fund, which would prescribe the amounts in question.

Rules against direct aggressive intervention should not be too difficult to police. However, greater difficulty would arise in preventing indirect aggression such as might occur, for example, if a country

---

[12] By 'external reserves' is meant gross reserves of gold and foreign exchange excluding reserves held in the currencies of group members.

were to subsidize capital export, thus driving down the exchange rate and promoting a favourable trade balance.

Greater difficulties arise in connection with the question of defensive intervention. As has been pointed out, the efficacy of wider margins in promoting equilibrating shifts in capital flows and inventory movements, as well as in permitting prompt adjustment to changes in the long-term equilibrium rate of exchange, would only be realized if monetary authorities took advantage of these margins and allowed actual exchange rates to move rather readily to the neighbourhood of the limits or to whatever level was required to restore equilibrium. On the other hand, where disequilibria were clearly of a short-term character, and where the countries experiencing deficits were adequately provided with reserves or other means of official financing, it might be preferable that exchange fluctuations should be ironed out through official intervention so as to avoid unnecessary disturbances to foreign trade industries and misdirection of certain types of investment.

On the whole, Fund experience with freely fluctuating rates would seem to indicate that even deficit countries, if given full rights of 'defensive' intervention on exchange markets, would be likely to intervene too much rather than too little in defence of their rates; surplus countries would surely be even more reluctant to sacrifice exchange stability to the correction of their surpluses, since their refusal to allow their rates to rise would increase the downward pressure on the rates of the deficit countries. There is, therefore, a case for examining various possible rules that would limit the right of monetary authorities to intervene defensively on exchange markets. Unfortunately, since rules have to be somewhat general, it seems impossible so to devise them as to permit all interventions that would be justifiable, and to prohibit all interventions that would be unjustifiable, in the circumstances of the particular case.

One possibility—a fairly radical one—would be to provide a 'margin within the margin'. Thus, if the margin of permissible exchange rate variation was 5 per cent on either side of par, there might be an inner margin of, say, 3 per cent on either side of par, within which monetary authorities would not be allowed to intervene for stabilization purposes on exchange markets.[13] Between

---

[13] While margins would be expressed in terms of spot exchanges rates, any rule regarding official intervention would apply to forward as well as spot markets.

3 per cent and 5 per cent from par, they could intervene defensively. In the case of countries with very low or very high reserves, quantitatively limited exemptions from the prohibition to intervene within the inner margin could be granted *ad hoc* by the Fund, as suggested above for aggressive intervention.

Another possible approach—which could be combined with the foregoing—would be to permit a country to practice defensive intervention in any quarter only after its exchange rate had moved during that quarter in a given direction by, say, 1 per cent.

Since an important objective of any widening of margins would be to reduce the necessity for restrictions on trade and payments, a minimum limitation on the right of defensive intervention might be to provide that countries could not impose such restrictions (at least on current transactions) unless their exchange rates were within 1 per cent of the lower limit and must progressively remove them if their exchange rates rise more than 1 per cent above that limit. (As before, exemptions to this rule might be granted *ad hoc* to low-reserve countries.)

WIDER MARGINS WITH FIXED PARITIES

It has occasionally been suggested[14] that any adoption of wider margins should be accompanied by a removal of the right presently enjoyed by countries of changing their par values with the consent of the Fund, if this is required, to meet a 'fundamental dis-equilibrium'. If such an arrangement were adopted and could be enforced the effect would be

(a) to intensify (probably very considerably) the equilibrating influence on capital flows of wider margins, since the limits of variation would now be announced to be absolutely immovable; and

(b) to prevent wider margins from being used to facilitate—except within the band itself—permanent changes in exchange rates.

In these circumstances, the role of wider margins with respect to longer-term disequilibria would be that of providing more time for an adjustment process to be carried into effect through the instrumentality of demand and incomes policies.

[14] E.g. by G. N. Halm in *The 'Band' Proposal: The Limits of Permissible Exchange Rate Variations*, Special Papers in International Economics No. 6 (Princeton, 1965).

Whatever be the advantages or disadvantages of this solution, it appears to the writer to be one which countries are most unlikely to accept. Circumstances arise in which devaluations of more than 5 per cent appear to be inevitable and necessary, and these circumstances, whether they consist of an uncontrollable upsurge of wage rates, a bout of inflation, or a grave deterioration in export markets, cannot be abolished by an international agreement to behave as if they did not exist.

THE U.S. DOLLAR, WIDER MARGINS, AND THE PRICE OF GOLD

It has been assumed in the foregoing that any widening of exchange rate margins would be achieved by a widening of the margins for each currency *vis-à-vis* the U.S. dollar, the latter remaining interconvertible with monetary gold at, or very close to, par. Under this arrangement, the value of the dollar could vary less than that of any other currency in terms of currencies in general. For example, if a currency other than the U.S. dollar was weak and was allowed to sink to its floor *vis-à-vis* the dollar, it could, in the extreme case, fall to a discount of 5 per cent *vis-à-vis* the dollar and 10 per cent *vis-à-vis* all third currencies, and in the most probable case (where third currencies were some at a premium, some at a discount *vis-à-vis* the dollar) would fall to a discount of 5 per cent *vis-à-vis* other currencies in general. On the other hand, if the dollar was weak and surplus countries allowed their currencies to rise to their ceilings, the maximum discount of the dollar *vis-à-vis* other currencies would be 5 per cent, and the most probable discount between 0 per cent and 5 per cent.

Moreover, under the arrangement envisaged, the role of the United States in the determination of exchange rates would remain a passive one. Whether or not the United States would get any advantage from the wider margins would depend on the extent to which other countries allowed their dollar exchange rates to vary within the margins.

It has sometimes been suggested, as a means of gaining greater and more assured flexibility of the dollar, that the dollar price of gold as well as dollar exchange rates should be allowed to vary within wider margins. This, however, would not achieve the desired result as long as other countries continued to peg their currencies on the

351

dollar. A wider spread for the dollar price of gold is presumably to be interpreted in the sense that the United States, while keeping buying and selling prices close together, could move them both to the vicinity of the upper limit when on balance losing gold through official conversions, and to the vicinity of the lower limit when on balance gaining gold. (To widen the spread between buying and selling prices would invite direct sales of gold outside the United States between countries wishing to sell and those wishing to purchase.)

Assume that the United States took advantage of the opportunity afforded by the wider margins of allowing the price of gold to vary. This would obviously have no direct effect upon exchange rates, which would be determined by the behaviour of other monetary authorities subject to such rules as might be adopted governing their intervention on the market within the permitted margins. However, it might conceivably exercise an equilibrating influence on the behaviour of other monetary authorities with respect to reserve composition. Thus, when the United States was in deficit and the dollar price of gold rose to its upper limit, countries would have an incentive to retain their reserve accumulations of dollars with a view to converting them when the price had fallen to par or below. Similarly, when the United States was in surplus and the dollar price of gold at the lower limit, other countries would have an incentive to run down their dollars and hold on as long as possible to their gold. This kind of offsetting behaviour in official conversions, however, could not be relied upon with any certainty, and would import an undesirable speculative element into the question of reserve composition.

The only way in which it would appear possible for the United States to be on the same footing as other countries with respect to wider exchange margins would be for all, or a large number of countries, including the principal trading countries, to peg their currencies not to the dollar but to gold, in such a way as to keep the price of gold in terms of their currencies—or of their currencies in terms of gold—within a range of, say, 5 per cent above and 5 per cent below par, subject to the same set of rules with respect to market intervention as were previously suggested for dollar exchange rates.

Such a system would work most easily if there were an integrated free market for monetary and nonmonetary gold. Arbitrage between exchange and gold markets would ensure that the exchange rate between any pair of currencies would be equal to the ratio of the market prices of gold in terms of the respective currencies. Then a monetary authority would sell gold only when the market price of gold in terms of its currency was rising and preferably only when it was near its upper limit, and would buy gold only when this price was falling and preferably only when it was near its lower limit. Arbitrage between exchange and gold markets would ensure that if the mutual exchange rate of any two countries diverged from par by more than 10 per cent the country whose exchange rate was at a discount would sell gold through the market to the one whose rate was at a premium, thus financing the deficit of the former and the surplus of the latter.

Under this system, if the United States were obliged to sell reserves its exchange rates *vis-à-vis* other deficit countries would be close to par, and *vis-à-vis* surplus countries at a discount of 10 per cent, while under the system in which countries peg on the U.S. dollar, its rate *vis-à-vis* other deficit countries would be at a premium of 5 per cent and *vis-à-vis* surplus countries at a discount of only 5 per cent. Since, under the latter system the market price of gold in terms of dollars would be free to vary over a range of 10 per cent, countries might be tempted to sell dollars for gold on the market when the gold price was low and sell gold for dollars when the gold price was high, even if the point had not yet been attained at which the United States itself was obliged to offer gold for dollars or vice versa.

MODIFIED OR PARTIAL ADOPTION OF WIDER MARGINS

Considerations could be given to widening exchange margins by a lesser amount than the 5 per cent on either side of par with the U.S. dollar that has been envisaged here. However, if it is accepted that the main potential advantage of the system is not that it reduces balance-of-payments disequilibria in the short run but that it facilitates prompt if partial adjustment of exchange rates to changes in their long-term equilibrium level, it will be appreciated that this advantage cannot be reaped to any significant extent unless the widening is substantial. A 4 per cent margin would give the advantages discussed to a significant degree, and would have the merit, as compared with a 5 per cent margin, of limiting the amount of exchange rate variation that could take place without a definite judgment on the part of the international community that a fundamental (rather than, say, a cyclical) disequilibrium existed. It could also mean that countries with persistent inflationary tendencies might sooner get into a position where they had to discuss their policies with the Fund. With margins of 3 per cent or 2 per cent, it becomes increasingly doubtful that the advantages claimed for exchange flexibility could be achieved unless (a) countries could be induced to refrain entirely from intervention within the margin, and (b) (at least in the 2 per cent case) the wider margin were associated with some scheme for an automatic gradual adjustment of the par values themselves.

As regards suggestions for a gradual and experimental widening of margins from the present 1 per cent upwards, it should be appreciated that a 2 per cent margin would shed rather little light on the manner in which a 5 per cent margin might be expected to work.

The question arises whether and in what way it would be possible for the system of wider margins to be adopted by some countries and not by others. It has already been suggested that the relative merits of wide and narrow margins might vary considerably as between countries of different types. Presumably all countries would enjoy the same legal rights as to the margins within which their exchange rates would be allowed to vary, but some might be exempted from the obligations with respect to refraining from official intervention within the wider margins discussed in a previous section on condition that they renounced in some way their right to use their wider margins. It has already been suggested that countries in a group desiring to maintain their mutual exchange rates at par might be allowed to do so provided that the exchange rates of the group as a whole varied in relation to their aggregate reserves in the manner required by the intervention rules.

Other exemptions are possible. For example, a country might be exempted from the rules restricting official intervention within wider margins provided that it undertook to maintain its exchange rate within 1 per cent of par with the U.S. dollar (whether directly or indirectly via a third currency). One advantage of this arrangement would be to ensure that if a country intervened to prevent appreciation while in surplus it could not take advantage of the wider margin when in deficit.

354

More doubtfully, exemption from the intervention rules might be given to any country that undertook to maintain its currency within 1 per cent of par with the currency of any country that was adhering to the intervention rules. This would permit currency areas to exist *without* the proviso (specified above) that the exchange rates of their members be managed with reference to changes in the aggregate external reserves of the area as a whole.

One difficulty about all such exemptions is that countries could scarcely be expected to renounce for ever their rights to utilize wider margins. Some might, therefore, renounce use of the margins so long as it suited them to claim exemption from the intervention rules, e.g. so long as they were in payments surplus but later, when it suited them, e.g. when they were in deficit, might renounce the renunciation and claim to exercise their rights to utilize the wider margins. However, legal ways of handling this difficulty should not be impossible to devise.

Index

Aliber, R. Z., 343n.
balance of payments adjustment process, code of adjustment, 275–288
and par value system, 268–95
and reserve needs, 173–5
Bank for International Settlements, 113, 116, 117, 119, 268
Bernstein, E. M., 112, 112n.
bilateralism, 34
mitigations of, 35–7
Boissonneault, L., 336n.

Clearing Union, 111
clearing unions and discriminatory import duties, 41–2
and discriminatory restrictions, 43–4
Committee on the Working of the Monetary System, 96n.
Coombs, C. A., 249n.

Day, A. C. L., 96n.
de Vries, T., 96n.
discrimination, group, 37–9
domestic financial policies, dependence on exchange rate régime, 237–48

European Fund, 112, 113, 116, 268
European Payments Union, 41, 112, 113, 115, 116
exchange rates, depreciation and the domestic price level, 197–236
for current and capital transactions, 296–325

exchange rate adjustment, complementary financial policies, 213–228
and the wage-price spiral, 228–31
margins, effects of widening, 326–355
régime and domestic financial policies, 237–48

Fellner, William, 272
foreign exchange reserves, 107–9
forward exchange market, official intervention on, 249–67
Frisch, Ragnar, 14, 37–41
multi-compensatory trade system, 33–41

General Agreement on Tariffs and Trade, 175, 268, 269, 271
Gilbert, M., 184n.
gold revaluation, 106–7

Halm, G. N., 350n.
Harris, S., 270n.
Harrod, R. F., 95n., 114n.
Hicks, J. R., 78n.
Høst-Madsen, P., 184, 184n.

import restrictions, 1–24
optimal, 6–10
non-discriminatory, 10–11
International credit institutions, reserve creation, 110–20
international liquidity, conditional and unconditional, 104–5, 122–123
demand for, 100–1

distribution of, 103–4
effects on national policies, 97–9
flexibility in supply of, 101–3
need for, 95–6, 123–4
types of, 121–3
International Monetary Fund, 14, 15, 16, 17, 106, 111, 112, 114, 115, 116, 117, 119, 120, 175, 268, 269, 271, 273, 290, 293, 296, 297, 326, 348, 349, 354
changes in drawing policies, 134–137
changes in gold policies, 137–40
changes in repurchase provisions, 140–2
Compensatory Financing Decision, 126n.
creation of international liquidity, 121–60
general operations, 124–30
increase in resources, 147–57
investment, 142–7
quota increases, 130–4
international reserve assets, distribution and need for reserves, 184–6
need for, 95–6, 123–4, 171–94
stocks and growth, 175–84
use and acceptance of, 161–70

Johnson, H. G., 19
Junz, H. B., 335n.

Kenen, P. B., 107n.
Keynes, J. M., 270–1
Kreinin, M., 336n.
Kuczynski, M., 19, 296n., 317

Lerner, A. P., 13

Machlup, F., 272, 274
Meade, J. E., 13n., 14, 49n., 272
Mundell, R. A., 19, 239n., 249n., 340n.

Nurkse, R., 270, 272

optimal export duty, 58–60
optimal import duty, 54–8
optimal tariff, 49–75
and trade elasticities, 60–5
Organization for Economic Co-operation and Development, 175, 269, 273
Working Party No. 3, 269, 272, 274, 288

real income concept and tariff changes, 65–7, 76–80
Rhomberg, R. R., 240, 240n., 332n., 335n.

supply, responsiveness of, 27

Tinbergen, J., 225n.
Tobin, J., 273, 289
trade restriction, real income loss from, 76–92
transferability, selective, 35–7
Triffin, R., 95n., 108, 112, 112n., 114, 115, 116, 117, 119
Tsiang, S. C., 249n., 343n.

United Nations, Department of Economic Affairs, 95n.

welfare economic assumptions, 24–25, 49–50, 65–7, 76–80
welfare effect of import duty, 52–4,
White, W. H., 225n., 249n.
wider exchange rate margins, effects on capital flows, 328–33
effects on current account, 333–7
effects on demand and output, 337–8
effects on non-exchange policies, 338–42
intervention rules, 347–50
and the U.S. dollar, 351–3